FAITH GIVES FULLNESS
TO REASONING

SUPPLEMENTS TO
VIGILIAE CHRISTIANAE

Formerly Philosophia Patrum

TEXTS AND STUDIES OF EARLY CHRISTIAN LIFE
AND LANGUAGE

EDITORS
J. DEN BOEFT — A.F.J. KLIJN — G. QUISPEL
J.H. WASZINK†—J.C.M. VAN WINDEN

VOLUME XIII

FAITH GIVES FULLNESS TO REASONING

The Five Theological Orations of Gregory Nazianzen

INTRODUCTION AND COMMENTARY

BY

FREDERICK W. NORRIS

TRANSLATION

BY

LIONEL WICKHAM and FREDERICK WILLIAMS

E.J. BRILL

LEIDEN · NEW YORK · KØBENHAVN · KOLN

1991

Dedicated to Fred P. Thompson, Jr.
Man of vision and integrity

BR
65
.G836
N67
1990

Library of Congress Cataloging-in-Publication Data

Norris, Frederick W.
    Faith gives fullness to reasoning : the five theological orations
of Gregory Nazianzen / introduction and commentary by Frederick W.
Norris : translation by Lionel Wickham and Frederick Williams.
        p.   cm. -- (Supplements to Vigiliae Christianae, ISSN
0920-623X : v. 13)
    Includes indexes.
    ISBN 9004092536
    1. Theology--Early church. ca. 30 – 600.   I. Gregory, of Nazianzus.
Saint. Orations. Oration 27 – 31. English. 1990. II. Title.
III. Series.
BR65.G836N67   1990
230'.14--oc20   90-42554
                                                                                              CIP

ISSN 0920-623X
ISBN 90 04 09253 6

© *Copyright 1991 by E.J. Brill, Leiden, The Netherlands*

PRINTED IN THE NETHERLANDS

This is the answer we make perforce to these posers of puzzles. Perforce – because Christian people find long-winded controversy disagreeable and one Adversary enough for them. Yet our attackers made it essential, since remedies too must be made for diseases, if they are to learn that their wisdom is not complete and that they are not invincible in their lavish attempts to nullify the Gospel. For when we abandon faith to take the power of reason as our shield, when we use philosophical enquiry to destroy the credibility of the Spirit, then reason gives way in the face of the vastness of the realities. Give way it must, set going, as it is, by the frail organ of human understanding. What happens then? The frailty of our reasoning looks like a frailty in our creed. Thus it is that as Paul too judges, smartness of argument is revealed as a nullifying of the Cross. Faith, in fact, is what gives fullness to our reasoning.

ORATION 29.21
Gregory of Nazianzus, Constantinople, 380 C.E.

CONTENTS

PREFACE

The first notebooks for this commentary were started during a leave of absence arranged by the President of Emmanuel School of Religion, Fred P. Thompson, Jr., when The Catholic University of America announced that I had been awarded a Post-Doctoral Andrew W. Mellon Fellowship for 1981-1982. At that time Emmanuel, a graduate theological seminary, was barely twenty years old. No policy for faculty leaves of any kind had been established, but President Thompson had encouraged me to apply for the fellowship. Through his leadership a policy was created that not only permitted my acceptance of the award, but also grew into a full sabbatical program for the entire faculty. In the midst of such imposing financial pressures on private education and the continued decline of scholarship in seminaries, that was an unusual effort. For his foresight and persistence, the volume is dedicated to him.

Gratitude is also due the Andrew W. Mellon Foundation for their excellent decision to offer The Catholic University of America funds for a program in Early Christian Studies. During 1981-1982 I was deeply indebted to a doctoral seminar led by Thomas Halton, one devoted to Nazianzen's *Theological Orations*. Many of the interpretations contained in the commentary arose during that semester. The Washington, DC area with the Library of Congress and the Dumbarton Oaks Research Library provided abundant resources. I must also express my thanks to the Duke University Library, both for allowing me to investigate Leunclavius' translation of Elias of Crete and for making a microfilm of that work for my personal use.

Donald Winslow, then editor of the Patristic Monograph Series, had in his possession a new translation of Nazianzen's *Theological Orations*. After consulting its authors, Lionel Wickham and Frederick Williams, he sent me a copy. Wickham, Williams and I met at the 1983 Oxford Patristic Conference and decided that a combined project was feasible. They have made numerous important contributions to the commentary; I checked and corrected the Biblical citations from the Sources chrétiennes edition, added some further citations for the list which appears within the translation and offered some suggestions for the translation itself.

George Kennedy proved to be of inestimable value both in his written works and in conversation. Each aspect of ancient rhetoric one learns creates in some way a deeper understanding of Gregory Nazianzen.

I owe much to research assistants Phil Kenneson and Chris Rollston for their criticisms and Bob Parsley for preparing the indices. It is a joy to watch promising seminary students develop scholarly skills. I also appreciate the assistance of John Egan, Rowan Greer, Charles Kannengiesser and the Christianity, Judaism and Antiquity Seminar at Notre Dame, and William Schoedel. Errors that have persisted are mine; there would, however, have been more without these people's help.

An appointment as the Tuohy Distinguished Visiting Professor of Religious Studies at John Carroll University in the Fall of 1988, although specifically involving another project, allowed time to use their library for further revisions of this manuscript.

Finally I am honored that the editorial board of ''Supplements to *Vigiliae Christianae*'' accepted my work in their series.

Frederick W. Norris
30 January, 1989 Eastern Feast of Gregory Nazianzen

ABBREVIATIONS

AC	*Antike und Christentum*
Barbel	J. Barbel. *Gregor von Nazianz: Die Fünf Theologischen Reden: Text und Übersetzung mit Einleitung und Kommentar* "Testimonia, Band III" (Düsseldorf, 1963)
Bernardi	J. Bernardi. *La Prédication des Pères cappadociens: Le prédicateur et son auditoire* "Publications de la Faculté des Lettres et Sciences humaines de l'Université de Montpellier, XXX" (Montpellier, 1968)
ByZ	*Byzantinische Zeitschrift*
Byzan	*Byzantion*
CAG	*Commentaria in Aristotelem Graeca*
CH	*Church History*
Elias of Crete	J. Leunclavius. *Gregorius Nazianzenus, Operum tomi tres. Aucit nunc primum Caesareii, Eliae Cretensis Episcopi, et ipsius Gregorii librorum aliquot accessione* (Basileae, 1571)
Focken	J. Focken. *De Gregorii Nazianzeni Orationum Carminum Dogmaticorum Argumentandi Ratione* (Numburg [?], 1912)
Gallay (1969)	P. Gallay. *Gregor von Nazianz: Briefe* "GCS 53" (Berlin, 1969)
Gallay (1974)	P. Gallay. *Grégoire de Nazianze: Lettres Théologiques* "SC 208" (Paris, 1974)
Gallay (1978)	P. Gallay. *Grégoire de Nazianze: Discours 27-31, Discours Théologiques* "SC 250" (Paris, 1978)
GCS	*Die griechischen christlichen Schriftsteller der ersten Jahrhunderte*
Gregg and Groh	R. Gregg and D. Groh. *Early Arianism: A View of Salvation* (Philadelphia, 1981)
Gregg	R. Gregg, ed. *Arianism: Historical and Theological Reassessments. Papers from the Ninth International Conference on Patristic Studies: September 5-10, 1983; Oxford, England* "Patristic Monograph Series, 11" (Cambridge, MA, 1985)
Hanson	R.P.C. Hanson. *The Search for the Christian Doctrine of God: The Arian Controversy 318-381* (Edinburgh, 1988)
Jaeger	W. Jaeger. *Contra Eunomium Libri*, 2 vols. Second edition "Gregorii Nysseni Opera" (Leiden, 1960)
JThS	*The Journal of Theological Studies*
Kennedy (1963)	G. Kennedy. *The Art of Persuasion in Greece* "A History of Rhetoric, Vol. I" (Princeton, 1963)
Kennedy (1980)	G. Kennedy. *Classical Rhetoric and Its Christian and Secular Tradition from Ancient to Modern Times* (Chapel Hill, NC, 1980)
Kennedy (1983)	G. Kennedy. *Greek Rhetoric Under the Christian Emperors* "A History of Rhetoric, Vol. III" (Princeton, 1983)
Kopecek	T. Kopecek. *A History of Neo-Arianism*, 2 vols. "Patristic Monograph Series, 8" (Cambridge, MA, 1979)
Mason	A. Mason. *The Five Theological Orations of Gregory of Nazianzus* "Cambridge Patristic Texts" (Cambridge, 1899)
Moreschini	C. Moreschini. *Gregorio Nazianzeno: I Cinque Discorsi Teologici* "Collana di Testi Patristici, 58" (Roma, 1986)
Mortley	R. Mortley. *From Word to Silence: The Way of Negation, Christian and Greek*, 2 vols. "Theophaneia, 31," (Bonn, 1986)
Otis	B. Otis, "Cappadocian Thought as a Coherent System," *Dumbarton Oaks Papers* 12 (1958), pp. 95-124
PG	J. Migne. *Patrologiae cursus completus: series graeca* (Paris, 1857-1866)

PL	J. Migne. *Patrologiae cursus completus: series latina* (Paris, 1844-1855)
PW	*Real-Encyclopädie der classischen Altertumswissenschaft*
RAC	*Reallexikon für Antike und Christentum*
Rep. Naz.	*Repertorium Nazianzenum, Orationes. Textus Graecus, I: Codices Galliae,* ed. by J. Mossay (Paderborn, 1981)
RHE	*Revue d'histoire ecclésiastique*
RHPhR	*Revue d'histoire et de philosophie religieuses*
Sesboüé	B. Sesboüé, G.-M. de Durand, L. Doutreleau. *Basile de Césarée Contre Eunome I and II,* "SC 299 and 305" (Paris, 1982- 1983)
Sinko (1917)	T. Sinko. *I. De Traditione Orationum Gregorii Nazianzeni* "Meletemata Patristica, II" (Cracoviae, 1917)
SC	*Sources chrétiennes*
SVF	J. von Arnim. *Stoicorum Veterum Fragmenta* (Leipzig, 1905-1924)
II. Symp. Naz.	*II. Symposium Nazianzenum Louvain-la-Neuve, 25-28 août 1981,* ed. by J. Mossay (Paderborn, 1983)
TRE	*Theologische Realenzyklopädie*
TS	*Theological Studies*
TU	*Texte und Untersuchungen*
Vaggione	R. Vaggione, trans. and ed. *Eunomius: The Extant Works* "Oxford Early Christian Texts" (Oxford, 1987)
VC	*Vigiliae Christianae*
Walz	C. Walz. *Rhetores graeci* (London, 1832-1836)
Wickham	L. Wickham, "The *Syntagmation* of Aetius the Anomean," *JThS* N.S. 19 (1968), pp. 532-569
Winslow	D. Winslow. *The Dynamics of Salvation* "Patristic Monograph Series, 7" (Cambridge, MA, 1979)
Wyss	B. Wyss, "Gregor II (Gregor von Nazianz)," *RAC* 12, pp. 793-863

INTRODUCTION

Life[1]

Gregory Nazianzen never lacked privilege. He was born at Arianzus into a wealthy, land owning, curial family that was established within the Hellenized upper class of Cappadocia.[2] The exact date of his birth is difficult to ascertain, although sometime between 325-330 are the years most fully accepted.[3] We do not know as much about the other siblings as we wish. His younger brother Caesarius received advanced education. According to Gregory's comments in the funeral oration for Caesarius, the young man excelled in geometry, astronomy and mathematics, but chose medicine as his profession. At one time he was a physician in the court of the emperor at Constantinople, at another treasurer of Bithynia; yet he died in mid-life without achieving much that had been hoped for him.[4] His death left Nazianzen with both sorrow and time-consuming inconvenience. When his brother was alive, Gregory did not worry with matters concerning family property. Upon the death of Caesarius, however, Nazianzen was faced not only with the personal loss but also

---

[1] For the purposes of this commentary an abbreviated sketch of Gregory Nazianzen's life suffices. The finest compact treatment is in Hanson, pp. 699-707. P. Gallay's biography, *La Vie de Saint Grégoire de Nazianze* (Paris, 1943) and J. Szymusiak's adjustment of the chronology, "Pour une chronologie des discours de S. Grégoire de Nazianze," *VC* 20 (1966), pp. 183-199 will aid those who demand more. C. Ullmann, *Gregorius von Nazianz der Theologe* (Gotha, 1867) is still useful as is A. Benoît, *S. Grégoire de Nazianze. Sa vie, ses oeuvres et son époque* (Marseille, 1876 [reprint Hildesheim, 1973]). For the interrelationships of family, friends and acquaintances see M.-M. Hauser-Meury, *Prosopographie zu den Schriften Gregors von Nazianz*, "Theophaneia, 13" (Bonn, 1960).

[2] In *Or.* 7.8, *PG* 35, 764A-D Gregory notes that his brother Caesarius had been offered "a seat in the Constantinopolitan senate," an offer that suggests the family may not have attained senatorial rank previously. *Ep.* 7, *PG* 37, 32C-33C and Gallay (1969), pp. 8-9 and *Ep.* 249, Gallay (1969), pp. 177-183 = Gregory of Nyssa, *Ep.* 1, *PG* 46, 999C-1009A give evidence of the curial status. See T. Kopecek, "The Social Class of the Cappadocian Fathers," *CH* 42 (1973), pp. 453-466. *Or.* 18.39, *PG* 35, 1037A-1038C states that Gregory the Elder almost singlehandedly provided the funds for the church building at Nazianzus.

[3] J. Mossay, "Gregor von Nazianz," *TRE*, Bd. 14 (Berlin, 1985), p. 165, notes on the basis of the Suda and the Byzantine tradition that Gregory might have died in 390 at about ninety years of age, but he settles on the dates 329/330 as more likely. Hanson, p. 701, n. 94, faults Benoît for preferring the earlier date of birth in order to make certain that Gregory the elder was not a married bishop begetting children.

[4] Even though *Or.* 7, *PG* 35, 756A-788C is a panegyric and thus contains many standard comments, underneath the usual form one can discover a number of things about the young man and the family. For a fuller description of Caesarius, see O. Seeck, "Caesarius von Nazianz," *PW* 3.1, 1298-1300.

with the need to look after the family estate and that of his brother. People whom he did not know pestered him unmercifully for some part of that inheritance.[5] Gregory's sister, Gorgonia, also described in a funeral sermon, was virtuous, particularly long-suffering and both a good wife and mother.[6] Nazianzen does not often speak of her as he did his brother, but her death left him as the only child and thus put an added burden on the relationship with his parents by leaving him alone to care for his parents in their old age.

His mother, Nonna, had a strong Christian influence on his life and that of the entire family.[7] She came from a Christian home and was instrumental in her husband's conversion.[8] Gregory's father had belonged to the Hypsistarii, a religious sect whose worship involved what Gregory called "a mixture of Hellenic error and Jewish legal fantasy." Its members in some way employed fire and lamps in their liturgy, observed the Sabbath, kept certain food laws, yet rejected circumcision.[9] Their sole object of veneration was the Almighty; they apparently refused to call God "the Father."[10] The elder Gregory's family had been a part of the sect and evidently found its tenets important, for Nazianzen's paternal grandmother disinherited his father when the Elder became a Christian. Later, however, she changed her mind.[11] Before the Elder's family become involved with the Hypsistarii, they may have worshipped various Hellenistic deities, since in at least one place Nazianzen refers to the previous "wandering" of his father.[12] Yet as bishop of Nazianzus Gregory the Elder held doctrinal positions that were similar to those of the so-called Cappadocian fathers. He once was gulled into accepting an Arian confes-

---

[5] *Carmen de vita sua* II, 367-385, *PG* 37, 1053-1056. For a new English translation of this poem see D. Meehan's *Saint Gregory of Nazianzus: Three Poems: Concerning His Own Affairs, Concerning Himself and the Bishops, Concerning His Own Life*, "The Fathers of the Church, Vol. 75" (Washington, DC, 1987). C. Jungck, *Gregor von Nazianz: De vita sua* (Heidelberg, 1974) provides an excellent introduction to, German translation of, and commentary on the one poem.

[6] *Or.* 8, *PG* 35, 789-817A.

[7] *Carmen de vita sua* II, 57-81, *PG* 37, 1033-1035.

[8] *Or.* 7.4, *PG* 35, 757D-760B. *Or.* 18.7-12, *PG* 35, 973B-980B, devoted to his father, further describes her piety and virtue. For a fuller description, see F. Dölger, "Nonna. Ein Kapitel über christlichen Folksfrömmigkeit des 4. Jahrhunderts," *AC* 5 (1936), pp. 44-73.

[9] *Or.* 18.5, *PG* 35, 989B-992B.

[10] Gregory of Nyssa, *Against Eunomius* 2.5, Jaeger 2.327.

[11] *Or.* 18.5, *PG* 35, 989C-992B. Kopecek, "The Social Class of the Cappadocian Fathers," *CH* 42 (1973) pp. 455-456 correctly notes that an Iranian-Persian background of the Hypsistarii has not been demonstrated. Thus the thesis of E. Ivanka, *Hellenistisches und Christliches im frühbyzantinischen Geistesleben* (Vienna, 1948) that the family belonged to an Iranian-Persian "country aristocracy" is most probably faulty.

[12] *Carmen de vita sua* II, 51-56, *PG* 37, 1033.

sion, but he apologized for his error and withdrew the acceptance.[13] His
years of service were marked by deeds of kindness, care for those in his
congregation and sensible teaching of the faith, rather than by acute
penetration into the theological problems of the day.[14]

The younger Gregory had the advantage of education from early years
well into young adulthood. His first school terms were spent at Nazianzus,
a city of Cappadocia little known to us, but of sufficient size to have decent
institutions, including a primary school.[15] The family, however, sent
Gregory on to Caesarea in Cappadocia for further studies at a secondary
level.[16] He may have first met his life-long friend Basil there. Nazianzen
indicates that he had known Basil before their paths crossed again at
Athens, but the record is not clear about their initial encounter.[17]

Education in advanced disciplines, philosophy and particularly rhetoric
was undertaken in Palestine, certainly at Caesarea,[18] then Alexandria
and finally Athens. Those three centers brought him into contact with various Hellenistic and Christian traditions. The first two cities had been the
homes of accomplished Christian teachers for well over a century. Palestinian Caesarea was the workplace of Origen, Pamphilus and Eusebius,
and probably still housed at least parts of the rather extensive library used
by the three.[19] Nazianzen's knowledge of catechetical orations by Cyril
of Jerusalem, a possible source for some of his comments in the *Theological
Orations*, may have been gained during his stay in Caesarea. Alexandria
had long been one of the most important centers of learning in the ancient
world. There the echoes of Origen would have strengthened the Caesarean influence Gregory had received. Doubtless the conflict between
Athanasius and Arius was part of conversation in Christian circles when

---

[13] *Or*. 18.18, *PG* 35, 1005C-1008A.

[14] *Or*. 18.15-29, *PG* 35, 1004A-1021B. See A. Zeigler, "Gregor der Ältere von Nazianz, seine Taufe und Weihe," *Münchener Theologische Zeitschrift* 31 (1980), pp. 262-283 for
more information concerning Gregory's father.

[15] *Or*. 7.6, *PG* 35, 761A-B indicates that both Gregory and Caesarius were first educated in the schools at Nazianzus. Also see J. Szymusiak, "Les sites de Nazianze et Karba-
la," *Epektasis: Mélanges patristiques offerts au Cardinal Jean Daniélou*, publiés par J. Fontaine
et C. Kannengiesser (Paris, 1972), pp. 545-548 and F. Trisoglio, *San Gregorio di Nazianzo
in un quarantennio di studi (1925-1969) Rivista lasalliana* 40 (1973) (Torino, 1974), pp. 39-43.

[16] Gregory the Presbyter, *The Life of Gregory Nazianzen*, *PG* 35, 248C. Also see *Or*.
43.13, *PG* 36, 512A-C.

[17] *Or*. 43.14, *PG* 36, 513A-C says only that the time in Athens brought him a more
perfect knowledge of Basil, although Basil was not unknown to him before that period.

[18] In *Or*. 7.6, *PG* 35, 761A-B Gregory states that he "studied rhetoric in the then
flourishing schools of Palestine." Jerome, *De vir. ill.* 113, *PL* 23, 707A remarks that Nazianzen was a student of the rhetorician Thespesius at Caesarea in Palestine.

[19] Jerome, op. cit., notes that Euzoius, a fellow student of Nazianzen in Palestinian
Caesarea who later became the bishop of that city, worked diligently to restore the library
by replacing papyrus rolls with vellum codices.

Nazianzen studied in the city, even though he may have been a student during one of the periods when Athanasius was exiled. Perhaps he also had the privilege of hearing Didymus the Blind.[20]

In Athens, probably by 350, Nazianzen sat under both the pagan Himerius and the Christian Prohaeresius.[21] The former was a renowned technical rhetorician who has left behind a number of orations.[22] Opinion about the quality of these works varies. Browning, having found them to be both verbose and often on schoolboy topics, concludes that "Himerius in the main displays a talent for saying nothing gracefully and at length,"[23] but Kennedy sees in Himerius one of the more talented rhetoricians of the fourth century. In his view Himerius was a poetic speaker whose Oration 48 "is to the Fourth Century what the poems of Pindar were to the early classical period." According to Kennedy, Himerius not only possessed great literary skills but also knew how to assess the value of enthymematic argument.[24] If Himerius had himself studied Plato, as Nock indicates,[25] and was capable of teaching his students poetic sensitivity and the proper use of enthymemes, then one source for the structure of Gregory's work is established.

Prohaeresius is more difficult to judge. He was a Cappadocian by birth and thus might have been known to Gregory's aristocratic family. Eunapius reports his uncommon ability to speak extemporaneously and his enormous capacity of memory.[26] He was the one Christian teacher known to us whom Julian excluded from the decree that Christians could

---

[20] *Carmen de vita sua* II, 128-129, *PG* 37, 1038 mentions his education in Alexandria only as an aside. J. Rousse, "Grégoire de Nazianze," *Dictionnaire de Spiritualité*, Tome VI, (Paris, 1967), p. 942 notes that a number of scholars have found a similarity between the Trinitarian and Christological contributions of Didymus, Nazianzen, and the other Cappadocians.

[21] Socrates, *H.E.* 4.26, *PG* 67, 529A and Sozomen, *H.E.* 6.17, *PG* 67, 1333C mention those two rhetoricians as teachers of both Basil and Gregory in Athens, but their reference to further study with Libanius at Antioch usually has been rejected. Mossay, however, "Gregor von Nazianz," *TRE* 14, p. 165 accepts it. In *Carmen de vita sua* II, 211-264, *PG* 37, 1044-1047 Nazianzen describes his life in Athens.

[22] Himerii, *Declamationes et Orationes cum Deperditarum Fragmentis*, ed. Aristides Colonna, (Rome, 1951). Eunapius, *The Lives of the Sophists* 95 gives some details about his life.

[23] R. Browning, "Himerius," *The Oxford Classical Dictionary*, 2nd ed. (Oxford, 1970), p. 516.

[24] Kennedy (1983), pp. 141-149. Kennedy provides a translation of the προθεωρία for *Or.* 9 that indicates Himerius presented a description of a marriage speech to his student Severus in which he described the first part as being composed of "polished enthymemes."

[25] A.D. Nock, *Sallustius: Concerning the Gods and the Universe* (London, 1926, [reprint Hildesheim, 1966]), p. xviii, claims that Himerius knew some of Plato's works at first hand, a knowledge not always evident in teachers of rhetoric.

[26] Eunapius, *The Lives of the Sophists* 63-79. Also see Jerome, *Chronica* a. 2378, *PL* 27, 691-692.

not hold positions in the schools since they did not share the outlook of the pagan literature they taught. Julian evidently made the exception because Prohaeresius had been his instructor, but his professor refused such preferential treatment. We are then safe in concluding that this Cappadocian was both a rhetorician and a Christian of some consequence. One of the reasons behind Gregory's vitriolic invectives against Julian well may have been that the two had studied under this same professor. Nazianzen and Julian shared so many common features that their differences needed emphasis.[27] Unfortunately what we would most like to know about Prohaeresius in reference to Gregory, that is, his view of the relationship between philosophy, rhetoric and Christian theology, remains a mystery. None of his treatises or orations has come down to us. He may have been helpful in bringing these aspects of education together for Nazianzen, but we cannot say.[28]

What can be said is that after two or three years in Palestine and Egypt pursuing higher studies, Nazianzen spent almost ten years in Greece. He took advantage of his status and wealth in order to pursue the highest levels of education available. In his autobiography he notes that when he was ready to quit the city, the crowd begged him to stay on at Athens and teach rhetoric; indeed it was willing to vote him first place in letters. The phrases imply that he was offered one of the prestigious positions there.[29] Although he seldom undervalues his rhetorical gifts, the aside may be correct. His talents were highly valued by various Byzantine writers. Indeed he is the church father most quoted within the Byzantine ecclesiastical tradition.[30]

---

[27] M. Kertsch, *Bildersprache bei Gregor von Nazianz: Ein Beitrag zur spätantiken Rhetorik und popularen Philosophie* (Graz, 1978) has demonstrated how much Gregory shared the philosophical positions and rhetorical attitudes that formed the basis of Julian's doctrines and those of the emperor's pagan teachers.

[28] Kennedy's conclusion, (1983), p. 141, that Nazianzen did not learn Christian theology from Prohaeresius is conjecture based on silence. Gregory often is unclear about his dependence on others except in occasional comments and pieces like his oration on Athanasius, *Or.* 21, *PG* 35, 1081A-1128C.

[29] *Carmen de vita sua* II, 245-264, *PG* 37, 1046-1047. Gregory notes in the same section that he was almost thirty when this outpouring took place. Thus it might have occurred about 360. Libanius, *Or.* 1.24-25 and 2.14, indicates by referring to "the three" in Athens that there were three state-paid sophists in Athens at the time. Eunapius says he met Prohaeresius in 362 while the old man was still teaching. Himerius apparently was also actively lecturing in the 360s. Perhaps Gregory was put forth as a candidate for the third chair, as a proper successor to one of his teachers, or as the shining star in one of the rhetorical schools.

[30] Wyss, pp. 799-800. G. Kustas, *Studies in Byzantine Rhetoric*, "Analecta Vlatadon, 17" (Thessaloniki, 1973), p. 21 notes that an anonymous commentary on Hermogenes' *On Ideas* contains scholia which use passages from Nazianzen as illustrations of Hermogenes' points. The commentary is printed in Walz, VII, pp. 861-1087 and the scholia are mentioned as Scholia Minora in the footnotes. Kennedy (1983), pp. 125-126, dates the

At Athens Gregory renewed a friendship with Basil that would lead each to the deepest sorrows and perhaps to the highest joys of his life. The two found they had common backgrounds, interests and goals. They made plans to set up a monastic community after leaving Athens, one in which they could study Christian writings and pursue the life of contemplation. When Basil left the city early, he put some strain on the relationship, but their united efforts could be productive. The *Philocalia* of Origen is probably the result of their mutual effort in Pontus.[31] If they assembled that piece, it offers striking evidence of their debt to the great Alexandrian. A general study of Nazianzen's writings can demonstrate the influence of Origen upon him.[32] Although the small monastic community at Annesi in Pontus with Basil was shortlived and perhaps more filled with tension than achievement, both men continued to be colleagues in various enterprises that brought their backgrounds and commitments together in common ventures. Their interpenetrating influence on each other provides an interesting insight into friendship in late antiquity.[33] Yet when the "orthodox" bishop of Caesarea, Basil, assigned Gregory to the dusty, noisy "stopping-place" of Sasima in 370 or 371, he created an affront that wounded Nazianzen deeply. For Basil placing Gregory in Sasima made sense because it was an important town on the border of a newly created province, a small city that commanded a well-traveled pass through the mountains. For Gregory being placed in such a waterless backwater in order to fight a church battle was inexcusable. He despised both cultural sterility and ecclesiastical politics. In his autobiographical poem Nazianzen remembered the pain of this incident and could not refrain from mentioning it even when he offered his famous panegyric to Basil after the Caesarian's death.[34]

---

anonymous commentator in the sixth century and also mentions that Pseudo-Zonaios, another sixth-century figure, cited Nazianzen's works as part of the classics, along with Homer and Demosthenes. Also see J. Noret, "Grégoire de Nazianze, l'auteur le plus cité, après la Bible, dans la littérature ecclésiastique byzantine," *II. Symp. Naz.* (Paderborn, 1983), pp. 259-266.

[31] M. Harl in the introduction to *Philocalie 1-20 et Lettre à Africanus*, "SC 302" (Paris, 1983) warns that only late manuscript titles and an unclear epistolary reference connect the *Philocalia* with Gregory and Basil. J. Robinson, in his edition *The Philocalia of Origen* (Cambridge, 1893) pp. vii-xiv, accepts Basil and Gregory as responsible for the selection. Gregory's *Ep.* 115, *PG* 37, 212C, Gallay (1969), p. 88, notes only that he sent a copy of it to a friend. Also see E. Junod, "Remarques sur la composition de la 'Philocalie' d'Origène par Basile de Césarée et Grégoire de Nazianze," *RHPhR* 52 (1972), pp. 149-156.

[32] C. Moreschini, "Influenze di Origene su Gregorio di Nazianzo," *Accademia Toscana di Scienze e Lettere la Colombaria: Atti e Memorie* 44 (1979), pp. 33-57 indicates Gregory's reliance upon Origen particularly in his sense of spirituality.

[33] See R. Van Dam, "Emperor, Bishops, and Friends in Late Antique Cappadocia," *JThS* NS 37 (1986), esp. pp. 68-73.

[34] *Carmen de vita sua* II, 389-399 and 439-462, *PG* 37, 1056-1057 and 1059-1061 and *Or.* 43.59, *PG* 36, 572C-573B.

The strong feelings exposed during this struggle were many. Gregory had a high sense of his own importance and was not at all appreciative of Basil's assigning him to such an uncultured town. Yet it was a greater blow to the friendship of so many years because it indicated clearly to Nazianzen—if not to Basil—that the Caesarian had turned to ecclesiastical politics as his life's work. For Nazianzen the battle between Anthimus, the Arian bishop, and Basil was not merely about doctrine; it was about worldly power. A political reorganization of Cappadocia had created some question as to which metropolitan would be in charge of the new districts.[35] The combat then concerned money and influence, not singularly faith. Gregory attempted to mediate the conflict, but only made matters worse.[36] Once again his personal difficulty in relating the life of "philosophy" with the life of action and his hatred of political squabbling in the church came to the fore. The events warped his view of Basil for some time, but in the last years of his life, he was able again to see Basil as both friend and preceptor. When Nicobulus, a relative, asked for Gregory's collected letters, Nazianzen sent not only those to him, but also a copy of Basil's epistles. He noted that he and Basil had respect for each other and that he preferred Basil's letters to his own.[37]

Other incidents could be added in order to paint the contours of Gregory's temperament. His experiences with colleagues at Athens make it certain that he did not enjoy the frivolity of student life. Some aspects of that "scholarly" community would have unnerved many, but when he remembers those days, he describes his own aloofness and condescension, attitudes perhaps based on an odd earnestness.[38] He also was unprepared for the disappointments of the monastic community that he and Basil attempted to create in Pontus. First, Basil left Athens early. Nazianzen's expectation had been that his friend would wait for him, so in disappointment he went back to his home in Cappadocia. When he did join Basil at Annesi in Pontus, the time together was intermittent and not altogether pleasant. Gregory's letters describing the stay possess a strange jocularity that either was meant to be a mild rebuke or that betrays an unusual lack of seriousness about and commitment to the enterprise.[39] Nazianzen was anything but a simple, even-tempered person.

---

[35] R. Van Dam, op. cit., pp. 53-68 carefully investigates the relationship between the parties in this imperial decision to partition Cappadocia.

[36] Ibid. See *Eps.* 40-48, *PG* 37, 81B-100C, Gallay (1969), pp. 35-45.

[37] *Ep.* 53, *PG* 37, 109A-B, Gallay (1969), p. 49. The best study of this conflict between old friends is still S. Giet, *Sasimes. Une méprise de Saint Basile* (Paris, 1941).

[38] *Or.* 43.15-18, *PG* 36, 513C-520C.

[39] *Eps.* 1-3, *PG* 37, 21A-24B, Gallay (1969), pp. 3-4 are odd. *Carmen de vita sua* II, 350-356, *PG* 37, 1053-1056 speaks of that time together as a soothing respite. Rufinus' translation of Eusebius' *H.E.* 11.9, *GCS*, Eusebius 2,2, ed. by Mommsen, p. 1015 describes the monastic venture.

He also fought the call of his father and the Christian community at Nazianzus to be an assistant in 361, at least an adjunct bishop in 374 and finally bishop in 382. Inner turmoil based on a longing for contemplation and study coupled with a sense of duty to his parents caused him to flee the responsibilities for a time and go to Basil's monastic retreat. He despised his father's tyranny in forcing ordination as a priest on him.[40] Taken together these incidents suggest that Gregory had problems with the demands of public life. He preferred the monastic life with its concentrated periods of prayer and study, but he knew he owed much to his family and should be involved in Christian service. He understood the necessity of pastoral duties, but often found them to be destructive of his contemplative endeavors. Yet his struggle with his father indicates a sensitivity concerning the nature of the church: tyranny has no place within it. It shows that Gregory had a sense common to Byzantine saints: contemplation first, service second.

The reservoirs of bile that he opened up toward others perhaps were self-generated by such conflicts. His own life was not fully appealing to him; his expectations of others were higher than what he himself could achieve. Any setback could unleash a torrent of abuse fomented by his own unease and his misreading of others.[41] His long autobiographical poem includes sections that seethe with self-pity. At times its organization and choice of metaphors are remarkably self-serving. He laments his many trials and compares himself rather favorably with Biblical heroes either directly or by allusion; he disdainfully refers to his battles with his father and haughtily rejects his opponents' charge that he abused canon law. Yet he can also be candid about his mistakes.[42]

Not all his life, however, was filled with the misuse of his temperament, skills and learning. After the death of his father and mother in 374, a retreat for about four years at the convent of St. Thecla near Seleucia gave Gregory a lengthy period of personal contemplation.[43] Then early in 379 he received the invitation to lead a small "orthodox" group at Constan-

---

[40] *Carmen de vita sua* II, 337-438, *PG* 37, 1052-1059 and *Or.* 2, *PG* 35, 408A-514C.

[41] H.-G. Beck, "Rede als Kunstwerk und Bekenntnis: Gregor von Nazianz," *Bayerische Akademie der Wissenschaften, Philosophisch-Historische Klasse* 1977, Heft 4 delightfully details Gregory's struggles with his rhetorical gifts, education and temperament.

[42] *Carmen de vita sua* II, 736-999, *PG* 37, 1080-1098 describes his struggle with Maximus the Cynic and shows his lack of judgment. In 954-999 he admits his errors although he says they were motivated by trust and grew out of ignorance. But in 1044-1061, *PG* 37, 1101-1102 he notes further weaknesses and does not wrap himself in a cloak of virtue.

[43] *Carmen de vita sua* II 545-549, *PG* 37, 1067. Hanson, pp. 702-703 says the monastery was in Seleucia in Cilicia. Moreschini, p. 11, places this retreat in Seleucia on the Tigris. There was a tomb of Thecla near Seleucia in Isauria, and a basilica dedicated to her in Seleucia near Antioch of Syria.

tinople,[44] a call that came after his monastic seclusion and that finally demanded all his talent and education. At least for a time it allowed him to bring into creative focus his sense of self and his expectations of others. He knew that he was prepared for theological debate and had a clear vision of his enemies in that conflict. On that count he neither surprised himself nor was he caught unawares by recognized foes.[45] The Arians controlled the major church edifices and probably were the Christian majority in the metropolis. Eunomius had visited the city on more than one occasion and did so again during Nazianzen's tenure there.[46] The so-called orthodox were outnumbered, but they had some hope in the new emperor. They met in a renovated house eventually given the name "Anastasia."[47] The emperor Theodosius had not yet officially declared his religious sentiments and thus the outlook for the orthodox community was somewhat uncertain if hopeful. They needed a champion who could combat the learned and eloquent leaders of Arianism in the capital city and quiet the theological bickering that had become common talk at many social events.[48]

The acceptance of this invitation well shows Nazianzen's complexity. He despised the life of a bishop at the level of administrative detail and always distrusted ecclesiastical politics. If these aspects were coupled with a town of little cultural life, he spent his animosity on those who even requested his presence in such a place. He had tried to evade his father's call to Nazianzus and had struggled with his hatred of Basil's attempt to place him in Sasima, but the opportunity at Constantinople was irresistible. There he could use his great rhetorical abilities in the service of ministry. That he did. Nearly half of the orations in his corpus are usually placed within the two year period in the metropolis, including the five *Theological Orations* here under investigation. Those particular orations were given at a most auspicious time, during the summer or the autumn of 380, that is, in between two important moves by emperor Theodosius. In February of 380 Theodosius had issued his *Cunctos Populos*, an edict

---

[44] J. Bernardi, "Nouvelles Perspectives sur la Famille de Grégoire de Nazianze," *VC* 38 (1984), pp. 352-359 has shown that a first cousin of Gregory, Theodosia, played a significant role in bringing him to Constantinople.

[45] For a concise description of this period in Nazianzen's life, see J. Mossay, "Gregor von Nazianz in Konstantinopel (379-381 A.D.)," *Byzan* 47 (1977), pp. 223-238. For a fuller description, particularly of the political climate, see R. Snee, "Gregory Nazianzen's Constantinopolitan Career, A.D. 379-381," unpublished doctoral dissertation, University of Washington, 1981.

[46] Kopecek, particularly pp. 494-497, notices that Eunomius and three Neo-Arian metropolitans were in Constantinople in 380. See Philostorgius, *H.E.* 9.18, *GCS*, Bidez; Winkelmann, p. 125.

[47] Sozomen, *H.E.* 7.5, *PG* 67, 1424C-1425D.

[48] *Or.* 27.2, *PG* 36, 13A-C.

which made the doctrine of Nicaea the official teaching of the Roman Empire.[49] In late November Theodosius would visit Constantinople and force Demophilus, the Arian bishop of the metropolis, either to assent to Nicene faith or to be driven into exile. Demophilus chose exile and thus Nazianzen's party became official Christianity in the capital.[50]

Gregory was suited for the preaching and teaching tasks in the capital, but he was not suited for other demands made on a bishop. He has left writings of stunning rhetorical and theological quality, but he has also left a record of inattention to detail, of insensitivity to motives and of inability to bear the reality of political life within the Church that he cherished. Although he overcame the challenge of Maximus the Cynic, a sly usurper supported by the Alexandrian bishop in an attempt to unseat Nazianzen, Gregory demonstrated in those events his lack of political *savoir faire*. The eloquent speaker, the insightful theologian, was poorly equipped as a bishop because in both personal and institutional affairs he often acted like a country bumpkin. He could either be duped and betrayed as by Maximus or attacked and pushed toward withdrawal as by his detractors among the "orthodox" at the Council of Constantinople.[51] These *Theological Orations* show that he expected nearly anything from his theological opponents; at times they evidence his ascription of the worst possible motives to the Arians or Pneumatomachians when he might have gotten a bit further had he appealed to their higher aspirations. What apparently always amazed him were the faults of those he considered his friends. That weakness was in his own temperament and not solely a part of his love for the monastic life. Basil also was at heart a monk. Yet he proved to be a deft political opponent of the later Arians and an attentive administrator among the "orthodox", one who anticipated difficulties from foes and friends alike. Gregory had no such gifts. At times he whined about their absence, or berated his enemies for their lack of virtue and their ineffective desire for good. Yet he could also plainly state his own deficiencies and take the blame, in the process winning back some sympathy.[52] We must not forget, however, that part of his problem lay in his distrust of tyran-

---

[49] *Cod. Theod.* 16.1-2.

[50] Sozomen, *H.E.* 7.5, *PG* 67, 1424C-1425D; Socrates, *H.E.* 5.7, *PG* 67, 573A- 576B; Philostorgius, *H.E.* 9.19, *GCS*, Bidez; Winkelmann, p. 125.

[51] *Carmen de vita sua* II, 736-999, *PG* 37, 1080-1098 and 1506-1918, *PG* 37, 1133-1163. J. Sajdak, "Quaestiones Nazianzenicae. Pars Prima: Quae ratio inter Gregorium Nazianzenum et Maximum Cynicum intercedat," *Eos* 15 (1909), pp. 18-48 has thoroughly discussed the relationship between Maximus and Gregory. Also see J. Mossay, "Note sur Héron-Maxime, écrivain ecclésiastique," *Analecta Bollandiana* 100 (1982) "Mélanges offerts à Baudouin de Gaiffier et François Halkin," pp. 229-336.

[52] *Carmen de vita sua* II, 1044-1061, *PG* 37, 1101-1102. In *Or.* 43.17, *PG* 36, 517B-520A he also notes his gullibility.

ny within the church, an issue that seldom if ever bothered Basil.

Perhaps the only suffering comparable to his problems with Basil over Sasima was his withdrawal from Constantinople, its council and his congregation. That resignation came not only from his ill health and temperamental rejection of petty arguments, but also from the apparent fact that he had become bishop of Constantinople in contradiction to Canon 15 from the Council of Nicaea, which forbid the migration of bishops from one see to another. After the death of Meletius, bishop of Antioch, who was serving as president, the council of 381 elected Nazianzen its president. Those in attendance clearly showed no interest in the Nicene canon which had been broken by many. But when bishops from Egypt and Macedonia arrived late only to find that Nazianzen had accepted the leadership of the council, they insisted that Gregory had received the "orthodox" bishopric of Constantinople after having been appointed bishop of two other cities, Nazianzus and the dreaded Sasima. Ecclesiastical politics once again reared its ugly head. Although Gregory had not taken office at Sasima, and had only served as an interim at Nazianzus, the appointments provided his opponents with an opportunity to raise questions of propriety. He offered to resign in order to demonstrate his own disinterest in the power of an episcopal throne and thus act as a model for those disputing the question of Meletius' successor as bishop of Antioch. He suggested the selection of aged Paulinus so that the schism in Antioch could be ended, but his actions and words were not persuasive. After the attacks, particularly from the Alexandrian contingent, his attempt to give up the see as an act of sacrifice was clouded. If he did not deserve the throne in the first place, his resignation well might indicate his acceptance of the judgment that previously he had gone against canon law. Satisfied that illness would serve as a neutral and acceptable ground, in 381 he gained release from his duties and left the city for Cappadocia.[53] In a letter[54] Gregory insisted that synods were such wicked gatherings that they endangered people's souls. He sensed that the great theological issues of his time were thwarted by such councils, which thrived on political power struggles. He was hurt and frustrated.

His frustration with ecclesiastical politics, however, was not ended. Upon his retirement to Cappadocia, regional bishops urged him to take over the leadership of the congregation in Nazianzus. For nearly a year he put them off. Then, serving as bishop, he suffered through another year's battles, some doctrinal and some administrative. Again charged

---

[53] *Carmen de vita sua* II, 1506-1904, *PG* 37, 1133-1162 and *Or.* 42, *PG* 36, 457A-492C describe these events.

[54] *Ep.* 130, *PG* 37, 225A-B, Gallay (1969), pp. 95-96.

with holding office contrary to canon law as the bishop of more than one
see, he finally retired to the family estates at Arianzus in 383. The last
years of his life were spent in literary pursuits, particularly poetry, epistles
to friends and probably some editing of pieces previously written. He died
in 390.[55]

Gregory will always be a perplexing person for the historian. Only on
occasion were his gifts and education yoked to appropriate tasks. He was
both a bumbling administrator who possessed few political interests or
skills and a talented literary figure who understood the relationship between philosophy, rhetoric and theology. Furthermore he consistently
challenged the grasping power of various bishops within the church. His
temperament never fitted him for the intricacies of church leadership, but
his orations, poetry and letters have influenced many. His attack on
ecclesiastical politics, however, must not be set aside as a quirk of his
character. He remains for millions of Eastern Christians one of the pillars
of orthodoxy—and that not without reason. Yet even as a theologian he
reveals deficiencies although not as many as Western Post-Enlightenment
definitions of ''theology'' would impose. He had large weaknesses, ones
which burdened his life because they worked against his uncommon
strengths. Although he was at times ungraciously forsaken by friends and
unfairly attacked by foes, the multiple demands made upon him were not
entirely different from those placed on others. A lack of either preaching
or administrative skills is still detrimental to the work of any pastor or
bishop. One need not be a poor administrator to challenge tyranny in the
church. The final judgment on his work, however, must be positive. It
justifies his claim to be the Theologian, a title he shares in Eastern tradition only with the apostle John.[56]

Writings

Gregory's works include poetry, epistles and orations. For any early
Christian writer to produce 17,000 verses is astounding given the lack of
such material from other Christian authors. The poetry is of mixed quality. In form it follows the classical patterns of Homer, Theognis and Euri-
pides. Its greatest weakness seems to be a lack of genuine creativity. At
times it has little literary or theological worth, but in specific instances one
of those aspects appears to be of redeeming value. The theological poetry,

---

[55] P. Nautin, ''La date du 'De Viris Inlustribus' de Jérôme, de la mort de Cyrille de
Jérusalem et de celle de Grégoire de Nazianze,'' *RHE* 56 (1961), pp. 33-35 has settled on
the 390 date.

[56] The title apparently first appears in the attribution of a citation to Gregory at the
council of Chalcedon in 451. *Acta Conciliorum Oecumenicorum* 2, 1, 3, 114, 14.

which deals with some of the same issues as the *Theological Orations*, is bland in terms of content even though at points its literary character is fairly high.[57]

Although Nazianzen possessed some poetic talent, he most often continued the classical forms, failing to demonstrate much inventiveness. The total contribution, however, is not without merit. The conformity to classical ideals may in part have been due to Gregory's insistence that Julian was totally mistaken: Christians were indebted to Hellenic culture and could employ its achievements.[58]

Knecht and Palla and Kertsch have taken the time to provide better texts, translations and commentaries for selected poems.[59] Wyss points out that the Theologian shows considerable skill in his elegies. The piece on human nature, *Carmen* I,2 14, retains its power to involve the modern reader.[60] Gregory's epigrams have been collected in various editions.[61] Most of them detail the plight of death or warn against the desecration of graves. Their form is similar to others from the period. Either the dead person, the grave monument, or the earth itself is the speaker. The pain and sorrow they express can still be gripping.[62]

The crowning poetic work from Gregory, one in which form and con-

---

[57] F. Trisoglio, "La poesia della Trinità nell'opera letteraria di San Gregorio di Nazianzo," *Forma Futuri: Studi in onore del Cardinale Michele Pellegrino* (Torino, 1975), pp. 712-740.

[58] One of the most thorough assessments is B. Wyss, "Gregor von Nazianz: Ein Griechisch-Christlicher Dichter des vierten Jahrhunderts," *Museum Helveticum* 6 (1949), pp. 177-220, reprinted in a special edition [newly—perhaps wrongly—titled "Denker" rather than "Dichter"] in the series "Reihe Libelli, Bd. 73," by the Wissenschaftliche Buchgesellschaft (Darmstadt, 1962). Also see Wyss, pp. 808-814. J. Sajdak, "De Gregorio Nazianzeno poetarum Christianorum fonte," *Eos* 18 (1912), pp. 1-30 and M. Pellegrino, *La poesia di S. Gregorio Nazianzo* (Milano, 1932) value the poetry highly as does J. McGuckin, trans. and ed. *Gregory Nazianzen: Selected Poems* (Oxford, 1986). H. Musurillo, "The Poetry of Gregory Nazianzus," *Thought* 45 (1970), pp. 45-55. D. Sykes, "The *Poemata Arcana* of Gregory Nazianzen," *JThS* NS 21 (1970), pp. 32-42, and "The *Poemata Arcana* of St. Gregory Nazianzen: Some Literary Questions," *ByZ* 72 (1979), pp. 6-15 find redeeming features in it.

[59] A. Knecht, *Gregor von Nazianz, Gegen die Putzsucht der Frauen. Verbesserter griechischer Text mit Übersetzung, motivgeschichtlichem Überblick und Kommentar* (Heidelberg, 1972). R. Palla and M. Kertsch, *Gregor von Nazianz, Carmina de virtute 1a/1b*, "Grazer Theologische Studien, Bd. 10" (Graz, 1985). F. Trisoglio, *San Gregorio di Nazianzo in un quarantennio di studi (1925-1965). Rivista lasalliana* 40 (1973) (Torino, 1974), section XIV "Le poesie" pp. 221-249 lists a number of authors who have dealt with sections of Gregory's poetry.

[60] Wyss, p. 813.

[61] *Anthologia Palatina* VIII. One of the most recent is *Epitaffi*, translation and commentary by C. Peri, "Jaca Book 23" (Milano, 1975).

[62] Wyss, p. 813 and Antonio Salvatore, *Tradizione e originalità negli Epigrammi di Gregorio Nazianzeno*, an appendix in "Antologia di epigrammi gregoriani (testo critico e traduzione), (Collana di Studi greci diretta da V. di Falco 33)" (Napoli, 1960). Also see F. Consolino, " 'Sophies amphoteres prytanin': Gli epigrammi funerari di Gregorio Nazianzeno (AP VIII)," *Athenaeum* 75 (1987), pp. 407-425.

tent are unmatched among early Christian authors, is his autobiographical poem, *Carmen de vita sua*.[63] Misch claimed that it could be favorably
compared with Augustine's *Confessions* and that it went beyond the bishop
of Hippo's work from a literary standpoint because of its poetic form. In
his view those qualities make it one of the highest points of autobiography
in all Greek literature.[64] Jaeger warned that even though its literary
character is high it does not contain the insights of Augustine's work.[65]
Otis, however, found Nazianzen's poem to be wanting in literary quality
and in insight into human sin.[66] Yet no one can read the poem without
sensing that both its maxims and personal observations add greatly to a
knowledge of human personality. It points up the complexity of Gregory
himself more than any other single work; it also represents something
original in autobiography.

   One of the most important claims about the poetry is the conclusion of
Sykes that Nazianzen, generally within his verses, evidences his classical
education and the good judgment when to employ that background and
when to rely on more Christian sources. According to Sykes, the Theologian normally wrote his poetry with the language of Homer and Calli-
machus, but in the so-called dogmatic poems his positions were taken
primarily from Scripture and Christian tradition. In the historical sections, Biblical heroes provided the models for daily living. Yet in those
verses that deal mostly with moral issues, the full depth of Gregory's classical education appears.[67] In the continuing debate over Nazianzen's
mastery of classical culture for Christian purposes, Sykes' observation is
crucial.

   Another significant claim is Louis Bouyer's assertion that Gregory's
poetry contains his greatest insights into Christian spirituality. Particular-

---

   [63] C. Jungck, *Gregor von Nazianz. De vita sua. Einleitung, Text, Übersetzung, Kommentar*
(Heidelberg, 1974) and D. Meehan, trans., *Saint Gregory of Nazianzus: Three Poems: Concerning His Own Affairs, Concerning Himself and the Bishops, Concerning His Own Life*, "Fathers of
the Church, Vol. 75" (Washington, DC, 1987).
   [64] G. Misch, *A History of Autobiography in Antiquity*, trans. from the 3rd ed. by E. Eickes,
Vol. 2 (London, 1950), pp. 600-624 offers a study of Nazianzen's autobiographical
poetry.
   [65] W. Jaeger, *Early Christianity and Greek Paideia* (Cambridge, MA, 1961), p. 80.
   [66] Otis, p. 123.
   [67] D. Sykes, "The Bible and Greek Classics in Gregory Nazianzen's Verse," *Studia
Patristica*, Vol. XVII, Part Three, ed. by E. Livingstone (Oxford, 1982), pp. 1127-1130.
The employment of classical materials extends further than style or vocabulary. Also see
his "Gregory Nazianzen as Didactic Poet," *Studia Patristica* XVI, Part 2, ed. by E. Livingstone (Berlin, 1985), pp. 433-437. A. Cameron, "Gregory Nazianzen and Apollo," *JThS*
NS 20 (1969), pp. 240-241 suggests that Gregory used an oracle of Apollo in one section
of the poetry.

ly the poem "On Virtue"[68] demonstrates that the Theologian found the Hellenic ideal lacking. For him Christian revelation and the monastic life held the highest goals for human existence. Contemplation, indeed divinization, is for Gregory the proper end of all human beings.[69]

On the basis of Ep. 53, Wyss notes that Nazianzen is the first Christian Greek writer to make a collection of his own letters.[70] That is one more indication of Gregory's sense of his own importance. His epistles further evidence his dependence upon classical culture,[71] but they sometimes strike one as advanced rhetorical exercises in which both the deeper views of the writer and those expected from the recipient are unavailable. That is true particularly of the letters addressed to Basil not long after Nazianzen's visit in Pontus. They appear to be more concerned with literary style than they are with an expression of personal feelings or a description of events. At least the attitudes present in them are ambiguous.[72] When, however, Gregory focuses his energies within epistolary form he can be both informative and moving. His advice to Nicobulus concerning the art of letter writing, if taken seriously by moderns, would raise the level of correspondence. How often we receive letters either too long or too short, lacking in grace but not utterly disgraceful, too cute to be beautiful and not understandable to specialist and average person alike. To write well in few words is still rare.[73] The letters also contain other doctrinal content. Nazianzen's Christological thought is only fully known through the theological epistles.[74] Without them we would not have such a detailed account of his attack on the Apollinarians.

From the standpoint of literary attainment and theological prowess, however, Gregory's orations are the basis of his fame. Kennedy insists that his panegyrics are the best since Demosthenes.[75] Byzantine literati

---

[68] *Carmen* II, 885-909, *PG* 37, 744-746. R. Palla and M. Kertsch, *Gregor von Nazianz, Carmina de virtute 1a/1b*, "Grazer Theologische Studien, Bd. 10" (Graz, 1985).

[69] L. Bouyer, *The Spirituality of the New Testament and the Fathers*, "History of Christian Spirituality, Vol. I" (New York, 1963), pp. 343-351. Also see J. Rousse, "Grégoire de Nazianze," *Dictionnaire de Spiritualité*, Tome VI (Paris, 1967), pp. 932-971.

[70] Wyss, p. 807.

[71] J. Lercher, "Die Persönlichkeit des heiligen Gregorius von Nazianz und seine Stellung zur klassischen Bildung (aus seinen Briefen)," unpublished doctoral dissertation, Der Leopold-Franzens-Universität, Innsbruck, 1949.

[72] *Eps.* 1-5, *PG* 37, 21A-29B, Gallay (1969), pp. 1-7. They may only have been a response to the call from Basil, *Ep.* 14, *PG* 32, 276B-277C, which describes their monastic retreat as filled with lovely sights and fragrances coming from its meadows. No retreat for desert fathers there.

[73] *Eps.* 51, 52, and 54, *PG* 37, 105A-109B, Gallay (1969), pp. 47-50.

[74] See Gallay (1974).

[75] Kennedy (1983), p. 237.

like Michael Psellos and John Siceliotes made such comparisons. Psellos praised Nazianzen's style;[76] Siceliotes used stylistic examples from Gregory where earlier commentators on Hermogenes had employed models from Demosthenes and other noted Greek rhetors.[77] Prizes are seldom awarded in the late twentieth century for invective, particularly the vitriolic type that Gregory wrote against the emperor Julian, but those two pieces are fine examples of the genre.[78] The bulk of the orations, however, presents theological themes in the form of homilies. Bernardi has insisted that not all the orations were delivered; some of them appear to be literary products from exordium to peroration.[79] Most were occasioned by feasts or topics; they are not sermons preached on Biblical books as much of the corpus from Chrysostom is. Gregory may have offered such homilies or at least composed some commentaries on the Bible.[80] Jerome spoke highly of Nazianzen's exegetical abilities.[81] Mason, while conceding that Gregory often showed interpretive skills above the common levels of his age, still suggested that he lacked the exegetical insight of Basil,[82] but Gallay finds his interpretive efforts illuminating and Hanson insists that of all the fourth-century interpreters, he is the one most

---

[76] See A. Mayer, "Psellos' Rede über den rhetorischen Charakter des Gregor von Nazianz," *ByZ* 20 (1911), pp. 27-100.

[77] See A. Poynton, "Gregory of Nazianzus and the Greek Rhetoricians, A Supplement to the Index of Walz *Rhetores Graeci*, Vol. 9," a typed manuscript given to the Library of Congress, April 26, 1934. In that list the Oxford scholar noticed, among other things, the illustrations drawn from Nazianzen that Siceliotes used in his commentary on Hermogenes' *On Ideas*.

[78] See C. Moreschini, "L'opera e la personalità dell'imperatore Giuliano nelle due 'Invectivae' di Gregorio Nazianzeno," *Forma Futuri* (Torino, 1975), pp. 416-432.

[79] Bernardi, pp. 93-260.

[80] Elias of Crete in Jacob Billius, *Eliae Cretensis Metropolitani Commentarius in Gregorii Nazianzeni, Gregorii Nazianzenii Theologi, Opera*, Tomus Secundus (Coloniae, 1690), col. 230A in his comments on *Or.* 2—Or. 1 in the Billius edition—speaks of a work he calls the History of Ezekiel the Prophet, perhaps a type of commentary on that Old Testament cycle. It is no longer extant.

[81] Jerome, *Ep.* 50.2, *PL* 22, 513 states with pride that Gregory and Didymus the Blind were his teachers of Scripture. His *Ep.* 52.8, *PL* 22, 534-535 has a strange account of how he asked Nazianzen a question concerning a phrase in Luke. Gregory told him he would understand the point best if he heard it in the midst of one of Gregory's orations where the applause would persuade him, even against his will, or he would feel a fool. Some secondary interpreters have castigated Nazianzen because of this text. For example see Wyss, "Gregor von Nazianz. Ein Griechisch-Christlicher Dichter," *Museum Helveticum* 6 (1949), p. 184. If Gregory meant it literally, he should be taken to task. But it is also possible that he was offering a humorous aside, not primarily a tactless comment on his manipulative power. Jerome at times could be even more humorless than Nazianzen. Gregory did speak highly of free will throughout his corpus. He also despised sophistry even as he accepted and employed it and better rhetorical skills. He was seldom if ever shy about his own gifts.

[82] Mason, pp. xiv-xv.

marked by a common sense approach. His exegesis is "both ingenious and honest."[83] The study of these five orations, particularly Oration 30, indicates that Nazianzen brought considerable hermeneutical skill and theological insight to the analysis of Scripture.[84]

Christian Paideia: *Philosophy, Rhetoric and Theology*

The most significant theme to arise out of the study undertaken for this commentary is the intricate interpenetration of philosophy, rhetoric and theology in the work of Gregory Nazianzen. It probably deserves a separate monograph, but here it can be sketched so that the reader will be aware of its importance in the educational debate between Gregory and his opponents. An explication of that theme under the rubric of *paideia* is appropriate but difficult. The foremost complication concerns the relationship between philosophy and rhetoric in ancient Greek education.[85]

It is a commonplace, found in modern news accounts and supported by some students of classical literature, that rhetoricians are the opposite of philosophers. The famous educational debate between Greek philosophical and rhetorical schools in the fourth century B.C.E. has often formed the context for such definitions of rhetoric and philosophy. Plato's attack on the sophists is assumed to be one primary feature of ancient education even into the late Roman period. Proper *paideia* is then philosophy vanquishing rhetoric.

Students conversant with ancient Greek literature often turn specifically to the *Gorgias* as the sharpest critique of rhetoric. There Plato attacked the sophists—particularly the famous Gorgias—as men who practiced things technical, who pursued an art without a subject. In Plato's view the practitioners of sophistic rhetoric used its techniques to argue any

---

[83] P. Gallay, "Grégoire de Nazianze le Théologien," *Le monde grec ancien et la Bible*, ed. by C. Mondésert, "Bible de tous les Temps, I" (Paris, 1984), pp. 313-334. Hanson, p. 846.

[84] For a comparison of the Cappadocians as exegetes, see H. Weiss, *Die grossen Kappadozier Basilius, Gregor von Nazianz und Gregor von Nyssa als Exegeten* (Braunsberg, 1872).

[85] Most of the monographs that devote considerable attention to rhetoric in the Gregorian corpus emphasize the rhetorical techniques Nazianzen employed. They do not focus particularly on the relationship of rhetoric to philosophy and theology in his works. See M. Guignet, *S. Grégoire de Nazianze et la rhétorique* (Paris, 1911), E. Fleury, *S. Grégoire de Nazianze et son temps* (Paris, 1930), and J. Plagnieux, *S. Grégoire de Nazianze Théologien*, "Études de science religieuse, VII" (Paris, 1952). R. Ruether, *Gregory of Nazianzus: Rhetor and Philosopher* (Oxford, 1969) rehearses previous research and thus offers few new insights on the question, except that she misunderstands Gregory as a rigid Christian apologist, one who found Greek religion, philosophy and culture to be blasphemous. In rebuttal, see my "Of Thorns and Roses: The Logic of Belief in Gregory Nazianzen," *CH* 53 (1984), pp. 455-464.

position. They avoided questions of ultimate values and made pragmatic choices uninformed by any eternal verities. No sophist could withstand the penetrating questions of Socrates, because there was no structure to, indeed, no unshakeable foundation for such positions.[86]

The *Gorgias* is as forceful as most of Plato's work. Yet its dialogue form and particularly its longer speeches represent his attempt to demonstrate that he could educate students for the various positions within the *polis* better than the rhetoricians who often trained children from the wealthy families. He engaged rhetoric at its weakest point, its shrinking into a practical study in which primary questions were often ignored. Within the *Gorgias*, however, Plato showed himself to be one who had command of the techniques of persuasion on which the rhetoricians based their view of *paideia*. More important, within his *Phaedrus* at crucial points Plato spoke of rhetoric and philosophy in terms of their similarities. Although he usually preferred the more philosophical term "dialectics," if truth were sought, he cared little whether the words used to describe that search were related basically to philosophy or to rhetoric. His underlying sense of *paideia* suggested that when certain conditions were met, the hostility between philosophy and rhetoric as two different systems of education could be avoided. What might be called a philosophical rhetoric would combine the two.[87]

Some students of Graeco-Roman culture have seen Aristotle's *Rhetoric* as in sympathy with Plato's views on philosophical rhetoric. The Stagirite's work begins with statements about the philosophical and logical basis of rhetoric and tries to maintain that level of discussion throughout. Aristotle is not always successful, but his insistence upon philosophical investigation and his concern for the relationship between philosophy and rhetoric led to the development of a position that at least in terms of length and depth was not provided by Plato.[88] Furthermore, J. Sprute has studied Aristotle's theory of enthymemes and shown that Aristotle saw enthymemes and syllogisms as two parts of the one technical structure needed to work with words and arguments. As the *Rhetoric* indicates, the relationship between the two forms is delicate. A syllogism, which deals with necessary conclusions, may be stated in a form different from its three parts of major premise, minor premise and conclusion. For

---

[86] Plato, *Gorgias* 449D-463D, 500B-501C.

[87] *Phaedrus* 259E-274B. Kennedy (1963), pp. 61-66, 74-79, and 82-114 describes Plato's philosophical rhetoric in detail.

[88] See particularly W. Grimaldi, *Studies in the Philosophy of Aristotle's Rhetoric*, "Hermes, Einzelschriften 25" (Wiesbaden, 1972), his *Aristotle, Rhetoric I: A Commentary* (New York, 1980), and L. Arnhart, *Aristotle on Political Reasoning: A Commentary on the "Rhetoric"* (De Kalb, IL, 1981).

the sake of an audience that listens to an oral argument, or for a general reader, such a formal demonstration may be presented in two parts: "if"—"then," or "it is thus"—"for." Either of those would be a syllogism in enthymematic form.

Yet probability questions, queries not susceptible to syllogistic argument, can be argued technically in that same enthymematic form. Thus when one hears or reads an enthymeme, one must be careful to see if it is a necessary demonstration presented only in two parts or a probability argument offered in two parts because it cannot be given syllogistic form.[89]

That distinction provides the bridge between deductive demonstrations and inductive presentations. It is the way over the chasm that separates what is often viewed as strict logic presented in syllogistic forms and probability arguments presented in rhetorical styles such as the use of questions or definitions. In terms of method it is crucial for understanding Nazianzen's debate with the Neo-Arians and is itself clearly developed within Aristotle's *Rhetoric*.

The quality of that treatise, however, has caused numerous problems, specifically in terms of the text itself. How often Aristotle actually lectured on the topic is difficult to ascertain, although it does not appear to have been his most pressing concern. Furthermore the later sections of the *Rhetoric* do not always agree with the earlier ones, thus leaving us with the strong possibility that we are dealing with an unedited set of notes. That chilling prospect leaves many queries unanswerable.

We are also confronted with the decision made by later students of Aristotle who found, copied and handed on his texts, ones who did not grasp Plato's view of philosophical rhetoric or the Stagirite's vision of the close relationship between philosophy and rhetoric. The *Organon*, the collection of Aristotle's treatises on logic as it normally appears in critical editions and translations, excludes the *Rhetoric* and the *Poetics*. That version of Aristotle has formed the basis for the study of this master in the West from the copying of the main extant Byzantine manuscripts until the present. Moraux's study of the Aristotelian manuscripts shows that as early as the 10th century the *Categories*, *On Interpretation*, *Prior Analytics*, *Posterior Analytics*, *Topics* and *On Sophistical Refutations* appeared together while the *Rhetoric* belonged to another manuscript tradition.[90] Thus it is

---

[89] J. Sprute, *Die Enthymemtheorie der aristotelischen Rhetorik*, "Abhandlungen der Akademie der Wissenschaften in Göttingen, Philologisch-historische Klasse, Dritte Folge, 124" (Göttingen, 1982). See Aristotle's *Rhetoric* 1356A-1359B and 1394B.

[90] P. Moraux, *Aristoteles graecus: die griechischen Manuskripte des Aristoteles* (Berlin, 1976). The 10th century manuscript which has the *Organon* as usually described is Florence Laur. 72.5. R. Kassel, *Der Text der Aristotelischen Rhetorik* (Berlin, 1971), pp. 2-18 lists fifty

not uncommon for modern interpreters to treat Aristotelian logic as restricted to the six works.

Porphyry may bear some responsibility for this arrangement. At least unlike his teacher, Plotinus, he insisted upon the importance of Aristotle's works on logic in determining the nature of the discipline.[91] His *Isagoge* is essentially an introduction to Aristotle's *Categories* that evidences knowledge of other treatises included in the normal *Organon*, particularly the *Posterior Analytics* and the *Topics*.[92] An overwhelming number of Greek manuscripts which include what most scholars consider to be the Aristotelian *Organon* begin with either the text of Porphyry's *Isagoge* as an introduction or with a commentary on the *Isagoge*, such as that of Ammonius, David, or Ps.-Alexander of Aphrodisias.[93]

Strong evidence for Nazianzen's dependence upon the Aristotelian logic of the usual Western *Organon* would be at hand if an anonymous piece had been written by him as some manuscripts claim. Yet the work, which includes a synopsis of logic and comments on the quadrivium, has no clear features that require him to be its author, even though a reference to "the divine Paul" and an allusion to Hebrews 7.9 suggest a Christian writer.[94] Good judgment demands that we leave the work anonymous.

---

manuscripts of the *Rhetoric*, none of which contains any of the usual pieces from the *Organon*. The oldest is Paris BN 1741 from the 10th century, which includes Aristotle's *Rhetoric* and *Poetics* in a collection of rhetorical treatises.

[91] A. Lloyd, "Neoplatonic Logic and Aristotelian Logic I and II," *Phronesis* 1.1 (1955), pp. 58-72 and 1.2 (1956), pp. 146-160 persuasively argues that much of the credit for reinstating Aristotle's "categories and predicables" goes to Neo-Platonists, not Stoics.

[92] *Porphyrii Isagoge et in Aristotelis Categorias Commentarium*, ed. by A. Busse, *CAG* IV,1 (1887).

[93] Moraux, *Aristoteles graecus*. For example see Athens 1067, Basel F.II.21, Berlin Graec. quart. 73, Bologna 3637, Escorial Phi III.10, Florence 72.5, etc.

[94] *Anonymi Logica et Quadrivius, cum Scholiis Antiquis*, ed. by J. Heiberg, "det Kgl. Danske Videnskabernes Selskab. Historisk-filologiske Meddeleser XV,1" (Kopenhagen, 1929), section 32, p. 26, lines 1-4. A number of early Christian writers use the adjective θεσπέσιος concerning apostles. *A Patristic Greek Lexicon*, ed. by G. Lampe (Oxford, 1961), p. 646 notes references in Clement of Alexandria, Eusebius and Cyril of Alexandria. Thus it provides no significant internal evidence for determining authorship.

The case against attributing the treatise to Gregory is twofold. First, the extended discussion of the relationships between dialectic, rhetoric, sophistic, and poetic—which is found in sections 64-67, see Heiberg, pp. 47-50—does not bring to mind specific analogues in the Gregorian corpus. There is no mention of enthymematic forms; in fact, rhetoric is described as growing out of falsehood and the lack of reason, more in agreement with the positions taken against sophistic rhetoric in Plato's *Gorgias*. Second, although four of the manuscripts Heiberg used for his edition attribute either the synopsis of logic or the study of the quadrivium to Gregory, six others mention Michael Psellos—one of them suggests Psellos or a monk named Euthymios—and another speaks of Psellos' disciples. Most important, the two oldest manuscripts, both from the eleventh century, Palatin. Heidelberg Greek 281 and Mutin. Estens. III C 11, as well as some of the later ones, are anonymous. See Heiberg, pp. v-xix.

Further study of the piece would doubtless uncover more information. It is of interest both to the history of logic and the history of Christian theology. Yet before we leave its connection with Gregory, we should note that certain copyists from the fourteenth through the sixteenth century as well as Johannes Wegelinus in the seventeenth century saw similarities of interest between such a treatise and the corpus of Nazianzen. The ἀπὸ φωνῆς appellation on some of the manuscripts does at least indicate that a commentary on Aristotle's logic appeared to those copyists as in the style and after the thought of Gregory. Furthermore, Leontius of Byzantium and John of Damascus found Gregory much to their liking and both are noted for their use of Aristotle. Thus any interpreter who views Nazianzen's work as often dependent upon Aristotle stands within a tradition that is both old and distinguished.

Although extant Greek manuscripts of Aristotle do not include the *Rhetoric* within the usual *Organon*, the collection of his logical works, evidence for a different understanding of Aristotelian logic exists. Moraux has offered some details about this tradition.[95] A group of late antique Neo-Platonic commentators on Aristotle treated both the *Rhetoric* and the *Poetics* as parts of Aristotelian logic. Ammonius at the end of the fifth or the beginning of the sixth century, in comments on the *Prior Analytics*, spoke about three types of syllogisms: the apodeictic, the dialectic and the sophistic.[96] In remarks concerning the *Categories* he also insisted that Aristotelian logic was divided into syllogistic and asyllogistic sections.[97] Ammonius' students Simplicius and Olympiodorus as well as Olympiodorus' student Elias distinguished three parts of the logic: the direct study of apodeictic method in the *Posterior Analytics*; the preparation for such investigation in the *Categories*, *On Interpretation* and the *Prior Analytics*; and the necessary correctives for various types of problems, ones discussed in the *Topics*, *On Sophistical Refutations*, *Rhetoric* and *Poetics*.[98] Elias mentions five kinds of syllogisms: 1) the apodeictic that are entirely true, 2) the poetic that are entirely false, 3) the dialectic that are more true than false, 4) the sophistic that are more false than true and 5) the rhetorical that are true and false.[99] Kennedy suggests that scholars in late antiquity, particularly in the Alexandrian circle, sometimes lectured on Aristotle's *Rhetoric* at the end of their discussion of the usual *Organon*, but none of

---

[95] P. Moraux, *Les Listes Anciennes des Ouvrages d'Aristote*, "Aristote Traductions et Études," (Louvain, 1951), pp. 177-183.

[96] Ammonius, *In Anal. pr. prosem.* 11.22-38.

[97] Ammonius, *In Cat.* 5.6.

[98] Simplicius, *In Cat.* 4.28; Olympiodorus, *Proleg.* 8.19; Elias, *In Cat.* 116.29ff.

[99] Elias, *In Cat.* 116.35ff.

those comments have come down to us. Perhaps none were published.[100]

Moraux warns that it is impossible to discover exactly when this broad-er understanding of Aristotelian logic first appeared.[101] He suggests that portions of Albinus' work indicate an interest in the different types of syllogisms[102] and that Diogenes Laertius describes a group of Stoics who separated logic into two sections, rhetoric and logic. Diogenes identifies Cleanthes as employing six divisions for his work: dialectic, rhetoric, ethics, politics, physics and theology. Evidently Zeno of Tarsus used a similar division.[103] Such an order implies a positive valuation of rhetoric and perhaps a connection between dialectic and rhetoric, between philosophy and persuasion, similar to that found in Aristotle. This view of rhetoric was available among the early Stoics in the third century C.E.

Some Arabic translations of and commentaries on Aristotle suggest a manuscript tradition that included the *Rhetoric* within the *Organon*. Aver-roës, the twelfth-century philosopher, wrote *Three Short Commentaries on Aristotle's "Topics," "Rhetoric," and "Poetics,"* which evidently came from a collection entitled *Short Commentary on Aristotle's "Organon."*[104] Interest-ingly the fuller work seems to have included, in the following order, an introduction based on Porphyry's *Isagoge*, then the *Categories, On Interpreta-tion, Prior Analytics, Topics 2-7, Posterior Analytics, On Sophistical Refutations, Topics, Rhetoric* and *Poetics.*[105] The actual commentary treats the *Rhetoric* as a discussion of logic.[106] Peters notes that Ishaq ibn Hunayn about 910 C.E. translated what is considered the normal *Organon* and the *Rhetoric*, but it is difficult to know if he or his apparent Syriac translation source put them together as one unit. A contents page lists the treatises in order with the *Rhetoric* following *On Sophistical Refutations*, but the *Rhetoric* was bound into the manuscript, Paris BN 2346, at a later date and placed be-fore the *Organon.*[107] Yet Margoliouth describes the Arabic translation of

---

[100] Kennedy (1983), p. 318. See B. Keil, "Zwei Identificationen," *Hermes* 42 (1907), pp. 548-563, who details this breakdown of animosity between philosophy and rhetoric in Neo-Platonic circles.

[101] P. Moraux, *Les Listes Anciennes des Ouvrages d'Aristote*, pp. 181-182.

[102] Albinus, *Epit.* 2, 3 and 6.8.

[103] Diogenes Laertius, 7.41 = *SVF* 3, p. 209, Fr. 3.

[104] *Averroës: Three Short Commentaries On Aristotle's "Topics," "Rhetoric," and "Poetics,"* ed. by C. Butterworth (Albany, NY, 1977), p. viii.

[105] Ibid., p. 5. Unfortunately Butterworth is unaware of the late antique Neo-Platonic interpretation of Aristotelian logic mentioned above. Thus he insists that Averroës himself changed the order and inserted treatises that do not belong in the *Organon*.

[106] Ibid., pp. 57-78.

[107] F. Peters, *Aristoteles Arabus: The Oriental Translations and Commentaries on the Aristotelian Corpus* (Leiden, 1968), pp. 26-27. R. Kassel, *Der Text der Aristotelischen Rhetorik* (Berlin, 1971), p. 90, n. 9 indicates that Peters was mistaken in his attribution of the manuscript. It is anonymous. For other differences in the Arabic manuscript tradition of Aristotle see R. Walzer, "Arabic transmission of Greek thought to medieval Europe," *Bulletin of the John Rylands Library* 29.1 (1945), pp. 160-185.

Aristotle's *Rhetoric* in Paris BN 882a as including only the *Poetics* in the same volume. It dates from the beginning of the eleventh century and depends upon at least one earlier Syriac translation that itself relied on yet an earlier Greek manuscript.[108] Wallace-Hadrill notes some Syrians produced translations of Aristotle's logical works that resemble the normal Western *Organon*, while other Syrians most interested in Aristotelian logic also translated the *Rhetoric*.[109]

Although the late antique commentaries, as well as certain medieval Arabic traditions that include the *Rhetoric* in the *Organon*, are neither the only nor necessarily the earliest evidence we have, they are significant because, as noted above, Aristotle in his *Rhetoric* states the relationship between rhetoric and dialectic. For him enthymematic arguments deal with audiences who must participate in decisions or with questions that defy more than probable answers. He saw a direct connection between his formal syllogisms and informal enthymemes and thus did not fully separate philosophy and rhetoric, logic and persuasion. He argued that the enthymematic form could be chosen so that the audience would itself provide the assumed premise even though the syllogistic form of an argument could be selected. In that case the conclusion was not a probable, but a demonstrable one. That same enthymematic form, however, could be used to present arguments that could reach only probable conclusions, not demonstrable ones.[110] That explanation of enthymemes provides the connection between the strictest logic of syllogistic operations and the less rigorous "logic" of probabilistic operations, ones that can be handled by rhetorical questions, authoritative proverbs, inductive method and grammatical analysis.

The possibility exists that some fourth-century C.E. philosophical schools, those which adopted Aristotelian logic as part of their curriculum, may have used the Greek manuscript and commentary tradition that included the *Rhetoric* among the logical works. An interpretation similar to that of Ammonius and his sixth-century C.E. inheritors may have appeared earlier, particularly since some second-century C.E. Middle Platonists like Albinus and early fourth- and third-century B.C.E. Stoics like Cleanthes and Zeno of Tarsus had already noticed a connection. If during Nazianzen's era the *Rhetoric* had been received in a manuscript and commentary tradition that included it among the logical treatises, any philosophical school interested in logic might have given careful con-

---

[108] D. Margoliouth, "On the Arabic Version of Aristotle's Rhetoric," *Semitic Studies in Memory of Rev. Dr. Alexandr Kohut* (Berlin, 1897), p. 376.

[109] D. Wallace-Hadrill, *Christian Antioch: A Study of Early Christian Thought in the East* (Cambridge, 1982), pp. 106-116.

[110] *Rhetoric* 1354A12-1357A31.

sideration to Aristotelian rhetoric in two ways. They might have studied Aristotle's use of enthymemes for the discussion of probability questions not amenable to formal demonstration and his use of them for public presentations where the audience was to be involved, but the question could be formally demonstrated.

In turn any rhetorical school might have been interested in logical problems and truth questions and thus the climate of suspicion between rhetoric and philosophy would be lessened, perhaps eliminated in important circles. According to Nock the latter was indeed the general situation. "There was little or no antagonism between rhetoric and philosophy under the Empire. Further rhetorical training tended to include some philosophy."[111] Therefore, when investigating a fourth-century C.E. figure like Nazianzen, no reason exists to employ the B.C.E. debate between philosophy and rhetoric, found in Plato's *Gorgias*, as the interpretative key. The better category is an eclectic sense of *paideia*, a philosophical rhetoric that includes Plato's *Phaedrus* and the broadest sense of Aristotelian logic, the normal *Organon* and at least the *Rhetoric*.

The development of this philosophical rhetoric, however, becomes difficult to trace not merely because any Greek manuscripts of the large Aristotelian *Organon* have been lost, or parts of the Neo-Platonic, Arabic and Syriac traditions are too seldom consulted, or Aristotle has too infrequently been studied on his own terms. Following that development of philosophical rhetoric is also problematic because much secondary literature has focused the history of rhetoric more on the study of treatises written about the subject than on an investigation of actual orations. There are obvious exceptions in which one author's work has been the central concern.[112] Some general histories, however, have been more interested in pieces describing the theory than those illustrating the practice. If a manual primarily offers technical advice, it is usually placed in the category of technical rhetoric. On that basis some of the great works have been hard to classify. For instance among the Latins, the writings of Cicero and Quintilian not only contain an overwhelming amount of practical advice but also some important points concerning the structure of so-called "philosophical rhetoric." Solmsen suggested that most ancient study of rhetoric was dominated by technical manuals. In his view the philosophical rhetoric of Plato and Aristotle did not receive either much attention or exposition because it was most often forced from the field by the technical concerns of later writers.[113] Kennedy in his one-volume

---

[111] A.D. Nock, *Sallustius* (London 1926; [reprint Hildesheim, 1966]), p. xix. He provides a general survey of this situation pp. xvii-xxxix.

[112] For example G. Kennedy, *Quintilian* (New York, 1969).

[113] F. Solmsen, "The Aristotelian Tradition in Ancient Rhetoric," *American Journal of Philology* 62 (1941) pp. 35–50 and 169–190, reprinted in *Aristotle: The Classical Heritage of*

history of rhetoric insisted that after falling into disuse during Hellenistic times Aristotle's *Rhetoric* did not play a serious role in the definition of rhetoric until the twentieth century.[114] For the purposes of this present work, his comment that "Christianity sought the truth, but no Christian writer specifically took up Plato or Aristotle's views of rhetoric" becomes important, as does his statement that while the Cappadocians were somewhat successful in bringing philosophy and theology together, they castigated classical rhetoric and did not make, "or seriously attempt, a synthesis of classical and Christian rhetorical theory."[115]

As far as the extant literature about rhetoric is concerned, Solmsen's views and Kennedy's first position have merit. Yet one of the questions that can be raised is the possibility of studying rhetorical treatises or orations to discover not only their technical devises but also their underlying logical structure. The point this procedure makes is rather simple. Some authors prefer to write novels rather than write about the theory of novels. Yet that does not force those in the discipline of literature to avoid describing the theory of a novel employed by a great novelist. Exploring the theory of rhetoric used by a great rhetorician can reach interesting conclusions. Using that approach one discovers that Gregory Nazianzen was a philosophical rhetorician. The claim can be demonstrated by an investigation of his orations rather than denied because he did not write a treatise on philosophical rhetoric. In the third volume of his history of rhetoric, Kennedy undertook such a procedure in describing the contributions of Nazianzen. As a result he provided a more succinct and penetrating analysis of Gregory's synthesis of classical rhetoric and Christian theology than any previous historian of rhetoric, a second position different from that taken in his one-volume history.[116] In a separate article he also noticed instances of Nazianzen's reliance upon Plato's *Phaedrus* particularly in the Theologian's second oration, indications that Gregory knew the Platonic treatise that first described the concept of philosophical rhetoric.[117] What is envisioned here is a fuller explication of the second position Kennedy sketched. It will be argued that Gregory did stand in the line of philosophical rhetoricians, a claim Kennedy first denied and then espoused.

Secondary studies of the Cappadocians often have either concentrated on the Platonic tradition employed by these teachers or have commented on the attack of Basil and Gregory of Nyssa made on Eunomius for his

---

Rhetoric, ed. by K. Erickson (Metuchen, NJ, 1975), pp. 278–309.

[114] Kennedy (1980), p. 81.

[115] ibid., pp. 81 and 143.

[116] Kennedy (1983), pp. 215-239.

[117] Kennedy, "Later Greek Philosophy and Rhetoric," *Philosophy and Rhetoric* 3 (1980), pp. 192-196.

use of Aristotle. Yet both de Ghellinck[118] and Peters[119] noticed the Cappadocians depended upon Aristotelian dialectic in their struggle with the later Arians. The most important work for investigating this question in relation to Nazianzen, however, is the doctoral dissertation of Focken, written at Berlin under Norden and Diels.[120] He looked at the uses of argument in Nazianzen and correctly showed how much Gregory depended upon his rhetorical education. In addition Focken indicated his own grasp of the relationship between rhetoric and philosophy by devoting an introductory chapter to these concepts. In his view, only the interpreter of the Theologian who understood the relationship between syllogistic deduction and rhetorical induction in Aristotle could see the intricate way in which Nazianzen employed Aristotelian logic.

Focken finds his primary examples of syllogistic deduction offered in enthymematic form within Oration 29, but suggests a similar analysis of Oration 31 could be offered. The employment of the enthymematic form means that an argument would be stated with two propositions, but it could be restated in the syllogistic form of three propositions. In Oration 29 Gregory argued that the Eunomians did not have a grasp of *paideia*, particularly at the level of understanding their own misuse of logic. Focken describes five passages within that oration, sections 2, 10, 11, 12 and 16, in which Gregory employs enthymemes. In the selected instances, the enthymemes could be stated as formal syllogisms and can be referred to various passages of Aristotle's *Prior Analytics*, Part I, particularly chapters 1, 4, 25, 32, 34, 36, 37, 38 and 41.[121] Focken's work makes it difficult to doubt that Gregory had studied Aristotelian logic and rhetoric seriously enough that he employed, in written or oral form for public audiences, enthymemes that could be backed by syllogisms. He used such techniques in order to defend his own positions and to attack the Eunomian or later Arian leaders who evidently prided themselves on and had the reputation of being masters in logical debate.[122]

---

[118] J. de Ghellinck, "Quelques Appréciations de la Dialectique d'Aristote durant les Conflits trinitaires du IVe siècle," *RHE* 25 (1930), pp. 5-42.

[119] F. Peters, *Aristotle and the Arabs: The Aristotelian Tradition in Islam*, "New York University Studies in Near Eastern Civilization, No. 1" (New York, 1968), pp. 18-22.

[120] Focken (1912). In a previous article, "Of Thorns and Roses: The Logic of Belief in Gregory Nazianzen," *CH* 53 (1984), 455-464 I have indicated the deficiency in some secondary surveys and the importance of Focken's work. D. Tsames, Η ΔΙΑΛΕΚΤΙΚΗ ΦΥΣΙΣ ΤΗΣ ΔΙΔΑΣΚΑΛΙΑΣ ΓΡΗΓΟΡΙΟΥ ΤΟΥ ΘΕΟΛΟΓΟΥ (Thessaloniki, 1969) deals with a number of the features presented in this section on *paideia*, but his observations are not as clear and penetrating as those of Focken.

[121] Focken, pp. 3-20.

[122] Socrates, *H.E.* 1.5, *PG* 67, 41A-B and Sozomen, *H.E.* 1.15, *PG* 67, 904C remarked about Arius' dialectical skills. Sozomen, *H.E.* 3.15 and 6.26, *PG* 67, 1085A and 1361D noted the reputation of Aetius for intricate argument and indicated that Eunomius

Yet Focken was able to take his argument a step further. Sections of Gregory's poetry contain examples of Aristotelian enthymemes that can be stated in syllogistic form. Examining *Carmen* IV, 16-20, 54-57 and 80-86 as well as *Carmen* II, 6-8, Focken demonstrated that formal Aristotelian logic as seen in the *Prior Analytics* stands behind some enthymematic structures within the poetry.[123]

There are further examples of Nazianzen's dependence upon Aristotelian logical principles for his attack on later Arian logical positions. At other places within Oration 29, ones Focken did not discuss, Gregory followed the Stagirite. In 29.15 he said the Eunomians gave evidence of their poor education since they confused the conditioned and unconditioned use of a single term. The phrase appears in Aristotle's *On Sophistical Refutations* 167a, 1.7. Nazianzen ridiculed the Eunomians in 29.12 for proposing ἀγέννητος as descriptive of God's essence because they showed themselves to be unaware of the principle: possession precedes deprivation, a principle that reflects Aristotle's *Categories* 12a, 26ff. Mathieu notes that the same section, 29.12, has statements that resemble claims in Aristotle's *Categories* 5 and *Topics* 1.15, 2.8, 4.4 and 7.1.[124] In 30.15 Nazianzen attacks the later Arians because they ignore the axiom that not everything predicated of a class can be predicated of every individual of that class, a principle stated in Aristotle's *Categories* 1a, 20ff.

Within Oration 29 Gregory's interest in logic is reflected in yet another way. By employing the liar's paradox as an example of two things that are contradictory and yet must be true, he took a position that recalls the title of a treatise by Chrysippus.[125] Diogenes Laertius notes that Chrysippus had composed numerous works on the subject, but one piece appears to have been written in rebuttal to the position Nazianzen espoused.[126] The Theologian's statement of the paradox, "I am now making a false statement," is a shortened form similar to the one that appears in Alexander of Aphrodisias' commentary on Aristotle's *On Sophistical Refutations* rather than the more conditional statement of it that one finds in Cicero or Jerome.[127] More important, Wyss[128] notes that the liar's paradox is handled

---

had similar skills. Socrates, *H.E.* 2.35 and 4.7, *PG* 67, 297B-C and 472C-473C spoke of that same reputation, but quite interestingly suggested that the later Arians misunderstood Aristotle's *Categories*.

[123] Focken, pp. 20-24.

[124] J.-M. Mathieu, "Étude Critique," *RHPhR* 40 (1981), p. 276.

[125] *Or.* 29.9, *PG* 36, 84D-85C.

[126] Diogenes Laertius, *Lives of Eminent Philosophers* 7.196-197 = *SVF* II, p. 7.34ff, (test. 15).

[127] Alexander, *Ad Soph. El. Comm.* 65b; Cicero, *Academics* 30 and 95-98; Jerome, *Ep.* 69.

[128] Wyss, p. 831. He also notices numerous other passages in which Gregory indicates his knowledge of Stoic philosophical and ethical positions.

in a way similar to that of Nazianzen in three Stoic fragments.[129]

Wyss points out three other indications that Gregory employs Stoic logic and epistemology.[130] First, the use of the distinction between silent or uttered reason: "How can you think of reason other than as our inner discourse, unspoken or expressed?"[131] comes from Stoic logic; the mention of Chrysippus in regard to the solution of certain syllogisms in 32.25 calls to mind the title of a work by Chrysippus that appears in the Stoic fragments[132] and the attack on such a treatise in 4.43. Second, the Theologian's reference to the principles of inductive science with the example of observed lunar cycles in 28.29 is reminiscent of yet another Stoic fragment.[133] Third, the dismissal in 25.6 of Stoic syllogisms with their "complete predicates" and "secondary accidents," is like that of Lucian.[134] Mathieu suggests that in 29.6 Gregory uses the phrase "not universally true," with a meaning that goes back to Stoic origins.[135] These examples imply that Nazianzen had studied Stoic logic and thus had indeed invested considerable time in attempting to unravel the logical puzzles that occupied his age. He was interested in the logic of more than one school and particularly with his concern for Stoic logic shows that he understood deductive validity not to be limited to Aristotelian syllogisms.

Focken, in his study, makes a second point. Throughout Oration 29 Nazianzen employs types of rhetorical induction to support his arguments. Sections 10 and 11 contain arguments that cannot be demonstrated syllogistically. There the Theologian uses Aristotelian enthymemes that are structured to deal with probability questions, queries that cannot be systematically proven. Section 12 includes various forms of rhetorical questions which produce much the same effect. Chapters 2 and 16 offer examples of arguments based on topoi or definitions. Passages from the poetry, *Carmina* II, 12-21, IV, 3-10, VIII, 32-43, VI, 53-74, V, 15-24 and elsewhere contain inductive rhetorical forms, while the use of topoi or definitions can be seen in *Carmina* VI, 37-40, IV 11-15, V, 15-33 and in other places.[136]

There is no doubt that Gregory depended upon his rhetorical education for his arguments. As a philosophical rhetorician he understood persuasion to be both deductive and inductive. He recognized that many great

---

[129] *SVF* II, p. 92, 280-282.
[130] Wyss, p. 831.
[131] *Or.* 28.13, *PG* 36, 41C.
[132] *SVF* II, p. 7, line 39, Fr. 15.
[133] *SVF* II, p. 28, line 18, Fr. 83.
[134] Lucian, *vit. auct.* 21. Also see *SVF* II, p. 168.2ff., Fr. 57 for the definitions of these concepts given by Chrysippus.
[135] Mathieu, "Étude Critique," *RHPhR* 40 (1981), p. 276.
[136] Focken, pp. 25-51.

questions were neither susceptible to the type of logic found in what we normally consider to be the Aristotelian *Organon* nor susceptible to the Stoic teaching about validity, but they could be approached through the larger Aristotelian *Organon* that included the *Rhetoric*, perhaps the only *Organon* known to him.

Although Focken's presentation is basic to the problems discussed here he neither argues for the conception of philosophical rhetoric nor clarifies the important two-fold use of enthymemes that Aristotle sees as a bridge between logic and rhetoric. Thus he does not emphasize the continuity between logic and persuasion and therefore does not provide the larger framework within *paideia* that is necessary to grasp the arguments between Nazianzen and the Neo-Arians.

Gregory employs, from that larger framework of *paideia*, other rules taken from rhetoric and grammar to assail the later Arian interpretations of Scripture. In at least seven places within Oration 30, he refers to rules from logic, common sense, grammar, or lexicography that his opponents have broken: 1) "It is impossible for the same thing to be, in a like respect, greater than and equal to the same thing,"[137] 2) "I cannot understand how what is common to two things could be the particular property of one of them alone. Nor, I think, can anyone else."[138] 3) "Deeds show disposition."[139] 4) "'Can' and 'cannot' have many meanings, not just one."[140] 5) "You also fail to distinguish meanings [of words]."[141] 6) "Your failure to recognize that 'until' is by no means the logical contrary of what lies in the future; it states the point up to which something happens, but does not deny what goes beyond that point."[142] 7) "When the natures are distinguished, the titles are differentiated along with the ideas."[143]

These latter principles again find their context in the tradition that had seen rhetoric as a part of dialectic. As a philosophical rhetorician, Gregory could rely not only on specific views of formal logic, but also on particular treatments of logical problems that usually fall under the category of rhetoric. Elias of Crete, an early twelfth-century commentator on Gregory, insists that Aristotle and Hermogenes were the major sources of these principles Nazianzen employs in his thirtieth oration.[144] In the

---

[137] *Or.* 30.7, *PG* 36, 112C.
[138] *Or.* 30.12, *PG* 36, 120B.
[139] *Or.* 30.6, *PG* 36, 109C.
[140] *Or.* 30.10, *PG* 36, 113C.
[141] *Or.* 30.4, *PG* 36, 108B.
[142] ibid.
[143] *Or.* 30.8, *PG* 36, 113B.
[144] Elias of Crete, pp. 94ff., particularly pp. 118-119. This Latin translation of the comments by Elias gives a much greater insight into the learning and judgment of the Cretan bishop than do the excerpts made by A. Jahn and printed in *PG* 36, 737-942.

middle of the twelfth century, two Byzantine commentaries on Aristotle's
Rhetoric, one by Stephanus and one anonymous, not only treat the work
as a portion of the *Organon* concerned basically with logic, but also attempt
to combine Aristotle's teachings about rhetoric with those of Hermogenes
and illustrate their interpretations with quotations from Christian writers,
particularly Nazianzen.[145] John Siceliotes, an early eleventh-century
teacher of rhetoric in Constantinople, provided a large commentary for
Hermogenes' *On Ideas*.[146] A. Poynton, in an index that lists almost eight
hundred references to Nazianzen that appear in Siceliotes, notes over
forty passages in which Siceliotes employs the *Theological Orations* as examples of Hermogenian principles.[147] Kustas indicates that an anonymous
commentary on Hermogenes' *On Ideas*, printed in Walz,[148] contains additional comments that Walz prints as Scholia Minora. These scholia use
the Theologian in particular as illustrative of Hermogenes' principles.
The oldest manuscript of the commentary dates from the tenth century,
but Kustas suggests parts of it come from the fifth or sixth centuries.[149]
A solid Byzantine tradition of interpretation viewed Nazianzen as dependent upon both Aristotle and Hermogenes for logic and rhetoric.

The fortunes of manuscript copying, however, have left us with more
than Byzantine witnesses who understood rhetoric as a logical discipline
and found the work of Hermogenes compatible with Aristotle's understandings. Sopater,[150] a fourth-century figure who apparently was a student of Himerius, the teacher of Gregory,[151] is credited with a number of
works. Two fragmentary treatises deal with μεταποίησις and προγυμνάσ-
ματα. There are also a prolegomenon to Aelius Aristides,[152] a piece titled
Division of Questions[153] and a commentary that treats Hermogenes' *On
Staseis*.[154] In the latter the introductory paragraphs indicate that Sopater

---

[145] *Commentaria in Aristotelem Graeca* XXI, 2 *Anonymi et Stephani in Artem Rhetoricam*, ed.
by H. Rabe (Berlin, 1896).

[146] Walz, VI, pp. 56-504. Kennedy (1983), p. 309 indicates a prolegomenon to that
work can be found in *Prolegomenon Sylloge*, ed. by H. Rabe (Leipzig, 1935), pp. 393-420.

[147] A. Poynton, "Gregory of Nazianzus and the Greek Rhetoricians," p. 7 of an unpublished supplement to the Index of Walz, IX. The passages from Gregory's *Theological
Orations* include the title of *Or*. 27, 27.3 and 9; the title of 28, 28.2, 3, 10, 19-22, 26-28;
the title of 29, 29.1-3, 6-7, 9, 16-19; 30.17; 31.10, 28, and 29. On pp. 11-12 Poynton also
lists references to Gregory found in other commentaries on Hermogenes' *On Ideas*.

[148] Walz, VI, pp. 861-1087.

[149] G. Kustas, *Studies in Byzantine Rhetoric*, "Analecta Vlatadon, 17" (Thessaloniki,
1973), p. 21. Kustas is not clear as to the date of the Scholia Minora.

[150] Kennedy (1983), pp. 104-109 provides an excellent description. Also see Glöckner,
"Sopatros, #10," *PW* IIIA, 1, pp. 1002-1006.

[151] Walz, VIII, p. 318.

[152] See Aristides *Opera* III, ed. by Dindorf (Leipzig, 1829), pp. 737-757.

[153] Walz, VIII, pp. 1-385.

[154] Walz, V, pp. 1-211.

saw rhetoric as part of logic. The body of the work shows that he had studied Plato's *Gorgias*, Aristotle's logical treatises other than the *Rhetoric*, Stoic views of the relationship between logic and rhetoric and at least some of Cicero's writings on rhetoric. References to Porphyry throughout the commentary indicate that Sopater thought the great Neo-Platonist agreed with his understanding of rhetoric and logic. If Sopater was indeed a student of Himerius, the teacher of Gregory, his works give us crucial insight into the education of Nazianzen. Although no two students of the same teacher will learn exactly the same things, the writings of Sopater strongly suggest that the Theologian's education in Athens should be placed within the tradition of philosophical rhetoric.

Sopater's commentary on Hermogenes' *On Staseis* strengthens the case of the Byzantine commentators that a positive relationship existed between that rhetorician and Gregory's orations.[155] Perhaps Himerius used Hermogenes' works in educating both Sopater and Nazianzen. Other rhetoricians had developed stasis theory before Hermogenes, but his treatise became the standard. Within that volume he laid out the various arguments that would often appear in the presentation of any case before a court or a deliberative body. If a person or an act came to the attention particularly of a court, if different persuasive arguments about that person or act could be made and if no decision had been reached, the στάσεις, the "situations" or "positions" would help form the structure of the case. The issue to be decided might be clear or unclear. If it were unclear, then the facts should be presented. If it were clear, i.e., if the facts were obvious, then the orator should offer either a definition of some incomplete understanding of the issue or a series of amplifications of the facts. Those amplifications could be divided into legal or rational inquiries. If they were legal matters, then specific questions could be put. What is the intent of the law? What inferences might be drawn from it? Is there a conflict or an ambiguity? If the questions are rational ones, pairs of queries might be raised. Does the matter under review concern the past or the future? Were the acts unintentional or intentional, beneficial or not, caused by the opponent or by someone else. Can blame be transferred to another or must one plead for mercy since the blame cannot be shifted?

In the development of the various topics Hermogenes shows a certain assumption of Aristotelian categories in an interrogative form, i.e., questions about Who? What? Where? When? and Why? as well as interest in the questions of justice, honor and expediency. His concern with the division of subjects into their essential parts and the demonstration of a case

---

[155] ibid.

indicates why Neo-Platonic philosophers and others fascinated by logic and the art of persuasion would find his works helpful.[156] The issues raised were often political or legal ones, queries that could not be put in syllogistic form. Probability questions, without formally demonstrable answers, dominated the entire process. Here was yet another area in which philosophy and rhetoric might come together to form the philosophical rhetorician.

Within Gregory's *Theological Orations* the influence of Hermogenes is evident as noted above. It involves, however, not only specific passages but also the structure of the orations. Oration 27, presented as an invective, employs stasis theory to make the case that the later Arians have got the facts wrong. His opponents, as apparently well-educated speakers, should know the simple rules of Aristotle about the choice of speaker, time, audience and topic. They, however, do not understand even such a simple set of rules, one known to any beginner in rhetoric. The Theologian supplies a refutation of their views and a defense of his own opinions. Oration 31 provides a similar plan. The later Arians charge that Gregory and his supporters are teaching a strange God, the Holy Spirit, of which Scripture is silent. Nazianzen does not immediately attack the claim as false. He first notes the difficulties, offers his own confession and then turns to Eunomian charges that his positions do not make sense. In section 21, however, he returns to the claim that Scripture is silent about the divinity of the Spirit. There he handles the questions with an intricate theory of why so little is said about the Spirit until the present post-Biblical age. And in section 29 he returns to the issue with a swarm of proof-texts from the New Testament.

For each *Theological Oration* knowledge of Hermogenes brings a fuller understanding of Nazianzen's outline. While Aristotle's sense of philosophical rhetoric and a working knowledge of various kinds of logic in late antiquity can provide the background for specific arguments, it is often Hermogenes' stasis theory that lies behind the organization or structure of each piece. Any grasp of the rhetorical exercises used in the schools will enhance one's recognition of Gregory's procedure, but the *staseis* used in a court of law or before a political deliberative body—much like the Aristotelian enthymemes that are a part of rhetorical induction—handle probability issues that, for the most part, cannot be put into syllogistic form to test their truthfulness. The Theologian often turns to such types of argumentation, particularly in the outline he follows for the argument of an entire oration. Eunomius' *Apology* follows similar plans, but con-

---

[156] Hermogenes, *On Staseis*, ed. by H. Rabe (Leipzig, 1913), pp. 28-92. Also see Kennedy (1983), pp. 80-86.

tinues to insist on formal demonstration of the truth of his statements. Gregory, however, knows that basic theological issues are not amenable to such rigorous proof, so he employs the best available tools provided by higher education in his culture for handling the questions involved. If God's nature is incomprehensible, how could theology be founded on demonstrable proofs? Again an important aspect of his quarrel with the later Arians concerns *paideia*; his opponents do not understand what the proper subjects of discussion are and thus do not know what manner of discussion to employ.

The final area in which Nazianzen's views of *paideia* are essential for the interpretation of the *Theological Orations* concerns epistemology, particularly the theory of language. For a philosophical rhetorician, a developed understanding of language would be a necessity. Gregory indicated that the principles of "inquiry" and "speculation" came from non-Christian sources, even though Hellenistic learning had to be stripped of its demons and errors.[157] For him language emerges from human "thought" or "inventiveness." Reality is organized into various "concepts" on the basis of the observed "facts." In the case of animals and men, all "that comes under the same species has the same concept."[158]

For Nazianzen the most important thing to remember about language is the distinction between facts and names. The truth, the essence of what one is investigating, is to be found in the "facts" not the "names." Names do not reveal nature.[159] There is a difference between "meanings" and "words." The "meanings" are what we look for.[160] "Things of the same and things of differing status can have the same name." Consider a dog and a dogshark. Both have the name "dog" applied to them; neither is more a "dog" by nature than the other. Yet they certainly are not the same creatures. "Homonyms" can thus be deceiving when one thinks a name designates a nature.[161]

Such examples demonstrate that language is a weak tool; it shows the known not adequately but faintly.[162] Indeed there are a number of truths found within nature and ourselves that far exceed our ability to discern them, let alone our power to express them in words. In all philosophical endeavors, our intellect and our senses are so limited, so open to wandering, that they do not provide exact knowledge.[163]

---

[157] *Or.* 43.11, *PG* 36, 508B-509A.
[158] *Or.* 29.13, *PG* 36, 92A.
[159] ibid.; 31.7, *PG* 36, 140C; 31.10, *PG* 36, 144B; 31.19-20, *PG* 36, 156A–B.
[160] *Or.* 31.24, *PG* 36, 160C.
[161] *Or.* 29.14, *PG* 36, 92B-93A.
[162] *Or.* 28.4, *PG* 36, 29C.
[163] *Or.* 28.21-30, *PG* 36, 53A-69C.

The eclectic character of these views is apparent. The suggestion that animals and men can be organized into species and put under various concepts is reminiscent of Aristotle's investigations of animals. Gregory does apparently know of those works, although it is difficult to demonstrate that he had studied them thoroughly. Oration 28.22-30 employs examples which bring to mind Aristotle's efforts. Wyss notes that Oration 31.10 speaks of τῆς περὶ ζῴων ἱστορίας and περὶ τὰς τῶν ζῴων γενέσεις, almost the titles for two treatises from the Stagirite.[164] The opinion that both the mind and the senses can be fooled far too easily is similar to Plato's views in *Phaedo* 66. The theory of language resembles the understanding of names being selected by convention rather than growing out of essence, an understanding found in Aristotle.[165] It also involves Epicurean conceptions that the things behind the words are more important than the words themselves.[166] Evidently the Theologian was aware of Platonic, Middle Platonic and Stoic attempts to explicate the opposing position that names designate essence.[167] Doubtless his mistrust of language as an exact tool was strengthened by grammatical studies that would have been an important part of his rhetorical education.

A thorough understanding of the debate between Nazianzen and the later Arians depends upon viewing Gregory as a philosophical rhetorician. A number of authors have described the Christian humanism, the Christian *paideia*, of the Cappadocians,[168] but Nazianzen is seldom invoked, first, because he did not write a refutation of Eunomius as Basil and Nyssa did and second, because it is not easy to see how much he participated in the Christian philosophy of the other two. Gregory neither provides extended discussions of his basic philosophical disagreements with the later Arians as Basil does, nor invokes metaphysical speculation as Nyssa does.

Yet like his fellow Cappadocians, Nazianzen relies upon his education in the struggle with Eunomians. He is convinced that if the Arians understood *paideia* correctly they would not argue as they do. If they grasped both the limitations of the human mind in speculative or contemplative matters and knew the proper principles of logic, rhetoric and grammar, they would not reach their conclusions. Any treatment of the heated exchanges that does not deal with this clash over the nature of *paideia* cannot represent fully the nature of the conflict. Gregory and the other Cappadocians were condescending in their attitudes toward the educational

---

[164] Wyss, p. 828; *Or.* 31.10, *PG* 36, 144B.
[165] *On Interpretation* 16A-B.
[166] Epicurus, *Letter to Herodotus* 37 and 75.
[167] Plato, *Cratylus* 430A-431E; Albinus, *Epit.* 6; Chrysippus, *SVF* II, p. 245, Fr. 895.
[168] See particularly Otis and Jaeger (1961).

backgrounds of Aetius and Eunomius. Such arrogance does not enhance their own positions any more than the Eunomian attack on Gregory's birth in a small town and his Cappadocian accent strengthens their views.[169] Yet the Cappadocians' sense of intellectual limitations and their understanding of rules for argument—both of which they view as lacking in their opponents—are not drawn solely from theological traditions. They grasped such things from their Hellenistic educational heritage as well.

The struggles with the later Arians about theological method make the most sense in this context. When Nazianzen prepared his *Theological Orations*, the conflict had begun to focus specifically on such questions. How could one defend a more probabilistic approach, a logic not limited to formal inference? By arguing for its sensibility and its piety. Throughout these orations Gregory employs the word θεωρία either as a concept of study and investigation or one of contemplation. He feels no compunction about insisting upon both. Oration 27 attacks the later Arians for not knowing basic rhetorical theory about any speech: not every speaker, concerning every topic, before every audience, on every occasion. It also ridicules his adversaries' lack of ethics and moral purity, at least emphasizing Aristotle's sense of the speaker's ἦθος, perhaps even as Sopater had done, invoking Cicero's concept of the *bonus orator*.[170] That is done both from the Hellenistic and Christian traditions. Oration 28 argues the main doctrinal issue, the incomprehensibility of God's essence, by rehearsing how little humans know about their own essence and the essences of things in nature. It criticizes a *via negativa* approach to knowledge and builds its case inductively on the basis of examples, but it develops the first major point, the speaker's ἦθος, by referring to Gregory's ascending the mount of contemplation, θεωρία, only to see the back parts of God. Indeed all the Biblical heroes who got close to or "saw" God never grasped his essence.

Then Orations 29-31 deal with Eunomian theological syllogisms, which Nazianzen finds wrongly formed, and groups of Scriptural passages, which he thinks are misappropriated by these later Arians because of their misunderstanding of context and grammar. Gregory employs principles from Aristotelian and Stoic logic, occasionally stated as they are found in treatises or fragments known to us. He often develops his arguments through Aristotelian enthymemes. Much of the time he involves his audiences in the arguments that could have been demonstrated through

---

[169] *Or.* 33.6-8, *PG* 36, 221C-225A.
[170] Sopater specifically mentions Cicero; Walz V, p. 8. See Kennedy (1983), p. 108 for the suggestion that Sopater understood that concept from Cicero.

formal inferences, through syllogisms proper. That is important because he must show that he has a command of logical procedures which his Neo-Arian opponents claim to have mastered. This focus on his opponents' reputation as expert logicians accounts for his preoccupation with theological method. In the full corpus of his orations he overwhelmingly prefers to preach rather than argue these important but fine points.

Within these orations he sometimes sees theology as concerned with questions of probability, questions which go beyond the powers of human intellect and language. These queries are basic to his confession of faith and can be dealt with only through enthymemes that have no formal syllogistic backing. The use of this second type of enthymeme fits his confession of God's incomprehensible nature while allowing him to argue for the appropriateness of his methodology. That use provides the bridge to other methods which concern probability questions. It affords him the opportunity of employing analogies with proper disclaimers and seeing poetry as essential for the task of theology.

Nazianzen, like Basil, Nyssa, Aetius and Eunomius, could be sophistic, technical and thus off the point. Yet his *Theological Orations* reveal that his sense of *paideia*, his education as a philosophical rhetorician, served him well. He could handle the theological methodology of his opponents because he had developed a different view of the nature of education, as well as a different view of the nature of theology. And in significant ways, he had joined those disciplines into an interesting harmony. He did not construct a neutral base from which he could argue polemically or apologetically with his Christian detractors and the pagan culture. For him faith gave fullness to reasoning. The bulk of his writings, particularly his orations, is not concerned with these questions of theological method. In skilled literary fashion they set forth the faith. Most of them appear within a liturgical context. Even Orations 38-40, which contain some of the same positions taken against the Eunomians, are preached around the festival of Epiphany and focus primarily on Theophany, Holy Lights and Holy Baptism. Gregory was fundamentally a confessional theologian, a preacher of the gospel. Yet he was not a crude fideist, unwilling to argue specific points with his audiences. His manner appears odd to many Western theologians, but it involves some of the same basic insights of Anselm or Aquinas when they are viewed as representatives of "faith seeking understanding."[171] The difference, particularly between his view and

---

[171] J. Plagnieux, S. *Grégoire de Nazianze Théologien*, "Études de science religieuse, VII" (Paris, 1952) views Gregory as a traditional theologian set within the church, dependent upon Scripture and tradition while working out his theological views through prayer and contemplation. For a similar view see T. Camelot, "Amour des lettres de désir de Dieu chez S. Grégoire de Nazianze: les logoi au service du Logos", *Littérature et religion* (Lille, 1966)

that of Augustine, appears in his connection of reason with the image of God, an image not lost in Adam's sin. On such a theological basis he can engage in various arguments that might appear to be foundational and apologetic, but in his view are built upon revelation and confession.

Although there is an originality in a number of his arguments, there is much that he owed to previous "orthodox" theologians, some of whom struggled against forms of Arianism. Numerous positions that Nazianzen takes in these orations had already been stated by Basil in his attack on Eunomius. Other points can be traced back to Athanasius[172] and earlier Christian writers. He could have borrowed a number of Aristotelian principles from Christian predecessors. Both Clement of Alexandria and Origen owed a debt to Aristotle.[173] Didymus the Blind, who might have been one of Nazianzen's Christian teachers while he was in Alexandria, actually formulated parts of his attack on the Manichaeans in syllogisms.[174] In any event Gregory's concern with the principles of logic is not reflected in many other early Christian theologians, including his own contemporaries, even though Origen appears to have had deeper interests in and mastery of logic than Gregory demonstrates.[175] Yet the Theologian's dependence upon Aristotle's understanding of the relationship between logical syllogisms and rhetorical enthymemes seldom if ever appears as clearly in earlier Christian literature. Gregory relies on the

---

[172] J. Szymusiak, "Grégoire le théologien, disciple d'Athanase," *Politique et Théologie chez Athanase d'Alexandrie*, ed. by C. Kannengiesser, "Théologie Historique, 27" (Paris, 1974), pp. 356-363.

[173] E. Clark, *Clement's Use of Aristotle: The Aristotelian Contribution to Clement of Alexandria's Refutation of Gnosticism* (New York, 1977) has detailed much of the Aristotelian influence in Clement although her study does not concentrate on Clement's dependence upon Aristotelian logic. G. Apostolopoulou, *Die Dialektik bei Klemens von Alexandria*, "Europaeische Hochschulschriften, Reihe XX, Bd. 29" (Bern, 1977) demonstrates both the rhetorical and logical influence of Aristotle on Clement. K. Pichler, *Streit um das Christentum: Der Angriff des Kelsos und die Antwort des Origenes*, "Regensburger Studien zur Theologie, 23" (Frankfurt-am-Main, 1980) has studied the way in which both Celsus and Origen belonged to a shared rhetorical and grammatical tradition, some of which goes back to Aristotle.

[174] Didymus employs a list of syllogisms in his *Contra Manichaeos* 2, *PG* 39, 1088B-1089B. The piece is somewhat mutilated and may be only an excerpt, but it is usually considered to be genuine. Scholars have had difficulty dating it, although most place it well beyond the period when Nazianzen might have studied with Didymus. Yet Didymus, as a good teacher, may have been using such techniques years before the publication of that treatise.

[175] L. Roberts, "Philosophical Method in Origen's *Contra Celsum*," unpublished doctoral dissertation, State University of New York at Buffalo, 1971 has shown that certain aspects of Stoic logic, not clear from Stoic texts and fragments, can be learned from Origen. That depth has not yet been found in Nazianzen. J. Rist, "The Importance of Stoic Logic in the *Contra Celsum*," *Neoplatonism and Early Christian Thought: Essays in Honour of A. H. Armstrong*, ed. by H. Blumenthal and R. Markus (London: 1981), pp. 64-78 also demonstrates that Origen had studied Stoic logic with some care.

Stagirite for the development of doctrine in terms of a faith response to questions of probability and an inductive rhetorical approach to theological argument and exegesis. His occasional use of Stoic logic and his partial acceptance of an Epicurean view of language fit well with his employment of Hermogenian rhetoric and his dependence upon an Aristotle who views arguments in terms other than syllogistic inference.

Methodologically, his conflict with the later Arians was complicated by the fact that they also relied upon some of the same general theological tradition that he does. Both Clement of Alexandria and Origen could be cited as claiming that language was a gift of God not the invention of men.[176] As part of their Platonic inheritance they insisted that names denoted essences. In many ways Nazianzen's dependence upon Aristotle's views of dialectic and rhetoric and a partial acceptance of an Epicurean theory of language allowed him to limit the Platonic dominance in Christian theology that Eunomianism embodied and rescue many important insights from Origen. Working on that project he is clearly a representative of what Florovsky calls the conversion of Hellenism.[177]

Kustas notes some Byzantine scholars saw rhetoric and theology as one.[178] As late antiquity worked toward a philosophical rhetoric, Byzantium recovered a rhetorical theology. Rhetoric itself could be referred to as a "sacrament," a μυστήριον. Precisely those who employed sentences from Nazianzen as illustrative of true rhetoric were involved in such constructions.[179] For them Gregory along with Basil and Chrysostom were the hierarchs of orthodox doctrine. And that orthodoxy was based in a rhetorical theology put together by a philosophical rhetorician like Nazianzen. It was doubtless those features that earned him the title "The Theologian."

It would be unbalanced to claim that Gregory was more than a philosophical rhetorician. He evidences neither a great interest in the metaphysics of Plato nor a full appreciation of all the Middle and Neo-Platonic appropriations of the larger Aristotelian *Organon* or Stoic logic. Nazianzen's prowess in rhetoric and his dependence upon the broader understanding of logic should not be missed. That claim, however, must be carefully defined. The Theologian is not the powerful metaphysician whom one discovers in reading the attacks of Nyssa and Marius Victori-

---

[176] Clement, *Stromata* 1.143.6, *GCS*, Stahlin, II, p. 89 and Origen, *Contra Celsum* 1.24, *GCS*, Koetschau, I, p. 74.

[177] G. Florovsky, "Christianity and Civilization," *St. Vladimir's Seminary Quarterly* 1.1 (1952), pp. 13-20 reprinted in *Christianity and Culture: The Collected Works of Georges Florovsky* (Belmont, MA, 1974), pp. 121-130.

[178] Kustas, *Studies in Byzantine Rhetoric*, pp. 117-126.

[179] Doxaprates, *Prol. Syll.*, 80.12-16 and John Siceliotes, *Prol. Syll.*, 394.12-14.

nus on later Arians. He may, however, have chosen not to be. His rhetorical theology does avoid the dangers of systematic foundationalist programs better than theirs, while it demonstrates his command of logic and grammar. His lack-luster reputation in some modern circles has probably been influenced by the twentieth-century misunderstanding of the Aristotelian heritage and the contemporary penchant for the philosophical justification of theological programs rather than Nazianzen's own lack of skill.[180] Historically, both worshipping Christians and students of culture have praised his efforts.

Two descriptive assessments must be avoided. Nazianzen is neither a literary figure who wrote and spoke well but understood little about the logical force of arguments nor a sophistic, technical rhetorician unworthy of modern attention. Both views do him an injustice. He was a talented philosophical rhetorician, who through that educational tradition grasped fundamental truths about both the content and the method of Christian theology. Had his approach been studied more carefully and followed more rigorously, theology might have avoided the serious problems which occur in foundationalist apologetic programs. His kind of rhetorical theology has many attractive features for any contemporary theologian.

Christian Doctrine: Trinity, Christology, Soteriology

Although the debate between Gregory and the later Arians becomes most clear when the question of Christian *paideia* is raised, no adequate description of the controversy appears until the question of Christian doctrine has been investigated. The debates between the two groups are theological. This section, however, can neither give a complete survey of Nazianzen's views on all matters nor exhaustively treat the selected topics. There is obviously too much within the corpus to attempt that.[181] What is envi-

---

[180] Gregory's approach involves the acceptance of "background beliefs" from his tradition and community. His attacks on opponents were "ad hoc," not systematic defenses of a "foundationalist position." These technical terms appear in R. Thiemann, *Revelation and Theology: The Gospel as Narrated Promise* (Notre Dame, IN, 1985) and G. Lindbeck, *The Nature of Doctrine: Religion and Theology in a Postliberal Age* (Philadelphia, 1984). The list of differences between their efforts and the Theologian's might be long and considerable, but the structural similarity is essential and striking.

It is one thing to insist that later Arianism was a theological tradition that grew into or out of worshipping congregations. It is another to demand that later Arianism developed a more cogent and persuasive theology. The latter descriptions often involve the acceptance of contemporary "foundationalist" programs as the standard of judgment.

[181] The number and size of even select studies on doctrines taught by the Theologian make such caution mandatory. H. Althaus, *Die Heilslehre des Heiligen Gregor von Nazianz*, "Münsterische Beiträge zur Theologie, Heft 34" (Münster, 1972); J. Draeseke, "Neuplatonisches in des Gregors von Nazianz Trinitätslehre," *ByZ* 15 (1906), pp. 141-160;

sioned here is a presentation of the points crucial for and contained in the *Theological Orations*.

In his general view of God, the Theologian confesses that the divine nature is incomprehensible. Forms of that assertion are probably the most oft-repeated statements within the *Theological Orations*.[182] For Nazianzen God's essence is unknowable not only for the average believer but also for the great heroes of the faith like Enoch, Noah, Abraham, Jacob, Elijah, Manoah, Ezekiel, Isaiah and Peter. Paul experienced things ineffable and thus may have known more about God than he could express. Both John and the Word himself intimated that such things were beyond our human power to bear or our world to contain. In any case no human has ever known God's inner nature.[183] Even the term "God," θεός, is itself a "relational, not an absolute term."[184] Gregory warns, however, against assuming that such a confession means he doubts God's existence. He finds himself unable to say God does not exist or God is evil, for in each case the word "'cannot' would mean impotence in God here, not power."[185] The principle which stands behind that view, "'cannot' in the sense of the totally inconceivable," is similar to the developed position of Anselm in his *Proslogion*.[186]

The Theologian's rejection of "composition," "conflict," "division," "disorder," and "dissolution," is involved in the denial of God's "corporeality."[187] Only through that denial can God be "boundless," "limitless," "formless," "impalpable," "invisible," "immutable," and "immortal."[188] Such positions echo those taken by a number of

---

A.-S. Ellverson, *The Dual Nature of Man: A Study in the Theological Anthropology of Gregory of Nazianzus* (Uppsala, 1981); Hanson, pp. 707-714, 781-787; S. Harkianakis, "Die Trinitätslehre Gregors von Nazianz," *Kleronomia* 1 (1969), pp. 83-102; J. Hergenröther, *Die Lehre von der göttlichen Dreieinigkeit nach dem heiligen Gregor von Nazianz, dem Theologen, mit Berücksichtigung der älteren und neueren Darstellungen dieses Dogmas* (Regensburg, 1850); K. Holl, *Amphilochius von Ikonium in seinem Verhältnis zu den grossen Kappadoziern* (Tübingen, 1904); F. Hümmer, *Des Heiligen Gregors von Nazianz, des Theologen, Lehre von der Gnade* (Kempten, 1890); F. Rudasso, *La Figura di Cristo in S. Gregorio Nazianzeno* (Rome, 1968); T. Špidlík, *Grégoire de Nazianze: Introduction a l'étude de sa doctrine spirituelle* (Rome, 1971); L. Stephan, *Die Soteriologie des heiligen Gregors von Nazianz* (Wien, 1938); J. Szymusiak, *Éléments de théologie de l'homme selon S. Grégoire de Nazianze* (Rome, 1963) and Winslow.

[182] *Or.* 27.10, *PG* 36, 24B-25A; 28.3-6, 10-11, 13, 17-21 and 31, *PG* 36, 29A-33B, 37C-40C, 41C-44B, 48C-53D and 69D-72C; 29.8 and 11-12, *PG* 36, 84B and 88D-89C; 30.2 and 17, *PG* 36, 105C and 125B; 31.8, 11 and 31, *PG* 36, 141B-C, 145A and 169A.

[183] *Or.* 28.17-20, *PG* 36, 48C-53A.

[184] *Or.* 30.18, *PG* 36, 128A.

[185] *Or.* 30.11, *PG* 36, 116C.

[186] Wickham, pp. 552 and 560 notices that sections 4, 12 and 17 of Aetius' work imply the same kind of argument.

[187] *Or.* 29.2 and 10, *PG* 36, 76A-B and 85D-88B.

[188] *Or.* 28.7-9, *PG* 36, 33B-37B.

Greek philosophers, particularly the developing Platonic tradition.[189] Yet Gregory sees them as related to his Christian tradition. No inspired teacher has ever taught that God is corporeal.[190] And each of the concepts listed above, both the nouns stated positively and the adjectives stated negatively as alpha-privatives, is in his view a correct inference from God's incorporeality.

Although Nazianzen insists that God's nature is incomprehensible, he is willing to make general statements about God that were a part of his Christian and Greek heritage. He does not deny all assertions about deity, only those from his Arian opponents that demand God's essence be encapsulated and clearly expressed in his being "unbegotten." For Gregory, God's titles could be gathered under the categories of power and providential ordering and related subsets under incarnational or non-incarnational acts.[191] He can say positive things about God's economy that indicate certain aspects of God himself.

On this basis Gregory refuses to say only what God is not; he rejects a *via negativa*. Any speaker must eventually say what the subject is.[192] What Nazianzen combats is the later Arian one-word definition of the divine essence, as if all other words or statements of Scripture and tradition either must be viewed as synonymous with it or must be deduced from it. God's nature, for him, is not so incomprehensible that God's existence, goodness, power, providential ordering and his lack of composition, conflict, disorder and dissolution are unknown. Perhaps the Theologian could argue for a number of these attributes as established, but in most cases he asserts them with a sense that there will be little or no disagreement about the appropriateness of his claims. Philosophical justification of these descriptions is not his concern.

An equal lack of interest in using philosophical argument to undergird his claims marks his use of Trinitarian formulae. Gregory apparently thinks that he is on firm Biblical ground when he refers to the three as Light, Light and Light or Father, Son and Comforter.[193] In a similar way he calls them the "ingenerate," the "begotten," and "what proceeds," or says "the personal name" of the "unoriginate" is "Father," the name of "the eternally begotten," is "Son," and the name of "what has issued, or proceeds, without generation" is "Spirit." In the same passage Gregory draws together a number of Biblical designations for God

---

[189] W. Jaeger, *The Theology of Early Greek Philosophers* (Oxford, 1947). C. Moreschini, "Il platonismo cristiano di Gregorio Nazianzeno," *Annali della Scuola Normale Superiore di Pisa* 3. *Ser.* 4.4 (1974), pp. 1370-1377.
[190] *Or.* 28.9, *PG* 36, 36C.
[191] *Or.* 30.19, *PG* 36, 128B.
[192] *Or.* 28.9, *PG* 36, 37A.
[193] *Or.* 31.3, *PG* 36, 136C.

and says: "These names of deity, of course, are shared."[194] In fact,
"monotheism is not defined as the sovereignty of a single person (after all,
self-discordant unity can become a plurality) but the single rule produced
by equality of nature, harmony of will, identity of action and the convergence towards their source of what springs from unity—none of which is
possible in the case of the created nature."[195]

When Nazianzen attempts to define more closely the relationships within the Trinity he uses at least three methods: reference to heretical errors, discussion of analogues and emphasis upon the economy of salvation. He warns: "it is equally as irreligious to make them [the three] a
combined personality, like Sabellius, as to disconnect them like the Arians."[196] Second, he indicates how difficult it is to find images within human knowledge that provide analogues for the Trinity. One might employ
a source, a spring and a river because that would involve no temporal
separation, no disruption of mutual connectedness and yet allow for three
distinctions in personality, but those images fail because they imply incessant motion and a numerical unit. Various Christians have used the images of the Sun, a beam and light. That picture, however, both depicts
composition and makes "the Father a substance but the others [the Son
and the Spirit] potentialities inherent in him." Once Gregory heard
someone suggest a sunbeam reflected off water onto a wall, but that illustration specifies the Sun as the source and introduces the problems of
"composition, dispersion and the lack of a fixed, natural stability." With
a touch of humor he notices the strangeness of thinking that any such analogy can be found in our world; it is much like searching for the living
among the dead.[197] Again he insists that our minds are too small to undertake the task of explaining the nature of God. Third, he notes that because God wanted to use persuasion and Himself understood how difficult
it is for humans to learn, He set forth Himself as Father clearly in the Old
Testament, but waited until the New Testament to make the deity of the
Son known. Now as the Holy Spirit dwells within Christians, the divinity
of the third person is becoming clearer.[198]

There is no philosophical justification for his Trinitarian views within
these orations. Philosophical concepts are employed, but in almost every
case the only clarification is provided in the use either of several terms in
the same paragraph, or of contrasting words in a phrase or a clause. The

---

[194] *Or.* 30.19, *PG* 36, 128C.
[195] *Or.* 29.2, *PG* 36, 76B.
[196] *Or.* 31.30, *PG* 36, 169A; See *Or.* 31.9, *PG* 36, 144A; *Or.* 30.6, *PG* 36, 112B; *Or.*
2.36-37, *PG* 35, 444B-445B; *Or.* 21.13, *PG* 35, 109A-C; *Or.* 34.8, *PG* 36, 248D-249A; *Or.*
38.8 and 15, *PG* 36, 320A-C and 328C-329B.
[197] *Or.* 31.31-33, *PG* 36, 169A-172A; *Or.* 31.10, *PG* 36, 144B.
[198] *Or.* 31.26, *PG* 36, 161C.

terms are apparently used analogically rather than foundationally. They are meant to illustrate not demonstrate. Nazianzen speaks of "the single Godhead's single radiance, by mysterious paradox one in its distinctions, distinct in its connectedness," but he does not define the terms or argue for their appropriateness. He uses the form of three repeated subjects, three repeated predicates and one reality, but supplies no philosophical context for his terms.[199] The same applies to his assertion that "the three are a single whole in their Godhead and the single whole is three in its individual distinctions."[200] Gregory claims that the three "do not have degrees of being God or degrees of priority over against one another," that "the Godhead exists undivided in separate beings."[201] In his view "it is their difference in, so to say, 'manifestation' or mutual relationship, which has caused the difference in names," but the "language here gives no grounds for deficiency, for any subordination in essence."[202] The unity of the Trinity is "by identity of power and essence."[203] That unity is real not like that of the human race which is "only a unity for speculative thought."[204] There is no "inequality of rank or nature" as his opponents suggest.[205]

This lack of philosophical justification for his Trinitarian doctrine is significant. First, Gregory employs the views of Christians before him. He refers to one who only recently passed away and had claimed that there were "three distinctions in personality, one Godhead undivided in glory, honor, substance and sovereignty."[206] Most commentators have identified the source as Gregory Thaumaturgus, but we cannot be certain. Nazianzen understands that there were differences within his contemporary Christian community, including the "orthodox," both concerning the status of the Son and the Spirit,[207] but he insists that he is on solid traditional ground in arguing for a Trinitarian position. Second, he calls attention to numerous Scriptural passages that teach the divinity of both the Son and the Spirit. In his view, the Bible itself is best understood when distinctions in the economy of salvation are made: the Son, the Son incarnate and the humanity as subjects or objects of various Scriptural state-

---

[199] *Or.* 31.3, *PG* 36, 136B-C.
[200] *Or.* 31.9, *PG* 36, 144A; See *Or.* 25.16, *PG* 35, 1220A-C.
[201] *Or.* 31.14, *PG* 36, 149A. See *Or.* 39.11, *PG* 36, 345B-348A.
[202] *Or.* 31.9, *PG* 36, 141D.
[203] *Or.* 31.16, *PG* 36, 152B.
[204] *Or.* 31.15, *PG* 36, 149B.
[205] *Or.* 31.20, *PG* 36, 156B.
[206] *Or.* 31.28, *PG* 36, 164D.
[207] *Or.* 31.5 and 14, *PG* 36, 137C-D and 149A, particularly where he distinguishes a number of parties among his "orthodox" friends as well as the Eunomian and Pneumatomachian "Christians".

ments. References to the divine work of the Spirit must also be taken into account.

Because Nazianzen usually avoids philosophical justification for his positions, it may not be appropriate to view him as the creator of a new Christian philosophy, a claim made for Basil and Nyssa. The Theologian attacks Eunomian *paideia* to point out its deficiency in dialectics and rhetoric. He employs philosophical terms in order to make Trinitarian thought plausible,[208] but his insistence on the incomprehensibility of God's nature, his analogical use of philosophical terms, his reliance on traditional Christian confessions and his Scriptural exegesis demand that he should be viewed not as a philosophical theologian or an apologist in any modern sense of those terms.

Yet it is must be noticed that he does not always rely strictly on revelation as contained in Christian scripture and tradition. Although he usually employs philosophical terms as analogues in his Trinitarian positions, at times those terms or concepts become fundamental to his doctrine. No Scripture indicates that God's nature does not include "composition," "conflict," "disorder," and "dissolution."[209] That sense is shared with what was a common Greek philosophical conception of divinity and what becomes classical theism. Gregory accepts those positions because no inspired teacher, no theologian within the Christian tradition, has taught that God had a body.[210] He evidently views these philosophical claims as necessary inferences from God's being incorporeal, but they exceed what the Biblical witness itself would claim. Yet in his view they represent what Scripture meant even though they are not words to be found in its pages.

This point, however, should be carefully qualified. Nazianzen can be highly critical of various positions taken by philosophical schools. Perhaps the most dense paragraph of criticism is to be found in the first *Theological Oration*[211] where he suggests attacks on positions taken by Pythagoreans, Orpheus, Plato, Epicurus, Aristotle, the Stoa and the Cynics. Furthermore Gregory rejects certain philosophical understandings of movement within the Trinity. He dismisses as ill-suited Plotinus' sense of the " 'overflowing of goodness,' 'as though a bowl had overflowed.' "[212] "The notion of involuntary generation (in the sense of some sort of unrestrained natural secretion)" is out of place as a description of the Godhead. A

---

[208] J. Draeseke, "Neuplatonisches in des Gregors von Nazianz Trinitätslehre," *ByZ* 15 (1906), pp. 141-160 studies four places in *Or.* 29.2 in which Neo-Platonic positions are mentioned. Two of them, however, are concepts Nazianzen rejects and the other two are more analogical than foundational.

[209] *Or.* 29.2 and 10, *PG* 36, 76A-B and 85D-88B.

[210] *Or.* 28.9, *PG* 36, 36C.

[211] *Or.* 27.10, *PG* 36, 24B-C.

[212] *Or.* 29.2, *PG* 36, 76C. *Enneads* 5.1.6.

mathematical model is also inappropriate if it is employed at all levels. Although there is "numerical distinction, there is no division of essence."[213] As I have argued elsewhere, his principle for appropriating Greek *paideia* is simple: "Avoid the thorns: pluck the roses."[214] Although not always unambiguous or consistent, he intends to distinguish the roses and the thorns on the basis of revelation.

Meijering has noted what is perhaps the most glaring error in Gregory's understanding of God.[215] Some might find his lack of philosophical justification or his partial acceptance of what became classical theism occupying that place, but the position concerning first cause probably takes precedence. Nazianzen claims that God is the "first and primal nature," "the primal being," and the "creative and sustaining cause of all,"[216] but he is not consistent about where causality fits within his Trinitarian scheme. On the one hand he can assert that the Father has no cause while the Son and the Spirit have a cause.[217] On the other hand he can equate "the primal cause" not with the Father, but with "the Godhead," "the sole sovereignty."[218] The importance of the argument about cause arises in the context of both polytheism and atheism, which lack a governing principle.[219] Furthermore Christianity has always claimed to worship one God, a confession Gregory also makes.[220] He evidently believes that a specific analogue makes his meaning plain. "A cause is not necessarily prior to its effects—the Sun is not prior to its light. Because time is not involved, they [the Son and the Spirit] are to that extent unoriginate—even if you do scare simple souls with that bogey-word; for the things which produce Time are beyond time."[221] Therefore, according to the Theologian, a confession that God has no cause but the Son and the Spirit do have one does not necessarily demand absolute priority for the Father.

The analogy does not solve the problem. Philosophical and systematic interests might have been better served had Nazianzen restricted causality

---

[213] *Or.* 29.2, *PG* 36, 76B.

[214] *Ad Seleucum* 1.61, *PG* 37, 1581 and *Carmen de vita sua* 1.472, *PG* 37, 1062. See my "Of Thorns and Roses: The Logic of Belief in Gregory Nazianzen," *CH* 53 (1984), pp. 456-458.

[215] E. Meijering, "The Doctrine of the Will and of the Trinity in the Orations of Gregory of Nazianzus," *God, Being, History: Studies in Patristic Philosophy* (Amsterdam, 1975), pp. 111-113, esp. n. 43.

[216] *Or.* 28.3, 6, and 31, *PG* 36, 29A, 32D and 72A; *Or.* 31.14 and 30, *PG* 36, 149A and 168C.

[217] *Or.* 29.3 and 11, *PG* 36, 77B and 89A.

[218] *Or.* 31.14, *PG* 36, 149A.

[219] *Or.* 29.2, *PG* 36, 76A–B.

[220] *Or.* 28.1 and 31, *PG* 36, 25D-28A and 72C; *Or.* 31.9 and 14, *PG* 36, 141C-144A and 149A, etc.

[221] *Or.* 29.3, *PG* 36, 77B.

to the one Godhead, not the Father, a name that designates one of the three persons. Moreschini indicates that a number of these passages are influenced by Platonic sources and thus represent a kind of Christian Platonism,[222] but as Meijering notes, that conflict is one which no consistent Platonist would allow.[223] Gregory's decision to speak of a cause, which sometimes is superior to what is caused and sometimes is not, proves to be arbitrary. Perhaps his interests do not lie in straightening out Christian doctrine by developing a philosophical theology; such categories are not fundamental to his positions. They are *ad hoc* explanations of a puzzle he finds in Scripture and tradition. The Biblical passages that claim priority for the Father can be appropriated as not demanding the subordination of the Son and the Spirit if this arbitrary choice is left in place. This position tries to counter the charge of "tritheism." Indeed Meyendorff[224] insists that much of the Eastern tradition—the Cappadocians, Pseudo-Dionysius and John of Damascus—takes the position that the Father is **the** "cause," αἰτία, **the** "principle," ἀρχή. Although it is an arbitrary philosophical position, it is one that expresses Biblical claims and became an important part of one tradition in Christianity.

Nazianzen approaches the debated relationship between the Father and the Son with great care. In his view any attempt to describe the exact process of the Father begetting the Son fails. While being unoriginate or unbegotten does mean being eternal, there is no reason to assume that being eternal is denied to the one who is originate or begotten. Begetting does not involve change since in terms of the Father begetting the Son, no body is involved. As the Father never began to be Father, so the Son has existed as Son from the beginning. The term "Father" itself always will be inappropriate if it is understood from the human context alone.[225] If the ingenerate and the generate are not the same, then one of them is not in the Godhead, a monstrous problem. In fact, the begetter and the begotten have the same nature since an offspring has the same nature as the parents. Opposing attributes can be ascribed to various objects without necessitating a difference of nature. Intelligence and lack of intelligence are opposites, but both can be predicated of humans.[226]

---

[222] C. Moreschini, "Il platonismo cristiano di Gregorio Nazianzeno," *Annali della Scuola Normale Superiore di Pisa 3*. Ser. 4.4 (1974), p. 1385.

[223] Meijering, op. cit.

[224] J. Meyendorff, *Byzantine Theology: Historical Trends and Doctrinal Themes*, 2nd ed. with revisions (New York, 1983), p. 183 notices that the Eastern tradition "attributes the *origin* of the hypostatic 'subsistence' to the ὑπόστασις of the Father—not the common essence." That priority of the Father was continually employed to rebut the charge of "tritheism." See Nazianzen, *Or.* 40.41, *PG* 36, 417A.

[225] *Or.* 29.3-5 and 9, *PG* 36, 77A-80C and 84D-85C.

[226] *Or.* 29.10-12, *PG* 36, 85D-89C.

How the Son was begotten is impossible to say. Asking if it were a voluntary or involuntary act, whether it were by will or by reason, is senseless, since humans cannot answer such questions about their own begetting. Even if we understood our own procreation, it would not necessarily follow that we would grasp the begetting of the Son.[227] Because we have so many questions about ourselves and about the wide variety we observe in creation around us, it is utterly ridiculous to claim we know the nature of God[228] and thus the nature of begetting.

The same is true of questions about the procession of the Spirit. Tight syllogisms, which demand deficiency, result in the Spirit being either an essence or an activity of the Son, or perhaps the Spirit and the Son being brothers. In Gregory's view these alternatives are ludicrous. He waggishly offers to explain the Son's begetting and the Spirit's proceeding if only the later Arians will explain the Father's being unbegotten. For him such attempts to pry into the ultimate mystery will drive everyone mad.[229] If an analogy is needed, however, one is available in Scripture. Adam was a creature of God; Eve was a portion of that creature; Seth was the begotten of Adam and Eve. Yet all shared the same nature. They were three different persons with one nature.[230] Furthermore, as concerns for salvation demanded that the Son be seen as divine, so it is with the Spirit. Baptism, worship and Scripture, indeed the reality of salvation, bear witness to or depend upon the divinity of the Spirit.[231]

Gregory's position is flawed, particularly in his descriptions of the Son's begetting and the Spirit's proceeding, because he employs illustrations from general nature or human nature in an equivocal manner. Begetter and begotten are of one nature, because that is the case with the offspring of parents. Three individuals can be of the same nature because Adam, Eve and Seth were of the same nature. Those are telling analogues for his position, but they blunt his attack on the Eunomians at another point. He cannot rebuke them for introducing human examples if he uses them himself. He could be held up to contempt in the same way he relishes exposing them. Either he should stop doing what he attacks them for doing, or stop attacking them for what he himself does. Had he been more careful to explain that his illustrations are *ad hoc* and neither systematic nor foundational, his position would have been defensible.

Nazianzen presents a complex Christological picture that has troubled

---

[227] *Or.* 29.6-8, *PG* 36, 80C-84C.
[228] *Or.* 28.21-30, *PG* 36, 53A-69C.
[229] *Or.* 31.7-8, *PG* 36, 140C-141C.
[230] *Or.* 31.11, *PG* 36, 144D-145A.
[231] *Or.* 31.4, 6 and 12-30, *PG* 36, 137B, 140B and 145B-169A.

many students of Christian doctrine. After arguing for the full divinity of the Son, he presents a threefold view of Jesus Christ, one which was found to be inconsistent by many fifth-century theologians in both the Alexandrian and Antiochene traditions. Primarily Gregory prefers to develop the picture of Jesus in terms of an economic or incarnational distinction. The various titles and incidents related to Jesus Christ should be divided: the more sublime expressions predicated of the Godhead proper, the lowlier ones of the compound, the New Adam, God passible for us. Some titles can be applied to both the transcendent and the human; others that are distinctly human belong only to what the Son assumed for us.[232] Yet according to Nazianzen, one would be well advised to go through all the titles, whether exalted or lowly, looking at them as God might, remembering God descended that we might ascend to become Gods. In each title never forget: "Jesus Christ in body and spirit the same, yesterday, today and forever."[233]

That twofold distinction is the dominant image. At one point Gregory even insists that the divine Son decides between the needs of the soul and the body so that "the one side has supremacy over the other, the better rules the inferior and the baser cannot rebel against the superior."[234] Although the sentences in context are straightforward, they do not make clear how human and divine are involved within the struggle. Could this sense of things lead to the suggestion that the human nature in Christ, being inferior, cannot rebel against the superior? In his powerful antinomies the Theologian confesses that the Son was tempted as man and conquered as God.[235] Such a confession might give the humanity no possibility of functioning as a subject. It apparently collapses the human will into the dominance of the divinity. Yet years ago Mason noted twelve passages within the *Theological Orations* in which Nazianzen's grammar and word choice introduce what that scholar found to be a nascent Nestorianism, a lack of clarity about the necessary "impersonality of his [Christ's] human nature apart from the divine."[236]

The most interesting passage, not in Mason's list, occurs in a section that deals with the interpretation of John 6.38. Gregory says the Son who comes down from heaven obviously does not oppose His will to the will of the One who sent Him, but "our merely human will does not always follow the divine: it often resists and struggles against it. This is the way

---

[232] *Or.* 29.18, *PG* 36, 97C; See *Or.* 30.1, *PG* 36, 104C.
[233] *Or.* 30.21, *PG* 36, 133A.
[234] *Or.* 30.20, *PG* 36, 129C.
[235] *Or.* 29.20, *PG* 36, 100C.
[236] Mason, pp. xvi-xix. The passages are to be found in *Or.* 29.18 and 19 and *Or.* 30.1, 2, 3, 7, 8, 9, 10, 12, 13, and 21, *PG* 36, 97B-C, 100B, 104C, 105B-C, 108A, 113A and C, 113D-116B, 117C, 121A, and 132C.

we interpret 'Father, if it be possible let this cup pass from me, but not what I will—let thy will prevail.' "[237] Unlike Athanasius, Nazianzen does attribute specific words, attitudes and acts to the manhood. In spite of Mason's attempt to explain the passages on the basis of poetic sense or grammatical slips, Gregory does make the humanity the subject of the anointing, the one who speaks of knowing the only true God, the only good (Mark 10.18; Luke 18.19) and the one who receives so many things mentioned in Scripture: life, judgment, inheritance of the Gentiles, power over all flesh, glory, or disciples.[238]

Winslow has suggested that, during his struggle with Apollinarians, Nazianzen repudiates this distinction between predication for the divinity and the humanity and insists upon one subject for all the attitudes and actions of Jesus Christ.[239] Winslow bases his opinion on the difference between the treatments of John 11.34-35 and 43-44 in Oration 29.20 and in Epistle 102.[240] In the first passage the Theologian attributes Jesus' not knowing where Lazarus was buried to the manhood; in the second he castigates the Apollinarians for attributing Jesus' not knowing to the manhood. Both interpretations are set in polemical contexts, the second formed around the debater's point. If the Apollinarians are so wise they should either stop dividing Christ's unity by themselves introducing two separate and conflicting natures or stop accusing others of making that mistake.[241] As a debater's point, it does not commit Nazianzen to a rejection of the position. He apparently kept his options open even within the debate with the Apollinarians.

Gregory never thought of himself as introducing two separate and conflicting natures with the result that the unity was threatened. His employment of "mixing," μίξις, and "blending," κρᾶσις, in the Stoic sense provided for the two elements to remain what they were, but to become one. His strong sense of unity in the person of Jesus Christ allowed him to use all three forms of predication—the Son, the Son incarnate and the manhood—without annihilating the oneness.

The complexity of Gregory's Christology, however, is not exhausted by

---

[237] *Or.* 30.12, *PG* 36, 120A; Also see *Or.* 30.5, *PG* 36, 109A.

[238] *Or.* 30.2, 9, 13 and 21, *PG* 36, 105B, 113C, 121A and 132C. See my unpublished Yale dissertation, "Gregory Nazianzen's Doctrine of Jesus Christ," 1970.

[239] Winslow, pp. 94-95 and his "Christology and Exegesis in the Cappadocians," *CH* 40 (1971), pp. 389-396.

[240] *Or.* 29.20, *PG* 36, 101A; *Ep.* 102, *PG* 37, 201A.

[241] See E. Hardy, *Christology of the Later Fathers*, "The Library of Christian Classics, III" (Philadelphia, 1954), p. 228, n. 16. The interesting aspect of the letter, although not the focus of this essay, is that some Apollinarians might be accused of dividing the manhood and divinity in Christ. This may be a popular position rather than one taken by learned Apollinarian leaders.

noting that this threefold predication continues throughout his works. Unlike many classical theists and various schools of ancient theology, Nazianzen does not speak consistently of a divinity aloof from Jesus' sufferings. The cry from the cross, "My God, My God, look upon me, why didst Thou forsake me?" must be carefully interpreted. "**He** is not forsaken either by the Father or, as some think, by his own Godhead, which closes up, afraid of suffering, and abandons the sufferer. Who applies that argument either to his birth in this world in the first place or to his ascent of the cross? No, in himself, as I have said, he expresses our condition. **We** had once been the forsaken and disregarded; then we were taken and now are saved by the sufferings of the impassible."[242]

For Nazianzen God suffers. Humanity is not inserted into the equation so that divinity will be kept from full involvement in incarnation. The Eunomian use of various Scriptural passages to insist on the secondary status of the Son is incorrect, but it should not always be challenged by attributing apparent weakness and anguish to the humanity. Yet Nazianzen can hedge even this important point. After listing a number of lesser acts and qualities, he insists everyone agrees that "expressions like these refer to the passible element not the immutable nature transcending suffering."[243] Although it is difficult to see this as consistent, Gregory does not himself view such statements as contradictory, perhaps because of the union. He can distinguish between the humanity and divinity as subjects, but he can also attribute everything to one person because of the intermingling. He is credited with being the first theologian to employ some form of περιχώρησις, interchange" or "to interpenetrate," for the two natures of Christ.[244]

One of the strongest reasons for this intermingling of divine and human in the attribution of words, attitudes and acts to Jesus is Gregory's soteriology. He describes the unity of Christ's person as a "single whole . . . by combination not by nature."[245] As mentioned above, his use of words for "blending," κρᾶσις, and "intermingling," μίξις, probably reflects a picture formulated by the Stoics who thought there were unions in which a new whole was formed without a change in the elements that composed it. That analogue was significant for Gregory, since in his view the incarnation meant the divine became human in order that humans might become divine. This doctrine of θέωσις, "divinization," is structural for his theology. The Son remained what he was; what he was not he assumed. He was emptied and then exalted that we might ascend. Through the

---

[242] *Or.* 30.5, *PG* 36, 109A-B; Mt. 27.46.
[243] *Or.* 30.16, *PG* 36, 125A.
[244] *Ep.* 101, *PG* 37, 181C.
[245] *Or.* 30.8, *PG* 36, 113B.

means of mind, the stronger side prevails, so that our thick corporeality will be overcome and we may be made God to the same extent that he was made man.[246] For our sakes, he became all we are except sin: body, soul and mind, everything that death pervades.[247] "Even at this moment he is, as man, interceding for my salvation, until he makes me divine by the power of his incarnate manhood."[248]

This is not to be understood in terms of some crude, physical theory, but more in terms of the complete identification of the Son with us because of our need for salvation.[249] Suffering itself is something which the Son takes on for our sake. We are saved by the passion of the impassible.[250] Full godhead and full manhood in the incarnate Christ are necessary for the salvation of humanity.

Interestingly, Gregory has no time for talk of "legal satisfaction." For him that is a humiliating idea, as if Heb. 7.25 would dare depict such a deity. Evidently in the Theologian's eyes no loving Father would require such satisfaction. Furthermore, a just God does not demand some kind of slavish prostration of Christ; the Son would not submit to such captivity. The Son is mediator and advocate, not one who accepts God's vengeance or God's tyranny.[251] In the same way that Nazianzen had resisted a Greek metaphysical distinction between deity and humanity to the point of endangering the incarnation or withdrawing the Godhead from suffering, he also does not develop a doctrine of sin that concentrates only on knowledge. Mankind cannot be saved by being taught the good and expected to do it. The brokenness of God's creation is much more severe than that. Even the sin of Lucifer was not merely satiation with the fullness of light; it was pride.[252] Human beings refuse willfully; their denials are their own choice.[253]

Christ, through his incarnation, can produce submission because he knows our rebellion, our passions which deny God, our thoughtlessness and our waywardness. He understands our impulses and emotions that indicate there is little or nothing of God in us.[254] The depth of our perversity has been complicated by the Evil One's tricks. He often "uses good for a bad end," enticing us to reach for what is less than perfect.[255]

---

[246] *Or.* 29.18-19, *PG* 36, 97A-100B.
[247] *Or.* 30.21, *PG* 36, 132B.
[248] *Or.* 30.14, *PG* 36, 121C.
[249] Winslow, esp. pp. 187-199.
[250] *Or.* 30.5, *PG* 36, 109B.
[251] *Or.* 30.14, *PG* 36, 121C.
[252] *Or.* 28.12, *PG* 36, 41A.
[253] *Or.* 30.10, *PG* 36, 116A.
[254] *Or.* 30.4-6, *PG* 36, 108B-112B.
[255] *Or.* 28.15, *PG* 36, 45C.

Yet under God's government, indeed with God within us, humans can respond to the fear of punishment, the hope for glory and salvation, and the practice of virtue. They may move toward perfection, closer to God himself.[256]

Nazianzen never views human nature as so defiled, as so deformed, that it could not become a participant in the divine nature. For him the central focus of soteriology means that both divinity and humanity were capable of some kind of interpenetration. θέωσις means that humans would become gods. The Biblical basis for this position is sparse. It may be implied in II Peter 1.4. People are called "gods" in Psalm 82.6, but the contextual meaning has nothing to do with Gregory's views. Even Jesus' apparent quotation of Psalm 82.6 in John 10.34, although closer to the points Nazianzen wants to make, is still not exactly support for what the Cappadocian claims. The Theologian's opinions are more likely to have come to mind in the conflation of the more poetic "he became poor that you might become rich" of II Cor. 8.9 with Phil. 2 and perhaps John 10.34, but there is no specific evidence. Winslow sees θέωσις not only as central to Gregory's entire theological enterprise, but also as a creative innovation in terminology on his part.[257] It is certainly the case that the word seldom appears before him and that the understanding distinguishes his view of salvation from that of the later Arians, yet it is also true that he is following the lead of people like Irenaeus, Origen and Athanasius rather than creating a new conception.[258] In any case soteriology, one of the few major Christian doctrines never decided by councils, is one of the most decisive factors in the conflict between the Cappadocians and the Neo-Arians.

Nazianzen takes positions on Trinity, Christology and soteriology that square in the main with his position as a defender of orthodoxy. In some ways that judgment is tautological since he became one of the three hierarchs of Eastern Orthodoxy, but his views are not without persuasive power even today. He usually undergirds his views by the exegesis of Scripture. Yet he offers no exegetical support for a teaching as important

---

[256] *Or.* 30.19, *PG* 36, 128C. Otis, p. 123 is incorrect to insist that Nazianzen shows no deep sense of sin like that found in Augustine. H. Althaus, *Die Heilslehre des heiligen Gregor von Nazianz* (Münster, 1972), pp. 118-122 views Gregory as closer to Augustine in the Pelagian controversy because Nazianzen's view of human nature and sin is more ontological and typological than the voluntary, moral view of the Pelagians. Against Althaus, however, it must be remembered that the Theologian emphasizes free will both in his doctrine of human nature and his Christology.

[257] Winslow, pp. 181-182.

[258] Irenaeus, *A.H.*, 5.4 has the general conception of Christ becoming human that humans might become divine. Origen, *Comm. on John* 2.2, *PG* 14, 109A and Athanasius, *On the Incarnation* 54, *PG* 25, 192B use forms of θεοποιέω, but not the noun θέωσις.

as "divinization" because he found it to be a true expression of Christian theology, true to the Bible's intent if not found specifically in its words. He provides innovations if he finds certain conservative views to be inappropriate. That is particularly true for his theory of doctrinal development.[259] He was a traditional yet creative theologian who eclectically employed philosophical concepts to illustrate his views. Although not always consistent, even at crucial junctures, he was seldom illogical or fideistic in a crude sense. The reason he employed had fullness, but for him faith gave such fullness to reason.

Opponents: Neo-Arians, Pneumatomachians, Pagans and Others

The two major groups, which Gregory saw as his heretical Christian opponents, were the later Arians and the Pneumatomachians.[260] Recent efforts to depict early Arians have led both to differing views of their major tenets and to increased discussion of their importance.[261] In terms of background the more traditional view that Arius was concerned with the monotheistic stance of Christian theology is important for later developments, particularly since Arius, unlike Aetius and Eunomius, supported the invisibility and incomprehensibility of God.[262] Yet the newer interpretation that Arius dealt primarily with soteriology[263] is also crucial for the later fourth century discussions. Soteriology was a point of strong disagreement between the Eunomians and the Cappadocians.

For our purposes here, however, the description of later Arianism—what is often referred to as Eunomianism or Neo-Arianism—is the specific focus. Fortunately, much ground-breaking research has been done in recent years.[264] The traditional view that the primary opponents in these

---

[259] *Or.* 31.26, *PG* 36, 161C.

[260] For Nazianzen's understanding of heresy see F. Trisoglio, "La Figura dell'eretico in Gregorio di Nazianzo," *Augustinianum* 25 (1985), pp. 793-832.

[261] See particularly Gregg, Gregg and Groh; C. Kannengiesser, *Holy Scripture and Hellenistic Hermeneutics in Alexandrian Christology: The Arian Crisis*, "Protocol of the Colloquy of the Center for Hermeneutical Studies in Hellenistic and Modern Culture, 41" (Berkeley, 1982), pp. 1-40 and his "Arius and the Arians," *TS* 44 (1983), pp. 456-476; R. Lorenz, *Arius judaizans? Untersuchungen zur dogmengeschichtlichen Einordnung des Arius* (Göttingen, 1980), and R. Williams, *Arius: Heresy and Tradition* (London, 1987).

[262] Athanasius, *De Synodis* 15, *PG* 26, 705C-708C and Philostorgius, *H.E.* 2.3, *GCS*, Bidez; Winkelmann, p. 14. T. Kopecek, in his response to C. Kannengiesser's presentation, *Holy Scripture and Hellenistic Hermeneutics* (Berkeley, 1982), pp. 51-68, makes much of this absolute difference between Arius and the later Arians.

[263] Gregg and Groh.

[264] E. Cavalcanti, *Studi Eunomiani*, "Orientalia Christiana Analecta 202" (Rome, 1976); T. Dams, unpublished dissertation "La Controverse eunoméenne," Institut Catholique de Paris, 1952; Hanson, pp. 598-636; Kopecek; Mortley, II, pp. 85-191; B. Sesboüé, *L'Apologie d'Eunome de Cyzique et le Contre Eunome de Basile de Césarée* (Rome, 1980);

five orations are later Arians still holds the field. Gregory never refers to his major opposition as Eunomians in the *Theological Orations* and only once in the five uses the name "Arians" as a contemporary reference.[265] Yet most of the positions he attributes to his antagonists can be found in the writings of later Arians. Kopecek's acceptance of Gregory's usual reliability in depicting later Arian doctrines is sound.[266] The comparison of positions from the fragments and works of Aetius, Eunomius and other Neo-Arians with views represented in these five orations indicates that in most instances Nazianzen presents later Arian arguments as they appear in their own works. He also states them in ways that correspond to the citations found in Basil's and Gregory of Nyssa's refutations of Eunomius' *Apology* and Nyssa's attack on his *Apology for the Apology*. Even though Oration 27 is primarily introductory, focused on what is necessary to be a true theologian, its section 8 warns that the opponents stress the importance of propositional statements of faith,[267] a position reflected in Eunomius' insistence that baptism owed its effectiveness to the "exactness of dogmas."[268] Oration 28 insists that the human mind is far too limited to know the divine essence or to give it an exclusive name; its section 3 warns that "perfect apprehension" of God's nature is far removed even for an "all super-celestial" being.[269] Arius evidently considered the ultimate nature of God to be ineffable to the Son and thus to all creatures,[270] but Epiphanius cited Aetius and Socrates quoted Eunomius as claiming that any Christian could know God's being as well as God himself knew it.[271] Oration 29 in many sections carries on a dialogue about the meaning of

---

Vaggione, and his unpublished dissertation, "Aspects of Faith in the Eunomian Controversy," Oxford University, 1976; Wickham, "The Date of Eunomius' *Apology*: A Reconsideration," *JThS* NS 10 (1969), pp. 231-240, and "Aetius and the Doctrine of Divine Emergency," *Studia Patristica* XII, "TU 108," ed. by E. Livingstone (Berlin, 1972), pp. 259-263. The most up to date bibliographies are to be found in Gregg, pp. 371-380 and Hanson, pp. 878-900.

[265] *Or.* 31.30, *PG* 36, 169A; *Or.* 20.5-6, *PG* 35, 1069C-1072D; *Or.* 33.16-17, *PG* 36, 233C-237A. In *Ep.* 202, *PG* 37, 332A, he mentions Eunomius as a threat even though the major focus of the epistle is on the Apollinarians.

[266] Kopecek, pp. 494-503.

[267] *Or.* 27.8, *PG* 36, 21A-C.

[268] Eunomius, *Apology for the Apology* 2.22, Jaeger 2.284; Vaggione, p. 126.

[269] *Or.* 28.3-4, 9, 11-12, and 17, *PG* 36, 29A-32B, 36C-37B, 40A-43B and 48C-49A.

[270] Athanasius, *De Synodis* 15, *PG* 26, 705C-708C. G. Stead, "The *Thalia* of Arius and the Testimony of Athanasius," *JThS* NS 29 (1978), p. 25 suggests that Athanasius' *Contra Arianos* 1.6, *PG* 26, 24A, which has ἀόρατος, "invisible," instead of ἄρρητος, "inexplicable," might be a misquoted text even though invisibility is also an Arian tenet.

[271] Epiphanius, *Panarion* 76.4, *GCS*, Holl III, p. 72 and Socrates *H.E.* 4.7, *PG* 67, 473B-C. Vaggione, pp. 170 and 179, lists the latter as an authentic fragment from Eunomius, but Wickham, pp. 565-566, n. 1 considers both the "folklore of apologists."

"begotten" and "proceeded" with particular emphasis on the former.[272] There is no question that the significance of γεννητός, "begotten," is a strong theme of later Arianism.

Kopecek's remark, however, that the ten points raised in Oration 30 came from a catena of texts circulated within the later Arian community is questionable.[273] Gregory himself says, "we shall group these explanations in numbered sections to aid the memory."[274] He does not suggest that the list was taken over from the Eunomians either in an oral or a written form. Although the ordering may not have originated in the Eunomian community, the content of the Scriptural interpretations represents its views. Some Scriptural references from eight of the ten sets Gregory discusses can be found in Eunomius' *Apology*—and the later Arian addition to that work, listed as section 28—the *Apology for the Apology*, the *Confession*, the *Fragments* and the *Thesaurus* from Cyril of Alexandria. Using Nazianzen's numbering of the ten sets these eight are: (1) Proverbs 8.22 in Oration 30.2, *Apology* 26 and 28, the later addition, the *Apology for the Apology* 2.2 and the *Confession* 3;[275] (2) 1 Cor. 15.28 in Oration 30.5 and *Apology* 27[276] (3) John 14.28 in Oration 30.7, *Apology* 11 and Cyril's *Thesaurus* 11,;[277] (4) John 20.17 in Oration 30.7, *Apology* 21, the *Apology for the Apology* 2.22 and Cyril's *Thesaurus* 10;[278] (5) John 5.22 in Oration 30.9, the *Apology for the Apology* and the *Confession* 3;[279] (6) John 5.19 in Oration 30.10, *Apology* 20 and 26;[280] (7) John 6.38 in Oration 30.12 and *Fragment* iii;[281] and (8) John 17.3 in Oration 30.13, *Apology* 17, 21, 25 and 26, and the *Confession* 2-4.[282]

Although the positions Gregory chooses for comment might have been taken directly from the writings of Eunomius, they may have arisen out of private and public discussions in Constantinople.[283] A close compari-

---

[272] *Or.* 29.3-16, *PG* 36, 77A-96B.
[273] Kopecek, p. 502.
[274] *Or.* 30.1, *PG* 36, 104C-D.
[275] *Or.* 30.2, *PG* 36, 105A-C and *Apology* 26 and 28, Vaggione, pp. 68-71 and 74-75; *Apology for the Apology* 2.2, Jaeger 2.10-11, Vaggione, p. 116; *Confession* 3, Vaggione, pp. 152-153.
[276] *Or.* 30.5, *PG* 36, 108C-109C and *Apology* 27, Vaggione, pp. 70-75.
[277] *Or.* 30.7, *PG* 36, 112C-113A; *Apology* 11, Vaggione, pp. 46-47 and *Thesaurus* 11, Vaggione, p. 183.
[278] *Or.* 30.7, *PG* 36, 112C-113A and *Apology* 21, Vaggione, pp. 60-63; *Apology for the Apology* 2.22, Jaeger 2.287 and 289, Vaggione, p. 126; *Thesaurus* 10, Vaggione, p. 182.
[279] *Or.* 30.9, *PG* 36, 113C and *Apology for the Apology*, Jaeger 2.384; *Confession* 3, Vaggione, pp. 152-155.
[280] *Or.* 30.10, *PG* 36, 113C-116B and *Apology* 20 and 26, Vaggione, pp. 58-61 and 68-71.
[281] *Or.* 30.12, *PG* 36, 117C-120B and *Fragment* iii, Vaggione, p. 178.
[282] *Or.* 30.13, *PG* 36, 120C-121B and *Apology* 17, 21, and 25-26, Vaggione, pp. 54-55, 60-63, and 66-71; *Confession* 2-4, Vaggione, pp. 150-159.
[283] Kopecek, p. 499.

son with Eunomius' fragments indicates that the opposition is genuinely later Arian, but it also shows that all the points argued were not assembled from any particular writings known to us. Two of the ten sets of Biblical quotations found in Oration 30 do not appear in Eunomius' writings as we have them. Again using Nazianzen's numbering, (9), centered on Heb. 7.25;[284] and (10), which concerns Mark 13.32,[285] are consistent with positions taken by Eunomius, but are not the focus of attention in extant pieces from him. The similarity of conception and Scriptural quotation strongly implies that the later Arian community is their source, but the lack of verbal parallels and the absence of certain points makes one question whether the specific issues represent direct quotations from Eunomius himself. Of course, Gregory's description of his opponents' teachings might have occurred in writings that were destroyed; he warns about their "elementary treatise,"[286] a type of literature we may possess only in the small chapter 28 added to Eunomius' *Apology*[287]. Given his sense of derision, that could be a condescending epithet, but it probably means that popular, simplified tracts containing the views of later Arianism had been circulated.

Whether or not the additional points represent doctrines taught by Eunomius or developed within later Arian circles cannot be answered with certainty, but either case suggests Gregory's *Theological Orations* are important for the history of Eunomianism. Since comparisons with Eunomius' fragmentary corpus indicate that Nazianzen tends to portray the opponents' views as well as Basil or Nyssa, the further developed issues may also be fair statements of views held by later Arians. Or, more interestingly, perhaps Nazianzen combats positions that had made their way into the salons, the parties, indeed, into nearly every corner of Constantinopolitan society.[288] This is significant for two reasons. First, we have in the *Theological Orations* debates with later Arian opponents that are not limited to the writings of Aetius or those of Eunomius. Nazianzen's five orations give a better sense of popular wrangling than do the textually based attacks of Basil and Nyssa. Second, because of that more popular character, these orations imply that later Arians were not merely a small cadre of highly polished dialecticians.[289] They formed a religious com-

---

[284] *Or.* 30.14, *PG* 36, 121C-124A.

[285] *Or.* 30.15, *PG* 36, 124A-B.

[286] *Or.* 29.1, *PG* 36, 73A-76A.

[287] Vaggione, p. 16 makes the connection between section 28 and Gregory's mention of an "introductory work."

[288] *Or.* 27.2, *PG* 36, 13A-C.

[289] C. Kannengiesser, "Arius and the Arians," *TS* 44 (1983), pp. 456-475 takes the view that the early Arian heresy basically came from systematicians and logicians, not so much from separate worshipping congregations.

munity that had wider interests than pure philosophical argumentation. We must not forget that Eunomius is said to have written a seven-volume work often referred to as a commentary on Romans.[290] As Hagedorn indicates, some later Arian circle produced a commentary on Job, edited pieces such as the *Clementine Homilies* and the *Apostolic Constitutions*, and probably produced the longer recension of the letters written by Ignatius of Antioch.[291] They could make themselves clear on many topics to any who wished to hear. Gregory notes that his opponents had great success and could be persuasive.[292] He and the so-called "orthodox" were forced to meet in a small chapel, Anastasia, while the Arian community controlled most of the larger churches and included much of the population.[293]

Some modern historians find it difficult to believe that the populace of Constantinople could understand the intricate detail in these theological arguments. Doubtless it was not easily accessible to the general public in the technical form found in Aetius' *Syntagmation*, but any reader will be impressed with the way Eunomius expressed basic positions in a much less technical manner than his teacher, Aetius.[294] And if the arguments Gregory combats represent yet another stage of popularization, we are then in touch with a different level of the debate. Certainly within those parts of society where enlightened discussion of pressing issues was the common fare, such arguments were pursued with fervor. And evidently enough of the higher level discussion could be simplified to make an appeal to popular audiences. The fundamental propositions and their Biblical bases, stated in less rigorous fashion, could be presented persuasively, perhaps in easily remembered patterns. Arius had produced poetry that allowed his positions to be grasped by the masses.[295] From studies of the Arian community in this later period, we know they developed liturgies that had common appeal.[296] Almost twenty years after Gregory's depar-

---

[290] Socrates, *H.E.* 4.7, *PG* 67, 473A mentions that work.

[291] D. Hagedorn, *Der Hiobkommentar des Arianers Julian* (Berlin, 1973), pp. xxxvii-lv.

[292] *Or.* 30.1, *PG* 36, 104C-D.

[293] Socrates, *H.E.* 5.7, *PG* 67, 573B-C; Sozomen, *H.E.* 7.5, *PG* 67, 1425A-B and Philostorgius, *H.E.* 9.19, *GCS*, Bidez; Winkelmann, p. 125.

[294] Vaggione, the newest edition of Eunomius' works, includes the Greek text, a fine English translation and an excellent introduction. His article, "Some Neglected Fragments of Theodore of Mopsuestia's *Contra Eunomium*," *JThS* NS 31 (1980), pp. 403-470 pointed out six new fragments related to Eunomius. Aetius' principal preserved work is most accessible in the text and translation of Wickham.

[295] His *Thalia* was probably a "dogmatic verse-composition" in popular rather than classical poetic form. See G. Stead, "The *Thalia* of Arius and the Testimony of Athanasius," *JThS* NS 29 (1978), pp. 20 and 40-51. M. West, "The Metre of Arius' *Thalia*," *JThS* NS 33 (1982), pp. 98-105 disagrees with Stead's assessment of the poetic form, but agrees that the piece was an intentional popularization of Arius' teaching.

[296] T. Kopecek, "Neo-Arian Religion: The Evidence of the *Apostolic Constitutions*" in

40000.0

ture from Constantinople, the persecuted Arians were still engaged in impressive liturgical processions at night, ones which involved antiphonal singing and special liturgical vessels.[297] All students of this debate must then be careful neither to think of the later Arian community as merely a philosophical circle nor to think of Nazianzen's *Theological Orations* as evening lectures given to the few who might have had both the interest and the education to follow them. Gregory strains not to make his orations too involved or too long. At times he knows he has stretched the limits, perhaps broken them.[298] Thus he uses the final sections of Oration 29 for a flight of eloquent oratory that lifts the spirit after the mind has struggled to follow the intricate enthymematic arguments.[299]

Other aspects of the later Arian community stand out within the *Theological Orations*. In Oration 29 Gregory introduces another topic: three stages of revelation. The Old Testament declared the divinity of God and hinted at the nature of the Son; the New Testament stated the Son's deity and suggested similar things about the Spirit; in their own era the nature of the Spirit had now become clear.[300] Although Gregory often skewers his opponents as innovators, this daring claim is itself an innovation. From what we know, others had not taken that position. Nazianzen, for all his ranting against Arian or Apollinarian change, leaves other alternatives behind. He not only viewed both the later Arian and the Pneumatomachian positions as improper expressions of the ancient truths of Scripture and the confessions of the Church, but also saw some "orthodox" statements and practices as older options which needed to be abandoned. The position of those like Basil, who did not confess publicly the divinity of the Spirit, had been taken perhaps because the time was not proper. Other things were not yet clearly understood; that development had waited,[301] but now the time was right. The denial of the Spirit's deity by both Eunomians and Pneumatomachians made its defense imperative.

As sketchy as these two passages are, they tend to strengthen the pos-

---

in Gregg, pp. 153-179 makes a convincing case for later Arians as worshipping communities. Kopecek, in his reviews (*JThS* NS 38 [1987], pp. 208-211 and *JThS* NS 39 [1988], pp. 611-618) of M. Metzger, *Les Constitutions Apostoliques*, Tomes I-III, *SC* 320 (1985), 329 (1986) and 336 (1987) disagrees with Metzger and defends the Arian authorship of the *Apostolic Constitutions*.

[297] Socrates, *H.E.* 6.8, *PG* 67, 688C-692A describes such events during the "orthodox" bishopric of John.

[298] Particularly *Or.* 29.17 and 19, *PG* 36, 96C-97A and 100A-B and *Or.* 30.1, *PG* 36, 104C-D.

[299] *Or.* 29. 19-20, *PG* 36, 100A-101C.

[300] *Or.* 31.26, *PG* 36, 161C-164B.

[301] *Or.* 43.68, *PG* 36, 585C-588C and *Ep.* 58, *PG* 37, 113A-117B, Gallay, (1969), pp. 52-54.

sibility that later Arianism was in many ways conservative, fundamentally based on earlier views rather than always being progressive, creating new options. Particularly in their resistance to a Trinitarian doctrine that demanded the Spirit be God, later Arians indicated their conservative leanings even though their baptismal practice was described by some as innovative. Perhaps even that single rather than triple immersion represented an earlier practice.[302]

Before we turn to a summary of the later Arian doctrine Gregory opposes, we must correct some misconceptions commonly found in secondary descriptions. Often the main tenets had been more carefully nuanced than has at times been recognized.[303] Both Aetius and Eunomius were misrepresented by their detractors, the Cappadocians and others, as demanding a total unlikeness of Father and Son. On the contrary, each could speak about a similarity between the Father and the Son in terms of will or activity,[304] although they did insist on an unlikeness of nature or essence. Wickham suggests that the Cappadocians made such sweeping charges not merely in an attempt to win "cheap verbal victories," but through a desire not to concede the selection of the field for the contest to the later Arians.[305] In any case on this point they misrepresented their foes. The Eunomians did not draw the inferences that the Cappadocians found necessarily connected with their positions. For that reason these opponents of Gregory are not called "Anomoeans" within this commentary.

Some secondary treatments also have extended the description of early Arians as philosophers and dialecticians to later Arians as well. That picture emerges in the fourth century. Nazianzen refutes them as lovers of syllogisms, as "logic-choppers."[306] Socrates, Sozomen and Philostorgius describe them as noted for their skills in debate.[307] Mortley often emphasizes the philosophical acuity of Aetius and Eunomius at points where both Basil and Gregory of Nyssa seem ignorant of the import of Euno-

---

[302] Socrates, *H.E.* 5.24, *PG* 67, 649A and Sozomen, *H.E.* 6.26, *PG* 67, 1361C speak of Arian baptism. Also see Kopecek, pp. 397-400.

[303] Wickham, p. 552, n. 1 says a common description of later Arians as teaching a "doctrine that the Son was totally unlike, ἀνόμοιος, the Father," stated by F. Cross in the *Oxford Dictionary of the Christian Church* (Oxford, 1958), p. 58, is false. Also see Hanson, p. 598.

[304] Eunomius, *Confession* 3, Vaggione, pp. 154-155 and Aetius according to Philostorgius, *H.E.* 4.12, *GCS*, Bidez; Winkelmann, pp. 64-65.

[305] Wickham, pp. 551-552.

[306] *Or.* 27.2, *PG* 36, 13B; *Or.* 29.21, *PG* 36, 101C-104A; *Or.* 31.18, *PG* 36, 153A.

[307] Socrates, *H.E.* 2.35 and 4.7, *PG* 67, 297B-300B and 472C-473C; Sozomen, *H.E.* 7.6, *PG* 67, 1428A-1429A; Philostorgius, *H.E.* 3.15, *GCS*, Bidez; Winkelmann, pp. 44-47.

mius' arguments.[308] Three adjustments of these descriptions, however, are in order. First, the skill in argument of Aetius and Eunomius, although great, is not without its weakness. Socrates warned that Aetius understood neither the purpose of Aristotle's *Categories* nor the tradition of its interpretation; he also found Eunomius verbose.[309] The Cappadocians often question later Arian logical and philosophical competence. Anastos points out a number of places in which Eunomius leaves himself open to criticism. He is not consistent in designating the Son either as begotten or created. He equivocally prefers to use both. Eunomius also waffles when he declares God to be incomparable and yet better than the Son. At times he demands that titles do not involve an identity of essence and at other times insists that different names demand different essences.[310]

Second, Aetius' *Syntagmation* insists that his "little discourse is based on the mind of Holy Scripture."[311] The disagreement about the meaning of certain Biblical passages, which is so clear in the *Theological Orations*, was probably basic to the debate in the 360s. Although neither Aetius' *Syntagmation* nor the writings of Eunomius contain all the Biblical references and discussions that occur in Gregory's *Theological Orations*, their systematic works are intended to show the way through various Scriptural claims. As noted above, some Biblical citations from eight of the ten sets Gregory treats in Oration 30 can be found in extant writings of Eunomius. Furthermore the Neo-Arian circle produced Biblical commentaries. Although Socrates warns that Eunomius' comments on Romans show him to be incapable of grasping its intent, the church historian does clearly indicate that Eunomius found Biblical exposition to be basic to the theological task.[312]

Third, even Aetius' *Syntagmation*, with its tightly constructed, sometimes cryptic, statements, is not expressed in formal syllogisms. Whatever the level of audience Aetius had in mind, whether advanced students or teachers, he chose an enthymematic form, that is, the presentation of one premise and a conclusion with the second premise to be supplied by the

---

[308] Mortley, II, pp. 141-191. I am not certain that either Basil or Gregory of Nyssa is as poorly informed as Mortley suggests. He paints them as unaware of developments in contemporary philosophy at points where they may be defending different positions because of the dangers they see in the views held by Aetius and Eunomius.

[309] Socrates, *H.E.* 2.35 and 4.7, PG 67, 297B-300B and 472C-473C.

[310] M. Anastos, "Basil's *Kata Eunomiou*, A Critical Analysis," *Basil of Caesarea: Christian, Humanist, Ascetic*, Part 1, ed. by P. Fedwick (Toronto, 1981), pp. 119-120.

[311] Wickham, pp. 540, 545.

[312] Socrates, *H.E.* 4.7, PG 67, 472C-473C. Wickham, p. 558, n. 1 insists on that Scriptural base for both Aetius and Eunomius.

reader or hearer. Each of the thirty-six propositions begins with an "if" clause. Such clauses are completed with questions or "then" clauses. Occasionally a problem is stated in a way that makes the implied three-fold syllogistic structure clear,[313] but in no case is an actual syllogistic form used. The type of enthymeme Aetius employs, however, is not the one in which probability questions incapable of formal demonstration are handled. His arguments are of the type in which the points could be proved through the three-fold syllogistic form, but, for the purposes of audience involvement, are presented in the two-fold enthymematic form. Eunomius is much easier to understand because he does not pack his enthymemes so tightly. He is more discursive in the development of his arguments, providing examples and other types of explanations, but his manner of argument (a lighter presentation of enthymemes for propositions that could be presented in syllogisms) provokes Gregory to his mode of response. In Nazianzen's view a number of important questions in theology must be handled "enthymematically" because they are probability questions that are not susceptible to formal, syllogistic demonstration. According to the Theologian, no one knows the nature of God. God's essence can be talked about confessionally, mystically and thus "enthymematically," but it cannot be demonstrated. For both Aetius and Eunomius, enthymematic argument is appropriate because of the rhetorical concern for audience response. Yet they insist that formal demonstration of their positions, even the description of God's nature, can be offered. This basic disagreement about methodology, about *paideia*, makes the debate most difficult. Both definitions of enthymemes rely on Aristotle's *Rhetoric*, particularly 1355A-1357B and 1395B-1396A, but the difference between the two is crucial.

That crucial difference in understanding *paideia* is perhaps more easily seen in the Eunomian theory of language, certainly one of its fundamental presuppositions. All parties to the debate found this to be important. The tenets of the later Arian linguistic theory must be assembled both from Aetius' *Syntagmation*, particularly sections 16-17, Eunomius' *Apology*, specifically sections 8 and 12, and fragments from his *Apology for the Apology* 1.5-10.[314] According to the these leaders of the later Arian community names designate essence. Of course that is not always true. Humans have used their powers of "thought," of "imagination," to create "utter-

---

[313] Wickham, pp. 541 and 545, propositions 5 and 6.
[314] Wickham. pp. 542 and 546-547; Vaggione, pp. 40-43 and 46-49, and Jaeger, esp. 1.238, 245, 270-271, 274, 276, 282, 284-285, 303, 313, 315-316, 323-324, 326, 328-329, 340-342, 344-348, 364, 367-368, 370-371, 385-386, 388, 398-399; Vaggione, pp. 105-114.

ances'' that are merely ''sounds.'' Once these inauthentic names have
been spoken, their meaning vanishes into the air with the cessation of the
noise. Authentic ''names'' and ''titles,'' however, depict the ''essence;''
they ''designate'' that ''essence.'' In such cases, the name and the essence
are identical.[315] Eunomius specifically states the methodological and theological significance of this theory of language. Authentic language was
not produced by human ''thought;'' God himself gave language to humanity. The Genesis account clearly taught that humans came into existence well after God had spoken. He designated the relationship between
true names and essences before people became involved with the apparent
naming of various creatures.[316] Therefore authentic names of all things
go back to God and are not subject to human invention. Philo is the most
likely source of this teaching, but the natural rather than the conventional
relationship of essence and names is supported by Plato, Albinus, Epicurus and Chrysippus each with different conceptions of God.[317]

The fundamental character of this theory becomes quickly apparent
when one turns to the later Arian doctrine of God. Since God himself revealed language, his essence is to be sought in his name. For the Neo-
Arians that name is ἀγέννητος, ''unbegotten'' or ''ingenerate,'' a name
not given in Scripture, but one clearly deduced from sophisticated
philosophical expositions of divine essence, particularly those found in
Neo-Platonic commentators on Aristotle. Mortley has demonstrated that
both Aetius and Eunomius probably followed the lead of philosophers like
Dexippus, Syrianus, or Alexander of Aphrodisias in developing the revelation of deity's essence by way of negation, a position that would later
be more fully expounded by Proclus. If nothing is prior to God, then he
is ingenerate. The use of an alpha-privative form does not involve a privation, the assumption of something that was previously there and then lost
as say in blindness, but involves the tightest linguistic expression of
the essence of anything, particularly deity.[318] The position had two
strengths. First, it depended upon recent contemporary developments in

---

[315] See the excellent description of this theory in Wickham, p. 560.

[316] *Apology for the Apology* 1.6, Jaeger 1.282, 284 and 302-303, 344-345; Vaggione, pp. 106-107.

[317] Philo, *Leg. All.* 2.14-15; Plato, *Cratylus* 430A-431E; Albinus, *Epit.* 6; Epicurus, *Letter to Herodotus* 75-76; Chrysippus, *SVF* II, p. 24, Fr. 895.

[318] Mortley, II, esp. pp. 128-159. Dexippus, *CAG* IV,2, p. 44, in discussing Aristotle says that the best definition of the essence of something can be arrived at by negation. Syrianus, *CAG* I, p. 61 and Alexander of Aphrodisias, *CAG* I, p. 327 teach similar views noting that privation is not necessarily involved when a negation is used. Proclus, *Platonic Theology* 2.5 perhaps offers the clearest and most pointed development of the position. Both Aetius' *Syntagmation* 19-20, Wickham, pp. 542 and 547 and Eunomius' *Apology* 7-8, Vaggione, pp. 40-43 expound such views.

philosophical circles and thus was in a sense up-to-date. Mortley criticizes both Basil and Gregory of Nyssa for being ignorant of those developments.[319] Second, it played on the Scriptural designation of the Son as "begotten" and thus "generate." It represented both the key position in the subordination of the Son and suggested itself as a quasi-Scriptural term. From the standpoint of argument this was a clever move, for it used an inference from Scripture to pass for actual Scriptural statement.

The significant connection, however, between the sophisticated theory of language, the sense of Biblical revelation and this philosophically astute definition of God's essence is not as clearly presented. God created language—particularly he gave essences their names—and thus provided the major premises for any discussion of his nature. On that basis, the development of deductive inferences from God-given names for essences is perfectly appropriate. Theology is thus propositional; theologians figure out doctrine through formal demonstration, i.e., through syllogisms, even if they may present their teaching for the sake of the audience in enthymematic form. Any attempt to see language as the invention of men after the nature of things had been set, as much more flexible and never exact, implies an acceptance of Aristotelian views of providence and subjective Epicurean theories about the origin of words.[320] This understanding of language is rooted in an attempt to make sense of Scripture, to interpret what it has to say to the contemporary era. Neither Aetius nor Eunomius planned primarily to set up a theological system that had only tenuous connection with the Bible. Aetius says his *Syntagmation* depends "on the mind of Scripture," κατ' ἔννοιαν τῶν ἁγίων γραφῶν, and Eunomius' works often have exegetical comments. For each of them, both Biblical concepts and Biblical words were inspired by God.[321]

But then why did God not give the name of his essence, ἀγέννητος, "ingenerate," in Scripture? Why, in fact, is it deduced from a philosophical discussion of how one reaches the truest definition of essence by way of negation, not privation? Is valid logical inference a form of revelation, given by God and not subject to the invention of men? What we have within the fragmentary corpus of the later Arians offers no clear answer to

---

[319] Mortley, II, pp. 160-191.

[320] Eunomius, *Apology of the Apology* 1.6, Jaeger 1.345-346, Vaggione, pp. 107-108, attacked Basil with those charges concerning Aristotelian and Epicurean doctrine. Kopecek, pp. 452-470 offers similar descriptions of the language theory on the basis of Eunomius' *Apology for the Apology*.

[321] *Syntagmation*, Intro., Wickham, pp. 540 and 545. J. Daniélou, "Eunome l'Arien et l'exégèse néo-Platonicienne du *Cratyle*," *Revue des études grecques* 69 (1956), pp. 412-432 shows the philosophical influence on Eunomius' theory of language, but as Wickham, p. 558, n. 1, indicates, it is the relationship to Scripture that is meant by the Neo-Arians themselves to be the strongest in any definition of theology.

such important questions, questions that should have been answered for
their presentations to be ultimately persuasive.

The grounds for choosing ἀγέννητος as the single name of God's essence are also not forthcoming.[322] Other alpha-privatives could fit the developed position of the Neo-Platonists. It seems obvious that the choice
of this word is linked to Scripture's designation of the Son as μονογενής,
the "only begotten" (John 1.14, etc.) and thus that its choice is based on
considerations other than the philosophical description of the way of negation. If that be the case, it is also difficult to see why some form of "uncreated," ἄκτιστος, should also not be the proper name for the divine essence, since Eunomius can again turn to Scripture in order to name the
Son a "created thing," a κτιστός, the "first born of all creation" (Col.
1.15). The selection of ἀγέννητος alone is arbitrary, based on a commitment to a subordinate position for the Son.

Furthermore the language theory developed in Neo-Arian circles involves a definite sense of synonyms and homonyms or equivocal terms,
perhaps taken from various rhetorical / grammatical writings. Eunomius
insists that synonyms vary in pronunciation or expression, but that they
are similar in meaning. Homonyms, however, are the same in pronunciation and expression, but differ in meaning. For example, if "Father" is
used of God, it is a homonym of what we as humans know of the word
"father." And if ἀγέννητος, "unbegotten," is the name God gave himself, the name that reveals his nature, then "light" when used of the
Father, the Son and the Spirit must be a homonym for the Son and the
Spirit. It has the same pronunciation and the same expression, but it has
a different meaning in each case, for the essence of each is different.[323]

By relying heavily on contemporary philosophical sources, often Neo-
Platonic interpretations of Aristotle, Eunomius encouraged the continued engagement with such teachings within Christian tradition. The
Platonic, subordinationist elements of Clement and Origen, particularly
the latter, were appropriated and expanded. Against this background Eunomius' argument for the deficiency of Son and Spirit becomes intelligi-
ble. There is no likeness or sameness of essence shared by Father, Son and
Spirit because the revealed names of their natures are different. The
Father is "unbegotten;" the Son is "begotten;" the Spirit "proceeds."

In his *Apology* Eunomius suggests two ways in which the difference in
nature can be demonstrated: first, by investigating the category of "es-

[322] M. Anastos, "Basil's *Kata Eunomiou*, A Critical Analysis," *Basil of Caesarea: Christian, Humanist, Ascetic*, Part 1, ed. by P. Fedwick (Toronto, 1981), p. 119.
[323] Eunomius, *Apology* 11, 16 and 19; Vaggione, pp. 46-47, 52-55, and 56-59.

sence,'' second, by investigating the category of ''work'' or ''created effect.'' Under the first category, all agree that God is prior to everything;
he is the maker who exists before everything made. The name ''ingenerate,'' which signifies this priority, is not produced by human ''invention.'' Neither is it subject to ''privation'' as if its alpha-privative form
implied some previous condition that was taken away. ''Ingenerate'' signifies God's character of ultimate priority. Being ''unbegotten'' is not a
mere part of his nature; it is not something different from him as if he were
composite; it is not something alongside him as something other than
what he is. It is his essence. If that be true, then any nature named ''begotten'' cannot be the same as one named ''unbegotten.'' Everything outside
the ''unbegotten'' essence is a ''thing made,'' a ''creature.'' This distinction, however, must be understood carefully. To say that the Son is a
''creature'' is not to say that he is like all other creatures. When applied
to the Son, the word ''creature'' is a homonym. It has the same pronunciation and expression, but not the same meaning. ''The first born of all
creation'' (Col. 1.15) is prior to all other creatures. Although the Son did
not exist before his generation, he is not like any other creature. His place
in the hierarchy is not acquired; it belongs to him by nature.

The Father and the Son are not the same because Being has no need
of Becoming. Generation always involves becoming. Yet it is not utterly
wrong to call the Son ''God'' as long as the speaker recognizes that, in
reference to the Son, the word ''God'' is a homonym. It has the same
sound and the same letters, but its meaning is different.

Eunomius' second line of investigation, that concerning the ''created
effect,'' also demonstrates that the Son is a ''thing created'' by the Father,
while the Spirit is a ''thing created'' by the Son. A ''created effect'' corresponds to the dignity of the ''essence'' that made it, but such a creation
cannot be identical with the ''essence'' of its creator because that ''created
effect'' begins and ceases; the ''essence'' of the creator does neither. Each
time the highest titles are applied to the Son, their appropriate application
is due to the Son's correspondence with his maker as a ''work'' of that
maker, the Father. In each case, however, the shared titles are actually
homonyms, not synonyms. The difference between an ''essence'' and a
''work'' must be acknowledged.[324]

Two features of the later Arian argument must be acknowledged before
it appears that Eunomius was only concerned with philosophical distinc-

---

[324] These paragraphs are intended to be a summary of the structure Eunomius gives
to his *Apology* 6-25, Vaggione, pp. 38-69, particularly sections 20-25. Along with Wickham, Hanson, Kopecek and Mortley are the most helpful secondary treatments of later
Arian doctrine.

tions. First, his writings are filled with interpretations of the Sacred Writings that make it clear he thought he was using philosophical categories to properly understand the Bible. There are over fifty passages of Scripture that are pertinent to the discussion of the Son in *Apology* 6-25.[325] Aetius described his *Syntagmation* as founded on the mind of Holy Writ[326] and Nazianzen's immediate later Arian opponents in Constantinople constantly refer to Biblical citations in presenting their views.[327] They think that any reader of Scripture will see clearly that the Son cannot be the same as the Father because so many lesser qualities and actions are attributed to him.

Second, Eunomius in his *Confession* specifically rejects the idea that the Son took up a manhood of soul and body.[328] Such a decision left him with no way to attribute the claims of Scripture to a fully functioning manhood. All such verses had to be predicated of the Son who was not divine in the way that the Father God was. Although much of the Antiochene School was repeatedly taken to task in later centuries for dividing the person of Christ—a claim not correct when their arguments are understood—those theologians with their emphasis on double predication did have a remarkable way of handling large groups of Scriptural claims about Jesus. Within this debate Nazianzen saw the strength of making the manhood a subject.

Eunomius' doctrine of the Spirit is in line with his views of the Son. He claims that the Spirit also exists by the will of the Father. As a "created effect" he began and can cease. Yet he must not be disparaged because he is the first and principal power of the Son; he is involved in sanctification. Although he is only third in rank, the implication is that the great titles could also be used of him as long as the speaker recognizes that they are homonyms. Because Eunomius himself subordinated the Spirit to the Son and the Son to the Father, Oration 31 from Gregory must be viewed as an extension of the debate with later Arians, not a discussion limited to Pneumatomachian opponents as some secondary literature suggests.[329] Oration 33, which was given months before the *Theological Orations*, attacked the "Arians" for their misunderstanding of the Holy

---

[325] See the references in Vaggione, pp. 38-69.
[326] Aetius, *Syntagmation,* Intro., Wickham, pp. 540 and 545.
[327] See particularly, *Or.* 29.18, *PG* 36, 97A-B, the ten clusters of texts in 30.2-15, *PG* 36, 105A-124B and the claim in 31.1 and 21, *PG* 36, 133B and 156C that it is unscriptural to speak of the Spirit as divine in the same way that the Father is divine.
[328] *Confession* 3, Vaggione pp. 156-157.
[329] See my article, "Gregory Nazianzen's Opponents in Oration 31," in Gregg, pp. 321-326.

Spirit, particularly at the point of baptism.[330] Eunomius' *Apology* shows that his dialectical rigor led him to attack suggestions of the Spirit as equal to the unbegotten God.[331] Yet again as in Oration 30, Oration 31 deals with arguments that are not known to us directly from Eunomius' writings. The questions that Gregory raises rhetorically as coming from his opponents appear to be genuinely later Arian, but they are much more concerned with the developments in the doctrine of the Spirit than are the sections of Eunomius' extant works. Such discussions might belong to parts of his writings that were lost or they may represent the second-level popularizations of such debates. In either case they indicate that one of the most significant emphases within popular Constantinopolitan Arianism during the 380s was the doctrine of the Holy Spirit.

Nazianzen's view, based on his liturgical practice as well as his theological understanding, demanded that the Spirit, who was God, be able to deify humans in baptism.[332] Θέωσις, "deification," is Gregory's fundamental explanation of salvation. Baptism into Father, Son and Holy Spirit is part of "deification" for him. For Eunomius, however, soteriology has nothing to do with any sense of becoming God. Even the generated essence, the Son, does not share properties with anything else, nor is the operation of its maker looked on as shareable.[333] Evidently for the later Arians the Sonship of the Only Begotten is fundamentally different from that of the Christian. There is no participation of essences, no mystical communion even at the level of knowledge.[334]

The church historian Socrates claims that some later Arians baptized "not in the name of the Trinity, but into the death of Christ."[335] Evidently that would not involve any participation in the essence of the Only Begotten, but would offer Christ as an example and baptism as a kind of burial with him. The *Apostolic Constitutions* speak primarily of that understanding of baptism.[336] The seventh canon of the Constantinopolitan Council in 381 also insists that Eunomians baptized with only one immer-

---

[330] *Or.* 33.16-17, *PG* 36, 233C-237A. Gallay, *La Vie*, pp. 252-253 places *Or.* 33 in 379. Bernardi, p. 165 dates *Or.* 33 in early 380. Yet both agree that *Or.* 33 was presented before the *Theological Orations*.

[331] Eunomius, *Apology* 25 and the Eunomian creed in 28, Vaggione, pp. 66-68 and 74-75 claim that the Spirit is the Son's noblest creation. Also see Basil, *Against Eunomius* 2.33, Sesboüé, pp. 136-139.

[332] *Or.* 33.16-17, *PG* 36, 233C-237A and *Or.* 31.28, *PG* 36, 164C-165A.

[333] Eunomius, *Apology for the Apology* 2.6-7, Jaeger 2.92-93; Vaggione, p. 118.

[334] See *Syntagmation* 29, Wickham, pp. 543, 548 and 565-566.

[335] Socrates, *H.E.* 5.24, *PG* 67, 649A.

[336] *Apostolic Constitutions* 3.17.1-4, 5.7.30, 7.40-44; M. Metzger, ed., *SC* 329, pp. 158 and 238 and *SC* 336, pp. 96-104.

sion.[337] At least some later Arian congregations had a different baptismal liturgy that did not include the trine immersion or a triune formula.[338] Sozomen considers Eunomian baptism not to be a recent innovation, but something that originated with Arius himself.[339] Early Arianism was much concerned with Jesus' place in salvation;[340] thus this baptismal practice well may have been inherited from Arius.

Unfortunately less has been published recently about the Pneumatomachians, the other major Christian opponents addressed in the *Theological Orations*.[341] Although various fifth-century figures indicate Macedonius, a bishop of Constantinople who died c. 362, was the leader, the proper name is Pneumatomachians. People holding the view that the Holy Spirit was not of the same essence as the Father and the Son were condemned in Egypt by 362, but in the 370s the apparent leader of the faction was Eustathius of Sebaste, an acquaintance of Basil. A former pupil of Arius, he became a defender of the homoiousion view, one which saw the Son and the Spirit as ''like'' the Father, but not ''of the same essence'' with the Father. The Pneumatomachian party had at least two wings. The first claimed both the Son and the Spirit were only ''like'' the Father; the second confessed the Son's essence as the same as the Father's, but denied such status to the Spirit.

Nazianzen's Orations 32 and 41, both probably written or given in 379, deal with Pneumatomachian issues.[342] Within the *Theological Orations* 31.5 and 13-14 have clear references to persons who accept the divinity of the Son, but not the divinity of the Spirit.[343] Nazianzen castigated

---

[337] W. Bright, *The Canons of the First Four General Councils of Nicaea, Constantinople, Ephesus, and Chalcedon*, Second Edition (Oxford, 1892), p. xxiv. The sixth fragment of Theodore's *Against Eunomius*, referred to by Vaggione, ''Some Neglected Fragments of Theodore of Mopsuestia's *Contra Eunomium*,'' *JThS* NS 31 (1980), pp. 427-428, deals with baptismal practices that were thought to be aberrant, but the only mention of the Spirit appears in a ''connective gloss'' added by the Syriac author Barhadbesabba whose writings contain the fragment.

[338] Kopecek, 397-400.

[339] Sozomen, *H.E.* 6.26, *PG* 67, 1361C-1364B.

[340] See Gregg and Groh.

[341] S. Papadopoulos, ΓΡΗΓΟΡΙΟΣ Ο ΘΕΟΛΟΓΟΣ ΚΑΙ ΑΙ ΠΡΟΫΠΟΘΕΣΕΙΣ ΠΝΕΥΜΑΤΟΛΟΓΙΑΣ ΑΥΤΟΥ (Athens, 1975), particularly pp. 13-63, surveys the history of this group. Also see W.-D. Hauschild, *Die Pneumatomachen* (Hamburg, 1967), P. Meinhold, ''Pneumatomachoi'' *PW* XXI,1, cols. 1066-1101, and Hanson, pp. 760-772. Hanson employs the term ''Macedonians'' for this group, not because Macedonius was actually related to the party, but because Pneumatomachians is such a pejorative term.

[342] *Or.* 32, *PG* 36, 173A-212C and *Or.* 41, *PG* 36, 428A-452C. J. Szymusiak, ''Pour une chronologie des discours de S. Grégoire de Nazianze,'' *VC* 20 (1966), pp. 183-189 and Bernardi, pp. 143-164, agree on a 379 date for these orations.

[343] *Or.* 31.5 and 13-14, *PG* 36, 137B-D and 148B-149A.

those who would accuse him of being a tritheist when they themselves on the same grounds are at least ditheists. Whatever reasons they can give for their positions will defend his.[344] Gregory sees that the Pneumatomachians hold contradictory views on this basic point. Yet he also understands that the defense of his Trinitarian position requires him to combat their teaching about the Spirit even if their doctrine concerning the Son is not much different from his own.

In arguing against the later Arian and Pneumatomachian positions, Nazianzen describes Christian theologians who have offered different understandings of the Spirit. His term for them is σοφῶν, a word which well may carry the ironic tone of those who think they are experts, but are not.[345] Yet it also may mean that Gregory recognizes these contemporary views have important historical foundations. He names no one, but includes positions he recognizes as "orthodox" although they are not what he wishes. Obviously those who see the Spirit as an "active process" or as a "creature" will be seen by the general public as "Christian" even though they are for Nazianzen "heterodox." Those are positions held by the later Arians. Other groups, however, exist within his "orthodox" camp. These folk, who view the Spirit as God, are willing to worship the Spirit in their minds, but they will not make a public confession of his divinity.[346] Although this party has no special name, it is difficult not to see Basil and his followers as the ones mentioned. Gregory and his disciples are those who confess publicly that the Spirit is God. In 380, as in any era, "orthodoxy" itself was no monolith.

Throughout these orations, Gregory also attacks certain aspects of pagan philosophy and religion. If Christians continue to discuss and debate their disagreements in public places, they will create enormous problems for explaining the faith to outsiders. Christians should at least respect their own mysteries as much as the pagans respect theirs and understand that language is contextual and communal. Worship must often take place in si-

---

[344] *Or.* 31.13, *PG* 36, 148B-D. Socrates, *H.E.* 5.4 and 8, *PG* 67, 569B-C and 576B-581A notes that although the "Macedonians" agreed to take part in the 381 council at Constantinople, they eventually rejected ὁμοούσιος as descriptive of the Son. Sozomen, *H.E.* 7.7, *PG* 67, 1429B-1431C says the "Macedonians" specifically rejected the Son's equality with the Father. Gregory's words in 380 indicate why the "orthodox" were pleased that the Pneumatomachians had been invited to the 381 council. Apparently it was thought that they might support a Nicene view of the Son. Perhaps the section of the party that rejected the Son's equality with the Father won the day, or some political or personal issue caused difficulties. At least at a later time these opponents were considered to have erred on both the doctrine of the Son and the doctrine of the Holy Spirit.

[345] *Or.* 31.5, *PG* 36, 137C. Barbel, pp. 226-227, note 10, insists the term must be ironic. That would indicate Gregory's feisty attitude even toward his "orthodox" supporters.

[346] *Or.* 31.5, *PG* 36, 137B-D.

lence or at least in closed confines.[347] When the Theologian argues for
the limitations of any human understanding of God, he includes sections
that attack pagan myths of creation and practices of idol worship.[348] And
in Oration 31, he mentions both the pagans who would reject his view of
the Spirit and those who would be closer to it.[349] For Gregory the discussion of Christian theology is always undertaken in a context that includes
pagan views, even though the actual debates most often will be heard
primarily by Christians.

Two other groups must be taken into account in sketching the background
of these orations. First, Gnostics, particularly Christian Gnostics, may account for part of the Theologian's concern with the "void" and the
"full." They certainly are the point of his aside that pushing the meaning
of "begotten" could lead to the silliness of a hermaphrodite god and the
many aeons.[350] The best text seems to attribute that silliness to Marcion,
but Hardy suggested that the attribution might be a slip for Marcus, the
Gnostic mentioned by Irenaeus.[351] Nazianzen hopes to tie the Neo-
Arians' sense of subordination within the Trinity to Gnostic speculations.
   He also desires to avoid the problems of modalism within his confessions of the Trinity. At one point he insists that the impiety equal to the
Arian error of dividing the natures is the Sabellian one of confusing the
persons.[352] Throughout the orations, particularly in his Trinitarian confessions or asides, he combats any sense of a unity in the Godhead that
would destroy the distinctions among the persons.[353] Yet it is clear that
he finds the Arian problem the most dangerous, both because he focuses
his attention upon it and also because he can say concerning the Trinity:
"It is better to have a meager idea of the union than to venture on total
blasphemy."[354] Although he does not openly attack the modalists—
indeed they are not an overriding concern in these orations—he must take
them into account. Eunomius accused his antagonists of all being related
to Sabellius, Marcellus of Ancyra and Photinus of Sirmium and thus
would have viewed the Cappadocian Fathers as teaching some type of
Sabellianism.[355] Basil in particular condemned Marcellus and his follow-

---

[347] *Or.* 27.2, *PG* 36, 13A-C.
[348] *Or.* 28.14-15, *PG* 36, 44C-45C.
[349] *Or.* 31.5, *PG* 36, 137B-D.
[350] *Or.* 27.10, *PG* 36, 24C; *Or.* 31.7, *PG* 36, 141A.
[351] E. Hardy, *Christology of the Later Fathers*, "The Library of Christian Classics, III"
(Philadelphia, 1954), p. 198, n. 11. The reference for Irenaeus is *A.H.* 1.11.
[352] *Or.* 31.30, *PG* 36, 169A. Also see *Or.* 31.9. *PG* 36, 144A.
[353] *Or.* 28.31, *PG* 36, 72C; *Or.* 29.2 and 12, *PG* 36, 76B and 89B; *Or.* 31.28, *PG* 36,
164D.
[354] *Or.* 31.12, *PG* 36, 148A.
[355] Eunomius, *Apology* 6, Vaggione, pp. 38-39.

ers in a number of letters.[356] It is likely that Nazianzen was aware of Marcellus. He lists "Galatians" among the heretics, doubtless referring to followers of Marcellus, and specifically mentions Photinus in a different list.[357] But he more often chooses to handle such issues under the name of Sabellius. On the basis of these investigations we can depict different groups of antagonists confronted in Nazianzen's *Theological Orations*. Although he neither mentioned the Eunomians by name nor referred to the Pneumatomachians by any title, he focused on later Arians as his major opponents within the larger Christian community and also found the Pneumatomachians defective in their doctrine. He tried to avoid Gnostic and modalist errors; at points he even chided "orthodox" supporters. Yet in spite of his concentration on internal Christian polemic, he wisely never forgot that paganism was an ever-present combatant whose influence was so strong that it should always be considered when Christians debated their own views.

The Manuscript Tradition

Because the authenticity of the *Theological Orations* as works by Gregory Nazianzen is still the best explanation of the evidence we possess,[358] the issue of concern here is the manuscript tradition. The Polish edition of Gregory's orations, a modern critical text of the entire corpus, was tragically delayed. Announced as an undertaking in 1913, Sajdak reported in 1930 that the work done by the Academy of Cracow was nearly complete. Sinko's section, which included the orations, had been finished for some time, but was awaiting publication until all parts of the corpus were ready.[359] The Polish project presents a difficult puzzle, for Mossay suggested that it was never ready for printing and consisted primarily of preliminary work. Mossay examined the papers of Sternbach, the leader of the project. What he found at the University of Jagellon did not represent completed work ready for publication. In his view the various

---

[356] Basil, *Eps.* 69.2, 125.1, 207.1, 263.5, and 265.3, *PG* 32, 432B, 545C-548A, 760C, 981A and 988C-989A.

[357] *Or.* 22.12, *PG* 35, 1145A and *Or.* 33.16, *PG* 36, 236A.

[358] I have argued the case in "The Authenticity of Gregory Nazianzen's Five *Theological Orations*," *VC* 39 (1985), pp. 331-339.

[359] J. Sajdak, "Die Scholiasten der Reden des Gregors von Nazianzus: Eine kurzgefassten Bericht über den jetzigen Stand der Forschung," *ByZ* 38 (1929-1930), p. 269 also indicated that L. Sternbach's edition of the poetry with a critical apparatus was ready for printing but S. Witkowski had not finished the letters. The failure to publish and thus the obscurity of the Polish project has caused many modern scholars to forget that Wilamowitz-Moellendorff first turned his students to Nazianzen and then suggested that the text of Nyssa needed attention.

optimistic reports from the 1920s onward were basically false. His final argument is that Sternbach's habits would not have allowed him to keep such important papers in his home from which they might have been taken by the Germans. In 1939 Sternbach was arrested as a person born to Jewish parents and died in a prison camp in 1940.[360] The exact state of what was available in 1939 may never be fully known because most of the participants are now dead.

In the 1950s Werhahn began to investigate what would be required to produce a critical text.[361] In the late 1960s and early 1970s Gallay published a modern edition of the letters in two volumes, one which includes the general correspondence and another which contains the theological epistles.[362]

Fortunately some of the preliminary studies undertaken by the Polish circle were published. Any look at the manuscript tradition begins with their efforts.[363] More important for the goal of a modern, critical edition are the preparatory investigations under the auspices of the Görres-Gesellschaft which are beginning to appear.[364] In 1971 that society along with the University of Münster agreed to underwrite a full critical text project for the poetry under the direction of Werhahn and Sicherl. In 1976 the first Symposium nazianzenum was held in Koblenz, September 27-28. Sicherl indicated that the project would be expanded to include the orations under Mossay's direction. Lafontaine agreed to take charge of the Armenian version of Gregory.[365] Others are responsible for overseeing work not only on the poetry, but also on the various versions in Armenian, Georgian, Coptic, Syriac and Arabic.[366] In 1981 Mossay published the

---

[360] J. Mossay, "Le professeur Leon Sternbach, byzantiniste et patriote," *RHE* 65 (1970), pp. 820-835. Also see G. Schnayder, "Editionis Gregorianae ab Academia Litterarum Cracoviensi institutae fata quae fuerint," *Studia Theologica Varsaviensa* 9 (1971), pp. 5-19.

[361] M. Sicherl, J. Mossay and G. Lafontaine, "Vers une Édition critique de Grégoire de Nazianze," *RHE* 74 (1979), pp. 626-627.

[362] Gallay (1969) and (1974).

[363] Among others see G. Przychocki, *De Gregorii Nazianzenii epistulis quaestiones selectae* (Cracoviae, 1912). J. Sajdak, *Historia critica scholiastarum et commentatorum. Gregorii Nazianzenii*, "Meletemata patristica, I" (Cracoviae, 1914); *De Gregorio Nazianzeno poetarum Christianorum fonte* (Cracoviae, 1917). Sinko (1917) and *De Traditione Indirecta*, "Meletemata patristica, III" (Cracoviae, 1923).

[364] M. Sicherl, J. Mossay, and G. Lafontaine, "Vers une Édition critique," *RHE* 40 (1979), pp. 626-640 offer a report on the work in process.

[365] J. Mossay, "Grégoire de Nazianze. Travaux et Projets récents. Chronique," *L'Antiquité classique* 46 (1977), pp. 595-597.

[366] M. Sicherl, J. Mossay, and G. Lafontaine, "Vers une Édition," pp. 626-640. Also see J. Grand'Henry, "Répertoire des manuscrits de la version arabe de Grégoire de Nazianze, Ie Partie," *Le Muséon* 97 (1984), pp. 221-222, "IIe Partie," *Le Muséon* 98 (1985), pp. 197-229, and "IIIe Partie," *Le Muséon* 99 (1986), pp. 145-170.

first in a proposed series of studies on the manuscripts of the orations.[367] August 25-28, 1981 a symposium dedicated to Nazianzen was held at Louvain-la-Neuve; its proceedings were published in 1983.[368]

Recently Gallay and Jourjon have produced the edition of the *Theological Orations* that is published in the Sources chrétiennes series. In spite of the overwhelming number of manuscripts that include at least some of Gregory's orations—Mossay estimated that they number between 1200 and 1500[369]—the selection made by Gallay and Jourjon is both fair and useful even though small.[370] Every student interested in Nazianzen is obviously pleased that the *Theological Orations* have received their attention. The edition improves the quality of the text and thus is the one used for this translation and commentary.

The question of most concern as an introductory matter is the order of the five *Theological Orations* within the manuscripts, both those in Greek and those in the various languages of translation. The arguments concerning the place of Orations 28 and 31 in the group must be discussed.

Sinko, on the basis of his careful analysis of Greek manuscripts, suggested that the bulk appear to be divided into two patterns: the consecutive numbering of Orations 27-31 and the removal of 28 into a different order, usually following 31, that is, 27, 29, 30, 31, 28. He put the manuscripts that he had seen into two groups, Family N, which contained fifty-two pieces and had the 27-31 order and Family M, which included forty-seven examples and had the order that removed 28 from the sequence.[371] Gallay and Jourjon employed six manuscripts from Family N, dating from the ninth through the early eleventh century. They also used four manuscripts from Family M, dating from the ninth and tenth centuries. Three of those place Oration 28 after Oration 31; one from the tenth century does not contain Oration 28.[372] Thus from Sinko's important studies and the SC edition one gains the impression that Oration 28 occupies an unstable place at least in the order of the five *Theological Orations*.

Yet the first thorough review of the extant manuscripts presents an even more complicated picture. It records the contents of the Greek manuscripts in France that include the orations. An overwhelming number of

---

[367] *Rep. Naz.*

[368] *II. Symp. Naz.*

[369] Mossay, "Vers une Édition," *RHE* 40 (1979), p. 629.

[370] J.-M. Mathieu, "Étude critique," *RHPhR* 40 (1981), p. 272, although somewhat critical of the three *SC* volumes he reviewed, has indicated his pleasure in Gallay and Jourjon's claim only to be preliminary, a claim he finds rare in incomplete modern editions.

[371] Sinko (1917), pp. 11-12 and 20-21.

[372] Gallay (1978), pp. 8-10 and 84.

those manuscripts contain all five orations in one of the two sequences Sinko described, but some early ones offer other orders. Paris 516, from the eleventh century, contains only Oration 28. Paris 519, written in 1007, includes only Orations 28-31. Paris 532, from the tenth century, has only Orations 29 and 31—together in sequence. A number of folios are misplaced in Paris 534, also from the tenth century, yet it contains only Orations 29, 30 and 28. Coisliniani gr. 241, from the tenth or eleventh century, includes only Orations 31, 29 and 30 with other orations interspersed between 31 and 29.[373]

The manuscript traditions of the translations present equally as complex a picture. The Syriac translations are the earliest evidence we have for Gregory's text. Some of them predate the Greek manuscripts by over two hundred years. Van Roey and Moors notice that Add. 17.146, dated to the sixth or seventh century, contains Orations 20, 28, 29, 30 and 31 in order, with Oration 27 following 31 only after five intervening orations. 20 is referred to as a sermon on divinity, 28 the second on theology, 29 the first on the Son, 30 the second on the Son and 31 on the Holy Spirit. 27 is known as the first against the Eunomians. Add. 18.815, from about the ninth century, contains only Oration 28.[374] In a separate article, which continues the study, van Roey and Moors notice that a group of eighth- or ninth-century manuscripts know a fourfold set of the *Theological Orations* that includes 27, 29, 30 and 31 in order and titles them one, two, three and four. Add. 14601, from the ninth century, includes 31, 29 and 30 in that order, but titles them the fourth, the second and the third. Yet Add. 14549, an eighth- or ninth-century manuscript, includes 28 and knows it as the second on theology.[375]

In correspondence Wickham mentioned that Peter of Callinicum, a sixth-century figure, in his *Against Damian* referred to Oration 20 as "the first on theology," 28 as "the second on theology," 29 as "the first on the Son," 30 as "the second on the Son," and 31 as "on the Holy Spirit."[376] Peter does not quote Oration 27; neither does he mention a group of five *Theological Orations*. Since *Against Damian* is not complete in the extant manuscripts perhaps he mentioned Oration 27 or the series in a lost portion.[377] In my view, however, his titles, which resemble those

---

[373] *Rep. Naz.*, pp. 46, 47, 53, 54 and 105.

[374] A. van Roey and H. Moors, "Les Discours de Saint Grégoire de Nazianze dans la Littérature syriaque," *Orientalia Lovaniensia Periodica* 4 (1973), pp. 121-133.

[375] A. van Roey and H. Moors, "Les Discours de Saint Grégoire de Nazianze dans la Littérature syriaque," *Orientalia Lovaniensia Periodica* 5 (1974), pp. 79-125.

[376] Letter, December 10, 1986.

[377] In their introduction to another piece written by Peter, R. Ebied, A. van Roey, and L. Wickham, *Peter of Callinicum. Anti-Tritheist Dossier,* "Orientalia Lovaniensia Analecta, 10" (Leuven, 1981), pp. 12-13 state that the *Against Damian* is not fully extant.

found on the various orations in some Syriac translations and some early Greek manuscripts, suggest that he may have known a series that put Oration 20 as the first and excluded 27. It is thus clear that sixth- through ninth- century Syriac witnesses know a number of ways in which the *Theological Orations* were comprised.[378]

Lafontaine indicates that in an Armenian collection, which he titles *Ad Quos* on the basis of the first words in Oration 27, the order is Orations 27, 20, 29 and then after an intervening title, Orations 30, 31, 28, 33, Epistles 101 and 102, and Orations 17, 32, 6, 23 and 22. Forty-one Armenian manuscripts from the twelfth through the nineteenth century preserve that order.[379] Lafontaine and Metreveli note that certain Georgian manuscripts, which date from the eighth through the eleventh century, contain some of the *Theological Orations*. Among the seven text types that they identify, two contain Oration 27 by itself, one includes only Oration 28 and another only Oration 31, while the final type has Orations 27 and 29-31.[380] Thomson describes an eleventh-century Slavonic manuscript, State Public Library, Leningrad, no. Q.p.I.16, that includes only Orations 27 and 28 from the *Theological Orations*.[381]

Grand'Henry lists four Arabic manuscripts at the monastery of St. Catherine in the Sinai of Egypt that contain parts of the usual set of *Theological Orations*. All four are from the thirteenth century and include only Orations 28-31 in sequence.[382] Another thirteenth-century manuscript, Cairo 617, contains Orations 28-31, while the eighteenth-century manuscript, Shath 648, contains only 29-31. Cambridge Add. 3292, a seventh-century manuscript, has only Oration 28.[383]

To further complicate matters Leunclavius' Latin translation of the commentary written by Elias of Crete indicates that Elias, a twelfth-century figure, knew the *Theological Orations* in an order that did not include Oration 31 on the Holy Spirit, but Oration 20 concerning ecclesiastical office. The sequence is 27, 28, 20, 29 and 30 with 31 beginning the orations outside the group of five.[384]

Therefore, when the most recent survey of only a portion of the extant

[378] For a concise history of the Syriac translations see A. de Halleux, "La version syriaque des Discours de Grégoire de Nazianze," *II Symp. Naz.*, pp. 75-111.
[379] Lafontaine, "Vers une Édition," *RHE* 40 (1979), p. 637.
[380] G. Lafontaine and H. Metreveli, "Les versions copte, arménienne et géorgiennes," *II. Symp. Naz.*, pp. 63-73.
[381] F. Thomson, "The Works of St. Gregory of Nazianzus in Slavonic," *II. Symp. Naz.*, p. 119.
[382] J. Grand'Henry, "Répertoire des manuscrits," *Le Museon* 97 (1984), pp. 226-227.
[383] J. Grand'Henry, "La tradition manuscrite de la version arabe des Discours de Grégoire de Nazianze," *II. Symp. Naz.*, pp. 113-114.
[384] Elias of Crete.

Greek manuscripts, short lists of some Syriac, Armenian, Georgian and Arabic manuscripts and the text used by a twelfth-century Byzantine commentator are taken into account, Sinko's suggestions about the sequences are too simplistic. Furthermore, from a logical standpoint, none of the orders of the orations in the Greek, Syriac, Armenian, Georgian, or Arabic manuscripts can be taken as final evidence for either the sequence in which the orations were first delivered or the order in which they were finally published. Early copyists might have edited the orations or given them another sequence for their own reasons. That would probably be true even if we had a simple choice between two well-attested orders. Obviously we should be alerted by the different sequences in the manuscripts to the possibility that the individual discourses that comprise the traditional *Theological Orations* could have been written and presented at different times. No final conclusion, however, can be drawn on the basis of the various orders alone, particularly when they are so complex even in the earliest manuscripts. Indeed this complexity of sequence within the manuscripts presently reported gives ample warning that we should withhold final judgment until the text project is complete. When that is finished, the orders may be even more varied than they are now known to be. The possibility most certainly exists that Oration 28 was free-floating with its own previous history, but Oration 27 has also been excluded from some of the manuscripts. In fact, Paris 567 from the eleventh century includes Orations 29, 20, 31 and 28 while it leaves out 27.[385] The place of Oration 28 within the *Theological Orations* will have to be accounted for now primarily on the basis of whether studies like those of Sinko and Bernardi have demonstrated both in the structure of Oration 28 and in its relationship to the other *Theological Orations* that it did not form part of the original unit. Without that kind of argumentation, the question is unanswerable.

Sinko insisted that he could discover from the text of Oration 28 that it had been given or written at another time and then brought into the group.[386] Bernardi agreed that Oration 28 was a later insertion and suggested that the opening sentences of Oration 29 refer back to Oration 27. The initial paragraph of 28, which outlines the entire group by mentioning issues found in 27 and then topics discussed in 29-31, is for Bernardi evidence of editorial work done to make 28 fit. Its opening lines and those of 29 are not in the style of the exordia from delivered discourses.[387]

The strongest arguments for proposing that Oration 28 was added to the original group do concern the style of these exordia. They well may

---

[385] *Rep. Naz.*, p. 67. The sequence is 29, 30, 31, 20, 28.
[386] Sinko (1917), pp. 11-12 and 20-21.
[387] Bernardi, pp. 182-185.

have been altered for publication from what they were when first presented. Bernardi, however, indicates that Oration 28, particularly in sections 3, 11 and 20, has echoes of a discourse presented orally. Thus his argument does not demand that 28 is solely a written composition and on that basis was not part of an original group of orations given at Constantinople in 380. In fact, Bernardi himself recognizes that these stylistic changes might have been made later in order to prepare for publication a series of speeches that had already been given.[388] Since neither he nor Sinko suggests that a person other than Nazianzen made those changes, even the editorial work they see present in the exordia could imply that Nazianzen at least intended the 27-31 sequence for publication.

Bernardi is, however, also concerned about the length of Oration 28. In his view it is too long to have been presented orally. Yet it is not much longer than Oration 31 whose length he does not question.[389] In the end, his and Sinko's suggestion that Oration 28 was an insertion depends primarily on their view that the opening lines of Oration 29 were not properly reedited and thus indicate a referral only to Oration 27.

The actual contents of Oration 28 could be explained in ways different from theirs. Its early rehearsal of what is to come in Orations 29-31 may or may not be a later editorial addition. Speakers have been known to indicate what they will treat on successive occasions.

The opening of Oration 29 does not demand that Oration 28 is an insertion. Bernardi fails to state the grounds on which he argues that those sentences can only refer back to Oration 27. The phrase "ready yet hasty argumentativeness" is too general to be limited to the opponents' positions mentioned in 27 alone. Oration 28 develops an attack on what might be called "hasty argumentativeness" in two ways. First, Gregory expands the bounds of disagreement with the later Arians partially through the employment of Clement of Alexandria's views in *Stromata* 5.12 and the arguments of Cyril of Jerusalem's *Catechetical Lectures*, particularly numbers 6 and 9.[390] In those writings and in Oration 28 the limitations of the human mind for encompassing the nature of God are emphasized. On the basis of Christian sources Nazianzen argues that our intellect is too small a tool for investigating God's nature. We cannot begin to grasp God's essence as He himself knows it. Second, from general knowledge, Gregory demonstrates that we have great difficulty understanding nature and our own existence. He had stated the fundamental point at issue, the restricted capacity of human understanding, in Oration 27.4,[391] but when he takes

---

[388] ibid.
[389] ibid., p. 184.
[390] ibid., pp. 184-185.
[391] *Or.* 27.4, *PG* 36, 16B-D.

more time—as in Oration 28—to spell out his views, Nazianzen intends
to establish that later Arian claims are based on "hasty argumentativeness."

The reasons Sinko and Bernardi offer for the insertion of Oration 28
into the order at the time of publication are not conclusive. This group
of five discourses does give some evidence of being reworked for publication, but there is no certainty that Oration 28 was a later addition. Thus
the theory of insertion of 28 into the group for publication cannot be used
as an indication that originally Gregory's arguments failed at the point
where he asserted human limitations of knowledge and the incomprehensibility of God's nature.[392] From the beginning of the debate with the
later Arians, the mystery of God and the weakness of human intellect are
supported by Nazianzen over against a full knowledge of God's essence
and a satisfaction in rigorous dialectical propositions defended by his opponents. Without Oration 28 the main points of the debate do not receive
extensive treatment.[393]

There is at least one more anomaly that must be discussed. Oration 28
differs from Orations 27 and 29-31 in an interesting respect. Gregory does
not use the dramatic form of presentation within it that he employs within
Orations 29-31. Nowhere in Oration 28 does he state his opponents' positions either in terms of questions and answers or statements with explanatory paragraphs. He offers no expressions of their opinions that could be
marked off and checked against extant later Arian works. The form employed is incessant rhetorical questioning. Nearly every structural section
of the argument begins with a number of queries.

That difference in form and structure does not necessarily demand that
Oration 28 was inserted into a previously existing group. Oration 27 has
a form different from that of Orations 29-31 in that it does not list opponents' objections either in their own words or paraphrased. The form of
Oration 28 also indicates that something unusual is involved. Although
its theme is essential for the series, its shape is not the same. Perhaps Nazianzen chose to emphasize the central theme of divine incomprehensibility
and human intellectual limitations by choosing a different form of presentation. That might be a wise choice from so skilled a rhetorician. It avoids
repetition of form while reemphasizing the same theme.

Some have also questioned whether or not Oration 31 is a part of this
same group. Jerome, Gregory's student, suggested Nazianzen wrote two
pieces against Eunomius and another concerning the Holy Spirit.[394] Ber-

[392] Bernardi, p. 185.
[393] J. Plagnieux, *S. Grégoire de Nazianze Théologien* (Paris, 1951), pp. 437-440 argues on
theological grounds that Oration 28 belongs in the series.
[394] Jerome, *De vir. ill.* 117, *PL* 23, 709A.

nardi warns that Jerome's statement must be taken with caution, since it is not clear that he had actually seen a copy of the *Theological Orations*.[395] Sections 3, 5-7, 10, 12, 14 and 22 of Oration 31 attack arguments that the Holy Spirit is one of the created things and not a part of the Trinity, a view expressed in Eunomius' *Apology* 25, in the Eunomian creed that appears as section 28 of the *Apology* and combated by Basil in his *Against Eunomius* 2.33.[396] More attention is paid to later Arian positions than those usually ascribed to the Pneumatomachians. Since we can trust Nazianzen's representation of later Arian views at those places where we have material from Aetius and Eunomius, it is not daring to accept his attack on the later Arians for belittling the Holy Spirit.[397]

Furthermore, we should not employ Jerome's words as the foundation for suggesting that the opening paragraphs of Oration 31 were added to make it appear as part of the *Theological Orations*. The internal argument of this piece only expands the opening sections of Oration 29: "Let us put our confidence in the Holy Spirit they dishonor but we worship." Other statements in Oration 29 point to the procession of the Spirit as another problem for his opponents.[398] None of the major students of these orations has suggested Oration 29 was not a part of the series presented in 380. Nothing stated in Oration 31 demands that it was presented at a different time and then added to the group.

If a decision about Oration 31 is based on the orders in the manuscripts, we are presented with different sequences that cannot be stamped primary or secondary. There is just as large a possibility that a scribe removed or rearranged it as that Gregory added it for publication.

It is also easy to see how Oration 27 might have circulated by itself or have appeared in a different order. The manuscript evidence for its separation is not yet as extensive as that for the exclusion or different placement of Oration 28, but its depiction of what is necessary for the discussion of theological issues warrants its free-standing position. Yet it could have formed a natural beginning point of these *Theological Orations* either

---

[395] Bernardi, pp. 181-182,

[396] *Or.* 31.3, 5-7, 10, 12, 14, and 22, *PG* 36, 136B-141A, 144A-D, 145B-148A, 148D-149A and 157A-C. *Apology* 25 and 28, Vaggione, pp. 66-69 and 74-75. Basil, *Against Eunomius* 2.33, Sesboüé II, pp. 136-139.

[397] Kopecek, pp. 495-496, n. 3, finds it difficult to accept that *Or.* 31 is directed against the Neo-Arians since we have little from them about their views of the Spirit. Yet he also claims, p. 500, that the similarity between other views found in Gregory and those still available from later Arian leaders "indicates that Gregory may certainly be trusted as a reliable source for Neo-Arian thought and dialectical strategy in 380." If that be true, then historians well might accept Nazianzen's insistence that in 380 Eunomians in Constantinople offered more developed arguments against the divinity of the Spirit.

[398] *Or.* 29.1-3, *PG* 36, 73A-77B.

in the original sequence of presentation or in the order reached for publication.

In the end we must admit we cannot demonstrate whether or not these five orations were given at Constantinople in one particular series. Editors and copyists could have decided that Oration 28 overemphasized the point and thus have moved it to a later position. Or it might not have been in the original group presented in 380. Oration 31 could have been an addition edited for publication as could Oration 27. The conundrum of the original order of presentation or publication has not been solved. The approach of this commentary will be to withhold final judgment on the original sequence and yet follow the 27-31 order that is implied by the orations themselves, particularly in the opening paragraphs of Oration 28. Fortunately both the Maurists, the Migne edition and the Sources chrétiennes edition have used that sequence. More will be said within the commentary about the internal support and weighty logic behind that order. Until the extant manuscripts, both Greek and translation, have all been examined, it represents a well-attested and well-argued alternative.

Commentary and Translation

This commentary does not attempt to trace out every possible allusion to or each quotation from Hellenistic learning, Christian Scripture and early Christian tradition. It is also based in part on the judgment that some earlier studies particularly of philosophical backgrounds have relied too heavily on single words as evidence rather than larger blocks of argument.[399] The main purpose of the comments is to elucidate the structure of each oration within the narrow late fourth-century debate between Gregory and his opponents. The notes in the Migne and the Sources chrétiennes editions, both important for the study of Gregory, are limited. Neither Mason, Barbel, nor Moreschini concentrates on the flow of argument within each oration or the immediate debate with opponents. Those who seek fuller explanations, however, should consult Mason for close philological insights, Barbel for extensive comments on the philosophical and Christian traditions behind particular points and Moreschini for the most up-to-date information.

The new English translation by Wickham and Williams was made some years ago on the basis of the Migne text and that of Mason. Williams translated Oration 27, Wickham Orations 28-31. Halton called their ef-

---

[399] H. Dörrie, "Gregors [von Nyssa] Theologie auf dem Hintergrunde der neuplatonischen Metaphysik," *Gregor von Nyssa und die Philosophie* (Leiden, 1976), pp. 21-23 utters a healthy warning.

forts to my attention in 1981 and Winslow, with the consent of the translators, made it available to me. The commentary employs it throughout.
For this present work Wickham and Williams have revised some sections
in light of the Sources chrétiennes edition.

With this translation the full text of the *Theological Orations* becomes
available in English for the first time. Hardy[400] noted in his adaptation
of Browne and Swallow's translation[401] that their work oddly deleted
some paragraphs. Unfortunately Hardy's translation also left out a few
lines. If we have repeated that strange mistake, the present translation
would supersede the previous ones for two reasons. First, it makes the argument between Gregory and the Eunomians about *paideia* accessible to
the reader who does not possess a knowledge of Greek. Second, the literary quality of this translation exceeds that of the other two.

Scriptural quotations and allusions are noted within the translation.
That notation has proved to be problematic. The extensive references for
the Sources chrétiennes text were difficult and time-consuming to assem-
ble, but they contain a number of misprints and some citations that have
no similarity to the passages within the orations. At times those references
include Biblical verses that include an important word mentioned in
Gregory's text, but do not have any resemblance to the point he makes.
Starting with the Sources chrétiennes references I have listed only those
that support the sense of a passage either by similar statement or inference
and have excluded those with no apparent connection. I have pointed out
those difficulties with the hope that if that edition is eventually reprinted,
the references may be corrected.

For the sake of grasping the arguments, statements in the translation
that represent Gregory's expressions of his opponents' views are set off in
separate passages and italicized. In Oration 30 that form is also used for
the Scriptural passages basic to the Eunomian positions. Statements
which occur in later Arian writings and are similar to Nazianzen's expression of his opponents' positions are discussed within the commentary. It
is important to remember, however, that italicized statements do not
mean the Theologian is quoting documents or necessarily stating views his
opponents held. He might be drawing inferences from their propositions
that they would never have drawn. Yet the commentary intends to show

---

[400] E. Hardy, *Christology of the Later Fathers*, "The Library of Christian Classics, III"
(Philadelphia, 1954), p. 125.
[401] C. Browne and J. Swallow, trans., *Saint Gregory Nazianzen, Archbishop of Constantinople, Select Orations and Select Letters*, "Nicene and Post-Nicene Fathers, Series II, Vol. VII"
(London, 1894).

that any description of later Arianism, particularly in its popular manifes-
tations in Constantinople, ought to make critical use of these orations.
Gregory is usually fair and accurate in his presentations of what can be
checked with the writings of either Aetius or Eunomius. Perhaps the statements not found in the works of the leaders were made by other members
of the community.

COMMENTARY

COMMENTARY ON ORATION 27

The manuscripts used for the SC edition contain titles either at the beginning or at the end of the oration which indicate that the copyists associated Oration 27 with an Eunomian opposition. The text itself does not name the opponents, but the translation of Rufinus, probably made before the end of the fourth century C.E., adds a comment in section one. For him the doctrine Gregory opposes represents *maxime Arrianos* (Gallay, p. 72, textual variant for 1.11). This discourse and the other four *Theological Orations* make it clear that later Arians were the primary antagonists.

The designation προδιάλεξις is closer to the contents of the treatise than διάλεξις. This piece introduces and discusses propriety in theology, i.e, what is appropriate to the discipline when its nature is understood. Yet those who titled the work διάλεξις or employed some form of the word in describing it were not far from the mark. The discourse brings forward definitions through rhetorical presentation in order to reach reasonable conclusions about the nature of theology. Its structure depends upon the close relationship between dialectic and rhetoric that is central to philosophical rhetoric.

27.1 The general tone of the first oration is ψόγος, "invective." That form of rhetoric was common to the fourth century C.E. Although it involved ridicule of the opponents, it was considered to be one aspect of the persuasive art, at least for the audience sitting in judgment. The modern reader may be offended by Nazianzen's incessant attack, but these *Theological Orations* are mild in comparison with his treatises against Julian (Orations 4 and 5). They breathe fire.

Because of the character of this treatise, it is more accurate to think of λόγος as a technical term with the meaning of "discourse" or "oration." Williams' translation "my words" is correct though general. This is not in the strictest sense a "homily." The play λόγος / λόγῳ sets the tone that marks Gregory's entire project. He offers a reasoned and literate discourse in response to those who are only clever in their use of logic and language. They take pride in their education, their ability to listen critically and their intelligence, but he questions each of those claims. For Nazianzen, one source of the Eunomians' error is their misunderstanding of the great Hellenic heritage of philosophy and rhetoric. He repeatedly addresses that deficiency throughout this series of discourses.

The quotation from Jer. 50.31 at the beginning presents the second source of disagreement. This oration, like the others, depends upon Gregory's sense of the Biblical basis for his position as well as its place in what he considers to be the best of Christian tradition. He employs phrases from I and II Tim. to expand his definition of "clever," thus giving his attack a quasi-Biblical cast.

The Maurist editors (*PG* 36, 12, n. 14) imply that the reference to οἱ . . . προσκνώμενοι . . . τὴν χεῖρα, "who have 'itching' hands," concerned the violent attack perpetrated by the supporters of Eunomius on Gregory and his small congregation. Moreschini (p. 43) agrees, but Gallay (p. 71, n. 2) correctly notes that the main point does not depend upon a background of boxing matches as Barbel (p. 39, n. 2) suggests, but is based on the sense of "itching" in II Tim. 4.3. That sense also provides one of the stronger pieces of evidence that this written work represents a spoken oration. According to Gallay's interpretation, Gregory looks out over his audience and sees some of his opponents who not only are eager to hear his arguments but also are writing them down to make certain they can refute what he says.

The charges and countercharges exchanged between the later Arians and the party of Gregory are grounded in an understanding of Scripture and tradition, but they also concern education. For Nazianzen, the opponents are sophists, or as Williams translates σοφισταὶ καὶ κοττισταὶ, "verbal tricksters" and "word-gamesters." Thus part of this theological argument renews the older disagreements between Plato and Gorgias. Only a sound knowledge of both the early debate between philosophy and rhetoric and the proposals for a philosophical rhetoric made by Plato and Aristotle can make sense of this series. Referring to the Eunomians as "sophists" is not merely name-calling. The issue is the nature of the relationship between dialectic and rhetoric.

Gregory's apparent asides concerning the later Arian rejection of a doctrine more noble than their own and their lack of compassionate deeds actually form part of the structure for this discourse. The first is picked up again in sections 2, 3 and 5; the second is emphasized in section 7 and alluded to in 9.

The SC text adds six words after the Jeremiah quotation, καὶ παίδευσιν καὶ ἀκοὴν καὶ διάνοιαν, "also [your] education and hearing and thought." They appear in manuscripts S, D, P and C, the group that Gallay considers the best, and also in B. Yet neither Rufinus' translation nor the other five manuscripts contain them. Mason (p. 1, n. 2) omitted the words because the manuscripts he consulted were weighted against that reading, but he rightly sensed that they fit the context. They indicate where the later Arians placed their pride: in their sense of *paideia*, in their ability to listen critically and in their intellectual capacity.

Wickham and Williams ("Some Notes on the Text of Gregory Nazianzen's *First Theological Oration*," *Studia Patristica* XIV, Part Three, "TU 117" [Berlin, 1976], pp. 367-368) correctly question the Greek form κυβισταί, "tumblers," that appears in the Maurist and now in the SC text. Gallay (pp. 72-73, n. 1) offers some attestations that might enhance its standing. Yet the Syriac translations that Wickham consulted are as early as—in some cases earlier than—the Greek manuscripts Gallay employed. Furthermore Gallay's claim that κοττισταί, "gamesters," is not properly attested had already been countered in the Wickham and Williams' article when they gave Johannes Malalas and other sources as parallels. Williams ("Acrobats and Geometry: Unwelcome Intruders in the Text of Gregory Nazianzen," *Glotta* LXV [1987], pp. 96-100) notes six further sources, including glossaries. The more vulgar form κοττιστής is probably the better reading since its derisive quality would be more stirring. Gregory does warn that such "laughable," γέλοιος, activity by his opponents deserves rebuke. The use of an unexpected colloquialism in such a setting and the ear-catching assonance are typical of Gregory's verbal power.

27.2 The Eunomians fancy "setting and solving conundrums." Gallay (p. 73, n. 3) suggests that Dan. 5.12 in the LXX forms the background of δήσωσιν ἢ λύσωσι, "setting and solving." A better reminiscence of the Daniel text appears in Oration 28.11. The later Arian concern with "conundrums," προβαλλομένων, becomes the focus again in 27.10, where the opponents are encouraged to "attack," βάλλε, selected philosophical riddles.

Nazianzen pictures their practice as a wrestling match without rules, performed at all the wrong places, even in the salons of women. Within Constantinople, noted both for its games and social life, the clashing scenes are apt. Gregory despises the popular success of the later Arians and attributes it to their theatrical interests. They do not take on true champions in tests of skill, but wheedle their way into the hearts of the untrained. Only a year later Gregory of Nyssa experienced this same kind of frivolous conversation about the problems facing the 381 council in Constantinople. He complained about how it had invaded the banks, the groceries, and the baths (*De Deitate Filii et Spiritus Sancti* [PG 46, 557]).

For Nazianzen silly talk and nauseating fare dominate later Arian gatherings. If these opponents are not stopped, either by successful attacks upon them or by their own change, they will make the great mystery of the faith into a "little finicking profession." (Mason's translation, p. 3, n. 12). The use of τεχνύδριον is related to the Theologian's employment of various forms of τεχνολογέω as descriptive of the Eunomians' whole approach (29.15 and 21; 31.18). The translation "social accomplishment" is justified by the context, which indicates the widespread affection for their gamesmanship. Yet there is also an underlying concern for the larger problem of *paideia* itself. In the following sections Gregory accuses his antagonists of not involving themselves in the proper educational process for theology. Principles and rules have been broken. When the essential structure of a competition is ignored, what could be a genuine contest becomes merely a show. Thus Nazianzen attacks the Neo-Arians because they do not understand the nature of the "game."

How much was Gregory's "heart torn within [him]" by the attitude and conduct of his opponents? In Oration 29.21 he does mention that he hopes for their conversion from logic-chopping to faith. In other instances, however, he displays his frustration and anger with both those who are behind these discussions and those who participate in them. He wonders out loud if the spies can be quiet long enough to hear him out and then appeals to their stubborn insistence on such discussions, indeed to their own self-interest.

Since he and his congregation had already been attacked in their chapel by his opponents (*Eps*. 77 and 78), perhaps he is justified in not expecting "the spies" to change. The sure way he quiets them through an appeal to their own concerns without dismissing his interests or those of his group shows understanding of human motivation and the art of rhetoric.

The shift from third to second person with οὐδὲν ζημιωθήσεσθε, "you can lose nothing," implies that this oration was presented orally. It suggests an actual situation in the small chapel. The tone is intensified by continued use of second-person verbs throughout the last part of this section.

Nazianzen's comparison of νεανικῶς, "youthfully," and γενναίως, "intensely," with ἀμαθῶς, "ignorantly," and θρασέως, "impudently," shows not only his skill in rhetoric, but also his grasp of the problem. The Eunomian doctrine is immature, but it might be better described as excessive. They teach with enthusiasm; in fact they act rashly. Gregory's method is skillful since the choice of words is from those that might have had positive meanings, but here are used ironically, to those that are unmistakable terms of rebuke. In his view people who claim to know all and to teach all are "stupid and arrogant."

This fiery language strikes the modern reader as appropriate only if Nazianzen had already decided that a change of heart for his adversaries within the audience was highly unlikely. He does direct much of his attention to his own congregation who revel in these attacks. Yet at times he backs away from his scathing rebuke and tries to influence the later Arians within the group, particularly in section 6. Given the strong words of Biblical figures, Gregory may sense that even his rebuke could help change his antagonists. The fourth-century context of invective, however, at least allows this language as a tool for the continued persuasion of his own congregation. Hearing their opponents confounded well might confirm their positions.

The *SC* edition cites Dan. 5.12 for the phrase δήσωσιν ἢ λύσωσι τῶν προβαλλομένων, "setting and solving conundrums," in 27.2.2-3. The relationship is tenuous. Only a form of λύω appears in the LXX text.

27.3 Philosophical discussions about God are not something cheap and common. They are not for everyone to lead, for everyone's participation, for every time, or for every subject. Kennedy, (1983, pp. 220-221) notices how much Nazianzen relies on philosophical rhetoric at this point. In a separate article ("Later Greek Philosophy and Rhetoric," *Philosophy and Rhetoric* 13 [1980], pp. 192-196) Kennedy demonstrated, on the basis of Gregory's Oration 2, that the Theologian had gained considerably from his study of Plato's *Phaedrus* and the concern for philosophical rhetoric expressed there. In 28.1 Gregory repeats cautions similar to those mentioned here, not merely because they are a rhetorical commonplace partially present in Aristotle (*Rhetoric* 1356A), but precisely because they form his plan of attack. He intends to demonstrate that the Eunomian misunderstanding of theology grows out of their lack of education. Anyone with a minimal grasp of *paideia* knows that this apparent commonplace is basic to the investigation of any topic. Barbel (p. 40, n. 5) notes that Oration 32.32 also deals with this sense of limitations for theology and that 32.18 and 29 relate that sense of limitation both to Christ and to angels, further evidence of the specific importance of this commonplace for theological efforts.

Williams' translation of θεωρία as "study" fits although some have emphasized the meaning of "contemplation," that is, spiritual meditation. (E. Hardy, *The Christology of the Later Fathers*, "The Library of Christian Classics, III" [Philadelphia, 1954], p. 129 renders διαβεβηκότων ἐν θεωρίᾳ as "past masters of meditation.") Here the general term is preferable; it signifies an interest both in proper education and in appropriate spiritual meditation. Gregory questions the Eunomians' ability to ascend the heights of Christian truth, but his quarrel also focuses on their mundane methods of investigating any truth. Since elsewhere in this section he employs the concept of purification, being cleansed in body and soul, at this point he uses θεωρία to refer to "study." For Nazianzen spiritual purification is the ultimate goal, but that emphasis does not minimize his debate with the later Arians about παίδευσις.

The person who pursues theology must have been educated, tested and presently be in the process of purification because the human condition makes it painstakingly difficult to raise philosophical questions about God at the right time. Purification is not only a Biblical motif, but also a principle that recalls Plato (*Phaedo* 67B) as Gallay (p. 76, n. 3) indicates. Once more Christian faith and Greek *paideia* combine. On those bases Gregory warns throughout these orations that humans never can escape their limitations. At best theological investigation goes on in silence within which one can become more judicious. Barbel (pp. 42-43, n. 7) points out that Oration 28.1 defines such "silence" more as "inner peace" than isolation. Therefore, others could participate, but only those who see the subject as a serious one, similar neither to entertainment nor to games of logic. Even then discussions should be restricted to topics that are within the grasp of the participants, both speaker and audience.

Nazianzen spells out the rhetorical commonplace with overtones of spiritual maturity and pastoral care. The threat of physical violence alone does not prompt these orations. Rather the Theologian sees the entire structure of human attainment, the whole process of learning, jeopardized.

27.4 The insistence on the rules of rhetoric: an educated speaker, a proper occasion, an appropriate audience and selected subjects could raise significant questions when applied to discussions about God. Does this insistence entail that God is to be thought about only under those carefully-controlled conditions? Gregory responds with a group of Scripture texts that indicate "it is more important that we should remember God than that we should breathe."

His opponents did not force on him the distinction between remembering God and discussing theology although he knows they would be quick to attack him on that point. His early involvement with Basil at Annesi in Pontus and his four-year stay at the convent of St. Thecla in Isaurian Seleucia already indicated his commitment to monastic spirituality and meditation. He clarifies that view more fully in the next oration (28.2-3, 12 and 28). Everyone should live in the presence of God at all times. Theology does not abrogate piety when it is true to itself, only when it is untimely and excessive. As parallel examples of his argument for propriety, Gregory speaks of 1) diet: too much honey, 2) seasons: a flower in winter, 3) dress: the exchange of men's and women's clothing and 4) deportment: laughter at funerals and crying at a drinking bout.

Even though seven of the ten manuscripts employed for the SC edition read εὐσεβές "piety," rather than ἀσεβές, "impiety," in 27.4.12, Gallay chooses the latter. It appears in D, P and C, three of the four from the preferred group M. Gallay selected wisely because the other reading is implausible. To say "I am not opposed either to theology, as if it were pious" makes little sense unless it were set in an ironic context.

For 27.4.18 all the manuscripts used for the SC text and the translation of Rufinus do not speak of "immoderate laughter," γέλω ἀμετρία, but of "geometry," γεωμετρία. Maximus (*Ambigua*, PG 91, 1212C-1213A) attempts to explain the "geometry" reading by offering a number of suggestions. All of them seem to indicate both that he had access only to the "geometry" reading and that he was troubled by its contents. Why "geometry" at a funeral? Elias (p. 7) recapitulates the arguments of Maximus, perhaps because of his own frustration with that reading. Gallay (pp. 80-81, n. 2), however, finds "geometry at funerals" to be a striking proverb, one worthy of the creative, literary mind of Nazianzen. Moreschini (p. 48, n. 23) notes the problems, but reads "la geometria." Whatever the reason γεωμετρία is certainly the difficult reading that could stand behind such a correction as γέλω ἀμετρία.

A conservative textual approach that demands much of proposed emendations is to be applauded. Here, however, context, parallels and early translations require the emendation of γεωμετρία to something like γέλω ἀμετρία. First, at the end of 27.5 Gregory offers a compact summary of the examples mentioned in paragraph 4. The clause, as translated, reads: "We must recognize that as in dress, diet, laughter and deportment there are certain standards of decency." This summary is not exact since it neither lists diet, dress and deportment in the order in which they appear in section 4, nor covers all the examples given in that paragraph. One aspect, however, is clear: Gregory himself refers to "laughter," γέλως. Therefore any emendation of 27.4.18 toward a reading of "laughter" rather than "geometry" takes its first cue from Nazianzen's summary of his own argument. This contextual observation, however, raises the possibility that the text was corrected to fit the summary. But Oration 11.5 (*PG* 35, 837B) contains the phrase γέλωτος ἀμετρία in a similar context and thus adds evidence that Gregory knows and uses this commonplace.

Second, W. Lüdtke ("Zur Überlieferung der Reden Gregors von Nazianz," *Oriens Christianus*, NS 3 [1913], p. 265f.) and P. Wendland, (*Berliner Philologische Wochenschrift* 20 [1900], p. 547) had proposed forms of the word for "laughter." Williams ("Acrobats and Geometry: Unwelcome Intruders in the Text of Gregory Nazianzen," *Glotta* LXV [1987], pp. 100-103) offers parallels for such an emendation.

Third, Williams and Wickham ("Some Notes on the Text of Gregory Nazianzen's *First Theological Oration*," *Studia Patristica* XIV, Part Three, "TU 117" [Berlin, 1976], pp. 368-369) base their emendation on parallels, but more specifically on two Syriac translations. The first is a tenth-century manuscript of what is reported to be an early seventh-century translation. It probably renders a Greek reading, γέλω ἀμετρία. The second is a sixth- or seventh-century manuscript of an even earlier translation apparently founded on a Greek reading, γέλοια μέτρια. The major Greek manuscripts used by the *SC* edition are from the ninth through the early eleventh century. Maximus gives us early seventh-century evidence of the reading γεωμετρία. Yet the Syriac translations take us back at least that far, probably farther if the second manuscript comes from the sixth century and is itself a copy of an earlier translation of an even earlier Greek manuscript. Evidence based on the fourth-century renderings of Rufinus is difficult to assess. He has what Gallay considers to be a deficient text of 27.1. Gallay's suggestion that the Syrians had such a poor understanding of Greek that they missed the beautiful proverb of geometry being out of place at funerals is implausible. Their translations are not such fumbling efforts elsewhere; they are often literal to the point of clumsiness in the Syriac itself. Therefore this is one place where the Syriac translations, the emendation by Greek specialists on the basis of parallels and the summary in the immediate context with its parallel elsewhere in the corpus of Nazianzen should be preferred.

27.5 Part of Gregory's reason for emphasizing the commonplace rules of rhetoric is that they could bring order to the chaos of his present situation. The "due season" of theology is not now. He appeals to his antagonists in the audience with arguments similar to those found in section 2. Again the main audience is his own congregation; the invective form is meant to solidify his position with them. The various asides suggest that the oration probably was presented orally, rather than composed in later leisure, and that opponents were among his hearers. Given Nazianzen's extensive education in rhetoric and his experience with the Eunomians, he knows that his attempts to chastise them as "brothers" most probably will not change them. His persuasive appeal is addressed to them only as those who must heed his warnings, yet he might have a sense that his harsh rebukes could convict them of their waywardness. Readers with queasy stomachs, inexperience in verbal or physical combat between family members, or within cultures in which fawning forgiveness follows harsh speech may have difficulty with this form.

Gregory appeals to reason and to the broad context in which these polemical exchanges between later Arians and his own group are taking place. The adaptation of a Platonic metaphor (*Phaedrus* 246B) warns about the wildness of human affairs when Reason, the rider and Discretion, the bit, are removed. For a horse-racing city like Constantinople, the metaphor is apt. Both the pleasure and expectations of the audience are heightened with the turn from a racing metaphor, with its carefully-confined course, to other boundaries. For Christians the boundaries of Egypt and Assyria bring to mind the deep sorrow of the Old Testament exiles.

Piling up images suited the rhetorical patterns of the age. The move from a race track to boundaries makes some sense even to a modern reader. The addition, however, of a spark fanned to a roaring fire and a wound invaded by flies is rhetorical flourish, perhaps an odd combination for a twentieth-century person, yet one expected by and given to Nazianzen's audience.

The Theologian calls his hearers not only to think about immediate concerns but also to remember the full context. Christian dissension enhances pagan argumentation. A religious polemic can never be understood as an internal matter alone; it always has evangelistic consequences. If the Christian community, which in Gregory's view has by far the better arguments, continues to wound itself through internecine warfare, the pagans may win the struggle.

Gregory seems unable as late as 380 to forget the problems of Julian's reign in the early 360s, which prompted his vitriolic invective in Orations 4 and 5. He also knows the strength of the pagan community at Constantinople. In his view no Christian of whatever stripe should forget the primary enemy. The pagans understand these conflicts and have enough sense of decorum to let only initiates know their innermost mysteries, even though their deities are demons and their overarching myths and liturgies are obscene. Since Christians are arguing about honorable titles, their approach should be no less proper.

The *SC* text for 27.5.28 contains a misprint, κα for καὶ.

The citation by the *SC* editors of Ps. 32(31).9 for 27.5.2-5 is strained. It depends upon forms of ἵππος, "horse," and ἄγχω, "restrain," that appear in both the LXX text and Gregory's words. Yet the main terms of the two passages are not the same.

27.6 Anyone who remembers the larger context and knows the communal nature of languages will grasp the problem. If pagans have been so dominated by bodily conceptions of deity that led them to depict the gods as crude and obscene, how will they tend to hear the internal debates of Christians about God's "generation," the "creation," or the "production from non-being"? The questions return to earlier paragraphs with their sense that the center of Christian faith is a mystery (cf. section 2, which alludes to I Tim. 3.16), one that can be divulged only to the holy in a holy manner (section 5). When the Eunomians display their penchant for "dissections and distinctions and analyses," τομὴν καὶ διαίρεσιν καὶ ἀνάλυσιν, they demonstrate their misunderstanding of theology and true philosophy. Theology is not a parlor game. Gallay (pp. 84-85, n. 1) notices that γέννησις, "generation," and κτίσις, "creation," in the Godhead are primary themes for the later Arians and that their error concerning "dissections and distinctions" becomes the focus of Oration 29.8. "Our way of thinking," φιλοσοφεῖν, recalls the "true philosophy," as Barbel (pp. 46-49, n. 17) notes. Christian appropriation of both the term and the contents of Greek *paideia* had a long history before Gregory. Thus Christian and Greek tradition warn that general discussion about God without care for developed spirituality and the attendant ethical deeds is questionable. Open debate before the morally and spiritually insensitive, who act as a "judge," ἐξεταστής, is utterly stupid.

The point also raises a specific aspect of the educational issue. Language is contextual and communal. Words do not express meanings in and of themselves. A pagan well might listen to the intra-Christian polemic, misunderstand its sense and decide that it basically proves his hideous theology to be correct. If the Eunomians are so well-educated, they should know such misinterpretations are not only possible but probable.

Nazianzen's appeal is both sensitive and sensible, but it does perhaps oversimplify the situation. The later Arians take their positions in consideration not only of Christian tradition, but also of the pagan audience. They are concerned, among a group of questions, that the growing discussions of Trinitarian positions threaten the Christian commitment to monotheism. Although Gregory may be horrified by the possibility that

"The Word" will be brought low by later Arian considerations, the Eunomians themselves are convinced that in denying the Son's sameness of essence they are protecting the transcendence of God and are making an appeal to the most advanced pagan worshippers as well as dealing with various soteriological themes. Ἀγέννητος, "unbegotten," appears as an attribute of the one deity who far supersedes the rough-hewn myths of the gods. A treatise from Sallustius (*De deis et mundo*, ed. by A. Nock [London, 1926]), probably a friend of the emperor Julian, offers evidence of such thought about a transcendent deity within educated non-Christian circles that may have been of concern to the Eunomians.

We would be wrong to think that the later Arian theologians or the worshipping Eunomian community itself feared that if the Son were not of the same essence as the Father, he would fall to the level of the immoral gods from pagan myths. Within their writings we can discover a pride in the place they gave the Son as the first-born of all creation, glorified before the ages, the mediator of God, indeed himself the God of all sensible and intellectual nature (Eunomius' *Confession* 3 and *Apostolic Constitutions* 7.33-38 and 8.12.6-7, 27, 50 [esp. in Vat. Gk. 1506]). Yet Nazianzen's fear that the pagans might misunderstand these internal debates is well-founded. Participation in non-Christian religions led people to hear Christian preaching and teaching in a way different from those in Judaism or Christianity. This truism does not mean, however, that Gregory's view of the Christian faith necessarily persuaded the best of pagan believers, or that it met the perceived needs of the general public. In 380 Gregory's group was small. The later Arians controlled most of the larger churches in Constantinople while the Theologian and his followers assembled in the small chapel, Anastasia.

Their immediate lack of success in the city, however, weakens any accusation that Nazianzen made rhetorical, i.e., sophistic appeals to the crowds in order to gain adherents at any cost. Sophistic argumentation for his views or for those of the Eunomians will have to be uncovered by looking at each case. Gregory believes his position stands on the best Biblical and traditional foundations and that it convinces because it relies on the best methods proper education can provide.

Gallay chose ἐξεταστής, "judge," over ἀκροατής, "hearer," in 27.6.3 even though only P and C read the former and Rufinus translated the word *auditor*. Ἐξεταστής appears in the margins as a correction in some of the manuscripts. Since the query is why an "audience hostile to our subject-matter" is allowed "to listen," the progression of the argument suggests that the concern should be: "Why do we appoint our accusers as our **judges**?" rather than "as our **hearers**?." They are already hearers.

27.7 Having warned his listeners about the dangers inherent in choosing the wrong audience for the discussion of theology, Gregory now turns to the character of the speaker, another aspect of the fourfold rhetorical commonplace. The statue of the theologian must be properly carved and polished. While the ''smoothing'' of a statue is certainly an apt metaphor for any oration given in a metropolis of late antiquity, Gallay (pp. 86-87, n. 3) notes that the picture may refer to Plotinus (*Enneads* 1.6.9).

In order to prepare themselves for their tasks, speakers must pay attention to the untamed tongue with its appetite for endless conversation at the wrong time before the wrong people about the wrong topics. Such an insatiable desire damages the orator's credibility. Furthermore, who will listen continually to a theologian who does not live virtuously? Some kind of discipline that sees life as a preparation for death and remembers the nobility bestowed in baptism is necessary to train the inferior nature. Theologians who avoid these demands open up all kinds of immoral possibilities to their hearers, thus giving license to impiety.

Once more these appeals depend upon both Christian and Hellenic tradition. Numerous phrases from Scripture appear, as does talk of baptism, ''the nobility of our second birth,'' τῆς ἄνωθεν εὐγενείας. Yet making life a ''meditation on death,'' μελέτην θανάτου, is a celebrated formula from Plato (*Phaedo* 81A), as Gallay (p. 88, n. 1) indicates. The theme itself recalls the rhetorical concern for the ἦθος of the speaker, emphasized by Aristotle (*Rhetoric* 1356A). Nazianzen describes ἦθος in terms of Christian virtues that reflect his concern for ascetic spirituality. He does not, however, call all speakers, all theologians, to the life of virginity or chastity. That life is one of two options, both of which are morally sound. The arguments from Christianity and Hellenism blend together properly.

Gregory quarrels with the later Arians because, in his judgment, they prefer to argue about theological words when the substance of their ultimate appeal to others depends upon the piety of their daily lives. Since attacks on the moral activity of opponents form a constant part of heresiological debate, we cannot be certain that the Eunomians were actually purveyors of impiety. The success their discussions had on street corners and in women's salons, however, did not enhance their moral status with an ascetic like Nazianzen. Neither did their physical attacks on him and his congregation. Although we err if we accept without question his description of life in the later Arian community as deficient ethically, we can say that for him, based on his rhetorical education and his sense of Christian discipline, the theologian's life speaks loudly.

The incessant interrogation of sections 6 and 7 gives force to the modern phrase, ''rhetorical questions,'' but the practice itself is not uncommon for ancient orators. A sense of mounting excitement was transmitted to the audience through such pounding at the opposition. Variation is provided by the more dialectical technique introduced in 8 through which answers to the questions are also provided.

Gallay includes the reading τοῦτο ποιήσωμεν, "Let us do this," in 27.7.3-4 on the basis of the best group of manuscripts, S, D, P and C. Although it may be superfluous for the meaning of the passage, its importance probably lies in its presence as an aside in a discourse presented orally.

For 27.7.26 the reading ἢ εὐσεβέστερον, "more piously," appears in S, D and P. The reading ἢ ἀσεβέστερον, "less piously," however, is also understandable. Gallay correctly prefers the first because of its presence in the better manuscripts. Yet the only sense of the passage comes from an ironic use of "more piously," a sense that conforms with the meaning of the secondary reading.

In 27.7.18 the *SC* editors cite Ps. 73(72).8 and Luke 18.14 as related to the phrase ἔπαρσιν καταβάλλουσαν, "our pride which comes before a fall." There is no relationship between the Psalms passage and the words of Gregory. A similar thought occurs in Prov. 16.18.

27.8   In virtuoso fashion Nazianzen turns to the later Arian penchant for speaking and dialectic by posing questions according to their usual practice. His shift to second person suggests that he focuses now on the Eunomian opponents in his audience. The form is Socratic, reminiscent of the Platonic dialogues which feature such repartee; the vocabulary comes from educated investigation of issues that can be found in the Platonic heritage. Williams wisely renders the text in a dialogical pattern, one which depicts the dependence upon the tradition of Socrates and Plato.

The topics chosen for this exchange do not seem to fit together well. On the surface, the comparison is confused. The first part, from John 14.2-4, emphasizes the many rooms in the heavenly mansion and the many ways which one might travel to reach God. The second part, from Mt. 7.14, speaks of the one way that must be taken in order to avoid destruction.

The two combined, however, make Nazianzen's point. The Eunomians reject other approaches—particularly his—and yet have chosen precisely the one which of necessity leads away from the goal. They accuse him and his supporters of poor "sense," "principle," or "doctrine," λόγος, and reject other ways of handling Christian teaching; they, however, follow the route not of "reason" and "study," λόγου and θεωρίας, but of "gossip" and "sensationalism," ἀδολεσχίας and τερατείας. Within the limits of a monologue, Gregory has set up a dialogue through which his antagonists might and his supporters shall grasp that intolerance and lack of Christian discipline has led his opponents to the worst positions on apparently contradictory points. The design allows the Theologian to illustrate his own concern with and command of this great intellectual heritage, the one which brought dialectic to its heights. In terms of form, he here demonstrates his acceptance of that Hellenic tradition and through it warns that the Eunomians are lacking in critical education.

Wyss, p. 832, notices that the concern with the unity of ethics can be found in Stoic writings, cf. *SVF* I, 373. Gregory's restatement of his opponents' position: Μίαν μὲν διὰ τὴν ἀρετήν, "One, because it is the way of goodness," is Biblical, Stoic and accepted by both parties in this dispute.

The reading in 27.8.28, ὡς μὲν αὐτοὶ οἴεσθε, "as indeed you yourselves claim," occurs in S, P, D, C and V. Its parallelism with the following phrase, ὡς δὲ ἐγώ φημι, "but as I say," fits the style and again emphasizes an oral presentation to an audience that includes opponents.

27.9 Having made his point through Platonic / Socratic development of both educational principles and Biblical texts, Gregory continues an admonition of Paul from section 8 and adds comparisons with other great figures within the faith. The irony of the concession, "Nevertheless, let us grant . . .," Ἔστω δέ, indicates his own assumption that indeed the later Arian leaders have not risen to the levels of Biblical heroes. Even worse they give responsibility to the uneducated and the undisciplined. If these lights of the Eunomian community are of heroic proportions they should know what it takes to become a theologian.

In making his point Nazianzen bursts forth in a rhetorical flourish of disparate images: spiders' webs, wasps' nests, earth-born warriors for heavenly subjects, gutter filth and effeminate, undisciplined males. Many of these pictures come from the stock of rhetorical education, learned in the earliest stages and refined by presentations required even in the advanced levels. Some modern classicists have criticized his teacher, Himerius, for concentrating on such topics even within his own speeches.

For Gregory the error of the later Arians continues to be the refusal to control their tongues. Such a lack of discipline shows that they do not understand proper education and that they have not grasped the meaning of Biblical warnings against such activity. Although their sense of dialectic is misguided and in most instances destructive, that disease could be loosed in two other areas. First, it could be used to eradicate many of the misunderstandings in philosophical traditions and second, it could be employed on questions of theology where undisciplined speculation has been unable to shake the great Christian truths.

S, P, D and C include ὑφάσμασιν, "webs" in 27.9.8, but it is omitted by A, Q, B, W, V, T and Rufinus. S, P and D belong to the family Gallay prefers. The word itself adds spice to the sentence.

For 27.9.4 the *SC* editors cite Ex. 2.3, 19.20 and 33.18-23. The initial reference should be Ex. 3.2.

27.10 The first remark makes sense to Gregory because the destructive, uninformed dialectic of the later Arians well might score a few points

against the misguided positions of great philosophers whom all the educated study. The second, however, has puzzled students and commentators.
Why does the Theologian suggest that a diseased dialectic can bring about
good when applied to these Christian issues? Some have had difficulty understanding how Nazianzen reached the conclusion that the doctrines of
the Trinity and Christology were so endangered by this Arian illness and
yet proposed "Resurrection, the Judgment, Reward and Punishment and
the passions of Christ," ἀναστάσεως, κρίσεως, ἀνταποδόσεως, Χριστοῦ
παθημάτων, as proper subjects for it.

One possible setting for these admonitions is the rhetorical school exercises. Students learned how to speak by writing, memorizing and giving
speeches on time-honored themes as well as frivolous topics. The more
sophistic the school the less concerned it was with the truth of any speech's
theme. In this context Nazianzen treats the Eunomians as beginning
pupils, anxious to gain fame through their oratorical skills. They consider
themselves well-educated, possessed of penetrating intellects (cf. section
1). Yet in his judgment, they are bumbling amateurs unworthy of treating
issues that would advance the discussion. They are sophists, not
philosophical rhetoricians. Let them babble about things their efforts cannot harm.

Gregory's specific attacks on various philosophical positions may have
come from handbook knowledge of the more famous schools. The five-
year period of silence required for initiation into the Pythagorean sect was
a well-known position, one which emphasized obedience to authority and
a severe ascetic life. The irony is clear. Loquacious Eunomians holding
forth on the topic of Pythagorean silence would be a sight to behold. Nazianzen himself held the ascetic life and silence in high esteem. He usually
enjoyed his periods of monastic retreat. Gallay (p. 94, n. 3) notes that the
Theologian did not reject silence for other purposes; he commended it as
one approach to worship and was himself silent for the Lenten season in
382 (*Or.* 32.14 and *Eps.* 107-114, 116-119).

The Orphic prohibition of beans was a famous topic of discussion in antiquity. Since Pythagoras was probably the source of that command, this
point allowed one interdiction to discredit a position held within two
schools of thought. Beans were a common source of food, but they were
also believed to have tremendous powers. Both educated people with interests in dreams, miracles, or magic and the uneducated with faith in
common superstitions often held that beans effected great changes. The
Pythagorean and Orphic communities tried to avoid such influence (cf.
T. Klauser, "Bohne," *RAC* 2 [1951], pp. 489-502). Gregory's point is
that the prohibition itself assumes the beans are magical. If the Eunomi-

ans could destroy that assumption, even though themselves diseased, they would kill a worse ill.

Nazianzen found the authoritarian claims of Pythagorean masters pretentious. He recognized that questioning of authorities was basic to the Socratic tradition, but he himself in these orations and elsewhere refers back to the Fathers of the Church as authoritative figures. Such ambivalence toward those held in honor raises interesting questions. Gregory attacked innovation as a horror introduced by his opponents and thus held a conservative view of what had been taught by great church leaders before him (cf. *Ep.* 101). He, however, expounded positions—particularly about the Holy Spirit's place in Trinitarian relations (*Or.* 31)—that were themselves innovations.

The call for his antagonists to turn their immature dialectical skills against Plato may seem odd since Gregory demonstrates his dependence on that philosopher and his tradition, at times even praising Plato or contemporary Platonists (*Ors.* 28.30 and 31.5). Yet Nazianzen's dependence upon philosophy is selective. He finds Platonic ideas, the teaching about the various wanderings of souls, the epistemology based on remembrance and the pederastic influence objectionable. Also he does not identify transcendent reality with Plato's idealism. The Theologian's understanding of the soul comes from Biblical texts, which do not speak of "re-embodiment" and "cycles."

Gregory selects in a similar fashion from his predecessors in the Christian faith. He and Basil probably assembled the *Philocalia* of Origen. Cappadocian Christology, specifically that worked out in Orations 29 and 30 by Nazianzen, relies heavily upon themes from the Alexandrian. The teaching about the "Re-embodiments and Cycles of our souls," τὰς μετενσωματώσεις καὶ περιόδους τῶν ἡμετέρων ψυχῶν, had been rejected by Origen (*Contra Celsum* 4.17 and 65-68, indeed *Contra Celsum* 4.17 is reproduced in the *Philocalia*).

Nazianzen does not base his epistemology on remembrance. He accepts the Socratic ideal of questioning (section 8), but often approaches problems through Aristotelian logic and rhetoric. Orations 28-30 demonstrate such dependence.

He rejects pederasty, a stance already implied in reference to "effeminate specimens of the male sex," τῶν ἀνδρῶν ὅσον κοῦφον καὶ ἄνανδρον, in section 9. A dismissal of the practice also occurs in Oration 4. According to Gregory pederastic influence was one of the serious failings of Platonism. It is tempting to suggest that Nazianzen finds the objectional activity most clearly in evidence within the *Phaedrus*. Kennedy ("Later Greek Philosophy and Rhetoric," *Philosophy and Rhetoric* 13 [1980], pp. 192-196) has demonstrated that Nazianzen's Oration 2 used a number of ideas from the *Phaedrus*, most importantly, the conception of philosophical rhetoric. Yet the ascetic, who criticizes the later Arians for their lack of ethical deeds, brooks no such love as that implied in the *Phaedrus*.

Epicurus' atheism, atoms and concern for pleasure struck the Cappadocian as unworthy of a philosopher. For Gregory praiseworthy philosophers were theists who found a sense of order or providence in the world and exhibited a concern for the development of virtues. In Oration 28.8 the Theologian mentions the theory of atoms developed by Epicurus as an example of absurdity. Epicurus' emphasis on pleasure is not physical joy, but Nazianzen may have found his equation of happiness and pleasure improper (cf. W. Schmidt, "Epikur," *RAC* 5 [1962], pp. 681-819). Gregory, however, espouses one lone aspect of Epicurean theory of language in his debate with the Eunomians. With Epicurus (*Letter to Herodotus* 37 and 75) he sees the basic meaning of words in the things that lie underneath those words, their πράγματα (cf. *Or.* 29.13). Eunomius (*Apology for the Apology* 1.6; Jaeger 1.345; Vaggione, pp. 107-108) had attacked Basil as using a theory of language which was similar to that of Epicurus and Aristotle but in many ways his words intend to saddle Basil with Epicurean and Aristotelian concepts of God and providence. Nazianzen, however, does not accept the single, natural meaning of words that Epicurus explains in his *Letter to Herodotus*. For him names are a matter of convention as Aristotle (*On Interpretation* 16A-B) indicated.

Perhaps the most interesting of the bishop's attacks is that on Aristotle. His reliance upon other aspects of the Stagirite's thought are obvious within these *Theological Orations*; he depends heavily upon Aristotle's logic and rhetoric. In this oration the influence of *Rhetoric* 1355B-1359B is prevalent. Gregory, however, rejects the Stagirite's view of providence, his teaching about the mortality of the soul and his insistence upon a type of humanism that centers on man alone. Nazianzen attacks Aristotle's weak conception of providence, a common view expressed by Christian theologians. Aristotle's positions on natural science and other issues often struck religionists as doing away with divinity. It is also possible that Gregory accepted the *De mundo* as genuine. His knowledge of the Stagirite is too extensive to be based upon handbook study alone. Thus this attack on a particular sense of providence may mean that some fourth-century C.E. corpus of Aristotle included the *De mundo*, although that is not the only place in which Aristotle discusses providence.

Nazianzen's reference to τὸ ἔντεχνον, "artificial system," must be carefully identified. Although he accepts much of Aristotle's logic and rhetoric, he also warns against placing too much emphasis upon anyone's syllogisms, including Aristotle's (*Or.* 32.25; *de virtute* 48-49; *Or.* 23.12). Since Gregory himself approaches theology at times in a negative mode, at times in silence and always with an awareness of the inability to conceive of God's nature, perhaps he has a deep distrust of any comprehensive system. For him human intellect is not an instrument of understanding strong enough to systematize theology and thus God. Theology is not amenable to rigid human organization; it is not a technique-oriented subject.

The "artificial system," τὸ ἔντεχνον, of his theological opponents is what disturbs him. In section 2 he warned that the later Arians tend to make "the mystery," τὸ . . . μυστήριον, of the faith into a "mere social accomplishment," a τεχνύδριον. He prays in Oration 29.21 that God will make his antagonists believers, not "logicians," τεχνολόγων, while in Oration 31.18 he notes that "according to [their] system," κατὰ τὴν σὴν τεχνολογίαν, Prov. 30.29 cannot mean what it says. In this instance Gallay (p. 97) translates τὸ ἔντεχνον as a reference to the overly subtle character of Aristotelian thought. Barbel (p. 57) locates the problem in the artificial character of Aristotle's logic. Those views can only be partially true since Nazianzen is dependent upon the relationship between syllogisms and enthymemes which Aristotle described in his *Rhetoric*. The Theologian is a philosophical rhetorician who participates in that larger understanding of Aristotelian logic, one that includes the *Rhetoric* among the logical treatises. He can rely on the lessons of technical logic as he often does. In Oration 29.15 he refers approvingly to the "logicians" as τοῖς περὶ ταῦτα τεχνολογεῖν. What he rejects is his antagonists' development of theology in terms of formal syllogisms described in the smaller Aristotelian *Organon*, their use of enthymemes primarily as tools for public presentation of demonstrable propositions.

Gregory, educated within much the same Greek tradition as the Eunomians, disagrees vehemently with that Eunomian decision. For him theology is fundamentally mysterious; it is not logical / propositional. Theology is a confessional endeavor best pursued through preaching and worship led by one who understands such things. The bulk of his orations outside this group are indicative of his decision. They do not contain the careful logical arguments involved in this set of five. Yet his opponents, particularly in the works of Aetius and Eunomius, offer a theology that views philosophy and logic as providing the structure for theology. In line with his sense of theology as confessional, his understanding of revelation as not being subject to foundational demonstration, Gregory insists that at its heart, what a modern would call "apologetics" or "philosophical theology" must be seen as a matter of probability questions that demand the use of enthymemes as tools for handling issues. The enthymematic form which he chooses for certain basic questions, however, is the second one described by Aristotle, one that is not subject to formal syllogistic treatment. Thus this attack on the "artificial system," τὸ ἔντεχνον, of Aristotle is specific, not a general dismissal of Aristotelian thought or technical logic. Behind the one phrase stands a pointed debate about the character of Aristotelian logic, the nature of *paideia* itself, indeed the purpose of theology (cf. Intro. *paideia*).

The bishop also finds deficiencies in the views of Stoics and Cynics. Elsewhere he praises their work, (*Ors.* 4.43; 43.60) but here he points out the haughtiness of the former and the greediness and crudity of the latter.

As a technical term τὸ κενόν, "The Void," had appeared in the writings of various philosophical and religious communities in antiquity. Aristotle (*Physics* 213A-217B) denied that there was a void beyond the known world, but the Stoic Cleomedes (*De motu* 1.1.5-8) claimed that there was a void which enclosed the world. Some Gnostics were concerned with such problems. Irenaeus (*Against All Heresies* 2.4.2) insisted that the Valentinians included everything within the Pleroma; the *Gospel of Truth* (17.4 - 18.11) indeed puts "oblivion" within the Pleroma. If τὸ κένον, "The Void," and τὸ πλῆρες, "The Full," form a pair as Hardy (*The Christology of the Later Fathers* [Philadelphia, 1954], p. 134) and Gallay (p. 97) indicate, they may have a Gnostic background. Any and all of these sources could be involved since Gregory found speculation about these themes to be a place where the Eunomian penchant for technical logic could be given free play.

Nazianzen puts interest in such topics together with other forms of error he rejects. He finds the structure and practice of Graeco-Roman religions silly. Their depictions of gods, sacrifices, idols and good and bad demons make no sense. These rejections raise interesting difficulties, particularly in interpreting parts of the Biblical witness. Origen (*Hom. on I Sam.* 28.3-25) struggled with the account of the witch from Endor. Gregory speaks of angels and devils in these orations. The problem, apparently, is that paganism still thinks devils do not have a Lord.

Nazianzen knows that the subjects he has mentioned had often been topics of philosophical or rhetorical exercises during late antiquity and had occupied the minds of students within various schools. Although his ironic introduction of a possible opinion held by his later Arian opponents highlights their overblown view of their own dialectical prowess, he does suggest a second set of themes that might better test their true abilities. For this second set of issues the verb changes from Βάλλε to Φιλοσόφει, from "attack" to "philosophize about." These are not errors to be thrown aside, but subjects to be given fuller attention. Most interpreters have had no difficulty including the first few themes in this list under such a description. Speculations about the universe or other universes, about matter and the soul, and about good and evil natures are useful exercises though incapable of garnering intellectual certainty. Properly done they should lead the speaker to a sense of the limitations he and his audience have. Yet the inclusion of resurrection, judgment, reward and punishment, and the sufferings or human passions of Christ seemingly forms an odd lot. Why would they not be harmed by ill-conceived dialectical treatment?

The theme of resurrection may be connected with what precedes and thus involve the nature of resurrection bodies rather than the event status of Jesus or Christians rising from the dead. Gallay (p. 97, n. 7) attempts to answer why these Christian topics pose no basic problem whether or not they are properly understood. In the preface of *On First Principles* Origen insists that full speculation about fundamental doctrines of the faith is left to the advanced. All can be saved by accepting Christian truth without further contemplation. Barbel (pp. 60-61, n. 43) quotes a passage from Oration 2.35 that indicates Nazianzen's acceptance of such views.

Obviously Nazianzen is concerned about heretical understandings of the faith. These five orations are focused on what he considers to be Trinitarian and Christological errors. He found such mistaken views to be more menacing than misunderstandings of other teachings. Perhaps the tale from Cyril of Scythopolis' *Life of Cyriacus* (12) is not far from the mark. That sixth-century monk tells how he asked Cyriacus if certain Origenist speculations about pre-existent souls and the final return were "moderate," μέσα, and "harmless," ἀκίνδυνα, as the Origenist monks said. They defended their views by quoting this passage from Nazianzen. Gregory indeed may have seen many theological speculations as inconsequential. Because revelation is not subject, at its deepest levels, to logical proof, a number of issues in theology cannot be harmed by amateurish logical treatment.

If nothing else, this present list—coupled with his concerns for the nature of the Father, the Son and the Holy Spirit—points up a major difference between his assessment of the theologian's task and that of many Western theologians. Interest in the sufferings of Christ, in how reward and punishment as well as judgment form the coherent structure of Christian faith, is marked in the Latin West, but the Greek East has often not viewed them as such central issues. Part of the reason for those differences may be Nazianzen's place as the Theologian, one of the three Hierarchs of Eastern Orthodoxy. As this section indicates he did not share the Western concerns.

27.10.7 has a misprint in the *SC* text: ἀφιλόσορον should read ἀφιλόσοφον.

Few treatises about the nature of theology come to us from the ancient church. That may be one reason this oration occurs alone in some

manuscripts. The organization of the entire work on the basis of the rhetorical commonplace concerning speaker, occasion, audience and subject
demonstrates the deep debt that Gregory owed to Hellenism and to his
education. Gallay (pp. 78-79, n. 1) notices that Harnack's question about
the Hellenization of Christianity arises from this oration, yet the aphorism
of Florovsky seems most appropriate: Gregory is christianizing Hellenism. He acknowledges his debt to Hellenistic education and strengthens
its insights through his sense of Christian revelation. Study and contemplation become one. If, however, he must choose, he chooses Christian
revelation.

His approach differs somewhat from that of Basil. The bishop of
Caesarea accused Eunomius of relying upon Aristotle rather than the
Scriptures (*Against Eunomius* 1.9), yet used Aristotelian logic to attack
some of Eunomius' positions (*Against Eunomius* 1.25). Even then he did
not make his debt to Greek logic and rhetoric clear. Although Basil's work
is a careful refutation of a writing by Eunomius and Gregory's oration is
a popular presentation before an audience of supporters and opponents,
Gregory acknowledges his acceptance of Greek *paideia*. His discourse does
not "despoil the Egyptians" while misrepresenting their positions. Ungraciously Basil's *Ad adolescentes* often succeeds at that task. Neither does
the Theologian decry the time he wasted in his youthful studies as the
Caesarean bishop does (*Ep*. 223). Nazianzen criticizes the Greek heritage
and suggests which aspects of it might be best explored through the Eunomian penchant for word games, but his critique depends upon an acceptance of other aspects, some of which are obvious in both the structure and
the content of this oration. He combats the later Arians because their faith
is false. They do not accept the Son as of the same nature as the Father;
but they also do theology poorly because they were educated poorly. All
three Cappadocians drink from Hellenic springs. Basil, however, appears
as a gifted christianizer of Hellenism as much from Gregory's great funeral oration (*Or*. 43)—which depicts him that way and demonstrates Nazianzen's debt to Hellenism—as from the Caesarean's own work.
Gregory's reliance on his education in philosophical rhetoric provides the
structure in these *Theological Orations* for his entire debate with the later Arians. As we shall see he does not at times possess the philosophical acuity
of Nyssa, but he makes his mastery of rhetorical education an integral part
of his grasp of Christian theology.

The Theologian's arguments with Eunomian opponents grow out of a
fourth-century debate with hostile listeners who are probably in the audience, but this oration contains good advice for students of theology in
any age. Attempting to understand God requires time, meditation and
study. Any theologian must give long years to the best education and the

heights of contemplation. Anything less misconstrues the subject, the discipline and its applications. As in almost any topic, the rhetorical commonplace of attention to the character of the speaker, to the audience, to the occasion and to the theme fits. In this sense a developed theology, which understands the relationship between dialectic and rhetoric while emphasizing the latter, need not be sophistic. It could follow the approach of philosophical rhetoric as a fundamental way in which theology can be true to its subject. Gregory's own view may be termed a Christian humanism in which the revelation of God in Christ through the Spirit forms the basis for a high evaluation of humankind. Thus he applauds education and depends upon Greek *paideia* at a number of crucial points, while placing everything in the context of Christian revelation and tradition.

The remaining *Theological Orations* provide the details of this way to do theology. In Oration 28 Nazianzen notes his opponents' misunderstanding of human intellectual limitations; in 29 he details their ignorance of how rhetorical enthymemes are used in argument. In 30 he attacks their poor knowledge of elementary logic and grammar employed in Biblical exegesis; in 31 he returns to their misappropriation of syllogisms. All these are educational deficiencies, but Gregory also addresses each oration to problems that concern the selection of Biblical texts, the exegesis of those texts and the continuity of Christian tradition.

The designation of this discourse, either at its beginning or its end, as Περὶ θεολογίας, "on the doctrine of God," is appropriate, even though such a title appears in Greek manuscripts that are dated no earlier than the ninth century. Within the oration Gregory focuses on the incomprehensibility of God's nature and develops the topic in two ways. First, he argues that Biblical heroes did not know God's nature. Second, he shows that humans do not understand fully either their world or themselves and therefore could hardly grasp God's essence. The argument is mounted inductively, often formed of enthymemes that deal with the issue as a probability question. The Theologian does not demonstrate God's incomprehensibility syllogistically by concentrating on the meaning of the terms; he presents his case forcefully through numerous examples.

Expanded titles on manuscripts Q, P and D, employed in the SC edition, suggest that the oration was given at Constantinople. Such late comments, however, prove nothing about original situations; they do not state anything other than tenth-century opinions about where Nazianzen spoke this piece. If these traditions are true, they give no answer to three important questions. Did Nazianzen originally offer Oration 28 as the second in the series? Did he present it in some other order within the original group? Or did he give it on a different occasion and then add it to the series for publication?

The manuscript tradition only heightens the mystery. The place of Oration 28 within the *Theological Orations* was discussed in the Introduction (pp. 76-78). Although the manuscript evidence supports no firm conclusion about the original order, there are both external and internal reasons for arguing that this oration occurred second in the series. Externally the Syriac manuscript Add. 17.146 and the Syriac writer Peter of Callinicum, both from the sixth century, refer to this oration as "the second on theology," thus suggesting that it occupied this place in a series from a relatively early date in at least one manuscript tradition. This Syriac evidence is the earliest we have, for the Greek manuscripts are dated no earlier than the ninth century. Internally Gregory uses Oration 27 to discuss the nature of theology in terms of the rhetorical commonplace concerning speaker, occasion, audience and topic. He plays on the need for purification, study and contemplation when he speaks of the orator's ἦθος, "character," but he does not fully develop either his sense of θεωρία, "study" and "contemplation," or the incomprehensibility of God's nature. In 28.2 he continues the discussion of ἦθος by describing his ascent up the mount, his meditative experience. This continuity of approach between Orations 27 and 28 is not dependent on the opening comments in 28.1 alone.

Nazianzen also speaks of contemplation in order to focus on the major theme in the debate with the Eunomians: God's incomprehensible nature. The most skilled devotees, those whose meditation and purification are beyond reproach, do not know God's nature (28.2-3, 17-21). In 27.9 Gregory conceded for the sake of argument that the later Arian leaders were themselves equal to Elijah, Moses and Paul. That allowed him to question their wisdom in giving the inexperienced responsibility, in trying "to mold other men into holiness overnight." Now he expands his attack by withdrawing the concession of 27.9. If they are like the Biblical heroes, they should know God's nature is unknowable. Since, however, they claim to explain his essence, they are not like the giants of old.

In the rest of the oration, Nazianzen demonstrates that his claim concerning God's incomprehensibility is not a fideistic circle, but a sensible conclusion. Only the foolish say they understand the nature of God when they find the nature of things so close to them unfathomable. His arguments are sensible, but they are *ad hoc* and thus neither foundational nor systematic.

A full presentation of theology in the midst of the debate with the Eunomians demands attention to contemplation and a reasoned defense of the claim concerning divine incomprehensibility. The first challenges later Arian piety; the second questions their *paideia*. Without this oration the series would not have a discourse devoted specifically to the main topic: God's unknowable nature. Oration 28 expands themes noticed in Oration 27, while focusing on what Gregory perceives to be the primary issue. Therefore, although it cannot be proved and indeed more research on the manuscripts may make it more questionable, there is a legitimate case that 28 belonged to the original plan and was the second in the series. At the very least it was a part of an early published series available in the sixth century.

28.1   The opening phrase of Oration 28 recalls 27.1 in which Nazianzen mentions the purification or cleansing of the theologian. Gregory's rehearsal of the famous fourfold rhetorical principle, which he takes as fundamental knowledge for any educated person, has a different purpose in this discourse. This time Nazianzen does not employ the forms of πᾶς, "everything," with the negative as he did in 27.3, παντός, πάντοτε, πᾶσιν, πάντα or as Williams translated it, "not for everyone . . . every occasion . . . every audience . . . all its aspects." Instead he uses descriptions of the speaker, occasion, audience and subject, with the two issues of θεωρία and παίδευσις again being highlighted. "Contemplation" is crucial (28.2), but so is "learning." No cultured person thinks of speaking about any topic without attention to the fourfold principle. When the discourse is to be about God, however, the fundamental concern will demand proper meditation.

Gregory's argument against the Eunomian understandings of θεωρία and παίδευσις dominates this mild form of ψόγος, "invective." He does not attack with the sharpness of his invectives against Julian, but even his confession of the relationships within the Trinity still serves this form. The later Arians claim to be well-educated and to have plumbed the depths of theology. For them theology is full of "distinction," διαίρεσις, which they purvey before the unlearned (27.6). The *Syntagmation* of Aetius is comprised almost entirely of enthymemes that can be stated as formal syllogisms. Eunomius' *Apology* and his *Apology for the Apology* include numerous conundrums as do the remarks that may come from later Arian popularizers (cf. *Ors.* 29-31). Yet these opponents are unable to accept the "mysterious paradox." In spite of their claims to knowledge, they do not know the "one in its distinctions and distinct in its connections," τὴν ἔλ-λαμψιν ἑνικῶς διαιρουμένην, καὶ συναπτομένην διαιρέτως. The play on different forms of διαιρέω evidences his disagreement with his antagonists. They make endless "distinctions," but miss the ones in the doctrine of the Trinity that count.

28.2 Moses' ascent up the mount provides the Biblical basis for Nazianzen's description of his own "character," ἦθος, in terms of "contemplation," θεωρία. Gregory mentioned Elijah, Moses and Paul within a similar discussion of ἦθος in 27.9. Ascending involves the level of purification and contemplation already achieved. He himself would like to reach the heights, but his eagerness is tempered by his sense of inadequacy, a sense based on his education within both Hellenic and Christian tradition. Plato knew only the pure could handle the pure (*Phaedo* 67B forms the context of 27.3); so did Moses.

Gregory's view is unmistakable. He, like Origen (*On First Principles*, Preface), allows the outward ceremonies of religion to provide for common people's needs, but there are levels above them and, sadly, levels below them. True theologians ascend to grasp the truth, while beasts snap and tear at sound teaching. The introduction of various animals from Old and New Testament references offers a string of Biblical allusions that cast aspersions on the character of later Arian theologians. "Chop-logic," σόφισμα, and "purity / impurity," κατὰ τὴν ἀξίαν τῆς καθάρσεως / οὐ καθαρῶν, are the dual concerns.

In 28.2.5 the *SC* editors refer εἰ μέν τις 'Ααρών, "Is any an Aaron?" to Ex. 19.24 and 24.9. Only the first citation applies.

In 28.2.32 they refer τῶν μεγάλων, "the big [vineyards]" to Ps. 80(79).8-11 (9-12). There is no connection.

28.3 Any good speaker must make some attempt to establish his own "character," ἦθος. Since Gregory apparently is speaking at the chapel Anastasia within the "orthodox" community, he boldly describes his own contemplative experience in contrast with that of his attackers, despite his anxiety about worthiness. At the height of contemplation he was unable to see the essence of God. No one could see more; not even a heavenly being can gain a "perfect apprehension," τῆς τελείας καταλήψεως, of God's nature as perhaps later Arians claimed they could (Eunomius, Fr. ii, Vaggione, pp. 170 and 178-179; *contra* Wickham, p. 565-566, n. 1).

This daring comparison between his attainments and those of his opponents strikes the modern reader as logically suspect even if sophistically effective. Those who worshipped at the chapel had already accepted his contemplative superiority. The comparison of the later Arians to unthinking beasts in section 2 and his claims for similarity to Moses in section 3 encourage his followers, but the harshness of the contrast and the *ad hominem* nature of the two arguments hardly appear to persuade his foes. Perhaps on the basis of his rhetorical education and his sense of Biblical prophets, he had reason to expect that such attacks could have a positive effect upon his foes. His call for their reconciliation to God in 29.21 strengthens that suggestion. But the strongest influence doubtless would be on those who had already accepted such a view of his character.

Underneath this section lies not only an appeal to Scripture and classical *paideia* but also one to Christian tradition. The point about the inability of humans to see God in his essence had been made by Clement of Alexandria (*Stromata* 5.11) and Cyril of Jerusalem (*Catechetical Orations* 6.5). Barbel (pp. 66-68, n. 9) cites similar opinions from early theologians. Basil had used such argumentation (*Against Eunomius* 1.10). Gregory accepts the principle his friend defended and borrows many of the specific Scriptural references and the arguments that formed its base.

Gallay (pp. 106-107, n. 2) notes the similarities between Nazianzen's sections 2-3 in this oration and section 2 from Gregory of Nyssa's *The Life of Moses*. The resemblances suggest the way in which the Cappadocians worked together on various projects. Since Nyssa's treatise followed these discourses by nearly a decade (390-392 C.E.), any borrowing probably was by Nyssa. Both treatises are concerned with the incomprehensibility of God's nature; both illustrate the point through reference to Moses' ascent as the type of spiritual enlightenment.

In 28.3.2 only W, P, and C read Ἔτρεχον; the others read Εἶχον. The context suggests that "running" makes more sense of talk about an ascent than does "having."

28.4   Gregory moves quickly to the next step in his argument. Leaving the *ad hominem* attack behind, he explicates the principle of God's incomprehensible nature. In the latter portions of this paragraph he perhaps follows some of Origen's speculations (*On First Principles* 2.4.3, 2.9.1) about celestial beings, but finds such thoughts unsatisfying. Little is known about these creatures, thus little can be asked. The claim of the Eunomians to know God's nature is, however, open to investigation.

The traditional interpretation has been that Nazianzen here refers to a comment from Plato (*Timaeus* 28C), but he does not name Plato. A number of commentators have based that identification on the similarity of this section to Clement of Alexandria's *Stromata* 5.12, a passage in which Plato is named and *Timaeus* 28C apparently is cited. Pépin ("Grégoire de Nazianze, Lecteur de la Littérature hermétique," *VC* 36, [1982], pp. 251-260), however, has shown that the actual words are closer to a Hermetic fragment. Elias of Crete, the twelfth-century commentator, (p. 22) suggested that the opinion reflected both Plato and Hermes. Whatever the source of the question, the point is to cast doubt on later Arian confidence in their conception and in their expression of God's essence. To that end Gregory attacks the unnamed pagan sage for a sophistic trick. An authority who says: "I know, but I cannot tell you," may not know. The statement can cleverly cover ignorance. Nazianzen turns this argument in a different direction in section 7. If the Eunomians know what God's essence is, they should be able to say clearly what it is, not merely what it is not. The designation of God's nature as ἀγέννητος, "unbegotten," is also a trick.

As Gregory sees it, full knowledge of God's nature is impossible for humans since their view is obstructed by their fleshly condition. The problem is not one of language or attitude, but one of mental power, for such knowledge is beyond even those prepared by contemplation. The Theologian hesitates to speak with finality about the ability of incorporeal natures to know God in himself, but even then he suspects that such creatures only grasp more than humans do, not everything about God.

28.5   To further ground his basic principle Nazianzen returns to Scriptural citations. God's peace passes understanding (Phil. 4.7); so does even an "exact knowledge," ἀκριβὴς κατανόησις, of creation. The Psalmist (8.3[4]) indicates only that he will see the fixed order of the universe, not that he has already seen it. If God's peace and an "exact knowledge" of creation surpass human capacity, surely the transcendent cause of that peace and creation is incomprehensible. This *a fortiori* argument dominates the discourse and will be supported by further comments on the Bible, nature and human nature.

Gregory devotes the rest of this paragraph and section 6 to a disclaimer.

By insisting on the inability to conceive of God's essence, he is not denying the existence of God. The background for this interjection appears to be a disagreement within various philosophical traditions about whether one could know the existence of something if one does not know exactly what it is. Nazianzen takes up the principle that existence is possible to demonstrate even when the nature of the thing in question is unknown. This principle is consistent with the rest of his exposition since there is no disagreement with the later Arians about the existence of God, self, or creation. As he will try to show, however, the nature of humans and of creation is not yet fully understood.

28.6 The mention of God as τὴν πάντων ποιητικήν τε καὶ συνεκτικὴν αἰτίαν, "the efficient and essential cause" or as Wickham translates it, "the creative and sustaining cause of all," indicates Gregory's general philosophical reading. Aristotle (*De Generatione et Corruptione* 324B, *passim*) speaks of efficient causes, but so does Plotinus (*Enneads* 6.3.18 and 28). Pseudo-Aristotle also mentions essential or sustaining causes (*De mundo* 397B). Stoic fragments contain similar teachings (*SVF* II, 144 and 1016). Mason (p. 29, n. 5) correctly notices that φυσικὸς νόμος refers not to natural law, but to "the natural consequence upon ourselves of the observations which we make." Pairing "instinctive law" with "sight," ὄψις διδάσκαλος, or what is taught by observation, makes that point.

Nazianzen does not argue against inferences, against any use of syllogistic argument. He is persuaded that looking at the orderliness of the universe leads one to posit the existence of God. Thus he turns to the example of the lyre and its maker, most prominently displayed in Plato (*Phaedo* 73D). Anyone, in his view, who would not follow reason along that path shows poor judgment. As Hanson indicates (p. 708, n. 119) here Nazianzen does not draw a line between "revealed and natural knowledge of God." What in later developments of natural theology will be called the argument from design for the existence of God he finds persuasive. In that sense he apparently does put forth a type of foundationalism, one that is rather common within his culture and one in which he finds no danger. But this clear point does not destroy the fact that throughout most of his presentation, he avoids foundationalism of any sort. Here his acceptance of this proof of the existence of God is *ad hoc*, not systematic. He makes no attempt to build a strong natural theology on which he can found his sense of revelation. Indeed the bulk of his attacks on the Neo-Arians comes from his sense that knowledge of God, particularly God's nature, is beyond the ken of humans.

There are observational or "instinctive proofs," ταῖς φυσικαῖς ἀποδείξεσιν, for the inference that God exists, but there is no proof that anyone has fully understood God's nature. To infer that God exists is not to comprehend his nature. "Whatever we imagined or figured to ourselves or reason delineated is not the reality of God," οὐδὲ τοῦτο εἶναι Θεόν, ὅπερ ἐφαντάσθημεν, ἢ ἀνετυπωσάμεθα, ἢ λόγος ὑπέγραψεν.

The methodological principle here is important. Fantasizing, making mental models and thinking things out do not override faith (cf. section 28). Intellectual activities may lead us part of the way; they may even point to God's existence, but God's essence is beyond our powers of conception, let alone our powers of expression (section 4). Enfleshed humans do not have the capacity to grasp God's nature except in faithful acceptance of the mystery. This is the crux of the argument with the later Arians who may have claimed that they knew and could describe God's essence in itself (see section 3). As Socrates (*H.E.* 4.7; Vaggione, *Fr.* ii, pp. 170 and 178-179; *contra* Wickham, pp. 565-566, n. 1), quotes Eunomius "God does not know anything more about his own essence than we do, nor is that essence better known to him and less to us; rather, whatever we ourselves know about it is exactly what he knows, and, conversely, that which he knows is what you will find without change in us." If Eunomians did not make that remarkable claim, at least for them, God had revealed his essence in his name, ἀγέννητος, "unbegotten," which they knew and could describe.

28.7 If, however, one insists on employing the proofs of deductive argument to form a conception of God, what are the results? Here ironic praise of his opponents as accomplished philosophers and theologians, along with the introduction of the second person pronoun, indicates again the strain of the situation and suggests the presence of the antagonists within an audience attentively listening to a spoken oration.

The introduction of corporeality as the example of what results from poorly-disciplined deductive argument does not demand that the later Arians claimed bodily quality for God. The extant writings from Aetius and Eunomius nowhere present that conception. Perhaps some members of the Eunomian community in Constantinople at a base, popular level had begun to claim that God was corporeal. We know that both in Egypt and in Palestine in the last decades of the fourth century there were Anthropomorphists who read Scripture literally and thought of God in bodily terms. The salon conversations in Constantinople and the elemental discourse, both so scathingly rebuked in Oration 27.2, might have been that vulgar, but there is a more probable explanation of this example. Disproving the bodily character of God, a position which the later Arians would most likely take themselves, opens up one argument and gives weight to another. First, in section 9 according to Gregory, knowing that God is incorporeal—as all inspired Christian teachers have insisted—does not give understanding of God's nature. By arguing against God's having a "body," σῶμα, in section 7, Nazianzen has introduced the principle involved in his attack on the alpha-privatives like the more important "unbegotten," ἀγέννητος, without tipping his hand as to the exact focus of that attack. The impending force of his argument is purposely hidden by using as an example a doctrine with which his opponents agree. Second, in section 12 Gregory insists that we cannot grasp God's nature precisely because we have bodies. We are corporeal; all our judgments are affected by that corporeality, particularly investigations of what the nature of an incorporeal object might be. This is a classic *reductio ad absurdum* argument that gains its force not only from the cadence of short and long sentences and the combination of questions and exclamations, but also from the reference to holiness or "be[ing] worth worship," σεπτόν. If it is indeed an argument accepted by most of the audience, then its value for section 12 is heightened even though all *reductio ad absurdum* arguments lack logical validity.

28.8   The tone does not shift radically in this section. Gregory still points out the irrationality of corporeality and employs two puns to emphasize his position, ones which Wickham has caught in his translation: "Talk of God's body has no solid body to it," σῶμα οὐχ ἕξει . . . ὁ περὶ τοῦ σώματος λόγος and "immaterial, . . . born along the circular drift . . . to suit their free-drifting, self-constructing argument," ἄϋλον . . . τὴν κύκλῳ φορὰν φερόμενον . . . κατὰ τὴν αὐτόνομον αὐτῶν τοῦ λόγου φορὰν καὶ ἀνάπλασιν.

The Theologian also introduces Jer. 23.24 and Wis. 1.7 for comparison. Scripture denies God's corporeality. So does tradition. Basil (*Hom.* 3.7) had linked the attributes of being "uncontained," ἀπερίγραπτος, and "incorporeal," ἀσώματος, as had other earlier theologians.

Barbel (p. 78, n. 25) asserts that no one known to him ever claimed that God had an angelic or supra-angelic body. If that be true, then Gregory is considering opinions that are hypothetical. Although popular theology often asserts strange doctrines, the best evidence suggests no later Arians had offered such views. Barbel's comment supports the interpretation that Nazianzen, in section 7 and now 8, intends to attack positions that the Eunomians themselves attack. He wants to win their support on those points before contesting other issues they hold dear. But he plans to force them into conceding that some of their doctrines imply God has a body, particularly their conundrums that deny divinity to the Son (cf. *Or.* 29.8).

The "fifth element," πέμπτον σῶμα, in the sense of a "fifth essence," πέμπτη οὐσία, had been rejected by Origen (*On First Principles* 3.6.6 and *Contra Celsum* 4.60) and is Aristotelian as Cicero (*Academica* 1.7.26) indicates. Among philosophical authors, Theophrastus (*de Igne* 4-6) had questioned its existence although he eventually supported it. Strato (*Fr.* 84,

Wehrli edition) rejected it and Xenarchos wrote an entire book against the concept (P. Moraux, "Xenarchos, 5," *PW* IX A2, 1423ff. summarizes the fragments.) Moreschini (p. 65, n. 43) also suggests it may have a Stoic background and that φλυαρίας βυθός, an "abyss of nonsense," is probably proverbial although it harkens back to Plato (*Parmenides* 139D).

In 28.8.8-9 Gallay accepts the emendation of Wyss (*Hermes* 73, [1938], p. 360ff.) that the reading should be ἀντιπαρεκταθήσεται, similar to *SVF* II, 157 and 471 and notes that Wickham found evidence for such a reading in the Syriac translations he investigated. This suggests once more that the Syriac translators were knowledgeable, a claim that Gallay questions in his remarks concerning variants for Oration 27.4. J.-M. Mathieu ("Sur une correction inutile [Or. 28,8, lignes 8-9 Gallay]," *II. Symp. Naz.*, pp. 53-59), however, argues for preserving the ἀντιπαρατεθήσεται reading both as sensible, in line with Neoplatonic influences in Nazianzen's work and as more plausible because it avoids the emendation.

28.9 The word play represented by ἄϋλος, "immaterial," αὐλή, "fold," does not advance the argument any more than the play on a fifth element did. But such verbal gymnastics met the rhetorical expectations of his audience.

Gregory's argument deals primarily with God as a body, the issue introduced in section 7. Here he states what he and the later Arian theologians agree upon: God is not corporeal. Eunomius (*Apology* 12) rejects a bodily generation, σωματικὴν τὴν γέννησιν, of the Son by the Father and thus denies the description "bodily" to each. Gregory's reason for introducing that argument is to criticize the use of alpha-privatives as predicate nominatives. Just as ἀσώματος, "immaterial," does not designate God's "essential being," neither do ἀγέννητος, "ingenerate," ἄναρχος, "unoriginate," ἀναλλοίωτος, "immutable," and ἄφθαρτος, "immortal." The later Arians employed the contrast between ἀγέννητος, "unbegotten," and γέννητος, "begotten," to claim that the nature of the Father was different from the nature of the Son (Eunomius, *Apology* 7-11).

That context makes Nazianzen's point interesting. He insists that if one were to find a group of subjects described by the same predicate nominatives, the subjects themselves would not necessarily be of the same nature. Men, cows and horses are all "corporeal," "begotten," and "mortal," but they are not of the same nature. Such argumentation is persuasive, but may later haunt Gregory, for he has demonstrated that different natures can be described with the same adjectives.

More important, Nazianzen criticizes the way of negation, the *via negativa*. Saying what something is not cannot express what it is. He thus imposes upon himself and others the demand to make some positive statements about God's nature. In Oration 31.31-32 he muses about his own attempts to find a positive figure for the Trinity. He discovers only a few analogies, yet each of them contains a major defect. Positive elements can be described, but each one must be carefully qualified. By criticizing the way of negation, he has opened up a counter to the more sophisticated philosophical foundations of the later Arian choice of ἀγέννητος, "unbegotten," as the word which designates the nature of God. He can reject that move not only because ἀγέννητος is an alpha privative and thus a privation, but also because the selection of a *via negativa* as the definitive way to speak of God's nature is equally flawed (cf. 29.12).

Once more he emphasizes the need for education and contemplation to understand what can be known about God. "The full reality is left to be grasped, philosophically treated, and scrutinized by a more advanced theorist of God," Ἀλλ' ὅλον τὸ εἶναι περιλαμβάνειν λείπεται προσφιλοσοφεῖν τε καὶ προσεξετάζειν τῷ γε νοῦν Θεοῦ ἀληθῶς ἔχοντι καὶ τελεωτέρῳ τὴν θεωρίαν. Again θεωρία includes both proper study and deep contemplation.

28.10   This section is an exercise in logic that turns on the mutually exclusive character of certain terms and propositions. It rests on the Biblical passages mentioned in previous sections and is informed by the Hellenistic discussions of God's enclosing, but not being enclosed. Its purpose is to demonstrate that Nazianzen's sense of God's incomprehensibility is the most reasonable. Here the enthymematic form of argument appears with the force contained in two of its primary aspects. First, Gregory takes positions that are amenable to deductive, syllogistic treatment. Although his arguments appear in pairs: "If . . . then," the minor premise of the more formal style could be provided. Second, he expects his hearers to supply the missing premise and thus employs the enthymematic form as a way to involve them in a complicated but demonstrable argument.

In section 5 Nazianzen emphasized that knowledge of a thing's existence does not entail knowledge of its nature. Now he leads his audience toward the conclusion that the inability to answer the query about spatial location demands that Christians recognize the limitations of human reason. The principle, which he deftly mentions at the end of the section, is a telling one. Comprehension itself is a form of limitation. To know something we must be able to enclose it in some way both in terms of our observations and our concepts. With God, particularly at the point of his nature, that is impossible although other factors can be known as He makes them known. Gregory assumes that none of those listening to his argument would accept the other conclusion to which his inferences lead: there is no reasonable way to talk about the existence of God.

28.11   In good rhetorical fashion the Theologian apologizes for this rather formidable set of arguments he has offered. He prefers noble simplicity. Part of his sentiment involves the common rhetorical demurral against eloquence rather than a rejection of literary skill or logical presentation. Ironically, well-educated rhetoricians often began their speeches with an eloquent rejection of eloquence, thereby demonstrating their cultured dependence upon rhetoric. Another aspect of Gregory's plan, however, involves his preference for confessional theology and liturgically oriented homilies rather than logically oriented lectures. Within his corpus, no other treatises are as tightly argued as these five.

Nazianzen sees his opponents continually breaking the rules of rhetoric and logic while creating a desire on the part of hearers to participate in such machinations. In order to counter them, he takes the risk of dialectical, i.e., enthymematic, argumentation. The rest of his homilies outside the *Theological Orations* indicate that he preferred a much less rigorous style for general preaching. He evidently decided to raise the issues in this manner within these orations in order to show that his opponents were not good dialecticians. Sections 7-10 are a subtle demonstration of their foolish deductive reasoning. The ultimate purpose of his arguments, however, is to establish the incomprehensibility of divinity. Discussion of the problems inherent in corporeality, alpha-privatives, a *via negativa* and spatial location is meant to demonstrate the inability of human intellect to fathom God.

The Theologian deals cautiously with that human weakness. Possibly relying on Plato's *Phaedrus* 247A, he refuses to attribute "resentment," φθόνος, to God. In other places within this series and the corpus, he does insist that eventually we will know even as we are known (section 17; *Or.* 45.3) Participation in God, becoming gods, is the goal of human beings (*Or.* 30.4). Thus God and His plan are not malicious, for eventually we will ascend to the heights. Even now we can know that God is ultimately good, a description found in Scripture and in Neoplatonists like Plotinus, but in this worldly existence, with its fleshly hindrances, we are incapable of fully comprehending the essence of God.

The incomprehensibility of God's nature is a basic position taken by such figures as Justin (II *Apology* 6), Clement of Alexandria (*Stromata* 5.81.2-82.4) and Origen (*On First Principles* 4.3.14) well before the Arian debate. During the later stages of that debate, not only Nazianzen but also Basil (*Against Eunomius* 1.10) and Nyssa (*Apologetic Explication in the Hexaemeron* 1.72) make the same claim. Later it becomes the focus of sermons by John Chrysostom (*On the Incomprehensible Nature of God*). In the West Marius Victorinus (*Theological Treatises on the Trinity*) holds similar views at the end of the fourth century. There is thus a common consensus among certain Christian leaders that this was one of the fundamental errors, perhaps the critical mistake, of later Arian theology. Interestingly Arius (*Thalia* [Athanasius *De Synodis* 15]) confessed the incomprehensibility of God's essence. The Neo-Arian claim for the comprehensibility of God's nature is therefore one important point in which they differed from Arius.

In 28.11.5-6 the *SC* editors refer τὸ ἐνεργοῦν τὰ τοιαῦτα δόγματα σκότος, "the darkness which activates dogmas like these," to John 3.19 and 1 Thess. 5.4. The reference is not helpful because the only connection is the word "darkness," σκότος. The mention of Isa. 1.11 as background for τοῦ πλήρους, "fullness," in 28.11.18 is also strained.

28.12   For Gregory there is graciousness in our limitations. We will always yearn for God because knowledge of him requires all that we have and more. Yet because we cannot know his nature in this life, we will not suffer Lucifer's fate while we are here on earth. We cannot become satiated.

This interpretation of Lucifer on the basis of Isa. 14.12-14 appears in Tertullian (*Against Marcion* 5.11 and 17) and Origen (*On First Principles* 1.5.5). In the battle against Arianism, Athanasius (*Against the Arians* 3.25) and Basil (*Against Eunomius* 1.16) also employ it. Later in the West a number of comments on the connection between Lucifer and the Isaiah passage refer to Jerome's *Vulgate*. Jerome (*Eps.* 50 and 52), who studied with Nazianzen and admired Gregory's interpretation of Scripture, may have been influenced by him in his translation of Isa. 14.12.

Gregory closes the argument introduced in section 7 as part of what is almost a ring composition. God is incorporeal; we are corporeal. Thus no matter how learned and contemplative we might become, "some corporeal factor of ours will always intrude itself." We in our bodies can neither grasp nor express a bodiless God. The force of this argument against his opponents rests in what Nazianzen sees as a contradiction. The Neo-Arian theologians insist that God is without a body, that his begetting of the Son is not bodily. But they forget that all human knowledge is tainted by bodily intrusions.

Although A, Q, B, W, V, D and P read προβεβλημένοις in 28.12.25, Gallay suggests περιβεβλημένοις from S, C and T. The sense of the word "pent in" as Wickham translated it, particularly in context with the quotation from Lam. 3.34, "prisoners of the earth," strengthens that judgment.

The reference to Ex. 10.22 for γνόφος in 28.12.18 is strained because it does not relate contexts but a single word.

28.13   How do we know that such limitations exist? When we try to depict or define the primary elements or the greatest virtues, even mind and reason themselves, we find ourselves constantly involved in material concerns. These two groups of examples, taken from nature and human nature, form a small outline for the last sections of this treatise, but Gregory treats them in reverse order. Paragraph 22 asks about how we know our human nature, while paragraphs 23-28 investigate what we know of nature. By taking this tack, Gregory avoids a crude fideism that claims our problems in knowing God are absolutely incomparable. According to Nazianzen we should expect difficulties in grasping the essence of God when we have such problems understanding nature and ourselves.

The further we go in such investigations, the more we tire of the intrusion of bodily analogies. That is true at these lower levels and thus should be anticipated as we contemplate deity. When the human mind struggles to reach God, it puzzles out two different principles: either it grasps material things that can be seen and makes them gods, or it looks at the beauty and order in nature and honors a grand God who surpasses them.

As Wyss (p. 831) notes, the conception of "reason" as "inner discourse, unspoken or expressed," Λόγον δὲ τίνα παρὰ τὸν ἡσυχάζοντα ἐν ἡμῖν, ἢ χεόμενον, comes from Stoic logic. Moreschini (p. 72, n. 76) sees parallels with *SVF* II, 36 and 1017.

A series of references to Biblical texts, which the SC editors suggest, is tenuous or misprinted. John 9.5 for φῶς, "light" in 28.13.1 would refer the word to Jesus, not the Godhead. John 4.16 for ἀγάπη, "love," in the same line is a misprint for 1 John 4.16. Ezek. 1.4 and 12 for φορᾶς, "movement," and Rom. 5.5 for χύσεως, "dispersal," relate single words and not contexts in 28.13.4.

28.14   The first principle involves paganism, an adversary never to be forgotten even in the midst of internal Christian polemic. Baffled by their own limitations, people worshipped what they saw. When they tired of being unable to grasp God and rejected their intellectual limitations, they worshipped what they could touch and handle. With time and because of tradition, they have even been persuaded to worship other men. Thus one danger for those who do not admit their mental deficiencies in discussing the nature of God is the descent into paganism. One unspoken inference is that the later Arians may themselves fall into such an abyss if they do not give up their exalted claims about God's essence. They may end up in a polytheism of various levels of deity.

In 28.14.12 A, Q, B, W, V, T, P and C read φύσεως, "nature," while only S and D read αἰτίας, "cause," with φύσεως in the margin.

28.15   Paganism may have begun with the worship of heavenly elements, but it has gone beyond honoring men to the worship of vices and strange beasts. What began as a wholesome desire for God was twisted by the Evil One, so that rational creatures worshipped their inferiors.

Gregory recognizes that his debate with the Arians is set within the larger context of Christianity's struggle with entrenched paganism. He borrows heavily from early Christian apologetic literature. Gallay (p. 130, n. 1) points out that section 14 repeats a number of themes found in Wis. 13-15. Barbel (pp. 90-95) in a series of notes shows that these themes are found particularly in Clement of Alexandria (*Exhortation to the Greeks* 2.26.4 and 4.55.3, 56.1 and 63.4) and Origen (*Contra Celsum* 5.10). Nazianzen's own invectives against Julian, Orations 4 and 5, are the most pointed attacks within his corpus, representing the Apostate as an deadly threat to the Christian community.

The Theologian also asserts that the history of the human race shows how those who have tried to puzzle out God's nature with their limited intellects have arrived at depraved conceptions of deity. What is to stop those apparent Christians, who rely on their intellectual power to fathom the depths of God, from suffering such consequences? The Eunomians certainly have not stooped to these levels, but the principle which motivates them is the same one that has been the basis of the highest and the most sordid pagan religions. When they create a theology that says it can define God's nature, the danger is idolatry. For any deity thus comprehended is a limited one, a god of our own composing.

28.16 If acceptance of the first principle—making gods out of what a limited intellect can grasp—leads to paganism, reliance upon the second principle—discovering the transcendent God in the order and beauty of what can be grasped—opens up a far different vista. When the second principle is invoked, the truly reasonable, ὁ λόγος, concentrates on things seen in order to search for that which provides their continued existence and order. Even the most reasonable of pagans have grasped the importance of that search.

Gallay (p. 134, n. 1), Barbel (p. 96, n. 44) and Moreschini (p. 76, n. 84) suggest that the non-Christian who asked Τί τὸ ταῦτα κεκινηκὸς καὶ ἄγον τὴν ἄληκτον φορὰν καὶ ἀκώλυτον; "What set these elements in motion and leads their ceaseless, unimpeded flow?" is Plato in his *Laws* 10.896A-897C. Wyss (p. 831) points out the similarity to Chrysippus (*SVF* II, 543). Elias of Crete (p. 42) suggested Oppian. Although I have not found the exact question anywhere, the important feature is Nazianzen's positive reference to a pagan writer after his attack on paganism in the preceding two paragraphs. In this way Gregory again recognizes his debt to certain non-Christian philosophers and thus refuses to view all Greeks as an idolatrous lot. Given the larger context of pagan society, distinguishing between wise and foolish pagans is important.

Sinko (pp. 17-18) noted that sections 15 and 16 resemble Oration 6 from Cyril of Jerusalem's *Catechetical Orations*. Although no evidence exists for contact between the two men, Jerome (*De vir. ill.* 113) tells us of a period in which Nazianzen studied at Caesarea. Since Cyril became the bishop of Jerusalem about 349 C.E., a time nearly corresponding to Gregory's stay in Caesarea in Palestine, Nazianzen may have heard of

Cyril's reputation during his residence in Palestine and obtained a copy of the orations later.

Sinko's position concerns resemblance not dependence. There is a likeness in genre and an occasional similarity of motif, but no apparent quotation. Gregory's arguments in sections 15 and 16 are not the same as Cyril's in Oration 6; nor is the correlation between sections 22-30 and Cyril's Oration 9 precise, but the similarities are striking. Since the Theologian shows no reluctance in relying on the work of many other Christian writers, he may have drawn from Cyril's work at these points.

For 28.16.3 both Mason (p. 46, n. 6) and Gallay (p. 132, n. 3) prefer προσβάλλων, "looked on,"—as Wickham renders it—to προσλαβὼν, "received." Gallay's list of attestations mentions only B for the first and P for the second reading, leaving his sources and reasoning unclear.

28.17 Having warned specifically about the evils of paganism—but having praised a specific pagan's view of God—and having implied that any conceptions based upon our limited intellect may lead to idolatry, Nazianzen senses he has cleared the way for a "fresh start." He can now restate (cf. section 4) the basic point of this oration: no human can find out what God is in his nature, as long as that person is enfleshed. A look at Basil's *Against Eunomius* 1.9-15, 2.4 and 9 or Eunomius' *Apology* 8-20 and his *Apology for the Apology* 1.5-8, 2.4 shows the centrality of this point. If Vaggione (pp. 170 and 178-179) is correct (*contra* Wickham, pp. 565-566, n. 1) that Socrates (*H.E.* 4.7) quotes a statement from Eunomius, then Eunomius claimed that "God does not know anything more about his own essence than we do, nor is that essence better known to him and less to us[.]" Nazianzen's view could hardly be more diametrically opposed. From his perspective, however, the principle of God's incomprehensibility does not entail that we shall never "know even as we are known," (1 Cor. 13.12). When we have returned to God, then we shall have that final knowledge, but in this world we can attain only relative understanding. Even the Biblical heroes obtained nothing but partial knowledge while they were on this earth.

Barbel (pp. 283-287) provides two excursus, one on νοῦς, "mind," and the other on εἰκών, "image." He brings together many passages in which the centrality of these themes in Nazianzen are made evident. Greek philosophy, particularly forms of Platonism and Stoicism, influenced these concepts. But Scriptural background is not lacking. Paul warns that flesh and blood will not inherit the kingdom. At times he almost equates πνεῦμα and νοῦς (1 Cor. 1. 14-16). Paul not only speaks of Christ as the εἰκών of God (2 Cor. 4.4); he also talks of a resurrection in which humans take on the εἰκών of the man of heaven, the second Adam, Christ (1 Cor. 15. 45-49). Christians, educated in the philosophical milieu of late antiquity and engulfed in Scripture as Gregory was, needed little imagination to find parallels between philosophy and Scripture. The Theologian was assisted in such comparisons by those before him, particularly Clement of Alexandria and Origen.

In 28.17.11 the *SC* editors refer ἀπαύγασμα, "light," to Heb. 1.3. The relationship is one of a single word and not a context.

28.18 The next three sections expound a theme found in Oration 27.9. There Gregory warned about the speed with which the Eunomians attempted to mold theologians. His charge was that they somehow felt themselves to be lofty, to be on a plane with champions of the faith. Here his point is more basic. Biblical heroes were in the best position to know the nature of God, but in each case there is, in Nazianzen's judgment, no evidence that they did in fact have such knowledge while they were in the flesh. In Oration 27.9 Gregory had mentioned Elijah, Moses and Paul as those who had more sense than to educate theologians in such short periods of instruction. Here the list is expanded and the theme deepened, for neither Enoch, Noah, Abraham, Jacob, nor those mentioned previously ever grasped the nature of God.

The Maurist editors and evidently Elias of Crete (p. 46) read οἶκος, "house," for εἶδος, "vision," in 28.18.14. Mason (p. 49. 1. 4) printed εἶδος because of the manuscripts he used. He suggested that פְּנִיאֵל in Gen. 32.30(31), εἶδος θεοῦ in the Septuagint, may be the background text for such a reading. The manuscripts employed by Gallay all support εἶδος. As he indicates (p. 137, n. 4) the correctors appear to be influenced by בֵּית־אֵל in Gen. 28.19, οἶκος θεοῦ in the Septuagint. Scribal error is possible. If the reading is εἶδος Gregory himself is conflating the two Genesis passages. The *SC* editors' Biblical references should mention Gen. 32.30(31).

In 28.18.19 Gallay reads γεννητῆς, "begotten," rather than γενητῆς, "created," taking S, D, C, A, Q and T over B, V and D. One of the manuscripts, however, that he finds more reliable, P, also reads γενητῆς. If the preferred reading is γεννητῆς, this is an instance like 29.2.11 in which Gregory uses γεννητῆς with the sense of γενητῆς. The context demands the meaning "created" since the sentence speaks of Jacob's body. This reading, however, may be disputed by more research into a greater number of manuscripts.

The *SC* editors' reference in 28.18.4-5 to Gen. 6.8 for Τοῦ δὲ Νῶε καλὸν ἡ εὐαρέστησις, "Noah's distinction lay in his being 'well-pleasing' to God," probably should be the LXX of Gen. 6.9.

28.19 Gregory continues his argument by citing Elijah, Manoah, Peter, Isaiah and Ezekiel as heroes who neither saw nor spoke about "God's nature," φύσιν [θεοῦ]. Cyril of Jerusalem's *Catechetical Orations* (9.3) have similar thoughts about Ezekiel. The inclusion of Manoah demands an interpretation since the Septuagint text of Judges 13.22, which

Nazianzen quotes, states that Manoah and his wife "had seen God," θεὸν
ἑωράκαμεν. Probably from the context of the passage that talks about an
angel of the Lord in verse 21 and the background of John 6.46. Gregory
insists that this leader and his wife only saw a "vision of God," φαντασίας
θείας. In such an interpretation, Manoah's words mean that anyone who
actually sees God in this life will die.

28.20   The Apostle Paul fits the Theologian's argument because 1 Cor.
12 might mean that he did not speak about what he saw in the third
heaven. He certainly indicated that our earthly knowledge of heavenly
things would be only partial. Even the Word himself said some things
could not be borne now and only later would be made clear.

This list in 18-20 is impressive, although two of the examples demand
careful attention. On the surface Manoah's words seem to contradict
Gregory's position, but in context they do not. Nazianzen also hesitates
in describing Enoch's situation. The most he claims is that there is no certain evidence for Enoch's knowing God's nature before he was taken up
into heaven. In effect Gregory successfully rehearses deeds and words of
important Biblical figures, including the incarnate Word, to support his
view that, according to Scripture, humans do not have the power to comprehend God's essence.

28.21   The basic problem is a simple but persistent one. Employing the
human intellect to search out ultimate reality involves too small a tool for
too great a task. People must have the possibility of knowing ultimate reality at some time, since, as Nazianzen said in section 17 – based on
Scripture – we will know as we have been known. Now, however, fleshly
senses cripple human minds because raw intellect cannot be brought into
contact with pure reality. In this existence humans are always at the mercy
of their impressions of reality, which they know to be perplexing and
faulty.

The epistemology that informs this discussion of the senses, intellect,
impressions and ultimate reality comes from Plato. Gottwald (*De Gregorio
Nazianzeno platonico*, [Vratislava, 1906], p. 37) correctly finds resonances
with *Phaedo* 661 and 83A, *Philebus* 20D and 65A, and *Phaedrus* 247B. Gallay (p. 143, n. 2) also sees similarities in *Phaedrus* 262C and *Theaetetus*
200A.

By adding Solomon, Paul and David to his list of Biblical figures, Nazianzen strengthens his point. These heroes also did not see God or discover
his nature. Solomon, so blessed with wisdom, only found how far off Wisdom was from him. Neither David nor Paul could penetrate the judgments of God, let alone his essence. The inference is clear. How can later
Arians claim to know God's nature when the giants of the faith confessed
their inability to understand even God's judgments?

For 28.21.20 P, C, B and Q read σοφίαν rather than σοφίας. Although the first is the more difficult reading, the meaning is not measurably affected by choosing the second.

The *SC* editors refer βάθεσι, "depth," in 28.21.19 to 1 Cor. 2.10 and Rom. 11.33. There is no contextual relationship to the first passage.

28.22 Perhaps that inference should be enough, but the limitations on human knowledge can be supported from other sources as well, limitations introduced by at least one of these Biblical heroes. David sang about his own unfathomable nature. Surely people who insist that they can name and describe the nature of God should have no difficulty explaining human nature.

The questions Nazianzen raises are not meant to be answered. Their purpose is to uncover ignorance. They indicate a subtle mind that has given thought to human nature, one which has puzzled over these matters without breaking through to solutions. This foray into analogous areas does not involve the creation of large apologetic constructs that would justify the incomprehensibility of God. God's nature is not demonstrated to be unknown because our nature is incomprehensible. The argument is simpler and more powerful than that. If a person finds the obvious questions about human nature puzzling, a nature more open to our immediate investigation, it is odd that such a person would claim to have deep knowledge of a more complex nature.

Wyss (pp. 828 and 831) notices the similarities of the observations about nature in 22-30 to writings from Aristotle and the Stoics. Moreschini (p. 84, n. 132) finds echoes of the Stoics in this section, particularly in the talk about ears and voices (*SVF* I, 74 and II, 138-139). Sinko (pp. 13-17) has pointed out the common themes mentioned in sections 22-30 and the topics discussed in Cyril of Jerusalem *Catechetical Orations* (9). Although the outline Nazianzen follows is his own, both Christian works do share a concentration on Job and a concern for Arian opponents. General philosophical knowledge, Scripture and Christian tradition are woven together to present an unavoidable conclusion: humans know little about nature.

28.23 The same kinds of epistemological problems appear when one turns to explicating the nature of animals. In generic terms Gregory sketches the great variations among animals. How did such differences occur? To offer answers to his queries would be long and tedious, as he admits, yet these sections increase the force of his argument. First, they recall various Biblical passages that question human knowledge of nature. Gallay (p. 149, n. 2) points out the similarities between these observations and Job 38-40. Thus the Biblical basis of both the observations and the type of argument is apparent. God demanded such knowledge of Job before he would allow that human to question his judgments. Second, the point concerning *paideia* here takes yet another turn. How could anyone of sufficient education claim to know the nature of God when no one is able to explain the variations in the animal kingdom? Eminent researchers, such as Aristotle, had written extensively on animals, but had not fully explained all the differences among the species. The implication is again that only the arrogant and ignorant would claim to have arrived at such knowledge of God if similar knowledge of nature is unavailable.

After indicating his sense of Platonic epistemology in 21 and expanding that concern through a look at human nature in 22, Gregory further displays his rhetorical education and skill. One image is piled upon another probably to the delight of his audience. The more tedious logical arguments of the early paragraphs (1-10) fit the fashion for Constantinopolitan sermons with their "tortuous conundrums" (11), but they are "too labored," thereby forcing the restatement of the main principle and a "fresh start" (16-17). The rehearsal of views from Biblical heroes and their implications supports the primary point in a different way (18-22). Now Nazianzen meets the expectation of his hearers by a flight into rhetorical commonplaces. In these sections, mounting toward the confessional conclusion, the Theologian paints picture after picture drawn both from stock images and from obscure sources. The theme for 23-30 is unified: mortals do not understand the intricacy of nature; the presentation is also deft, perhaps even dazzling. The heavier argument has ceased; the light variations on a single theme begin.

28.24   A full investigation of the animal world would be tiresome, but Gregory knows how to display his learning. A knowledge of the natural world evidently was a standard part of any rhetorician's education. Illustrations such as these dot many ancient orations and were employed for different purposes. There is no certainty that Nazianzen had given careful attention to works like Aristotle's in order to have clear and colorful examples for his speeches, even though in Oration 31.10 he speaks of περὶ ζῴων ἱστορίας and περὶ τὰς τῶν ζῴων γενέσεις, nearly the titles of two works by the Stagirite: *The History of Animals* and *The Generation of Animals*. What he uses are commonplaces. He introduces marine life, specifically fish. Although they are enclosed in a medium dangerous to people and most mammals, they are suited for water because of their special and yet different characteristics.

Next Nazianzen discusses three types of birds. The τέττιξ, "cicada," is, perhaps for a modern reader, a strange example of a song bird. It evidently fits Gregory's categorization because it flies and sings. Homer spoke of them in the *Iliad* 3.151-152. Their sweet music is also a theme in Hesiod *Opera et Dies* 582 and *Scutum Herculis* 393, and in Simon Atheniensis 173-174. Being plentiful in Greece, their introduction here would have been pleasing to the audience. The swan appears not because of its voice, but because of the melodious hissing of its wings in flight. In both cases the question concerns the origin of the song. Thus Nazianzen leaves to the side the noises birds have been taught to make by imitating humans. The query concerns music untaught by trainers.

The examples of a peacock's lovely tail and a woman's skill at weaving indicate the tenuous logical grouping of these images with each other and with the previous concern for song. They are intended to evoke a more emotional response, but they do add strength to the main point of how little humans know about things found in nature.

Although the sense is not changed radically, it is best to include ἀποχωρήσεις καὶ, "roam in migration," as Wickham translates it, in 28.24.6. That follows B, W, T, S and C as Gallay (p. 150, l. 6) does. Mason (p. 58, l. 9) also included that reading.

28.25   If one understands all things in nature, what is the explanation of instinctive intelligence? Again the fine rhetorical flourish, laced with commonplaces, carries the hearer. Gregory chooses examples both from Greek oratory and Christian Scripture. By comparing nature's builders with humans of great technical and artistic skill, he pictures human limitations in yet another way.

Piled up images were weighty according to rhetorical canons, persuasive devices meant to drive home the point. People who do not know the source of instinctive knowledge in other creatures and cannot begin to duplicate the feats of birds, bees and spiders should not claim to know God's nature. Nazianzen is not disparaging human intelligence, for it not only forms part of humanity's claim to being in some way heavenly, but also serves as the instrument to make his case concerning human limitations.

His references to these men of science and art indicate his education, but more important they show his ability to call to mind the careers of generally accepted masters in order to strengthen his argument. Euclid, the geometrician, is often a painful memory for the modern reader. Palamedes, now viewed as legendary, but then as the historic companion of Agamemnon, was credited in certain accounts with inventing letters, chess, the discus and dice, as well as the various movements of armed phalanxes in battle. Zeuxis was noted for his employment of shading and smooth transition in colors used to depict the human body. Polygnotus may have been the first Greek painter of great reputation because his figures were not so rigidly postured and were transparently clad. Faces he painted looked more life-like; the way he grouped figures was often copied by other artists. Parrhasius' painting depicted the expressiveness of hu-

mans without shading; his figures were remembered for the flowing outlines in which they were captured. Aglaophon, also a painter, gained a
reputation for his use of color. He was said to be the father of Polygnotus
and was perhaps the first to depict Nike with wings.

Greek mythology saw Daedalus, the model artist, craftsman and inven-
tor, as the creator of much more than Gregory mentions. Carpentry tools,
superb metal work like the golden honeycomb in the temple of Aphrodite
on Eryx and the design of temples in many lands were attributed to him.
28.26 Gregory extends his exposition by turning to plant life. His Neo-
Arian opponents would have difficulty defining the nature of plants, how
they grow and offer such aid. Reason can recognize God's handiwork, no
mean feat, but it cannot offer explanations or identify causes.

Once more there are resonances with Job, both in the intent of the arguments and the specific examples. Job 38.4-7 speaks of the earth's foundation; the rest of the chapter mentions water in verses 16, 25-26, 28-30 and
34-38. These descriptions, however, could come from other authors or
personal observations. Gregory knew of hot springs and their healing
aspects.

28.27 The sea provides further proof of reason's weaknesses. Natural
philosophers are of no use because their ideas are far too small to contain
explanations of the massive sea. The κύαθος, "pint-pot," is a strong,
derisive image for at one time it was a small cup holding only about one-
twelfth of a pint. The cause behind the sea's great movement and yet its
obvious boundaries is given by Scripture, Job 26.10 (LXX) and Jer. 5.22:
God keeps it in place. Only the luxurious wealth and variety of God himself could have devised such a whole in which opposites work together:
rivers are always moving and seas go nowhere.

28.28 The sea, however, has limitations that the air does not. By turning to the air and beyond, Nazianzen can now let argument and reason
soar beyond themselves. As Moreschini (p. 91, n. 140) notes, Gregory
returns to a striking Platonic image, *Phaedrus* 248C, to describe this flight.
In mounting rhetorical power he also pulls together themes found in
almost any praise of God's creation within ancient Christian literature.
Resemblances to Cyril of Jerusalem's *Catechetical Orations* (9) and Basil's
Hexaemeron come easily to mind. Gallay (p. 162, n. 1) specifically mentions
Hexaemeron, homily 5, but again the bulk of the material comes from Scrip-
ture itself, particularly Job 26 and 38.

Finally Nazianzen states the principle that has informed this oration,
indeed, the entire series. It deserves attention because in some form it has
influenced much Christian theology. The phrase, Πίστις δὲ ἀγέτω πλέον
ἡμᾶς ἢ λόγος, "Faith rather than reason shall lead us," is similar to the
Latin *fides quaerens intellectum* associated with Anselm. Mason (p. 66, n. 17)

found its thought much like Augustine's *credo ut intelligam*, but there are also striking dissimilarities. The Theologian's position is not based on an understanding of human nature as depraved, its image of God destroyed. He neither promotes a weak conception of sin, nor undervalues the present powers of human reason.

The closer parallel for Nazianzen's approach is probably to be found in a much-studied section of Irenaeus (*Against All Heresies* 2.24-28). Schoedel ("Theological Method In Irenaeus," *JThS* NS 35 [1984], pp. 31-49) shows that Irenaeus assembled Jewish and pagan sources to argue for an unenclosed God, one whose nature was incomprehensible, by pointing out how little we know about things at our feet or before our eyes. Irenaeus particularly employed concepts from the Sceptics and from the medical studies of empiricists like Galen. With those references he claimed that we must accept revelation found in Scripture and let faith lead, for reason is befuddled at what it finds. Irenaeus' view, however, is not one which demands a God of the gaps; instead it forms a defense against Gnostic dualism and speculation.

Gregory's view is a much more nuanced one, if for no other reason than that he takes greater pains to develop the position. Like Irenaeus he uses widespread handbook knowledge of nature and then of human nature to make his case for our limited success in dealing with things close at hand. For him the balance between reason and faith is a delicate one. He confesses the priority of faith but is much concerned with the Eunomian misunderstanding of reason. Faith does lead, but it leads most effectively when the lessons about reason have been learned. In what seems to be a heightened sense of the paradox, the Theologian finds the most learned to be those led by faith. As an entire exercise these *Theological Orations* always represent a twofold argument with the later Arians. They have neither understood how faith leads, nor have they grasped the capability and limitations of reason. If one has carefully examined the inability of human intellect to grasp fully the essence of self and nature, then faith's confession of its inability to comprehend God's essence is not a leap into the abyss. But neither does Nazianzen's argument with the Eunomians represent a carefully-constructed apologetic program that puts faith in the background, only to be brought back when the intellectual task is completed. Faith informs the entire project. It is in this context that the insistent play upon the word λόγος finally reaches its goal. This sermon or discourse makes sense because it has reasonably investigated the limitations of human intellect. That should answer the charge of later Arians that Nazianzen and his group are foolish.

Gregory's position does not deny that one can learn of God by looking at nature. He has mentioned in various sections (13-16, 26-28) that observing nature leads one back to God; thus he does use a type of natural theology, but only on an *ad hoc* basis. He does not employ it as an over-arching apologetic that operates without faith. He seeks no neutral foundation for his program. The immediate focus is on the Eunomians' claim that in testing theological statements by means of their restatement in terms of formal syllogisms, they had reached an understanding of God's ultimate nature. In their view God had revealed the foundation in His name as "unbegotten," ἀγέννητος. With their power of logic, with their rules of inference, they could then make known even further intricacies of His nature. For the purpose of involving their audiences or readers they often presented those propositions in enthymematic form, that is, in the two-statement rather than the three-statement form of syllogisms, but they intended that those two statements could be made into syllogisms for the sake of demonstrating their positions.

Within that context Nazianzen attacks two points. First, no well-educated person claims the ability to know and express God's essence when that person cannot penetrate the essence of self and nature. When self and nature are not always subject to syllogistic demonstration, how could God's essence be subject to such testing? As Oration 20 makes clear, both Gregory and those in his community at the chapel Anastasia were being ridiculed as too provincial and backward to understand the arguments of the urbane later Arians. The Theologian's response is that the Eunomians themselves suffer from poor education. They claim knowledge of dialectic and its syllogisms, but do not understand philosophical rhetoric, particularly its importance for questions where logical certainty is not possible. They have no firm grasp of *paideia*. Secondly, Nazianzen faults their understanding of Christian tradition. This theme is always present, particularly in the selection and interpretation of Biblical passages. But in Orations 27 and 28, the major emphasis is on the first point, the lack of education among the Neo-Arians and thus their inability to understand the relationship of faith and reason.

The Biblical citation for 28.28.19-20 δεσμεύων ὕδωρ ἐν νεφέλαις, "binds up the water in the clouds," is Job 26.8 not 26.28 as the *SC* apparatus reads. The reference to Sir. 48.3 for 28.28.21 is either a misprint or a mistake. Mt. 5.45 as the reference for 28.28.30 is a parallel only in word, not in context.

28.29   Once the lesson of reason's limitations has been learned by examining its inability to understand things at our feet, once we have taken the measure of ourselves, then we can hope to ascend and approach the heavenly with a proper sense of humility. The phrase τὰ ἐν ποσὶν ἀγνοῶν, "ignorant of what lies at your feet," in contrast with the stars, represents an old Hellenistic proverb. Pliny (*Natural History* 18.252) had employed it. Plato (*Theaetetus* 174A) told the humorous story of Thales falling into a hole while looking at the sky. A bemused female slave found it odd that anyone so interested in the heavens should be so oblivious to what was at his feet and before his eyes. Van Unnik ("Theological Speculation and Its Limits," *Early Christian Literature and the Classical Intellectual Tradition: In Honorem Robert M. Grant*, "Théologie Historique, 54" [Paris, 1979] pp. 33-43) details how important that proverbial stance was to Irenaeus (*Against All Heresies* 2.28) in combatting Gnostic speculation. Here it holds the later Arians up to ridicule because they have neither grasped the content of the proverb nor known how often it is repeated in Hellenistic and Christian sources. Their claim to have mastered *paideia* is false.

Another principle, one rooted in education, is enunciated here. As Mason (p. 67, n. 8) points out, "there could hardly be a better description of inductive science." Wyss (p. 831) notes the similarity of Nazianzen's principle to Stoic teaching (*SVF* II, 83). Gregory concedes that his opponents know much about the world. They have learned what the science of that day taught inductively about various heavenly bodies, but unfortunately, observing orbits and making rules about them still does not explain the cause of those movements. Again the problem is that the later Arians, for all their claims to *paideia*, do not know the limitations of what we might call "inductive science."

28.30 In fact they do not even know their own Greek literature well since they seem to be unaware that Plato (*Republic* 508C) viewed the sun as having the same place in sensible things as God does in ideal things. If they had searched out the depths of *paideia*, even the wealth of their own limited educational tradition, they would have known their inability to explain the nature of the sun, the moon and the seasons. Although they continue to be unable to give clear descriptions of what makes the heavens move and hold together, they still feel confident in making their claims about God.

Homer (*Iliad* 18.239, *Odyssey* 31.7) and Hesiod (*Theogony* 9.56) both speak of the sun as ἀκάμαντος, "unflagging." Mason (p. 68, n. 14) notes that the use of φερέσβιος, "bringer of life," and φυσίζωος, "life-begetting," by poets as descriptive of the sun is unknown to him. Wyss (p. 855) suggests *Orph. lith.* 301f. as the source for the φερέσβιος image.

Eunomians have forgotten that it is poets, not logicians, who "speak reasoned truth not metaphor" when they hymn the sun. The inference, stated in section 31, reminds later Arians that only such poetic hymnody, such "reasoned truth," can be employed in speech about God. Internally consistent, but humanly bound syllogisms shatter when their subject is God. It is the philosophical rhetorician, not the logic-chopping rationalist, who most clearly sees the subject of theology and can express it. That rhetorician knows and loves the poets who can form enthymemes for probability arguments, but beyond that use words to evoke and inspire. The 17,000 verses written by the Theologian were meant not only to show that a Christian could master classical forms but also to illustrate that theology and poetry have much in common.

Gregory, in discussing the heavenly bodies, warns against astrology. This raises once more the possible popular malformations of later Arian doctrine. Nothing in the writings of Aetius or Eunomius suggests that they depended upon astrological schemes for their doctrine or practice, but most popular audiences in the ancient world would have included some who planned their lives according to the stars.

Kennedy ([1983] pp. 225-226) finds sections 22-30 to be a high point within Oration 28, perhaps within the series. Descriptions of the Father in terms of his creation here go well beyond any usual sense of the sophist's art.

The *SC* citation of Ps. 46.4 for 28.30.25 is a misprint for Ps. 147(146).4.

28.31   The subject of angels, their nature as incorporeal, as "wind" and "fire," taken from Ps. 104(103).3-4, allows Gregory to sum up his previous discussions. In paragraph 4 he mused about the knowledge of God's nature that incorporeal beings might possess. In section 7-11 he dealt with the incorporeality of God so that he could state his important principle in 12: no corporeal human can fully understand incorporeal divine nature.

The absurdity of the claim to know God's ultimate nature should now be apparent. Humans have great difficulty describing the heavenly bodies without breaking into poems and hymns. Only that type of language is appropriate for the vast number of incorporeal beings like angels. Therefore, one should neither demean hymns to the Trinity, nor use only logical propositions for speaking of God, Christ and the Holy Spirit. None should be surprised that humans are overwhelmed with their own inadequacies when they desire to speak of God.

The *SC* editors list John 20.11 as a reference for παρακύψωμεν, "bend our gaze," in 28.31.6 but the contexts offer no match. Much the same is true of the reference to Dan. 10.13 [LXX] for ἀρχαγγέλους, "archangels," in 28.31.16, Eph. 1.21 for δυνάμεις, "powers," in 28.31.18 and Heb. 1.14 for λειτουργούς, "ministers," in 28.31.26. Jud. 9 for ἀρχαγγέλους, "archangels," in 28.31.16 and Rev. 4.5 for νόας, "minds," in 28.31.18 have little or no connection.

In these first two orations of the series as printed in the *SC* edition, Gregory has laid a foundation for his arguments in the last three. The later Arians have demonstrated that they do not understand even the most elementary aspects of education. They show no knowledge concerning the first principles of rhetoric; only certain subjects before certain audiences at certain times from certain speakers are appropriate. In the first discourse Nazianzen also tests Neo-Arian advancement in contemplation and holy living and finds them wanting. Their grasp of *paideia* and the Christian life is faulty.

In the second oration he goes to great lengths to investigate their education from another perspective. Do they know enough about reason to have established its limitations? They claim to understand much, but they have neither been patient enough nor thorough enough to learn how little they understand about themselves, the world around them and second-level natures. No one can be wise who claims to know exactly the nature of the all-transcending essence of God and yet cannot explain creation in detail. No Christian should be trusted who asserts what Biblical heroes did not claim.

The situation Gregory faces makes him explicate his own approach more fully than he does in other orations. Here he must argue both παίδευσις and θεωρία. From a modern viewpoint, many would not be able to follow his *ad hoc* argument for the design of the world as a clear evidence of God's existence. He neither mentions the horrors of nature that question the wisdom or the compassion of a designer, nor does he seem to be aware of other attacks on that position. But his rejection of the *via negativa* as the one way to knowledge, his comments on the restricted character of inductive science, his valuation of poetry as carefully-reasoned language and his reasonable examination of human intellectual limitations make his case strong even for modern readers.

His basic approach also commends itself as viable for the modern era. He roots his position in the confession of his tradition and community: faith leads rather than reason. But in a series of *ad hoc* attacks, rather than a systematic explication and justification of a neutral foundation, he combats the later Arian claims that he and his congregation are uneducated and that their own reputation as gifted dialecticians is deserved. Gregory is not a crude fideist; neither is he a rigid systematician nor a foundational apologist. What he embodies is the *fides quaerens intellectum* stance of a Christian philosophical rhetorician, yet one that, unlike much theology in the West, does not disparage human intellect with a doctrine of original sin and near total depravity. His position uses finely-honed intellect to grasp the limits of human understanding without trusting that intellect to create a foundation for faith. That is an impressive model for any age.

COMMENTARY ON ORATION 29

The titles on the manuscripts cited in the SC edition are nearly the same. In most instances this oration is designated as Περὶ Υἱοῦ λόγος α', "On the Son, Oration One" although twice it is also referred to as Βιβλίον Β', "Volume Two," and once Βιβλίον δεύτερον, "Second Volume." The various sequences of the five orations within the manuscript tradition suggest that this was the first discourse on the Son, since in a number of manuscripts it precedes Oration 30. Its listing as Βιβλίον Β' or Βιβλίον δεύτερον represents two variations: manuscripts S and P, in which Oration 28 follows Oration 31, and manuscript C, in which Oration 28 is not included. In both sequences Oration 29 is the second oration within the series.

29.1   In the Introduction (pp. 76-78) I have discussed the positions of Sinko (pp. 11-12 and 20-21) and Bernardi (pp. 182-185), who argue that the opening sentences of this oration refer to Oration 27. They may both be correct that this discourse was clumsily edited, but nothing in its second sentence demands that it originally followed Oration 27 rather than Oration 28. The first two statements of 29.1 have censorial aspects. Without the first sentence the opening section makes sense and contains no necessary reference to anything preceding. The observation about the ease of attacking another's position and the difficulty of establishing one's own is a commonplace that occurs as early as Demosthenes (*Olynth.* 1.7). Gregory promises to reverse the process by first giving reasons for his view and then arguing against those of his antagonists, but he does not follow that plan in any detailed way. He only states his position in section 2 and then attacks the later Arian doctrines in 3-16.

The comment about the Holy Spirit suggests topics that will be taken up specifically in Oration 31. The prior sentence stated the Theologian's summary of disagreements with his detractors. Supporting one's view in such debates requires a person both religious and intelligent, ἀνδρὸς εὐσεβοῦς καὶ νοῦν ἔχοντος. Thus the conflict with the Eunomians continues to be focused on the relationship of faith and reason, on piety and *paideia*. That theme lies just under the surface of this entire oration and is mentioned again in section 21.

Nazianzen's opponents had evidently circulated a type of elementary or "introductory treatise," λόγον εἰσαγωγικόν, that met the needs of the less educated, though Gregory found it deceptive. Gallay (p. 178, n.1) thinks first of the *Thalia* of Arius, a piece that was poetic and probably effective. Philostorgius (*H.E.* 2.2), the Neo-Arian historian, noted that

Arius had written poetry "for the mill, the sea, and the road" and then had set it to music. Vaggione (p. 16) makes the attractive suggestion that section 28 of Eunomius' *Apology*, which is a separate work, fits this description. It is an introductory summary. The Theologian's rebuke of Eunomians for arguing in salons and on street corners (27.2) indicates that they had success in popularizing their ideas. Nazianzen may be referring to other specific works which circulated among such popular audiences; his phrasing of later Arian positions might recall them. Some of the statements are similar to Eunomian fragments that Vaggione includes in his edition. Since we have Aetius' technical *Syntagmation* and Eunomius' more discursive apologies, we know later Arianism appealed to different types of audiences. The Theologian recognizes he has much to accomplish if he is to refute their efforts. Some of his own theological poetry reaches out to a wider public through a pleasing medium. In these orations he undertakes the task of arguing enthymematically before a general audience. Part of the audience has been educated in the nature of dialectic, knows its connection with rhetoric and thus sees that the orations demonstrate the learning of the speaker. Within that group both friend and foe will be more concerned with the logical moves. Another part of the audience, however, has not been educated in such matters and thus will be more susceptible to the massing of pictures and the appeals to popular "orthodox" piety, whether or not such attempts prove to be ultimately convincing.

29.2 The discussion of anarchy, polyarchy and monarchy or as Wickham translates them: "atheism, polytheism and monotheism," calls to mind the full context of Hellenistic religions. As in 28.13-15 Gregory is ever aware that wrangling within Christendom weakens faith and gives paganism the victory by default. But he also emphasizes an agreement, found among the groups claiming to be Christians, that monarchy or monotheism is the basic principle.

The description of that monotheism, however, points up disagreements. For Gregory that monarchy is not limited to or circumscribed by one person. Unity can exist when there is "equality of nature, harmony of will, identity of action, and the convergence towards their source of what springs from unity," φύσεως ὁμοτιμία συνίστησι, καὶ γνώμης σύμπνοια, καὶ ταὐτότης κινήσεως, καὶ πρὸς τὸ ἓν τῶν ἐξ αὐτοῦ σύννευσις. Although this is impossible for created nature, within the Godhead there can be "numerical distinction" without "division in being," ἀριθμῷ διαφέρῃ, τῇ γε οὐσίᾳ μὴ τέμνεσθαι. Nazianzen assumes the Eunomians are troubled by the lack of unity in a Trinitarian conception that holds the Son to be equal in some significant way to the Father. They are concerned that a plurality of gods results, one which represents a return to polyarchy or polytheism. Eunomius (*Apology* 25) insists that the Spirit be counted as a third, i.e., as occupying a third rank. For him that position is true to Scripture and implies the avoidance of polytheism.

The recent work of Gregg and Groh has rightly emphasized soteriology in early Arianism. Their thesis also suggests, less convincingly, that concern for monotheism was not an important feature of Arius' theology as most secondary works have argued. Here Gregory indicates that his Neo-Arian opponents have difficulty with a monotheism described in Trinitarian terms. According to him the Eunomians see μοναρχία, "monotheism," as limited to the one πρόσωπον, "person." If he is representing them fairly—he is usually trustworthy—monotheism is a concern of later Arians.

Gregory also seeks to defend the oneness. In his view, however, many problems can be avoided if Christians will limit themselves to Christian terms and thus speak of the Son as begotten, the Father as unbegotten and the Spirit as proceeding. The construction of syllogisms that bring the oneness of God and the unbegotten Father, the begotten Son and the proceeding Spirit into conflict is for Nazianzen a major error.

Nazianzen discusses select phrases from philosophy that he views as appropriate and inappropriate. The proper talk about the original monad moving into a dyad and finally a triad, μονὰς ἀπ' ἀρχῆς, εἰς δυάδα κινηθεῖσα, μέχρι τριάδος ἔστη, is probably an echo of Plotinus, as Moreschini ("Il platonismo cristiano di Gregoria Nazianzeno," *Annali della Scuola Normale Superiore di Pisa*, Ser. III, IV.4 [1974], pp. 1390-1391) indicates. Plato (*Timaeus* 41d) has often been cited as the source for the improper phrase "overflowing of goodness," ὑπέρχυσιν ἀγαθότητος. But Whittaker ("Proclus, Procopius, Psellus and the Scholia on Gregory Nazianzen," *VC* 29, [1975] p. 309) sees in this passage an indirect quotation of Plotinus' *Enneads* 5.2. Rist ("Basil's Neoplatonism," *Basil of Caesarea: Christian, Humanist, Ascetic* [Toronto, 1981], pp. 215-216) agrees but also notes that the title cited by Nazianzen, περὶ πρώτου αἰτίου καὶ δευτέρου, "On Primary and Secondary Causation," is not the title given to Plotinus' work in Porphyry's edition. Rist suggests that Gregory had access at least to the 5.2 section of the *Enneads*, perhaps more. Wyss (pp. 833-834) finds evidence of 5.1 and 1.6 in the full corpus of Nazianzen.

The significant phrase is οἷον κρατήρ τις ὑπερρύη, "as though a bowl had overflowed." Barbel (p. 130, n. 9-10) surmises that the reference may be to an unknown Neo-Platonist since there is no exact correspondence to known Neo-Platonic texts. Whittaker (pp. 309-313) notices how often commentators on Gregory speculated about the source of the κρατήρ τις, which is not part of the Plotinian passage. More specifically he shows how they treated the lines just prior to the indirect quotation. Some referred back to what they knew from the writings of Proclus. Perhaps Nazianzen depended upon some Neo-Platonist unknown to us, one upon whom Proclus also relied. But the most likely source is still Plotinus.

A, Q, B, V, C and a hand correcting W read γενητῆς rather than γεννητῆς for 29.2.11. Although there is often confusion about these forms, here the reading of W, T, S, P and D is preferred. According to Gallay (Intro., p. 22) S, P, D and C have the consistently better readings. Thus in this case the weightier evidence supports γεννητῆς. Context, however, demands that Gregory was arguing against the later Arian position of a γενητὴ φύσις, a "created nature," in the sense that the Son's nature as the begotten one makes him the first of the creatures. If γεννητῆς is the reading preferred, it offers some evidence that Nazianzen did not distinguish carefully between the meanings of the two words, for here he intends "created" even if he might have employed γεννητῆς. Further investigation of the manuscript tradition may change the data. See a similar example in 28.18.19.

29.3 In his translation Wickham wisely marks the various questions that Nazianzen employs as dialogical foils. They may come from his opponents and often can be identified as later Arian even though Gregory nowhere in this oration calls them Eunomian. Barbel (p. 128, n. 1) suggests Eunomius himself as the subject, but Eunomius (*Apology* 10 and 16) argues against referring to chronological or bodily aspects in any discussion of God's nature. The immediate adversaries are probably those popularizers who were responsible for the elementary treatise (29.1) and who were carrying on discussions in salons, on street corners, in market places, in nearly any inappropriate place (27.2). Yet the basic arguments of this oration also may apply to Aetius or Eunomius rather than only to the popularizers of later Arianism. These subtle leaders do not employ the older Arian formula, ἦν ὅτε οὐκ ἦν, "there was when he was not," with a chronological referent. In Nazianzen's view, however, they still make the category mistake of employing language out of context.

According to Gregory in 28.4, they miss what even Plato or the writer of Hermetic literature had understood: God's nature cannot be expressed in human language. In that passage Nazianzen criticized the Hermetic writer for failing to recognize that God's nature cannot be conceived by limited human intellect. The later Arians continue to raise questions in which the words used are cemented in the context of creation and thus are bonded to the wrong meanings. The issue is the understanding of language, particularly the point that meaning is determined by context. In section 6 Gregory refers to the previous arguments raised by his opponents, 3-5, as concerned with one problem: Τοῦτο μὲν δὴ τοιοῦτον, "So much for that objection."

The examples concern time and involve the old Arian formula, ἦν ὅτε οὐκ ἦν, "there was when he was not." Gregory attacks the connotation of chronology by demonstrating that words and phrases such as "when," "before," "after," and "from the beginning" are all time-bound. Even the attempt to go beyond time, to suggest that there is a "supra-temporal" realm, τὸ ὑπὲρ χρόνον, creates difficulties if the explanation refers back to time for its bearings. Perhaps Nazianzen is aware that his opponents, particularly Aetius (*Syntagmation* Intro.), had attacked the supporters of Nicaea as "chronists," χρονῖται, as those obsessed by "time." For Gregory expressions that originate in contexts dominated by "time" cannot be put into a context "before time" and still be used to speak of priority. If Father and Son "transcend time," ὑπὲρ τὸ πότε ταῦτα, they transcend categories of priority even when those categories apparently have been stripped of their chronological references.

This discussion shows a resemblance to the approach of twentieth-century linguistic analysts. The similarity rests in the understanding of meaning based in context. That likeness itself comes from the grammatical training rhetoricians received not only at the secondary, but also at the highest levels of study. Much of Nazianzen's argument with the Eunomians concerns the differences in their conceptions of language and context. Yet the resemblance to modern linguistic analysis must not be allowed to create deceptions. For Gregory theology is not a language game judged only by its internal coherence rather than its relationship to reality as generally perceived. In his view even though "being unoriginate," ἄναρχος, demands "being eternal," ἀΐδιος, it is not necessarily the case that "being eternal" necessitates "being unoriginate." Usually cause precedes effect, but not always. The sun and its light are simultaneous. For the Theologian an analogy from creation shows how the relationship between Father, Son and Holy Spirit might operate. As he noted in 28.30 even a pagan writer (Plato) understood that God is to the immaterial world as the sun is to material world. In fact, most of the arguments in Oration 28 use analogies from the created world to illustrate the limitations of human intellect.

Yet the similarity to twentieth-century arguments can act as an aid to understanding the disagreements between Nazianzen and his opponents. In his *Apology* 12 and 16-19, Eunomius details his view of language. The main point rests on the relationship of names and essences, "by the distinction in names manifesting the difference of essence," ταῖς τῶν ὀνομάτων διαφοραῖς καὶ τὴν τῆς οὐσίας παραλλαγὴν ἐμφαίνοντας. Aetius (*Syntagmation* 16) emphasizes the same basic position, one that probably finds its most striking exposition in Plato's *Cratylus*.

In spite of his careful arguments against the Eunomian theory of language, the Theologian here introduces a problem that will plague his understanding of the Trinity: δῆλον δὲ τὸ αἴτιον οὐ πάντως πρεσβύτερον τῶν ὧν ἐστιν αἴτιον· οὐδὲ γὰρ τοῦ φωτὸς ἥλιος, "But clearly a cause is not necessarily prior to its effects—the Sun is not prior to its light.'' Gregory provides both a principle and a model he thinks will allow him to designate the Father as the cause without requiring priority over the Son. Meijering (*God Being History: Studies in Patristic Philosophy* [Amsterdam, 1975] pp. 111-113, especially n. 43) indicates that in 30.1 and 31.23 and 33, however, Nazianzen insists nothing is the cause of God since such a cause would be superior to God. The Theologian uses arbitrary definitions of αἰτία, "cause," and οὐσία, "being" in order to fit the needs of his arguments. Meyendorff (*Byzantine Theology*, 2nd. rev. ed. [New York, 1983], p. 183) notes that much Eastern theology depends upon Nazianzen's distinction in its defense of monotheism, but Meijering appears to have the stronger argument against the loose philosophical case. Gregory's problem is actually a Scriptural one. In 31.14 he speaks of the Godhead, not the Father as the primal cause. Yet because Scripture, especially the Gospel of John, speaks of the Father as God, the Theologian keeps the tension intact.

The *SC* editors suggest Heb. 1.2 as a reference for 29.3.20-21, but there is neither similar word usage nor a matched context.

29.4   The disagreement about language applies to the question about begetting. In Gregory's view begetting is subject to change and thus implies less than full divine status for the Son only if it is bodily. For him bodily begetting recalls pagan mythologies. He had dealt with the problem of corporeality in Oration 28.7-9. Although the sophisticated teachers of later Arianism reject such crudities—Eunomius (*Apology* 12 and 16) scoffs at those who think of a body when they discuss God—perhaps the Constantinopolitan popularizers drew such inferences. Anthropomorphists in Egypt and Palestine did attribute bodily aspects to God during the 390s. In any case the later Arian leaders find γέννησις, "begetting," to involve ἐμπαθής, "passion," even when bodily conceptions are excluded. Aetius' *Syntagmation* is a philosophical presentation of the unequivocal and essential differences between "unbegotten" and "begotten." Eunomius (*Apology* 9) warns that if God is essentially "unbegotten," then he "could never undergo a generation which involved the sharing of his own distinctive nature with the offspring of that generation," οὐκ ἄν ποτε πρόσοιτο γένεσιν ὥστε τῆς ἰδίας μεταδοῦναι τῷ γεννωμένῳ φύσεως. For such a position would entail διαίρεσις, "division," μερισμός, "separation," and even ἀφθαρσία, "corruption." All those concepts are blasphemous when applied to God.

Nazianzen's question, "how can he be God, if he is a creature?," πῶς Θεός, εἰ κτίσμα; must be properly understood. On the basis of Prov. 8 and Acts 2, Eunomius (*Apology* 12, 15, 17-18) calls the Son a ποίημα, a "thing made," and speaks of him as "having been created," κτισθείς, or as a "creature," κτίσμα. In his *Confession* 3, he refers to the Son as οὐκ ἄκτιστον, "not uncreated," and thus as a created being. Another Eunomian confession, which is not from Eunomius himself but is included in his *Apology* as section 28, calls the Son a κτίσμα, a "creature." That confession insists that the Son is also οὐχ ὡς ἓν τῶν κτισμάτων, "not like any other creature," a view similar to Eunomius's claim (*Apology* 15) that the essence of the only begotten is not like that of the things made out of nothing. As both Aetius (*Syntagmation* 4) and Eunomius (*Apology* 11 and 21) taught, the nature of the Son is not like that of the Father. His essence is certainly not equal to the Father's essence. Nevertheless, the Son is not a creature like all other creatures; for the later Arians the Son is no mere man. Eunomius (*Apology* 21) claims that in his teaching about the Son he does not remove the "Godhead of the Only-begotten," οὐ γὰρ ἐπ' ἀναιρέσει τῆς τοῦ μονογενοῦς θεότητος. He and his party "confess that the Lord Jesus is himself 'Only-begotten God,'" μονογενῆ μὲν γὰρ ὁμολογοῦμεν θεὸν καὶ τὸν κύριον ἡμῶν Ἰησοῦν. Therefore Gregory's question, if addressed to the skillful teachers of later Arianism, lacks sophistication. Perhaps popularizers in Constantinople were claiming that the Son was not divine in any sense and thus was never to be called God. In either case Nazianzen's quarrel with Eunomius concerns the type of Godhead, the kind of divinity Jesus was confessed to be.

The Theologian's *reductio ad absurdum* argument might please his supporters, but as a logical argument it fails. Yet even if the question and the absurd inferences were rejected by his opponents, the Eunomian category mistake that formed the basis of disagreement remains. In Gregory's view, the later Arian community continues to speak of God in terms dominated by human attributes. Their discussions do not take into account the way in which all words ascribed to God must be cleared of their human associations.

29.5   The debate over context is also involved in the discussion of fatherhood. Eunomian conundrums similar to those mentioned here are found in Cyril of Alexandria's *Thesaurus* 5 (*PG* 75, 57B-C and 60D; Vaggione, p. 180). For Nazianzen, it is clear that every human father was first a son. Each was born from a pair of parents, developed and then became a father. God's fatherhood is different. The human context of the word "father" does not apply when the word is used of him. To demand that having-begotten and having-been-begotten must involve a beginning is to fall back into the problem of context and grammar once more. No verb tense in Scripture is to be taken out of context, for examples abound where the meaning of tense-form is changed by context.

The countercharge to which Gregory alludes again concerns the educational level of the Eunomians. Their objections are "labored." They do not understand what "scholars," φιλόπονοι, have established about tense usage. Similar points reappear in Oration 30 where Nazianzen deals not so much with his opponents' general philosophical and logical deficiencies as with their specific exegesis of Scripture.

Interestingly each party in this dispute refers to the other as those who misunderstand time. The Theologian calls his antagonists φιλοχρόνοι, ones who have a "penchant for time," while Aetius (*Syntagmation* Intro.) names his opponents οἱ χρονῖται, "the Temporists." That problem continued from the older Arian debate. The formula ἦν ὅτε οὐκ ἦν, "there was when he was not"—which Gregory in section 3 asserted was wrong—meant "before time began" for early and certainly later Arians. Eunomius (*Apology* 10) notes that time had to do with the stars and thus not with the Unbegotten or other intelligent beings. In much of his argument, however, it is difficult to tell whether the begetting of the Son is in or out of time. Perhaps at a popular level, the arena which also concerns Gregory, such subtle distinctions were lost. As he indicates in section 3, words with a time referent: "when," "before," and "after," confuse the debate.

29.6 Nazianzen turns to a conundrum about will and voluntary acts, one raised by his opponents and alluded to in paragraph 2. Similar puzzles appear in Cyril's *Thesaurus* 7 (*PG* 75, 96C, 97B and 100A; Vaggione, pp. 180-181). If the Father begat the Son involuntarily, then he must have been in someone's power. If voluntarily, then the Son is of the will and not of the Father. This particular phrasing of the issue is not found in either Aetius or Eunomius, but the latter (*Apology* 12 and 23-24) does state that the Son was begotten by the will of the Father, the second position in the conundrum.

The gamesmanship involved is clear. Gregory first attacks the conundrum by derisively employing yet another *reductio ad absurdum*. If the Son is begotten voluntarily, then the will must be some kind of mother who takes the place of the Father. He applauds his antagonists' inclusion of will in the process since that at least involves intentionality rather than passivity, but he offers two counter-positions about the Father and the Son. If the terms are applied in the same way either to the questioner's physical father or to the creator God, they destroy natural fatherhood and the God of creation. His opponents would not admit the loss of either.

The puzzle succumbs to reason when the grammar is unpacked. "The participles refer to a subject of motion; the nouns designate the motion itself," τὰ μὲν ὁ κινούμενος, τὰ δὲ οἷον ἡ κίνησις. Characteristics belong to the subject, not to the act of the subject.

Mathieu ("Étude critique," *RHPhR* 40 [1981], p. 276) notices that Nazianzen employs οὐ πάντως in the phrase οὐδὲ γὰρ ἔπεται πάντως with the sense of "it is not universally true." Wickham translates the phrase "it is not a necessary concomitant of it." That sense of οὐ πάντως appears in Stoic logic and thus indicates again how Gregory's education in logic was rather extensive and not limited to Aristotle alone.

29.7 In the Theologian's view, the best way to point out the absurdity of the voluntary / involuntary conundrum is to apply it to areas where its results will threaten positions held by his opponents. Thus he expands his comment concerning God and His creation by turning attention to whether or not the Father is God voluntarily or involuntarily.

He adds a special twist by introducing the query πότε, "when." Much as the later Arians claim, any question about "when" that focuses on the Father being God must deal with a subject before the creation of time. But even at that stage the word "when" creates problems of priority, ones which are inappropriate to a discussion of God. Other possibilities either inject division within God or posit some other God. If the conundrum wreaks such havoc in a discussion of God the Father, why should it be invoked in debates about the relationship of the Father and the Son?

When his antagonists shift ground by asking πῶς, "how," the Father begat the Son, they are trapped in similar problems. The response (cf. Eunomius *Apology* 12 and 23-24) that the Son is begotten by the will of the Father fails because humans do not effect things by will or by reason. The opponents' apparent claim that begetting occurred by the will **and** the reason of God seems to be new, for neither Aetius nor Eunomius in any extant writings employ the Father's λόγος, his "reason," as an answer to how the Son was begotten.

29.8 If Oration 28 was delivered as the second in the series, then sections 6-7 of this speech follow its argumentation and section 8 restates its primary position (cf. 28.4). The incomprehensibility of God's nature can be defended by pointing out the deficiencies in human knowledge about things closer at hand. Denying to God something which we have not understood about ourselves is ridiculous; indeed, some things we grasp about our nature may not be applicable to God. The principle stated in this way allows Nazianzen to shield himself from the charge he makes against his antagonists. He does not compare humanity and divinity as if they were members of the same class. Rather he attacks the level of knowledge later Arians possess. If they do not understand some aspect of their own nature, how can they rightly claim to understand an aspect of God's nature that appears similar but in fact is not?

A relationship to Oration 28.8-10 and 13 also appears in the demand that his opponents "drop the habit of treating the incorporeal nature as if it were a body," τὸ ὡς περὶ σώματος διανοεῖσθαι τῆς ἀσωμάτου φύσεως. The leaders of later Arianism would not accept this description of their positions. They know that the incorporeal is not embodied. But it is odd how often they ascribe attributes to divinity that are more appropriate for an entity with a body, particularly in their conundrums. Popular positions taken by Neo-Arians might have fallen headlong into the corporeal trap.

Approaching God's innermost nature in silence and Biblical confession is fundamental to Gregory. Gallay (p. 193, n. 2) indicates that this same theme of silence is treated in Oration 20.11. It can also be found in 28.4 and 20. Scriptural praise appears in 28.19.

The *SC* editors refer 29.8.28-30 first to Mt. 11.27 and Luke 10.22 and then to Ex. 14.20 and Mt. 17.5. The first set has no connection either through exact wording or context. The second does match some words, but the contexts are unrelated.

29.9 Nazianzen's main principles, nestled in section 8, still must be applied to other conundrums raised by his antagonists. The dilemma, whether the Son existed or not when he was begotten, is another category mistake. It might be relevant to human existence, but even humans are in one way present before conception and in another way existent only at conception or birth. Since the Son exists from eternity, no point of beginning can be posited before eternity. Any such suggestion would nullify the definition of eternity and perhaps even present problems of being and non-being for the Father.

Once again this formulation of the issue does not appear either in the extant writings of Aetius or Eunomius. Aetius (*Syntagmation* 10) comes close to arguing that the Son did not exist when the Father begat him, but both the form and the substance of his presentation is different. The force of his point comes from what he sees as an absurdity: "it is impossible for begotten nature to exist in unbegotten essence," γεννητὴν γὰρ φύσιν ἐν ἀγεννήτῳ οὐσίᾳ οὐκ ἐνδέχεται εἶναι. Eunomius (*Apology* 12-15) also supports only one side of this conundrum. For him the Son did not exist before He was begotten.

What Gregory attacks directly is neither the position the Neo-Arians defend nor their method of argument. Instead he concentrates on the form of the puzzle, the assumption that in each case one of the alternatives must be true. For him the later Arians of Constantinople show their lack of *paideia* by not investigating their logical conundrums with sufficient thoroughness. Some classical problems in logic do not fit the form of their argument. The three examples he uses: whether or not time itself is in time, the liar's paradox and whether one is present to oneself, all offer alternatives that are both false. On the basis of those examples, he claims, however, that one should not be surprised if a puzzle includes two true statements.

Thus, for Nazianzen, Aristotle's law of the excluded middle is not a universal logical principle. When two contradictories are juxtaposed, both could be true or false, not just one true and the other false. Stoic logic was noted for its concerns with these paradoxes, but whether Gregory had studied that school's teachings in great detail is unclear. He represents the liar's paradox in a way Chrysippus probably opposed (cf. Diogenes Laertius, *Lives of Eminent Philosophers* 7.196-197). Yet Wyss (p. 831) notes that *SVF* II, 280-282 are similar to Nazianzen's position.

The main issue, however, is clear. The Theologian faults Eunomian logical acuity both in its popular and "learned" forms. He disagrees with Sozomen's assessment (*H.E.* 3.15 and 6.26) that Aetius was a skillful logician. He certainly finds a Neo-Arian "introductory treatise" (section 1) to be wanting. His attack on the *paideia* of later Arians, begun in Oration 27 and generally grounded in Oration 28, is here supported by a closer look at the logic behind their conundrums.

There is another flaw, from Gregory's perspective, in the Eunomian puzzles. Temporality is injected into discussions of the Trinity, discussions that should involve only eternity. As noted elsewhere, the problem of time sequence within the relationships of the Trinity appears to be at least one area in which the later Arians and Gregory thoroughly misunderstood each other. Both Aetius (*Syntagmation* 27) and Eunomius (*Apology* 20) think that "cause," αἰτία, demanded the priority of the Father. Gregory agrees as he states in 29.2 and 10, although he tends to speak of the "inoriginate," ἄναρχον, rather than the "uncaused." But for him such priority does not demand different essences.

29.10 Eunomius (*Apology* 20-21) claims that the Father and the Son are different because one is "ingenerate," ἀγέννητος, and the other "generate," γεννητός, but he insists that the "only-begotten," μονογενής, Son is "divine," θεότης. Thus one later Arian denies Gregory's conclusion. Nazianzen's poorly nuanced response, however, does have a point. Even in Eunomius' formulation, the divinity of the Son is not the same as that of the Father. Gregory of Nyssa (*Against Eunomius* 1.15, Jaeger 1.79) explicitly argues this position in response to Eunomius' *Apology for the Apology*: "Anything that does not properly exist is the same as anything unreal," πᾶν γὰρ τὸ μὴ κυρίως ὂν ἐν ῥήματι μόνῳ.

The same type of problem is involved with the Theologian's concession that "what has no origin and what is created cannot be identical in nature," οὐ γὰρ ταὐτὸν τῇ φύσει τὸ ἄναρχον καὶ τὸ κτιζόμενον. Eunomius (*Apology* 15) claims that the Son has been created, but that he is not a creation like those things created out of nothing. The Eunomian confession, not from Eunomius himself but included as section 28 of his *Apology*, makes basically the same point. Nazianzen probably accepted Basil's contention (*Against Eunomius* 2.20) that Prov. 8 should not be used to support the position that the Son is a "creature," κτίσμα. Basil refused to admit Prov. 8.22 as the definitive description of the Son because the statement is made only once in Scripture, it appears in a book that is often obscure and some of the Hebrew texts do not read "he created," but "he begat." Unfortunately Gregory's careless concession that something created is not of the same nature as something inoriginate, already mentioned in section 4, only complicates the issue since he does not mention or interpret Prov. 8.22.

When Nazianzen uses the similarity of nature between parents and offspring as an argument for the sameness of essence between the Father and the Son, he is again misguided. Basil (*Against Eunomius* 2.32) employed it against Eunomius; thus it is an older statement in the debate, but it remains unconvincing. When Gregory consistently attacks the later Arians for invoking human and time-bound analogies and then invokes such analogies to support his own position, he refutes his own attacks on the Eunomians. His argument, however, is an interesting one because it relies not on an enthymeme that can be turned into a formal syllogism, but an enthymeme that requires inductive rather than deductive method for its verification. Fathers and children can be said to have the same nature because anyone looking at the evidence would have to concede that. To contradict the claim one would need to provide counter examples from the world rather than an analysis of the argument's structure. The enthymeme is composed of two statements and deals with a probability that must be argued inductively. It is not an enthymeme that can be supported syllogistically.

Nazianzen's rejection of "ingenerate," ἀγέννητος, as definitive of God's nature also reflects Basil's *Against Eunomius* 1.15, but it is a better formed argument. For Gregory, the Eunomians offer no convincing reasons why ἀγέννητος names God's "nature," φύσις, rather than being only one of a series of properties like "immortality, purity, and immutability," τὸ ἀθάνατον, καὶ τὸ ἄκακον, καὶ τὸ ἀναλλοίωτον. Obviously they are not all different essences, for then God would be "composite," σύνθετος, a characteristic no one in the debate would admit.

This section, following the persuasive demonstration of later Arian misuse of logic in 9, fails. Only one of the four major arguments is well formed, while the others concede points that would please the opponents. Yet as much as any other section in this oration, this one evidences the frustrating problems that marked the disagreements. The goal of avoiding long discussions and complicated presentation also may have affected this paragraph.

Gallay reads καινέ, "new," rather than κενέ, "empty-headed," in 29.10.7, taking the evidence of B, V, T and P over that of A, Q, W, S, D and C. That seems odd since he (p. 22) claims that S, D, P and C form the more reliable family of manuscripts. His choice might be on the basis of sense. Eunomius (*Apology* 15) claims that his views are from the saints who spoke of old, πάλαι. Each party in the dispute avoids presenting its claims as new. Thus to address an opponent as ὦ καινὲ θεολόγε would sting. But the immediate sense of the passage: "make your choice of the alternative blasphemies," ἑλοῦ τοίνυν τῶν ἀσεβειῶν ὁποτέραν βούλει, suggests that κενὲ is the better reading. The "empty-headed" selection of "alternative blasphemies" is what the context demands. Since most of the better witnesses support that reading, it should be accepted.

In 29.10.12-13 Q, B, W, V and T omit γεννήτορος καὶ, making the sentence read, "it is in the nature of an offspring." The better witnesses have the fuller reading, which Wickham translated, "it is in the nature of an offspring to have a nature identical to the parent's." That seems preferable according both to sense and to manuscript evidence.

29.11 The later Arians reject "immortality, purity and immutability" as descriptive of God's essence because those properties are found in other beings, but the Platonic tradition claims that "matter," ὕλη, and "form," ἰδέα, are also "ingenerate," ἀγέννητος. There is no general agreement that ingeneracy is a property of God alone.

Adam's creation by God, his coming into existence without parents, did not exclude him from the human race. The example apparently supports Nazianzen's argument about the begotten Son, but it is weak at two points. First, the parallel between Adam and the rest of mankind best fits an argument that the Son was like the rest of creation. Second, the illustration is an analogy from human nature about divinity, the type of analogy Gregory rebukes when his opponents employ it. Yet it is also interesting since it is another example of an enthymeme that defies syllogistic formulation. It relies on the Biblical story of creation rather than the definition of terms or the argument's structure. Again the Theologian is directly concerned with a type of induction rather than deduction, a probability argument rather than a demonstrative one. Basil (*Against Eunomius* 1.15) argued that "unbegotten" or "ingenerate," ἀγέννητος, was not descriptive of God's nature. Gregory, in order to fit the point with his analogy of Adam, insists "unbegotten" only means God has no parent. That tends to correct the parallelism and bring the connection between Adam and mankind to the fore.

Nazianzen's debate over the use of human analogies could be sharpened in this section, but he does employ his arguments in an *ad hoc* rather than in a systematic way. They are meant to assist one in thinking about the unthinkable. When they are introduced, they do not function as limits on God's being, but only as models for better understanding. Gregory's approach is not basically apologetic or foundational, but confessional. In Oration 28 and again in section 8 of this oration, he warns of using knowledge about ourselves as definitive of God, but emphasizes the absurdity of claiming to know God in ways we do not know ourselves.

Nazianzen, as in Orations 27 and 28, confesses that being "begotten" is "no lesser thing for the Son," οὐκ ἔλαττον τῷ Υἱῷ, than being "unbegotten" is a "high thing for the Father," μέγα τῷ Πατρί. We humans do not understand this fully because of our present condition. Only the purified, only those who have passed beyond this life, will be able to think properly about the begetting of the Son.

What the Theologian sees as his antagonists' stunted spirituality represents a major issue. When Gregory recalls these features, he offers no aside; on the contrary, he states his basic commitment and approach. The different orders in the manuscripts for these *Theological Orations* suggest that Gregory himself might not have included Oration 28 in the series and put it in the published order. It is also possible that an editor thought it was out of place and deleted it, or an editor found it pertinent and put it in. A number of different sequences occur in the manuscript tradition that further complicate the problem of discerning what the original order may have been. But without the educational and contemplative setting of Oration 27 and the argument concerning human ignorance and divine incomprehensibility in 28, the specific points of Orations 29-31 lack introduction and context. The statements concerning spirituality in this section indicate the significance of that theme and the integration of the entire argument in these orations.

In 29.11.25 Gallay reads χαμαιπετέσι, "earthbound," with A, Q, B, W, V, T and S against χαμαιερπέσι in D, C and the correctors of S, and against χαμερπέσι of P. The difference in meaning is slight. Lampe (p. 1512) uses this instance as evidence for Nazianzen employing the word, but also notes that χαμαιρ(ρ)ιφής appears in Gregory's poetry (*Carmen* I.2.32.141). Both the Maurists (*PG* 36, 89A) and Mason (p. 90, l. 4) support Gallay.

In the *SC* edition 29.11.17-18 is referred first to 1 John 3.2 and 1 Cor. 13.12, then to John 1.5 and finally to Wis. 9.15. There is no contextual relationship and seldom even a similar word.

29.12 The conundrum raised by his opponents is similar to that which appears in Cyril of Alexandria's *Thesaurus* 10 (*PG* 75, 132B-C; Vaggione, p. 183).

The disagreement of the parties over the meaning of "unbegotten" is the theme of this section. For later Arians, it describes God's "essence," οὐσία. For Gregory and his followers, it describes a "personal characteristic," ἰδιότης, something outside the essence. The logically weak aside about being one's father's father might have had some rhetorical effect. The basic structure of the sections, however, is twofold.

First, if "ingenerate" and "God" are to be interchangeable then both these terms must be either "relative," τις, or "absolute," μηδείς. "God" is a relative term and "ingenerate" is an absolute one; thus they cannot be used synonymously. As Mason (p. 91, n. 1) indicates, the Greek usage of "god" as a relative term created a problem for the absoluteness of God. Was he God before there was a creation to which he could be related? The philosophical question is forceful, but Nazianzen's grammatical point is sound. Within logical systems, terms are interchangeable only if they are of the same type. Relative and absolute terms are not.

Second, "since conditions are prior to privations, and privations take away condition," ἢ ἐπειδὴ πάλιν αἱ ἕξεις τῶν στερήσεων πρότεραι, καὶ ἀναιρετικαὶ τῶν ἕξεων αἱ στερήσεις, from Gregory's vantage point the later Arians are in the difficult position of claiming that in some way the essence of the Son, "begotten," is prior to that of the Father, "unbegotten," and is also in the process of being destroyed. The conclusion is an obvious absurdity meant to ridicule his opponents. The logical principle seems to be adapted from Aristotle (*Categories* 12A). This is yet another difficulty the Eunomians have created by choosing an alpha-privative as the name of God's essence. Eunomius, however, (*Apology* 8 and *Apology for the Apology* 1.9-10, Jaeger 1.391 and 399; Vaggione, p. 114) refuses "privation," στέρησις, as descriptive of God being "unbegotten," ἀγέννητος. His immediate support for "unbegotten" has its weaknesses, since here he only asserts that the impious alone would think God is deprived of anything. That does not explain why an alpha-privative is the name of God's nature. But as Mortley (II, esp. pp. 130-139) shows, a much more technical, philosophical development lies underneath Eunomius' remarks. Dexippus (*CAG* IV.2, p. 44), Syrianus (*CAG* IV, p. 61) and Alexander of Aphrodisias (*CAG* I, p. 327)—and later Proclus (*Platonic Theology* 2.5)—distinguish privation and negation. The famous Aristotelian example of blindness, which presupposes the state of sight before its existence, is the position Nazianzen accepts. There is, however, a second understanding in which negation can be predicated of states or things that are indefinite. For Dexippus such negation defines the "truest essence of a thing." This forms the backdrop against which Eunomius makes his claim. To say God is ἀγέννητος is not to introduce a privation, but to use a negative in order to reach the truest nature of the indefinite or infinite being referred to in the discussion. Nothing exists before God; he is "ingenerate" or "unbegotten." The alpha-privative defines the absolute priority of God. In some ways this might be seen as an ultimate foundation for a *via negativa*, a way to knowledge of God that interestingly Gregory had rejected in *Or.* 28.9. Distinguishing between "unbegotten" as a term for negation rather than privation would not have impressed him.

Mortley (II, pp. 141-142), who does not discuss Nazianzen, is probably correct that Basil missed this technical point, because Basil (*Against Eunomius* 1.9) primarily attacks Eunomius for using Aristotle's *Categories* rather than Scripture. Mortley is also correct that Nyssa raises the issue of privation being the loss of a previous attribute. But he struggles to discover who might have made that argument in such a way that Eunomius himself (*Apology for the Apology* i.9, Jaeger 1.391; Vaggione, p. 114) rails against those who say God is unbegotten through privation so that God has lost something.

Obviously Nazianzen has made that claim here in a *reductio ad absurdum* attack on the Eunomian use of the term. If it is true, as Mortley (II, p. 140) claims, that Aristotle never says in the *Categories* that privations are secondary, then we must still search for the commentators on Aristotle or other philosophers who would have made such claims and thus influenced Nazianzen. Although Gregory's purpose is ridicule, he has connected privation with priority in a way that reverses the position Eunomius took. The alpha-privative is secondary; if it is applied to a doctrine of God, it would make the Son, "begotten," prior to the Father, "unbegotten," and in danger of perishing. The church historian Socrates (*H.E.* 2.35) provides some assistance in searching for the philosophical tradition behind this gibe. He suggests that Aetius misconstrued Aristotle's *Categories* because he did not understand its intent. In Socrates' view Aetius did not know the Ephectic interpretation of Plato and Plotinus which would reveal the sophisms of the *Categories* and thus explain how generation could occur without beginning and the begotten be co-eternal with the unbegotten. If such an Ephectic tradition within Scepticism as Diogenes Laertius (9.70) describes was still available in the fourth century C.E., then Nyssa and Nazianzen are not to be seen as philosophical hacks when they follow an interpretation different from that of Eunomius. For them explanations of the relationship between begotten and unbegotten and perhaps the secondary priority of privations had been argued within a philosophical tradition that they accepted even if only at a handbook level. It is probably part of the contemporary debate as Mortley (II, pp. 131ff.) hints when he attempts to describe it. The view of Nyssa and Nazianzen is a different reading of Aristotle's *Categories*, but not necessarily a particularly uninformed one.

With these two arguments Nazianzen has once more leveled his attack against the grammatical and logical acuity of his adversaries. They employ language and logic without understanding the difficulties inherent in those subjects. For him their confused positions are rooted in their lack of *paideia*.

Mathieu ("Étude critique," *RHPhR* 40 [1981], p. 276) notes that lines

29.12.12 and 17-18 reflect knowledge of Aristotle's *Topics* 106A-107B, 113B-114A, 124A-125B and 151B-153A as well as his *Categories* 3B. That increases the evidence of Gregory's dependence upon Aristotle.

For 29.12.17 Gallay reads εἰσαχθῆναι with A, Q, B, W, V, T and S against ἀντεισαχθῆναι supported by D, P, C and the corrector of S. The meaning is not changed by either reading; both have the sense of "have been brought in." Probably ἀντεισαχθῆναι is to be rejected since ἀντίκειται appears in line 16 and ἀντικειμένας directly after the reading in question. Those forms may have influenced copyists. Both the Maurists (*PG* 36, 89B) and Mason (p. 91, l. 8) support Gallay's reading.

29.13   The argument: "unless God has ceased to beget, the begetting must be unfinished and at some time stop; but if it has stopped, it must have started," εἰ μὲν οὐ πέπαυται τοῦ γεννᾶν ὁ Θεός, ἀτελὴς ἡ γέννησις, καὶ πότε παύσεται; εἰ πέπαυται δέ, πάντως καὶ ἤρξατο, occurs in a slightly different form in Eunomius' *Apology for the Apology* 2.15 (Jaeger 2.224; Vaggione, p. 122) and in Cyril of Alexandria's *Thesaurus* 5 and 10 (*PG* 75, 60D, 69C-D, and 129A; Vaggione, pp. 180-181 and 183).

The importance of Biblical exegesis in these debates shows itself here. The Theologian is not certain what Prov. 8.25 means and thus wants to be especially careful in answering whether begetting has stopped and at some point started. With that qualification, the issue becomes whether or not the Eunomian argument depends upon logical necessity. The principle, they argue, relates beginning and end. "What is going to stop must have started, what is not going to stop cannot have started," εἰ γὰρ ἦρκται . . . τὸ παυσόμενον, οὐκ ἦρκται πάντως τὸ μὴ παυσόμενον. Gregory, however, insists that there are examples that do not fit those conditions.

E. Hardy, (*The Christology of the Later Fathers* [Philadelphia, 1954], p. 169) and Barbel (p. 151) take the οὐκ in οὐκ ἄρα ἦρκται κατ' αὐτοὺς τὸ παυσόμενον to mean "not true" while Mason (p. 92, n. 12) reads it as "never [have had a] beginning." Wickham's translation, "**Their** argument then, that something which is going to end requires a beginning is untrue," fits the previous phrase, "what is going to stop must have started."

In positive rebuttal, Nazianzen introduces yet another aspect of his own position. Names are often used of species. All individuals that can lay claim to the species classification deserve the name. Therefore, if it can be demonstrated by argument and witnesses that the Son belongs in that species, then he should be given the name. For the ultimate truth is to be found in "facts," πράγμασιν, and not in "names," ὀνόμασιν.

Here Gregory states some principles basic to his disagreements with the Eunomians. He has a much different theory of the relationship of language and reality from the one they employ. He shares his view with Basil (*Against Eunomius* 2.4): reality is prior and language follows. Classifications of facts, or states of affairs, πράγματα, are fundamental. The position is somewhat similar to that of Epicurus (*Letter to Herodotus* 37 and 75) in which the things that underlie a word are what constitutes its meaning, but in the end Epicurus defended a natural meaning of names. Nazianzen's view follows Aristotle (*On Interpretation* 16A-B) who sees names established by convention, by arbitrary designation alone. The later Arians depend upon an opposite view, that names determine essence, a view found in Philo (*Leg. All.* 2.14-15), Plato (*Cratylus* 430A-431E), Albinus (*Epit.* 6), Epicurus (*Letter to Herodotus* 75-76) and Chrysippus (*SVF* II, 895) and shared by early Christian writers like Clement of Alexandria (*Stromata* 1.143) and Origen (*Exhortation to Martyrdom* 6).

Nazianzen's further reliance on Aristotle is also clear. The species / individuality distinction is one the Stagirite often employed within his studies of nature. Gallay (pp. 204-205, n. 1) also indicates that the word ὁμώνυμον, which so often means "homonym," here reflects its usage as "equivocation" in Aristotle (*Categories* 1A). Fundamentally different presuppositions have made the exchange between the Eunomians and Gregory difficult. Nazianzen views his opponents as both illogical and unfaithful. His sense of reality as well as his understanding of Christian doctrine is offended by their claims. According to his judgment, if an individual deserves inclusion within a species, then it should not be given the name of the species in an equivocal fashion. The "facts," πράγματα, will determine that judgment. When they are known, the name follows. Similar views on the relationship of reality and language are found in Oration 31.24.

29.14   In the extant works of Aetius and Eunomius, there is no reference to the argument about the use of the word "dog" for a dog or a dogshark, but that analogy, perhaps brought forward by the later Arians at Constantinople, is the topic of discussion in this section. No "facts" about a dog or a dogshark demonstrate that one deserves the name "dog" more than the other. "Things of the same and things of differing status can have the same name," ἐν ὁμοτίμοις πράγμασι καὶ διαφόροις ἡ κοινωνία τῆς κλήσεως. One is no less a dog than the other, when one remembers that the reality is not in the name.

The analogy contradicts the Eunomian position if they remember their own principle about language—here unstated, but present early on in the debate (Eunomius, *Apology* 12 and Basil, *Against Eunomius* 2.4): names designate natures. If the dog and the dogshark are called "dog," and if the reality is in the name, then they have a parity of nature. To placard their position for the general public, Neo-Arians should use the analogy of a picture and a real man. It emphasizes disparity. Nazianzen points up their illogical position by employing once more the term ὁμωνυμία in Aristotle's sense from *Categories* 1A, "equivocation," or as Wickham translates it, "ambiguous names."

Gregory is quick to see that there is a deeper difference than the philosophical questions. The argument here is not entirely about *paideia*, but fundamentally about worship. In Nazianzen's view refusing adoration to the Son is blasphemous; he must not be given second place in reverence. That is the central nerve of the controversy for the Theologian, but the complexity of the situation arises once more. Eunomius does not refuse worship or reverence to the Son. In his *Confession* 2-4, he uses the same formula for belief, πιστεύομεν εἰς, "we believe in," to introduce his position of God, the Son and the Spirit. He also insists that the Son, although receiving a derivative glory, is "glorified throughout eternity by the Spirit and every rational and begotten essence," δοξαζόμενον ὑπὸ τοῦ πνεύματος δι' αἰῶνος καὶ πάσης λογικῆς καὶ γεννητῆς οὐσίας. In his *Apology* 21 he says he has no intention of taking away the "Godhead," θεότην, of the Only-begotten. Later Arians were a worshipping community that honored the Son, as the *Apostolic Constitutions* indicate (Kopecek, "Neo-Arian Religion: The Evidence of the *Apostolic Constitutions*," in Gregg, pp. 158-179).

The most interesting comment in this paragraph is Nazianzen's ascription of the word "similar," ὅμοιον, to his opponents' vocabulary. Aetius (*Syntagmation* 4) flatly rejected the use of ὁμοιούσιος, "of similar essence," as well as ὁμοούσιος, "of same essence," for the Son. Eunomius (*Apology* 21-22) denies that those words or their derivatives could be used of the Son as his antagonists employed it, but in section 24 he speaks of "similarities," ὁμοιότητα, between the Son and the Father based not on "essence," οὐσία, but on "activity," ἐνέργεια, or "will," βούλησις. Thus it is a mistake to refer to either Eunomius or perhaps these Constantinopolitan Eunomians as Anomoeans without careful qualification. Gregory of Nyssa (*Against Eunomius* 1.6 and 18, Jaeger 1.37 and 90) employs that epithet of the school, but the position taken by Eunomius, and evidently by his followers, must be treated fairly and not crudely caricatured. The leaders of later Arianism confessed a similarity between Father and Son, but not a similarity in essence.

29.15 Aetius (*Syntagmation* 27-28) had argued for a relationship of "cause," αἰτία, and "essence," οὐσία, similar to the argument raised here by Nazianzen's opponents, expressed in terms of "cause" and "nature," φύσις.

The logical duel continues with the introduction of another principle from Aristotle's *Categories*, again 1A. Gregory does not deny that there are some ways in which the Father is superior to the Son. The issue, however, is whether or not an individual can belong to a species or a class only if it shares all the characteristics of every member of that species or class. Aristotle found that to be a false conclusion. Members of a class, individuals in a species, do have particular characteristics that are not shared by all within the group. Thus, conceding some differences in particulars does not demand that the individuals in the species be reclassified.

Another way to state the principle, also found in Aristotle's *Categories* 1A, is to see the fallacy as arguing from the particular to the general, from a conditioned to an unconditioned use of a term. The formal syllogism, which lies behind the opponents' enthymeme, can lead to strange conclusions if the rules for avoiding fallacies are not applied. Following their sense of things, we could say that if one man is dead, humankind is dead. In Nazianzen's view this is the kind of stupidity which the later Arian syllogisms involve. They have not learned their logic.

29.16 The final logical dilemma could be constructed from Eunomius (*Apology* 23) where he argues that the essence of God is unbegotten and that of the Son is begotten. Thus the Son must be an "activity," ἐνέργεια, of God's will.

This conundrum is again set in the form of two exclusive alternatives that are designed to be unacceptable to Gregory and his party. In section 9 Nazianzen had warned that a form with two alternatives, which supposedly exhausted the possibilities and were contradictory, could not be trusted. Here he proposes a third alternative, but also argues that the two posed by his opponents are neither contradictory nor destructive of his position if either one is conceded.

The use of σχέσις, "relationship," within Trinitarian teaching does not first appear in the works of Gregory. *The Dialogue on the Trinity* 1.25—a treatise often attributed to Athanasius but probably written by Didymus the Blind—spoke of such a relationship between the Father and the Son. The Theologian may have been taught by Didymus while he was studying in Alexandria. Here σχέσις offers an option not employed earlier in these *Theological Orations*. It provides a strong alternative to the dilemma of "essence," οὐσία, or "activity," ἐνέργεια.

Although Nazianzen can accept either part of the original dilemma, he finds the use of ἐνέργεια as descriptive of the Son or of God's begetting of the Son to be "decidedly odd," ἄτοπος. His basic approach to *paideia*, however, allows him to accept even that. All these terms can be explained "if we follow common sense and the meaning of the terms," κατὰ τὰς κοινὰς ἐννοίας, καὶ τὴν τῶν κλήσεων τούτων δύναμιν. Proper thought and correct grammar, reality as seen from the facts and meaning drawn from context, will permit these puzzles to be solved.

Having occupied himself from section 3 through 16 with the logical puzzles of his antagonists, Gregory now suggests they turn to Scriptural texts—a play on λογισμός and λόγια. Since his opponents have not been persuasive in their use of logic perhaps they can win the argument if they concentrate on the words of Scripture.

29.17 In staccato fashion Nazianzen points out Biblical phrases that form the basis of his position. The words are taken from throughout the Old and New Testaments with a concentration on the Gospel of John. They reflect Athanasius' refutation of Arius and Basil's attack on Eunomius. Gregory views the "Son's Godhead," τοῦ Υἱοῦ τὴν θεότητα, as the same as that of the Father—in section 16 he spoke of it as ὁμοούσιος. Thus he would not accept the claim of Eunomius (*Apology* 21) that the "Godhead of the Only-begotten," τῆς τοῦ μονογενοῦς θεότητος, was left intact in Eunomian teaching. He agrees with Gregory of Nyssa (*Against Eunomius* 1.15, Jaeger 1.79) that a less than equal Godhead is in fact not real Godhead. If the Son did not exist properly with the Father from the beginning, then he did not exist and thus is not God as the Father is God.

The logical formula—"perfection does not result from addition," Οὐ γὰρ ἐκ προσθήκης τὸ τέλειον—implies yet again that his opponents have misunderstood the principles involved in these arguments. No divine being, whether Son, Spirit, or Father reaches perfection through added traits. In reference to the Son, the subject of this section, perhaps we see here a hint of the προκοπή doctrine, the "advancement" theme of early Arianism, that was founded particularly upon Luke 2.52 (cf. especially Gregg and Groh for the importance of this view in early Arianism). Gregg ("Cyril of Jerusalem and the Arians," *Arianism: Historical and Theological Reassessments* [Cambridge, MA, 1985] pp. 85-109) has shown that Cyril of Jerusalem's *Catechetical Orations* are a rich source for specific arguments that formed part of the structure for early Arian doctrine, particularly the teaching concerning προκοπή, "advancement," in the life of Christ. Προκοπή is not part of the teachings represented in the extant works of Aetius and seldom appears in the writings of Eunomius. When Eunomius speaks of it, he explicitly rejects it (*Apology for the Apology* 3.4, Jaeger 2.116). Yet some popularized forms of later Arianism in Constantinople might have used it. The play on the form of the early Arian saying, ἦν ὅτε οὐκ ἦν, "there was when he was not," is picked up from section 3 and restated in terms of the Scriptural passages alluded to in the first part of this paragraph.

With these Biblical texts Gregory reminds his audience that part of the disagreement with later Arianism concerns the handling of Scripture. It is not that he and his party treat Scripture and the Eunomians do not. To make the better case, a group must be able to handle all the texts. Nazianzen argues that the later Arians ignore Biblical descriptions of the Son's equal Godhead.

29.18 He also refutes the interpretation of Biblical passages they find fundamental for their views. In the same staccato style he lists their passages, some of which he will carefully investigate in Oration 30, but his major attack on the later Arians is here twofold. First, he contends that a proper hermeneutic, one that goes beyond the letter and operates with appropriate reverence, can indicate the true interpretation of each passage. The nature of that hermeneutic has already been seen in this oration. It investigates the definition of each word in context and the grammatical relationships of the words. Thus it is not without concern for the literal text. In many ways it is the structure and content of rhetorical education that provided these principles of interpretation. And yet the content is confessional, set within the house of faith. The Son is God. For Gregory no logic can properly attack that position.

Second, Nazianzen offers a Christological principle from which he can make sense of these two groups of passages. The loftier references should be attributed to the Godhead, the divine Sonship, and the lowlier to the compounded condition that resulted from the incarnation when the divine Son was made man. Such a distinction allows the list of verses in section 17 to apply to the nature of the Son within the Godhead and the list in 18 to apply to the human condition which he assumed.

This principle does specify that a full humanity with will and intellect was assumed. Other confessions, which appear earlier in the corpus (*Ors.* 2.23; 22.13; 38.13), and the later famous correspondence concerning the Apollinarians (esp. *Ep.* 101) indicate that, in Gregory's view, the Son had to assume body and soul to save mankind. This soteriological principle dictates the Christology. Here the intended subject appears to be the Son. In his pure essence within the Godhead, the lofty titles apply to him. The lowlier titles and predicates may be applied to that same Son as long as the needs of οἰκονομίας, "salvation," are understood. For those reasons he was emptied and made man. The position taken is much like that of Athanasius, one which will be expressed later by Cyril of Alexandria, but in Gregory's case, the emphasis upon the soul of Christ—found in Origen—keeps him from finally accepting an Apollinarian Christological solution.

These statements will not satisfy Nazianzen's adversaries. For them it is precisely the condition of being "compounded," σύνθετος, that proved the Son's Godhead to be less than the Father's. For Eunomius (*Apology* 14 and 19) the unbegotten God could not be "compounded," σύνθετον, because he is "uncompounded," ἀσύνθετον.

The *SC* Biblical references to Isa. 49.3 and 5 for δοῦλον, "servant" in 29.18.4;

to John 15.15 for ἔμαθε, "he learned," in 29.18.5 and to John 9.4 for ἀπέσταλται, "he was sent," in the same line; to Mark 14.33 for τὸ ἀγωνιᾶν, τὸ ὑποδύεσθαι, "was in agony, was subject to things," in 29.18.11 and to Mark 15.39 for ἀνθρωπισθέντι, "was made man," in 27.18.25 have no contextual connection and in some instances not even any similar word usage.

29.19 Having finished the dense argumentation based on his education in philosophical rhetoric with its concern for logic, contextual definition of words and grammatical relationships, and having stated his Christological principle for Scriptural exegesis, Gregory now reveals his rhetorical skill and confessional sensitivity. The apparent contradictions between the Son's nature and God's economy are enfolded in moving, poetic expressions. For the next two sections the Theologian bursts forth in hymns confessing the apparent paradoxes as one might in the midst of worship. It is fascinating that his most pronounced logical treatise should include these phrases. He emphasized the need to operate at a particular level for a specific audience in Oration 27. His arguments in Oration 28 were broadly based in order to persuade his hearers of human limitations and divine incomprehensibility. In this oration, however, he senses that confessional rhetoric is as appropriate as logical analysis. For him the logical conflict provides the context for these confessional paradoxes.

The form has rhetorical balance, sometimes of phrases, but usually of clauses or sentences. The emphasis in this section is on the divinity of the Son, since his opponents are primarily concerned with that issue. Yet in most if not all cases, what is said here is similar to such confessions in Orations 2 and 38 as well as the theological epistles 101, 102 and 202, which are focused on the Apollinarians and thus on the humanity of Jesus. Ridicule is also a part of the tone, because he finds the later Arians to be blasphemous about the nature of the Son. Their own salvation is in jeopardy if, as they claim, the Son is not of the same essence as the Father.

Soteriological concerns dictate the structure and contents of sections 19 and 20. Man and God became one in the Son, with the divinity being dominant so that humans could become God as much as he became man. Θέωσις, "divinization," is fundamental for Nazianzen's view of God's economy. The mystery of faith is that the "uncompounded," ἀσύνθετος, became man, or as Gregory said in paragraph 18, became "compounded," σύνθετος. The cause behind this mystery was salvation itself. For Gregory the purpose of incarnation, the reason God became man, was "in order that I might be made God to the same extent that he was made man," ἵνα γένωμαι τοσοῦτον Θεός, ὅσον ἐκεῖνος ἄνθρωπος. As best we can tell from the fragmentary evidence, the θέωσις theme played little or no part in later Arian theology. For them salvation did not come to humans in order that they might become gods. As Eunomius (*Apology* 7, 11, 15, 17 and 24) indicates, a gulf exists not only between the unbegotten

God and the begotten Son, but also between the created Son and the rest of creation. It can be properly inferred that for the later Arians, talk of mortal humans becoming "God to the same extent that he [the Son] was made man" well might be unintelligible.

The hermeneutical principle, employed by Gregory, would also be nonsense to a Eunomian. "Why do you take offense at what you see, instead of attending to its spiritual significance?" Πῶς σὺ προσπταίεις τῷ βλεπομένῳ, μὴ σκοπῶν τὸ νοούμενον; The rhetorical balance, which Nazianzen employs, also forms the bulwark of his faith, because God offers a "mystery," μυσταγωγέω, beyond our fullest comprehension. Statements of faith must balance the apparently contradictory; they must confess the paradoxical.

Such talk appears illogical to his antagonists, but for him it is the basic level at which truth can be discovered. That level is not dependent upon sophistic rhetoric, because it has an appropriate logical structure or analogue. Philosophical rhetoric is spelled out in Orations 27 and 28 and is employed in sections 1-16 of this oration as the basis for an attack on later Arian misuse of logic. Yet Nazianzen's position also relies upon a penetration into the greatest realities through the highest levels of contemplation. He warns the later Arians about what is at stake if they cannot confess the humanity and the divinity of Jesus Christ. For him the central issues of the gospel stand in peril; salvation itself could be lost.

In 29.19.16 Gallay reads ἐτέθη with A, S, D and C against ἀνεκλίθη supported by Q, B, W, V, T, P and the corrector of S. The text of Luke 2.7 is ἀνέκλινεν αὐτὸν ἐν φάτνῃ. Thus ἐτέθη is the more difficult and preferred reading.

There is no connection between 29.19.20 and Ex. 14.27 as the *SC* notes suggest. The Biblical citation for 29.19.22 should be Ps. 45(44).2(3), not 43.3 as the SC reference has it.

29.20   Midway through section 19 Nazianzen shifted from contrasts that listed first the divine Son and then the Son as the subject of what he assumed; he returns to that form throughout this paragraph in order to make one point: "If the first set of expressions starts you going astray, the second set takes your error away," Εἰ ταῦτα ἐμποιεῖ σοι τῆς πλάνης τὴν ἀφορμήν, ἐκεῖνά σου λύει τὴν πλάνην. In each case the salvific effect of the incarnation is predicated on the necessity of the Son being fully God. His weaknesses are attributed to the human condition he assumed.

Because Nazianzen develops thematically the dominance of Jesus Christ's divinity, there are times when the humanity is not given its due. Perhaps Jesus' baptism was to hallow the water, but if his victory over human tests was due to his divinity, then something crucial in the humanity is lost. Gregory, sounding much like Athanasius, does not state specifical-

ly in this confession that Jesus' human intellect struggled and submitted
to the will of God. Yet during the debates with the Apollinarians he relies
upon a doctrine of free will assumed within a full humanity. In fact, the
soteriological basis is cryptically involved in section 19 of this oration,
"what he was not he assumed," ὃ δὲ οὐκ ἦν, προσέλαβεν and can be
found as early as Oration 2.24 and then elsewhere. Origen's soteriological
formula, (*Dialogue with Heracleides* 7) "The whole man would not be saved
if the whole man were not assumed," Οὐκ ἂν δὲ ὅλος ἄνθρωπος ἐσώθη,
εἰ μὴ ὅλον τὸν ἄνθρωπον ἀνειλήφει, lies just beneath the surface.

   The point of this section, however, is that the doublets should provide
the principle through which the Eunomians may grasp the truth. If the
references to Jesus' humanity might lead them to think of him as nothing
more than a secondary divinity, then the references to his divinity should
change that view. If both sets of Biblical passages are accepted as descriptive, then he must be seen as both God and man in one. From Gregory's
vantage point, only this perspective with its incumbent acceptance of mysterious union can do justice to both lists of Scripture verses.

   We may assume, however, that Nazianzen's presentation did not persuade his opponents. Starting with a conception of divinity as permanent-
ly unbegotten, unchanging, incapable of begetting from its essence an
equal essence, the Eunomians would find Gregory's views of incarnation
and salvation to be nonsense.

The SC reference to Mt. 29.31 for 29.20.10-11 should be Mt. 14.25-32. John
18.37 indicates Pilate called Jesus a king; a similar thought but none of its words
appear in the clause of 29.20.11-12 that Jesus "is emperor over those who demand the tax." Isa. 53.4 as a reference for 29.20.26 is a misprint for Isa. 53.5.
Wis. 8.16 for 29.20.31-32 and Heb. 9.24 and 1 Pet. 3.22 for 29.20.38, although
they have some similar words, are not related contextually to the meaning of
Gregory's text.

29.21 Nazianzen feels pressed to respond more thoroughly to the logical
fallacies of his opponents, but his basic interest is in a proper balance between faith and reason. This section represents an elegant statement of the
principle of faith seeking understanding. Human intellect cannot encom-
pass the Godhead. As he argued at length in Oration 28, reason is too
small an instrument for that task. Yet no charge of careless fideism can
be brought against Gregory. He demonstrated reasonably for a fourth-
century author that the limitations of human intellect must be recognized
apart from its inability to handle theological issues. The human mind has
not fathomed the nature of the world or the essence of humanity. Furthermore, in spite of his own occasional mistakes within this oration, he has
shown the poor education of his antagonists. They do not have a grasp of
the logical principles employed in the most learned circles. They neither

handle Aristotle well, nor know the various positions that different schools had taken on the great logical puzzles even though they well may represent some interesting developments in a particular school (Mortley II, esp. pp. 130-139). As Nazianzen says elsewhere (28.28) the deficiencies of human intelligence appear in its inability to handle many problems, not just those of theology. If that be true, any group that claims to know the essence of God does not understand the critical weaknesses of humanity.

The Theologian, nevertheless, does not argue the deficiency of human intellect on the basis of reason in such a way that logical arguments will become the court of appeal for theology—without any concern for faith. Gregory avoids setting up a neutral foundation in order to validate belief. "Faith, in fact, is what gives fullness to our reasoning," ἡ γὰρ πίστις τοῦ καθ' ἡμᾶς λόγου πλήρωσις. The examples from nature and humanity are not intended to provide a foundation on which an apologetic or a polemic will be built. These points are *ad hoc* illustrations. They are meant to be persuasive, but they are not set out as a basis for reason systematically to justify faith. He prays that the opponents will be changed by God from τεχνολόγοι, "logic-choppers," to πίστοι, "believers."

1 Cor. 5.20, printed as a Biblical reference for 29.21.20, should be 2 Cor 5.20. Acts 24.16 for 29.21.25 shows only a one-word similarity rather than any contextual connection.

Oration 29 gives the clearest evidence of Nazianzen's education in logic. He has a command of dialectic that is too often overlooked. Although his attacks on the later Arians do not all hit the mark, he is repeatedly on target. Time after time he demonstrates that his education in philosophical rhetoric prepared him to deal with logical fallacies as well as contextual, grammatical mistakes. His case against the Eunomian lack of education is well taken. They narrowly defined the realm of logic, much more closely than Aristotle or the Stoics would have done, and then misused its principles. Furthermore they often misconstrued problems that could be solved on the reasonable basis of grammar and context.

The greatest weakness of Gregory's position is his attempt to provide analogies from human life. He does not make his *ad hoc* method clear as he will in Oration 31. Hints persist that what applies to humans may not apply to God, but then he rather flatly injects the analogy of parents and children to insist on the sameness of nature for the Father and the Son. To make that move, he should have been much more perspicacious. Groundwork for the difference between his use of human analogies and those of his antagonists is called for, but not supplied. His rejection of an overarching apologetic or a basic foundationalism should have been clarified.

Perhaps the greatest strength is again his delicate sense of the relationship between faith and reason. Once more he insists on confession and worship as the milieu. "Faith gives fullness to reasoning." Although he is prepared and does argue with his detractors about the nature of reason and logic, pointing out their misunderstanding of basic *paideia*, he demands the priority of faith. His flights of rhetoric transform maddening paradoxes into essential ellipses. He insists upon "both / and" rather than "either / or" formulae. He knows the limits of reason and avoids any project that would make reason the court of appeal in which faith must argue. The delicacy of his struggle with the Eunomians is only seen in this light. He must argue that their sense of logic, grammar and word usage in context is incorrect, but he must not argue that case as if faith can only make its appeal in the court of such technical considerations. Thus he breaks off his logical arguments and mounts the wings of confessional theology so that his approach will not be misconstrued.

His logical case and moving confessions are not without difficulty, but it is also not difficult to see how one major tradition of Christian faith honors this man as "the Theologian."

The manuscripts used for the SC edition usually title this piece "the second discourse on the Son," Περὶ Υἱοῦ λόγος Β' or something similar. As in the cases of Orations 28 and 31, manuscript P says this oration was given in Constantinople. But since P dates from 941 its comment is too far removed from the events to settle any questions of where and when the oration was first given.

30.1 Gregory begins with a reference to the two parts of Oration 29. For most of that discourse he pointed out the problems later Arians had with logic, the difficulties inherent in their conundrums, but he also offered in sections 17-20 a general refutation of their views by noting the Scriptural passages they relied upon and those his group found basic. Here he restates his interpretive, Christological principle of "allocating the more elevated, the more distinctly divine expressions of Scripture to the Godhead, the humbler and more human to the New Adam, God passible for our sake over against sin," τὰς μὲν ὑψηλοτέρας καὶ θεοπρεπεστέρας φωνὰς προσνείμαντες τῇ θεότητι, τὰς δὲ ταπεινοτέρας καὶ ἀνθρωπικωτέρας τῷ νέῳ δι' ἡμᾶς Ἀδὰμ καὶ Θεῷ παθητῷ κατὰ τῆς ἁμαρτίας.

According to this principle, the first group of texts concerns the essence of God and the second deals with the economic or salvific conditions that the divine Son took on for us. The major tenets of this Christology are similar to those of Athanasius. In each instance the Theologian emphasizes the unity of the subject. The new Adam is God made passible for us, not a human subject who fought the battle and won. The phrase Θεὸς παθητὸς κατὰ τῆς ἁμαρτίας, "God passible for our sake over against sin," is bold, but is similar to Gregory's poetic and confessional language elsewhere (*Ors.* 5.27; 45.19, 22 and 28). For him it is the suffering of God that gives full value to Jesus' death.

Kopecek (p. 502) has suggested that the ten points might come from a later Arian catena. That is possible, but this paragraph gives the suggestion little support. First, the Theologian says that he has grouped the explanations of Biblical verses into these numbered sections so that they can be more easily remembered. Second, the Scriptural passages mentioned in 29.17-20 are not the same as those stated here. Thus it is unlikely that Nazianzen is drawing on some specific source for the arrangement of these points. He does, however, treat verses that were fundamental to the positions taken by the Eunomian community. The ordering is probably his, the substance theirs.

Throughout this discourse we must pay attention to Gregory's grasp of hermeneutical principles. Oration 29 illustrated how much he depended upon philosophical rhetoric, that is, his training in the logic of Aristotle with exposure to other schools of thought and classical problems. There he also relied on tenets gained from his grammatical training, positions which resemble twentieth-century linguistic analysis. Here his rhetorical education will make itself known primarily in the lexicographical and grammatical principles he uses in the interpretation of texts. As in the previous orations, he carries on a running argument concerning the inadequate education his opponents received.

30.2   Prov. 8.22 forms the center of his first point. Because of its reference to a "created" subject made "at the beginning" it was doubtless a favorite text of all Arian communities. Eunomius (*Confession* 3, *Apology* 26—and the later Arian confession which appears as section 28 of the *Apology*) uses that text as proof that the Son was a "creature," κτίσμα. He can say (*Apology for the Apology* 1.4, Jaeger 1.71-73; Vaggione, p. 102) that the Son was of the same essence as creation, its "first-born" (Col. 1.15), but often he says the Son was not a creature like all other created things. He was that first created being through whom all else was made. As a creature he was not of the same essence as the Father, but in a significant way he is not to be compared with anything that was made through him (*Apology* 15, *Apology for the Apology* 2.6-7, Jaeger 2.76, 79, 82, 86-87, 91-92; Vaggione, pp. 118).

Basil (*Against Eunomius* 2.20) responded to the later Arian interpretation of Prov. 8.22 by indicating that the statement only occurred once in Scripture, that Proverbs was full of obscure sayings and that some Hebrew manuscripts read "begot," not "created." Gallay (p. 229, n. 2) suggests that Gregory has Basil in mind when he avoids certain views, "though they have been taken as forceful by some of our predecessors," εἰ καί τισι τῶν πρὸ ἡμῶν ὡς ἰσχυρὰ τέθειται, but he may have been thinking of Origen (*On First Principles* 4.4.1) when the Alexandrian refers to the Son as a κτίσμα, a "creature."

In Oration 29.15 Nazianzen dealt with the cause / caused conundrum and found it perfectly compatible with divinity. He employed two logical principles, first, that everything predicated of a class may not be predicated of each individual in that class, and second, that conditioned uses of terms must not be confused with unconditioned uses of terms. In that way he hoped to be able to say that the Father is greater than the Son in relationship to cause without conceding that the Son must be lesser than the Father in nature or essence. Meyendorff (*Byzantine Theology*, 2nd. rev. ed. [New York, 1983], p. 183) observes that Basil and Nazianzen used the position of the Father as cause to explain the monarchy in the Trinity. By attributing cause to the Father they established a defense against the charge of tritheism, but Meijering (*God Being History: Studies in Patristic Philosophy* [Amsterdam, 1975], pp. 111-113, n. 43) insists that this position concerning cause was chosen and defended without consistency. From a philosophical vantage point Meijering's view is difficult to dislodge, but Nazianzen's problem is a Scriptural one. The Gospel of John particularly speaks of the Father as the being behind everything. The Father is God. Thus the Theologian keeps that position although it cannot be explained with philosophical consistency.

Gregory offers another interpretation of "cause," one similar to that of Athanasius (*Orations against the Arians* 2.45) as Barbel (p. 172, n. 3) notes, but one inconsistent with his position in Oration 29.15. The Theologian applies his Christological and soteriological principle to the text. What the Son is in Himself has no "cause," αἰτία, since it is of the Godhead, which is "uncaused," ἀναίτιος. The incarnate Son, however, has a cause. He became man for us. The Proverbs text speaks of causal relationship, being created; thus it refers to the humanity that was assumed by the Son.

The difficulty of seeing Gregory's Christology exclusively in terms of either later Alexandrian or later Antiochene teachers becomes apparent in this section. The anointing of the humanity with divinity is a favorite Antiochene theme. Mason (p. 111, n. 1) conjectures that Nazianzen's Greek text of Prov. 8.23 translated the Hebrew verb as "anointed" rather than as "set up." That could explain the occurrence of the word in Gregory's exposition. When, however, Nazianzen restates his principle yet a third time—the second in this paragraph – he introduces a distinction that sounds much like a classical Antiochene Christology of double predication: "Whatever we come across with a causal implication we will attribute to the humanity; what is absolute and free of cause we will reckon to the Godhead," ὃ μὲν ἂν μετὰ τῆς αἰτίας εὑρίσκωμεν, προσθῶμεν τῇ ἀνθρωπότητι· ὃ δὲ ἁπλοῦν καὶ ἀναίτιον, τῇ θεότητι λογισώμεθα. That phrasing allows the "humanity" to act as a subject. Nazianzen often prefers to speak of the Son as the one subject, either in terms of his uncaused divine nature or in terms of his caused assumption of human nature for our salvation. He senses no necessity to avoid speaking of the Son, Wisdom, as "created" provided that his condition required for salvation is kept clearly in mind. Yet, as Mason (p. xvii) notes, his language varies, at times implying that the humanity is a personal subject, at times asserting that the one subject is the Son.

The Scriptural reference for 30.2.4-5 is 1 Kings 11.1-13 not 1 Sam. 11.1-8. Wis. 7.21 and 8.6 are not related to 30.2.6 contextually, but only by one word.

30.3 Nazianzen's preference for the Godhead as the subject of Biblical titles and terms, even the lowly ones, dominates this paragraph. The Son can be a "slave" or a "child of God" as long as the cause of those conditions is grasped. He became those things for our salvation. Yet the closeness of God and man in Jesus Christ can be represented as an "intermingling," μῖξις. Gregory uses the concept in the way some Stoics did (*SVF* II, 465, 468, 471, 473, 479-480), that is, to describe a mixture in which the ingredients remained what they had been, but became one.

For Nazianzen nothing in the essence of humankind excludes it from becoming God, from "being made God," γενέσθαι Θεόν. Furthermore, the salvific principle so often quoted from the theological letters is also present here. The Son "was subject to all that he saved," πᾶσιν οἷς σέσωκεν. In Epistle 101 Gregory put it negatively and positively: "what is not assumed is not healed and what is united with God, that indeed is saved." The Son became a full man. Section 21 of this discourse indicates that he became all we are: body, mind and soul, everything except sin. Here, however, the second aspect of soteriology is also evidenced. The intermingling of the humanity with the divinity is what effects salvation.

30.4   Nazianzen now turns to the second set of texts. The first cluster of passages in this set involves verses that contain the meaning "until," ἄχρι or ἕως. Eunomius (*Apology* 26-27) does not build his case on all the passages Gregory mentions, but he does insist that the Son will submit to the Father as Paul implies in 1 Cor. 15.28.

Nazianzen begins by interpreting 1 Cor. 15.25. His response to the later Arian treatment of these passages is interesting. It depends upon the meaning of "until," ἄχρι or ἕως, and "rule," βασιλεύειν. His opponents misunderstand how these words can be used in various cases. They do not recognize that the word signifies what happens up to a point without necessarily indicating what follows that point. The Son's nature need not be seen as secondary to that of the Father when one looks at Scriptural uses of "until."

Although Gregory lists this argument as a second point of the later Arians, he also may have in mind someone like Marcellus of Ancyra who was rejected, then supported by the West and much of Egypt as well as Asia Minor, but whom Basil condemned as a modalist. In taking his position, Marcellus employed I Cor. 15.24-28 as an important textual basis, as Lienhard ("The Exegesis of I. Cor. 15:24-28 from Marcellus of Ancyra to Theodoret of Cyrus," *VC* 37 [1983], pp. 340-359) indicates. Eunomius (*Apology* 6) saw Sabellius, Marcellus and Marcellus' student, Photinus, as significant enemies. In his *Apology for the Apology* 2.16 (Jaeger 2.246; Vaggione, p. 123) he accused Basil of teaching Sabellian doctrines. Nazianzen rejects Sabellian error in 30.6 and again in 31.30, but does not specifically mention Marcellus. He castigates the "Galatians," surely a reference to Marcellus' followers, in 22.12 and Photinus in 33.16, but both are mentioned in passing within lists of heretics. Here in sections 4 and 5, however, he does speak of a kingdom that will end and one that will not end, a position that has some overtones similar to doctrines taught by Marcellus. His major concern is to deny any sense that the Son is secondary and subjugated to the Father, a concern that is Christological, not ecclesiological.

In offering his own interpretation of "until" he operates much as a twentieth-century linguistic analyst by pointing out how context, not root meanings, must determine the sense of the word. He gives an example from Mt. 28.20 of his counterproposal for the interpretation of "until," ἄχρι, suggests that he could provide further instances and then offers Scriptural allusions as the examples for his interpretation of "rule."

Ps. 82(81).1 provides yet another basis for his sense of salvation as θέωσις, "becoming God." Its reference to "God in the midst of the gods," Θεὸς ἐν μέσῳ θεῶν, is for him a description of the Son bringing in the saved at the time of judgment. The Biblical text does not support that meaning, but Gregory reads it as a statement of his basic soteriological principle: God the Son became human that humans might become gods.

30.5 To get at the heart of the lexicographical problems, Nazianzen recalls a main principle: the economic distinction, the difference between the Son as He is in Himself and as He was when He assumed humanity. Because humanity is cursed, sinful and rebellious so must the Son be if He assumed our humanity. Thus the Son suffers in his Godhead, since we "are saved by the sufferings of the impassible," σεσωσμένοι τοῖς τοῦ ἀπαθοῦς πάθεσιν.

According to Gregory, the later Arians see the Son as "subordinate," ὑποτεταγμένος, to the Father and must account for that fact. He senses that they would respond by raising questions about his own positions. If one views the Son as not subordinate, then perhaps he is insubordinate, a "bandit" or an "opponent of God." Eunomius (*Apology* 22) views the Son as "subordinate," ὑποτεταγμένος, but he does not see him as opposing God. Indeed, in his works (*Apology* 23-24) he consistently speaks of the Son doing the Father's will, the will by which the Son existed and acted.

This section does show Nazianzen's supporters that his interpretative principle can explain texts basic to Eunomian views, but his arguments would hardly dislodge his antagonists.

Gregory's talk of Christ's "actively producing our submission, of setting us under his royal rule in free acceptance of our being ruled," ὡς ἐνεργῶν τὴν ὑποταγήν, καὶ ὑπὸ τὴν ἑαυτοῦ βασιλείαν τιθεὶς ἡμᾶς, ἑκόντας δεχομένους τὸ βασιλεύεσθαι, (section 4) or Himself subjecting all to God should not be taken as a denial of free will in humans or in the person of Christ. The power of Christ to attract human will is apparently the background. The priority of grace is never in doubt, for the active involvement of divinity in the incarnation is basic to the Theologian's Christology. Yet unlike some emphases in Western fathers, for Nazianzen there is no problem with asserting Christ's power in producing submission and also affirming human will and acceptance of that submission.

The inclusion of the word from the cross, taken from Ps. 22(21), may serve as a test case to demonstrate the complexity of Gregory's Christological views. The subject who is not forsaken by the Father or his own Godhead must be the human Jesus. Thus Nazianzen can speak of the man Jesus as a subject. He attributes the cry from the cross to Jesus the man (cf. 30.12), but not because the divine Christ had forsaken Jesus or that the Father, fearing suffering, had departed. There is a full human subject present who must act, but the divinity would not avoid such things and leave that human alone in his hour of pain.

Once again Nazianzen has posited an active human subject at a crucial point, in the garden of Gethsemane. A phrase in Eunomius' *Confession* (3) rejects a description of the incarnation that would involve taking up a full manhood of soul and body, οὐκ ἀναλαβόντα τὸν ἐκ ψυχῆς καὶ σώματος ἄνθρωπον. The subject of actions attributed to Jesus Christ must be the Son and thus all lesser actions or qualities prove the Son's lesser divinity.

For Gregory, however, the mystery is still that the impassible is involved in the passion, τοῖς τοῦ ἀπαθοῦς πάθεσιν. That mystery plays the central role within the economy of salvation. The Son rescues humanity by taking on our disobedience and dying for us. The Theologian does not in any case want to withdraw either the Father or the Son from death on the cross. His overpowering reason is the nature of salvation itself.

We must not assume that all later Arians found the "passion of the impassible" to be improper. Nazianzen does not explicitly attribute that position to them; he merely notes that some have had such thoughts, ὃ δοκεῖ τισιν. Aetius and Eunomius find the great difficulties involved in Trinitarian doctrine primarily at the level of the Son's generation. In our extant texts they seldom if ever speak of Christ's death. Furthermore, one Arian scholion to the Council of Aquileia says "Even in flesh like ours the impassible God, the Word, suffered and the incorruptible God endured corruption, in order that he might change our state to incorruptibility." (Gryson, *Scripta Arriana Latina*, "Corpus Christianorum Series Latina LXXXVII" [Turnhout, 1982], Fr. 20, p. 260). Later Arian worship and piety could make its confession in terms similar to those of Nazianzen.

The *SC* Scriptural references for this section are confused. 30.5.8-9 recalls Col. 1.18 and Eph. 5.23, not 1 Cor. 15.45. In 30.5.11-12 the quotation is from 1 Cor. 15.28, not Col. 1.18. 30.5.20-21 cites Ps. 22(21).1(2) not 1 Cor. 15.28. And the Biblical allusion for 30.5.29-31 is Ps. 22(21) as Gregory himself says, not Isa. 53.6.

30.6   This second point also involves a cluster of texts. According to the later Arians, if the Son learned obedience, cried, shed tears, begged, was heard and was God-fearing, he cannot be of the same essence as the Father. In one sense Nazianzen agrees. These things do not apply to the Son in his nature as the Word, but to his incarnation. The Son had to take on all these lowly, alien attributes in order to save mankind. By becoming everything we are, he can absorb and overcome the "meaner element," χεῖρον, in order that through his "intermingling," σύγκρασις, we can participate in what he is. Once again the soteriological principle of θέωσις, "deification," interlocked with a Christological principle of the divine Son's incarnate condition, bears the weight of Gregory's argument.

The proverb, "deeds prove disposition," ἔργον γὰρ ἀπόδειξις διαθέσεως, and Heb. 2.18 provide an added dimension to these principles, particularly the soteriological one. That dimension can be expanded to events in everyday life, rather than being limited to the concept of θέωσις, "deification," which often focuses on the final end. Humans may take solace in the fact that the Son's actions demonstrated his intention. He can help us because he himself has suffered and was tempted.

The rhetorical rejection of Sabellian doctrines of the Trinity, while castigating later Arian teachings concerning the same problems, is effective and perhaps needed. One way to view the 1 Cor. 15.28 passage was to see the Son as going completely back into the Father, much as a torch would be taken from a burning pyre and then put back into it with all loss of its individual presence. As noted above, Gregory seldom mentions the Sabellians and never in these orations refers to Marcellus of Ancyra or his pupil Photinus, but Eunomius (*Apology* 6) saw those three as archrivals. In Nazianzen's view of the Trinity, the Son and the Spirit never surrendered their individuality, although there was also a clear unity among them and the Father. Gregory's interpretation of 1 Cor. 15.28 through Col. 1.28 and 3.11 hits the mark. It is his concluding argument for the second point begun in section 4. Since Paul says God, not the Father, will be all in all and elsewhere writes "Christ will be all in all," the apostle supports the Theologian's position concerning the equality of essence between the Father and the Son and at the same time stands against the Sabellian error that in the end God alone will be all in all.

Gregg and Groh are correct to show that early Arianism was much concerned with questions of soteriology. Whether or not Arius was exclusively interested in such themes remains questionable. There is, however, no way to avoid the fact that Gregory and his later Arian opponents had differing views of salvation. Sections 4-6 are all focused on soteriology and the Christological positions resulting from it. Only from that context are the Trinitarian issues raised. For Nazianzen, the lowly attributes and actions mentioned in the Gospels do not demonstrate that the Son is less than God the Father; rather they indicate how fully the Son participated in human life. Some of the issues from the first stage of Arian debates are still in place. For Gregory like Athanasius, salvation demands the involvement of complete divinity. Θέωσις, "deification," cannot be achieved unless the Son is fully divine.

Unfortunately the Scriptural references in the *SC* edition for this section are also in disarray. Luke 22.53 and Eph. 5.8 have no contextual relationship with 30.6.22-23. The citation in 30.6.28-30 from Heb. is 2.18 not 2.8 and the final passage in 30.6.42-44 is Col. 3.11 not Gal. 3.28. Gallay's note 2, (p. 239) not only repeats the mistaken reference to Gal. 3.28 but also suggests that what stands in Gregory's text is a conflation of that passage with 1 Cor. 15.28.

30.7   For some odd reason, the third and fourth points are almost treated as a single argument. This is one place in which Kopecek's suggestion (p. 502) of a later Arian catena gains support. It seems unlikely that a clearly developed organizational scheme, devised to assist the memory, would lump these two points together. Perhaps there was a list of passages circulating within later Arian communities. One source for such positions, which employs both of these Biblical passages, is Eunomius' *Apology*. In section 11 he notes that the Son cannot be equal to the Father because in John 14.28 the Son specifically says the Father is greater than he. In section 21 Eunomius quotes the John 20.17 passage about "my God" and employs it again in his *Apology for the Apology* 2.22 (Jaeger 2.287 and 291; Vaggione, p. 126).

For the third point, those passages where God is said to be greater than the Son, Nazianzen invokes a logical principle. Surely if the Son were only referred to as less than the Father, the case would be closed. But there are other texts that speak of him as "equal," ἴσος, to the Father. The existence of two such sets of verses poses a problem since "it is impossible for the same thing to be, in a like respect, greater than and equal to the same thing," Τὸ γὰρ αὐτὸ τοῦ αὐτοῦ ὁμοίως μεῖζον καὶ ἴσον εἶναι, τῶν ἀδυνάτων. Μεῖζον, "greater," is not an absolute term, but a relative one. The key is the τὸ αὐτὸ ὁμοίως, "the same thing in a like respect."

This logical principle is preceded by two questions begun with εἰ, "if." Together they represent a type of dialectical exegesis in which enthymematic forms are employed to suggest the more formal syllogistic reasoning which lies behind the discussion of the texts. According to the classical treatment of Aristotle (*Rhetoric* 1355A-1357B and 1395B-1396A) the minor premise of a syllogism may be omitted from an enthymematic argument in order to bring the audience into the logical process. In some instances the parts of an enthymeme could be stated in full syllogistic form that displays the validity of one's case. Here the Theologian uses the enthymematic form in order to involve his audience in the reasoning process. Thus once again his disagreement with the later Arians concerns not only the substance of their arguments but also their form. He considers his opponents to be lacking in their grasp of *paideia* and shows that he can himself use the type of ethymemes they so love.

Their arguments can be deflected if proper distinctions are made. The Father is superior as to "cause," αἰτία, but the two are equal in "nature," φύσις, and "glory," δόξα. The hidden analogy is that of a son sharing the nature of the father, or of Adam sharing in humanity, models discussed in Oration 29.11 and by Basil (*Against Eunomius* 1.8).

Gregory's confession that the Father is greater than the Son since he is the "cause" creates difficulty. Traditionally it goes back at least to the Apologists and in terms of Nazianzen's background, directly to Origen. Gregory had already discussed the point in Oration 29.3, using an analogy from nature. The sun may be said to be the cause of light, but the sun and the light exist together at the same time. That analogue, available in fourth-century intellectual circles, provided the basis for considering his argument about Father and Son.

As Mason (p. xvii) indicates the Theologian's language "the [Son] considered as man," τοῦ κατὰ τὸν ἄνθρωπον νοουμένου, implies a human subject. That distinction in attribution is continued in the next section.

Gallay reads ἡμετέρῳ rather than ὑμετέρῳ in 30.7.9, preferring A, S, D, P and C over Q, B, W, V and T. That represents the better family of manuscripts (S, D, P and C) and the better sense of the passage. The phrase, "derivation from the uncaused does not mean inferiority to the uncaused," μὴ ἔλαττον εἶναι τὸ ἐκ τοιαύτης αἰτίας εἶναι τοῦ ἀναιτίου, is Gregory's argument, not that of his opponents.

For 30.7.1 John 14.17 is a misprinted reference to John 14.28. The point in 30.7.3 concerning Eunomian rejection of "equality," ἴσος, is best related to Phil. 2.6, not John 10.30, in 30.7.3.

30.8 The fourth point, how the Christ can say "my God," reemphasizes the tension in Gregory's two major Christological approaches. His grasp of soteriology often influences his decision to speak of the difference between the Son in his essence and the Son incarnate, but here the "duality," the fact that the Son is twofold, διπλοῦς, is worked out another way, because the context concerns attribution. The subject of some words or "titles," ὀνόματα, is the "visible," ὁρώμενος, not the "Word," λόγος. One way to deal with the Biblical statements and attributions that imply a lesser Son is to ascribe those passages to the humanity.

In section 6 Nazianzen had introduced "intermingling," σύγκρασις, as descriptive of the unity in Jesus Christ, the way in which the two natures are brought into "combination," σύνοδος. He also employs it in Ep. 101 during his attack on Apollinarians concerning the fullness of the human nature in the incarnate Christ. But Athanasius (*Against Apollinaris* 2.16) rejected the term σύγκρασις and Cyril of Alexandria (*Eps.* 44-46) rebutted the charge that he used it in his Christology.

The conception of ἐπίνοια, "idea," is important for the debate with the later Arians. Eunomius (*Apology* 8) views the term as signifying words that are human inventions, sounds that have no substance. For him, "unbegotten," ἀγέννητος, is not a sound, but the name of God's very being. It is not a "human conception," ἐπίνοια ἀνθρώπινη, but the name given by God himself for his own nature. In his *Apology for the Apology* 1.5-10 (Jaeger, esp. 1.238, 245, 270-71, 274, 276, 282, 284, 303, 313, 315-16, 323-24, 326, 328-29, 340-41, 344-48, 364, 367-68, 370-71, 385-86, 388, 398-399; Vaggione, pp. 105-14) Eunomius devoted considerable energy to an explication of section 8 of his *Apology*. Basil (*Against Eunomius* 1.5-7), however, uses ἐπίνοια to signify, in part, his argument that no human word could designate the essence of God. All the words used for God's essence are human words and do not describe God as he is in himself. Gregory of Nyssa (*Against Eunomius* 2.11-66, Jaeger 2.227-409) focuses a large part of his refutation on the concept of ἐπίνοια, again making the distinction between human conceptions in human language and the Eunomian claim that names designate God's essence. When Nazianzen speaks of ἐπίνοια in this section, he alludes to previous arguments in these orations. God is incomprehensible in his essence; what the Trinity is in itself must remain a mystery. As humans, however, we cannot avoid human conceptions and language. Therefore, when we look at the various sayings and titles of the Son, the duality, the "natures," φύσεις, must be distinguished in our "thoughts," ἐπινοίαι. The visible is the subject of some things, the Word the subject of others.

Gregory's example from Eph. 1.17 is not as "straightforward" as he assumes. At the end of this oration, section 21, his reference to "Jesus Christ" concerns the one subject "in body and spirit," not the assumed manhood. In that paragraph he uses the title "Christ" in two senses: first, "because of his Godhead," second as an "unction [which] belongs to his manhood." Thus his explanation of the passage from Ephesians does not necessarily take it away from the later Arians, who view it as indicating that the Lord Jesus Christ has a God, and therefore is not God as the unbegotten Father is.

30.9   In the fifth point, Gregory lists more features that apply to the "manhood," ἀνθρωπότης. This position is similar to that taken by the classical Antiochene school during the early Arian debates. Kopecek (p. 503) suggests that this string of Biblical passages is not found elsewhere in Neo-Arian writings. Eunomius assumes in his *Confession* 3 that the Son received glory, but the claim that the Theologian refers to here may be one of those prominent pieces of evidence indicating views held by later Arians in Constantinople that go beyond other witnesses.

Nazianzen counters that the humanity must at least be a passive agent who receives certain things, but he does not separate completely the human subject and the divine incarnate subject. As long as these attributes are not described as acquired characteristics, properties which become the Son's by grace, they can be said to be the Son's by nature. Gregory seldom employs double predication as a fully distinct way to approach Christology, for in his view it would weaken the force of the economic approach.

The latter part of the paragraph restates that economic approach as the counter to later Arianism, a position similar to that taken in classical Alexandrian Christologies. Nazianzen has no interest in distinguishing between the two Christological approaches and choosing only one. Such a decision comes primarily in the fifth century when further implications of the two Christologies appear in the debates between Nestorius and Cyril. The Theologian, because he sees the inner-workings of the Trinity as an ultimately incomprehensible mystery, does not select one alternative. Yet he prefers the economic distinction because of its importance for salvation. Θέωσις, "deification," demands a full humanity, but it does not necessarily require an active human subject even though it moves in that direction. The active human subject well may be included because of Nazianzen's commitment to free will in all human beings.

30.10   In his discussion of point six, Gregory's philological and logical skills become even more apparent. To interpret a verse like John 5.19 one must look closely at the meanings of "cannot," μὴ δύνασθαι. Eunomius (*Apology* 20 and 26) employs this Johannine text to prove the subordinate, secondary position of the Son. Because the Son can do nothing on his own, he is "entirely different," πάμπολυ διενήνοχεν, from the Father. To combat such a view, Nazianzen returns to dialectical exegesis. At least five different meanings of "cannot" appear in common speech and Scriptural quotations. First, "cannot" may mean a lack of ability to do something, but an ability which may vary with time and circumstance. Second, "cannot" could imply something that is generally true. Third, "cannot" might be used to express something that is reasonably or morally inappropriate. Fourth, "cannot" could have the sense of willful refusal. Fifth, "cannot" also may refer to the naturally impossible, yet miraculously possible.

Nazianzen sensitively notices that some texts which use "cannot" are difficult to put under one of the specific five groups which he has specified. Even the example of Christ's inability to heal certain people may apply to category three. Obviously unbelievers employed inappropriate reasonable or moral canons when they decided not to believe in him.

The example of the bridegroom could be interpreted Christologically in two ways, either the figure "in his visible body," ὁ σωματικῶς ὁρώμενος, or the one "known spiritually as the Word," ὁ ὡς λόγος νοούμενος. Mason (p. xvii) is concerned that this introduces two persons in Christ. Although the language does not speak of two persons, it does suggest double predication or attribution similar to the classical Antiochene views.

In 30.10.24 Gallay reads μή with A, Q, B, W, V, P and C against T, S and D and the Maurist editors. The μή is to be preferred because it is an insertion into the text of John 7.7 as we have it, one which reverses the meaning. That sense best suits Gregory's argument. He views the world's inability "not" to hate Christians as an act of will.

30.11   The John 5.19 passage, however, fits within yet another meaning, that is, "cannot" in the sense of something inconceivable.

This kind of logical or dialectical exegesis presents further examples of Gregory's disagreement with the later Arians about the nature of *paideia*. Any text has both an immediate context and some relationship to reality. Unless interpreters know how words like "cannot" may be employed, they will make poor choices. The different uses of "cannot" must be in mind lest the exegetes wrongly assume that only one meaning is possible for a particular text. An understanding of words and grammar, of context and meaning, is part of this debate with the Eunomians. They do not seem to grasp the various senses of a word like "cannot" because they have not examined the available options. Therefore, they continually show themselves to be uneducated.

Perhaps twentieth-century readers are better able to understand the nature of Gregory's arguments for two reasons. First, historians of rhetoric have recaptured the dialectical aspects of Aristotle's *Rhetoric*, thus enabling us to recognize philosophical rhetoricians like Nazianzen. Second, the grammatical, contextual basis of linguistic analysis has reminded us of the contemporary philosophical import of such concerns. The first is the more significant, but the second also is helpful.

When Gregory employs such sophisticated logical moves, however, he too often finds a meaning for the passages in John that agrees with the theological consensus which he accepts. He is most persuasive when he relies strictly on the immediate context of an individual passage. In section 7 he at least alludes to Biblical passages that speak of equality between the Son and the Father. There he bases his argument on Biblical context and logical principle, but here his discussion of "cannot" is less clearly tied to immediate context and thus is a weaker argument. To wonder how absolute Wisdom can be taught makes sense. But the *reductio ad absurdum* argument, which plays with the necessity of four worlds, lacks logical bite, although it doubtless had sophistic snap. We must, however, recognize Nazianzen's command of rhetoric, both in its philosophic and dialectical concerns and in its more sophistic interests, even if we do not always agree with his judgment.

The *SC* Biblical citation in 30.11.11 should be John 6.57 not John 6.58. The quoted words in 30.11.39-40 are all from Amos 4.13. Job 38.25 has no connection.

30.12   The seventh cluster of Biblical passages involves some of the most important Christological allusions to be found in these discourses. Eunomius (*Fr.* iii, Anastasius of Sinai, *Contra Monophysitas Testimonia* [*PG* 89.1181B-C], Vaggione, pp. 178-179) offers insight into this debate since he claims that the Son had his own will, one not in accord with the uncreated will of the Father, and builds his view on an interpretation of John 6.38. In his *Confession* (3) he rejects the assumption of a manhood complete with body and soul, the conditions necessary for a human subject. Nazianzen attempts to refute the position that the Son has a will different from that of the Father by attributing a will to the assumed man. He probably relies upon Origen's soteriological claim (*Dialogue with Heracleides* 7) that full manhood must be assumed in order for mankind to be saved fully and thus ascribes attitudes and statements to the manhood as a subject.

For Nazianzen the quotation from John 6.38 basically has two parts. If the first portion had not said that the subject was the one who came down from heaven, then the second would have been clear. A difference of will is simply understood when one thinks of the struggle between the human will and the will of God. Human wills often resist the divine will. That is what Mt. 26.39 means when Jesus, praying in Gethsemane, asks that the cup pass by him but finally submits his human will to the will of the Father. The man Jesus possessed a will that could resist God.

Jesus the man offers the prayer in Mt. 26.39. That is a crucial place for the manhood to be the subject. Yet Nazianzen still speaks in most instances of the Word made flesh, the Son incarnate, as the subject of attitudes and statements that are less than divine. In section 9 he suggested some possibilities of passive human reception; here he posits active human involvement. This is one of the few places within the corpus where he goes beyond Athanasius and becomes a figure who could be quoted not only on the Cyrillian side of fifth-century debates, but also on the Antiochene side, perhaps even by the Nestorian camp. Mason, in his introduction (p. xviii), noticed that this passage left Gregory open to charges like those leveled against Nestorius. Nazianzen's statements demonstrate that his Christology does not represent the distinct positions of the fifth-century quarrels. The Theologian still sees a human subject, actively involved in the person of Jesus Christ, as one way to explain specific Biblical texts. This interpretation allows him to interpret the verses about a will that could resist the Father.

Nazianzen refuses to view the divine Son as possessing a will that has desires other than those of the Father. Because the first part of John 6.38 speaks of Him who came down from heaven, then it must mean something different from the Matthew passage. Its point is that the Son has no will of His own which is opposed to the Father's. In Gethsemane or elsewhere the Son would have known his Father's purpose and would not have resisted it.

Gregory employs both a grammatical and a logical principle in dealing with the seventh point. The grammatical rule is: "There are many statements of this kind, which make a general negation and no affirmation," Πολλὰ γὰρ τῶν οὕτω λεγομένων ἀπὸ κοινοῦ λέγεται, καὶ οὐ θετικῶς, ἀρνητικῶς δέ. Not every statement that contains a negative can be turned into a positive.

For Gregory a logical rule confirms the interpretation that the grammatical rule applies to these texts: Πῶς γὰρ ἴδιόν τινος τὸ κοινόν, ἢ μόνου; "How could what belongs to two things be the particular property of one of them alone?" The principle is clear enough, but it is not exactly the point at issue. For later Arians, the Father and the Son do not share these particular properties, in this case the same will. Eunomians would agree with the logical rule, but deny that it applied to the Father and the Son. To make his case Gregory needs to show that his interpretation of John 6.38 is the most appropriate.

His sense of grammar is not based on a distortion of the verse. More important, the context of John 6.38, particularly verses 39-40, specifies what the will of the Father is: that the Son be preached about and believed in. Nazianzen's grammatical principle with examples is helpful, but the immediate context of the verse decisively favors his view. General grammar with its logical force opens the possibility for an interpretation other than that of the Eunomians, one supported by Biblical verses as examples, and then argued from the context of the passage in question.

The *SC* reference to Ps. 58.5 for 30.12.24-25 is a misprint for Ps. 59(58).3(4).

30.13   The eighth group focuses on John 17.3, which Eunomius (*Apology* 17, 21 and 25) found to be central. There is only one true God, the uncreated, the uncompounded. He is different from the Son. In Nazianzen's view, John 17.3 must be understood in the context of claims about other gods. In Orations 29 and 31 he makes mention of the pagan atmosphere in which all Christians live. Both with a view to the context of the passage and the contemporary situation his point is sound.

The debate about the Son's goodness is more complicated. Eunomius (*Apology* 21) claims that the Son is good, but he also insists that the cause of the Son's goodness is the Father. Some later Arians, however, may have read Luke 19.18-19 to mean that the Son was not good. Gregory's response is interesting in view of his Christology. "Consummate goodness . . . belongs to God alone, though the word 'good' can be applied to man," Τὸ γὰρ ἄκρως ἀγαθόν, . . . μόνου Θεοῦ, κἂν τοῦτο καὶ ἄνθρωπος ὀνομάζηται. The lawyer had called Jesus "Good teacher" and "had borne witness to his goodness as man," ὡς ἀνθρώπῳ τὴν ἀγαθότητα μαρτυρήσαντα. Although the language is not precise, Nazianzen apparently attributes the response of Jesus to the assumed manhood and not to the divine Son. Double predication is again at hand.

It is unlikely that any party in Constantinople confessed the Son as God, but refused that designation for the Father. What Gregory makes is a debater's point. If Baruch 3.35-38 is taken seriously and set within the framework of the Eunomian position, then the Father is not God, for those verses refer to the Son as God.

Nazianzen offers none of the often discussed New Testament texts that have been seen as naming the Son God (John 1.1, Rom. 9.5, the variant for John 1.18, 20.28, etc.). The fact that he uses none of these here demonstrates nothing, because it would be an argument from silence, but it does raise questions. We are left with an interesting puzzle. Perhaps the text of Scripture he studied did not include some of those variants or the tradition to which he belonged did not interpret them in that way.

John 14.16 has no close connection to 30.13.5-6. John 16.27, referred to in 30.13.6, is a misprint for Rom. 16.27.

30.14   The ninth point concerns Heb. 7.25, the Son's ability to intercede for us. Wickham is probably correct to emphasize the "legal satisfaction" milieu of ἐκδίκησις, which is often rendered only as "vengeance." It points up a significant difference between Gregory's view of salvation and a number of varied legal theories developed in the West. For him such conceptions are basically humiliating, unworthy of God. The Father does not seek vengeance (cf. *Or.* 45).

The problem with acts or attitudes predicated of the manhood is not solved here. Even though 1 Tim. 2.5 specifically attributes this intercession to the human Jesus, Gregory is unclear. One phrase apparently sees Jesus Christ, "as man," ὡς ἄνθρωπος, interceding for us. But the next seems to have the Son "with the body" he assumed, μετὰ τοῦ σώματος— probably a reference in short form to the whole assumed manhood, not just a physical body—as the subject of the intercession. Nazianzen does not participate in the fifth-century distinctions that formed the basis of disagreements between Cyril and Nestorius. His soteriology, which demands a full, functioning manhood, can support a human subject, but that same view of the economy also demands the intermingling of divine and human in order that humans may become divine. It involves a dominate divine subject.

By including two asides about the Spirit, Nazianzen warms his audience to the bold claims he will make in Oration 31. The Spirit also makes petition for us. The mediating or petitioning acts of Christ do not serve the Father's need for satisfaction. Neither is the Christ a slave groveling before his master. Such metaphors are also unworthy of the Spirit. This type of Trinitarian statement calls to mind five other places in these orations: the opening words of this discourse where the "power of the Spirit" is mentioned, the beginning and closing sections of Oration 29 where the Trinity is invoked and the Spirit is said to be honored among his supporters, but defamed among the opponents and the first and last paragraphs of Oration 28 where similar claims are made.

2 Cor. 5.20 uses πρεσβεύομεν, "intercede" or "act as ambassadors," of Christians while Eph. 6.20 attributes πρεσβεύω to its writer, but 30.14.5 uses τὸ πρεσβεύειν of Christ and thus bears no contextual relationship to those passages.

30.15 The tenth point deals with the ignorance attributed to Jesus Christ, here focused on Mark 13.32. Nazianzen again sees the argument as straightforward. Since the Son is called Wisdom at various places in Scripture, he must know. He cannot be the subject of ignorance. Some Scriptural assertions about the "son" should be ascribed "not to the divine but the human," τῷ ἀνθρωπίνῳ, μὴ τῷ θείῳ. Logic, grammar and the highest piety demand it. Logically "knowledge of one thing here necessarily involves knowledge of the other," ἔνθα ἡ τοῦ ἑτέρου γνῶσις ἀναγκαίως συνεισάγει τὸ ἕτερον, thus the Son would know. Grammatically, the "absolute use," τὸ ἀπόλυτον, of the term "son" "without relational qualification," ἄσχετον, suggests that the humanity is the subject. "Most piously," or as Wickham translates it, "in the most truly religious way," ἐπὶ τὸ εὐσεβέστερον, the manhood, not the Son of the Father, is ignorant.

Gregory finds it impossible to deal with all the claims of Scriptural texts unless the humanity is a subject to whom words and actions may be attributed. For him a Christology that depends exclusively upon the divine Son as the subject could explain some of these passages, but even the economic situation, the limitation which the assumed manhood brings to that divine Son, presents deep difficulties. If the Son incarnate is ignorant, is our knowledge of salvation limited? Is it sufficient? By employing the Son before the incarnation, the Son incarnate and the assumed manhood as subjects, Gregory retains all the possible options, although he leaves questions concerning a unitary subject unanswered.

Mason (p. 132, l. 4) prefers ἐν χρῷ to the ἐν χρόνῳ, which Gallay in 30.15.8 reads with all the manuscripts of his edition. The text used by Elias of Crete (p. 158) evidently read ἐν χρῷ as did the second hand of the Lincoln College manuscript. Mason senses that "on the surface" rather than "in time" is more forceful and more likely to have been misread by copyists. His arguments are strong. Further survey of manuscripts may support his reading.

30.16 A second explanation of the son's ignorance, if needed, allows the Father to have some kind of honor as the parent, the "cause," αἰτία. As in Oration 29.15, Gregory distinguishes between a shared "essence," οὐσία—here referred to as the "primal nature," πρώτη φύσις—and the "cause." That creates various philosophical problems, but it is the position he defends. Eunomius (*Apology* 7 and 21) equates αἰτία, οὐσία and ἀγέννητος, "unbegotten;" therefore, he sees the Son's "essence" as different from the Father's.

One of the "scholars," φιλόλογοι, to whom Nazianzen refers is probably Basil (*Ep.* 236) as Gallay (p. 259, n.2) suggests. Others in the circle were Gregory of Nyssa and Amphilochius of Iconium.

A group of texts indicate that human weaknesses are to be ascribed to the manhood, "not the immutable nature transcending suffering," οὐ τὴν ἄτρεπτον φύσιν καὶ τοῦ πάσχειν ὑψηλοτέραν. A significant ambiguity in Gregory's Christology appears here. In section 1 and elsewhere in his hymnic passages he finds no difficulty in speaking of the "passible God," θεὸς παθητός, the divine capable of suffering. Yet in this paragraph he wants to make a distinction and attribute such things to the manhood. He does not, however, withdraw the divinity from suffering and death (cf. section 5). Jesus did not cry out from the cross because either the Father or his own godhead had forsaken him. In a most interesting way, Nazianzen absorbs some aspects of a patripassionist position, while refusing to allow human weaknesses to be attributed to the Son. Again the soteriological emphasis on θέωσις, "deification," provides what explanation there is. The Son in Himself cannot be the possessor of these limitations since He shares the nature of God, the Father, who has none of them. If, however, mankind is to be saved, if people are to become gods, two conditions must be met. First, the Son must be fully divine or humans will not have the opportunity of becoming divine. Second, all human aspects must be assumed by the Son or humans cannot become divine. Furthermore, if all those aspects have been assumed, "body, mind, and soul" as Gregory says in paragraph 21, then the manhood can be a subject and can itself take over the limited attitudes and actions that Scripture predicates of the son.

The problems apparent in this section are the distinction between αἰτία, "cause," and οὐσία, "essence," and the ambiguity concerning the involvement of the "impassible" in things "passible." Both center on the equivocal use of terms. They probably represent the greatest unresolved philosophical difficulties in the Theologian's Christology, even greater than the continued use of single and double predication. Meijering (*God Being History: Studies in Patristic Philosophy* [Amsterdam, 1975] pp. 111-113, n. 43) notices how Nazianzen's view of the Father as the αἰτία, the "cause," of the Son differs from the views of Plotinus and Athanasius and is itself logically inconsistent. Meyendorff (*Byzantine Theology*, 2nd. rev. ed. [New York, 1983], p. 183), however, finds this use of αἰτία along with the employment of ἀρχή "principle," for the Father rather than the common οὐσία, "essence," to be an important contribution of Greek theology, one taught by the Cappadocians, Pseudo-Dionysius and John of Damascus. It well may be that in each case, the philosophical difficulties are accepted as unfathomable because both Scripture and tradition demand the ambiguities, but Meijering is correct that the position is philosophically arbitrary.

The *SC* Scriptural references for this section are confused. John 19.30 and 9.14 have no connection with 30.16.13. For τελειώσεως, "perfecting," the reference is Heb. 5.9; for ὑψώσεως, "exaltation," Phil. 2.9. In 30.16.14 Heb. 5.9 is a misprint for Heb. 5.8. Rom. 4.25 has no relationship with προσφορᾶς, "offering," in 30.16.15; Eph. 5.2 does.

30.17 The starting point for this theme involves the later Arian claim to know God's nature, his essence, his name. Eunomius (*Apology* 7-8 and 19) asserts that names reveal nature and that the Father's proper name is "unbegotten," ἀγέννητος. His teacher Aetius (*Syntagmation* Intro. and 1) consistently calls deity the "unbegotten God," ἀγέννητος θεός. For Gregory, the opposite condition applies: "God cannot be named," Τὸ θεῖον ἀκατονόμαστον. His nature is not encapsulated in a human word.

The "deductive arguments," οἱ λογισμοί, which support Nazianzen's position, already have been presented particularly in Oration 29. In Oration 28 he argued inductively that those who do not know everything about themselves and nature should not be taken seriously when they say they know God's essence. In Oration 29 he demonstrated, often deductively, that the later Arians were not the masters of dialectic they were seen to be. Here he evidently recalls some of those arguments in the poetic phrase, "No man has yet breathed all the air," οὔτε γὰρ ἀέρα τις ἔπνευσεν ὅλον πώποτε.

In 28.4 he had rebuked the Hermetic writer—and in passing perhaps Plato also—when he stated that God in himself could not be conceived, let alone expressed in language. Here he notes the ancient Hebrews' practice. They carefully wrote other symbols to stand in the place of a name for God. They would not have accepted the assertion that human speech could contain the name of God, that his nature could be expressed in human language.

The comment about the Tetragrammaton seems confusing as E. Hardy (*The Christology of the Later Fathers*, "The Library of Christian Classics III" [Philadelphia, 1954], p. 189, n. 50) suggests. The Massoretes wrote יהוה with the pointing for אֲדֹנָי. The meaning of Nazianzen's phrase, however, is that different written letters were used for the name "God." He might be referring to Greek translation manuscripts of the Old Testament, some of which have Hebrew letters for God's name as Barbel (pp. 204-205, n. 35) indicates. Fouad Papyrus 266 from the first century B.C.E. is a Greek manuscript in which the Hebrew Tetragrammaton appears thirty-one times in one hundred fragments (cf. Metzger, *Manuscripts of the Greek Bible* [Oxford, 1981], pp. 33-35 and 61). Jellicoe (*The Septuagint and Modern Study* [Oxford. 1968], pp. 270-272) indicates Origen and Jerome found the better Septuagint manuscripts to be ones that did not have the Christian innovation of putting the Greek κύριος in the place of the Tetragrammaton, but ones that rendered the divine name in Hebrew characters. The most likely referent, however, is the widespread practice in Hebrew manuscripts of writing the Tetragrammaton in palaeo-Hebrew characters much different from the normal Hebrew characters (For example cf. 11QPsa in Sanders, *The Psalms Scroll of Qumran Cave 11*, "Discoveries in the Judaean Desert of Jordan, 4" [Oxford, 1965], pp. 19-49). Gregory would have known that the "ancient" Hebrews wrote in Hebrew. Even if he himself could not read that language he would have been able to see the difference between the two scripts.

Because no human can know everything and none can penetrate to the "essence of God," οὐσίαν Θεοῦ, the "noblest theologian," ἄριστος θεολόγος, is not one who knows the whole, but one "whose mental image is by comparison fuller, who has gathered in his mind a richer picture, outline, or whatever we call it, of the truth," ὃς ἐὰν ἄλλου φαντασθῇ πλέον, καὶ πλεῖον ἐν ἑαυτῷ συναγάγῃ τὸ τῆς ἀληθείας ἴνδαλμα, ἢ ἀποσκίασμα, ἢ ὅ τι καὶ ὀνομάσομεν.

For Gregory, theology is a noble task, but one that involves more than a sense of logic alone. On the basis of his education in philosophical rhetoric, he knows the uses of syllogisms and enthymemes, but that education also helped him develop a literary and grammatical sense. Metaphors and similes abound in texts. As we have seen above, particularly in sections 4 and 10-13, Nazianzen finds meaning within context, indeed contexts that can rely heavily upon pictorial language. Thus for him the best theologian well might be called a poet-philosopher.

His descriptive phrases are careful and interesting. The verbs used for "collecting a faint and feeble mental image" and "gathered in his mind a richer picture," are συλλέγω and φαντάζω. The first, both in sound and form, is similar to yet different from συλλογίζομαι, which means "to gather together in logical form, to infer from premises." Συλλέγω emphasizes the smallness of the human mind when confronted with God. The second, φαντάζω, invokes the sense of imagination not by stressing the "fantasy" aspect, which an English transliteration might imply, but by pointing up the ability of mental images to present only "faint and feeble" pictures, different ones which "by comparison" would be "fuller" although they can never be "full." Modern concern with the religious imagination and literary form as fundamental for theology is no new topic. Certainly a fourth-century figure who wrote over 17,000 verses of poetry is justified in holding such a view of theology.

30.18 Although the nature of deity is incomprehensible and names do not reveal nature, three terms are closer to describing God's essence than any others: "He who is," ὁ ὤν, "God," Θεός and "Lord," κύριος. Thus his opponents cannot infer that the confession of incomprehensibility leaves one without any concepts or words for God. Yet these terms are either "relational, not absolute," λεγομένων ἐστί, καὶ οὐκ ἄφετος, as the last two, or "most strictly appropriate," κυριωτέραν, as the first, which emphasizes God's absolute existence.

Nazianzen does not make a large ontological claim by using ὁ ὤν, "the one who is," in order to borrow the conception from Hellenistic philosophical systems of his day. Had he been interested in that he well might have commented on the various philosophers who had made similar assertions. He notes that Plato, Aristotle and others come close to Christian truth when they compare God to the place of the sun in our universe (28.30), speak of the mind of the world (31.5) or ask about what gives everything movement (28.16). He is aware of the closeness of some philosophers to ultimate truth as he sees it. But here he uses the term ὁ ὤν because Scripture indicates God used it of himself.

As Barbel (p. 207, n. 40) observes, the etymology of θεός from θέειν had appeared in similar form not only in Plato (*Cratylus* 397D) but also in Theophilus (*To Autolycus* 1.4), Clement (*Stromata* 4.23 and *The Exhortation* 4), Eusebius (*The Preparation of the Gospel* 1.9) and elsewhere.

30.19 The sense of this paragraph about God is clear. Its purpose in the argument is to provide a twofold distinction of the "economy" or "providence," οἰκονομίας, for speaking of God, a division that is similar to the twofold distinction used for the Son. In that way the attribution of titles to God in himself or as he is in his providence supplies the model for attribution to the Son whether or not it is related to the incarnation.

The triune formula that closes this section is used elsewhere by

Gregory. Gallay (p. 266, n. 1) says it appears in Oration 42.15. In this instance it states the differences between the three without destroying their unity. "Names of deity are shared," κοινὰ θεότητος τὰ ὀνόματα. This time the distinctions are emphasized, but the designations of "un-originate," ἄναρχος, for the Father, "unoriginately begotten," ἀνάρχως γεννηθέντος, for the Son and "unbegottenly proceeding," ἀγεννήτως προελθόντος, for the Holy Spirit, are part of an attempt to form links as well as to specify individual characteristics.

Nazianzen employs the play on ἄναρχος / ἀνάρχως, "unoriginate" / "unoriginately," in order to emphasize the same nature of the Father and Son, but it is imprecise in depicting the Trinitarian relationship. There is no such parallelism between the Son and the Spirit; in fact, the repeated form stresses their difference, γεννηθέντος / ἀγεννήτως, "begotten" / "unbegottenly." Yet in Gregory's view, if the adjectival and adverbial use of "unbegotten" expresses the link between Son and Spirit, after the sameness of Son and Father has been stated previously, then the formula effectively indicates the sameness and difference in the Trinity. He may also depend upon his extensive arguments that "begotten" and "un-begotten" do not signify differences in the essence of Father and Son.

There are two misprints in the *SC* Scriptural references for this section. In 30.19.5 Ps. 57.13 should be Ps. 67.13 [LXX]; in 30.19.7 Isa. 1.19 should be Isa. 1.9.

30.20   What remains for this oration is to list the various Biblical titles for the Son, ones showing that he must be of the same essence as the Father. Gregory mentioned in the previous section that the names for dei-ty are shared by Father, Son and Holy Spirit. Interpreting the divine names given to the Son should close the circle of this presentation. If his opponents see that their fundamental texts can be explained either by at-tributing the less-than-divine characteristics to the Son in his incarnate condition or to the manhood which he assumed, they will only have caught half the vision. For the whole view, they must also look at the pas-sages that attribute divine characteristics to the Son.

These twelve titles, all given the Son in Scripture, form the basis for the claim that the Son is "of one substance," ὁμοούσιος, with the Father. One statement from Scripture is also crucial to Nazianzen's case, John 14.9: "he who has seen me has seen the Father." Eunomius (*Apology* 19 and 24) offers an explanation of "image," εἰκών, "light," φῶς, "life," ζωή, and "power," δύναμις. He insists that the basic categories for any discussion about the essences of Father and Son are ἀγέννητος, "unbegot-ten," and γέννητος, "begotten." Given that definition, any reference to both the Father and the Son as "light," "life," and "power" must mean different lights, lives and powers. Those words, when used of the Son, are homonyms. Eunomius (*Apology* 24) claims that the Son is the "image," εἰκών, of the Father "not because the image points to a similarity according to essence, but according to action," οὐ πρὸς τὴν οὐσίαν φέροι ἂν ἡ εἰκὼν τὴν ὁμοιότητα, πρὸς δὲ τὴν ἐνέργειαν.

The Christologies of Nazianzen and his Eunomian opponents have different bases, but somewhat similar approaches. Gregory begins with the confession that the Son and the Spirit are of the same nature as the Father and then attributes the lower statements, attitudes, or actions of the Son to a divided condition. Eunomius begins with the confession that the Son and the Spirit are not of the same nature as the Father and then attributes the apparently higher titles or characteristics of the Son to a divided condition. For Gregory the lesser statements could not mean that the Son is less than the Father; for Eunomius the greater statements cannot mean that the Son is equal to the Father. If there is a fatal weakness in Eunomius' view, it appears first in his rejection of any talk about the Son being equal to the Father (*Apology* 11). Nazianzen weakens his own case by only alluding to Scriptural references that demand equality rather than arguing them in detail. He thinks his opponents must explain these high titles from Biblical passages in their presentation of Christology. If the Son is secondary, unlike the Father in nature or essence, how is it that he can be given these titles in Scripture? From the Theologian's vantage point the later Arians have not dealt with the fundamental texts for his position. As noted above, Eunomius had offered his interpretation for many of these titles and had supported them to his own and to his community's satisfaction, primarily by treating them as homonyms.

Gallay reads γεύσεως, "tasting [the forbidden tree]" in 30.20.48, accepting A, D, P, C and S and rejecting Q, B, W, V, T and a corrector of S, which read ἁμαρτίας, "sin." The Maurists and Mason accepted ἁμαρτίας. Apparently Gallay's decision is reached on the basis of ἁμαρτίας being the more likely gloss for the more unusual γεύσεως as well as the appearance of γεύσεως in the better family of manuscripts: D, P, C and S. The sense is basically the same with either reading.

In 30.20.18 the Scriptural reference John 1.13 is a misprint for John 1.3. John 14.31 for 30.20.47 has no contextual relationship with the point Gregory makes.

30.21 To make fullest sense, the first sentence must refer not merely to the titles mentioned in section 20; it must begin Gregory's summation of the entire oration.

Nazianzen's reference to Christological principles that arise from Biblical texts offers interesting distinctions. Some titles, like those listed previously, can be attributed to either "the transcendent or the human," as Wickham translates it. Word for word the phrase emphasizes the soteriological point, τοῦ τε ὑπὲρ ἡμᾶς καὶ τοῦ δι' ἡμᾶς, "that above us and that because of us." This soteriological principle determines Christology. The

Son does not become man simply to acquire an instrument for being known. Incarnation is not a tool of epistemology. The Son becomes "all that we are, sin apart—body, soul, mind, all that death pervades," πάντα ὑπὲρ πάντων γενόμενος, ὅσα ἡμεῖς, πλὴν τῆς ἁμαρτίας, σῶμα, ψυχή, νοῦς δι' ὅσων ὁ θάνατος.

Such an understanding of salvation, which occurred "so that you may ascend from below to become God, because he came down from above us," ἵνα γένῃ Θεὸς κάτωθεν ἀνελθών, διὰ τὸν κατελθόντα δι' ἡμᾶς ἄνωθεν, forms the platform for his Christology. Because the Son became man that we might become gods, the titles always will be interchangeable. For example, although calling the Son "Christ" might refer to his Godhead, the needs of salvation allow us to speak of the one who anoints as man and the anointed one as God. Other Biblical titles fit those same conditions.

Heb. 5.2 as a Scriptural reference for 30.21.33 is false. Neither words nor context fit.

In this oration Gregory does not propose an overarching theory that distinguishes all the titles or Biblical passages as either belonging to the divine Son in Himself, to His condition as incarnate, or to the assumed manhood. For him neither Scripture nor tradition is so systematic that any particular title or verse must of necessity fall under one of these three subjects and one alone.

If his opponents use a passage to destroy one of the three Christological claims, then Nazianzen challenges the interpretation of that text. His quarrel with the later Arians focuses on their assertion that the Son is not of the Father's essence. Although that can be viewed as an ontological disagreement, it is important to note that in most instances Gregory's fundamental argument is soteriological. He can speak of God as incomprehensible and impassible; here he refers to the divine nature as "inaccessible," ἄληπτος, but his view of the divine essence is colored by his understanding of salvation. Only the passion of the impassible saves. If the Son is not divine, humans cannot become gods; θέωσις, "deification," is crucial. But that same soteriology demands a full manhood with intellect and will and thus the presence of a human subject.

Double predication can also protect the Son's divinity. Thus in some places the lowly acts and attitudes should be attributed to the manhood, but Nazianzen prefers in most cases to employ the distinction between the Son in Himself and the Son incarnate. In that way he can emphasize the sameness of Jesus Christ "yesterday, today, and forever."

The Theologian does not argue the ontological implications of his view of salvation. How can humans become gods? Is there not an inseparable gulf between the Creator and the created? His usual response to any questioning of how God could become man is to refer to the mystery and point out how the human mind is not a large enough instrument to understand many things about the divine. He apparently accepts and develops the traditional θέωσις principle of soteriology in similar fashion.

Within this oration he attacks the Eunomian interpretation of Scripture through what I have called a dialectical exegesis. He concentrates particularly on those passages his antagonists viewed as destructive of the Son's claim to be of the same essence as the Father and then provides a list of texts that support his outlook. Logical principles, grammatical rules and rhetorical practices are employed to demonstrate both the later Arians' lack of education and their misunderstanding of theology. When Nazianzen concentrates on immediate context his arguments are often persuasive, but his own case can be deficient. He does not support a position counter to the Eunomian interpretation of the higher titles for the Son, specifically Eunomius' contentions that the Son is created, but is not like any other creatures and that the higher titles given to the Son are actually homonyms; Gregory only asserts his own views. Although he points out the weakness of his opponents' education, the decisive factor is still the tradition he receives from his community, particularly his soteriology founded on θέωσις, ''deification.''

Within that emphasis on education and Christian tradition, he stresses literary and poetic skills as significant for expressing the mystery. This is more than a passing comment. His over 17,000 verses demonstrate his interest in poetry; the rhetorical and / or liturgical character of nearly all his other orations, including the invectives and the encomiums, point up his deep sense of life and theology as literary activities.

COMMENTARY ON ORATION 31

The title for this oration is Περὶ τοῦ ῾Αγίου Πνεύματος, "On the Holy Spirit." Manuscripts D and P indicate that it was given at Constantinople, but their comments reflect a tenth-century tradition and thus do not answer whether this oration was part of the original series as presented or published.

31.1 The rhetorical play on the word λόγος in the opening section is skillful if a bit florid by modern standards of style. The first appearance of ὁ λόγος means "the doctrine" about the Son; the second still refers to the teaching about Him, but also serves as a transition into the meaning "the Word" himself by alluding to John 8.59 and perhaps Luke 4.30. The third signifies "The Word" as its subject and recalls particularly the treatment of antagonists in Oration 28.2 where Gregory insists that brutish adversaries, who try to ascend the mount of contemplation, will be stoned. Nazianzen completes his explicit play on λόγος by calling the "arguments" employed to crush the opposition λόγους. The Biblical background for that wordplay is Ex. 19.12-13, which was the dominant image in Oration 28.2.

Other overtones may also be involved. When he refers to "the Word" as the Son, he probably expects his hearers to understand that the "Word" is "Reason" and thus is himself the best "argument." That is why the "arguments" of the antagonists can be overcome in the proper "doctrine" or "teaching" about the Son. That is why a "discourse" (cf. 28.1) is the appropriate means for expressing the "teaching" about the Son. Gregory assumes that most of his audience expects, follows and is pleased by these verbal gymnastics.

Although the allusion to Oration 28 suggests that at least for publication Nazianzen had included that discourse in the group, it leaves open the question whether Oration 28 was originally given in the series at Constantinople. The introductory sentences of 28.1 and 29.1 do not confirm Bernardi's speculation that 28 was added later because Gregory found his arguments defending God's incomprehensibility required more support (cf. Introduction, pp. 76-78).

A number of Nazianzen's opponents view the Holy Spirit as a "strange, unscriptural God," ξένον θεὸν καὶ ἄγραφον. With the beginning of that issue, a new complexity is added to these discourses. The question concerning a "strange, unscriptural God" was raised not only by the later Arians, who, according to Gregory, have a deficient view of the Son, but also by those who, in his opinion, have a "fairly sound," οἱ

. . . μετριάζοντες, view of the Son. This is a reference to a group known as the Pneumatomachians or Macedonians. At least one segment of that group accepted the divinity of the Son, but was resistant to any such talk of the Spirit.

The question about the Spirit's divinity forms the στάσις for this oration. The views of Hermogenes lie behind the outline. Here the issue is whether the Biblical facts support the statement that the Spirit is God. If not, why not? Nazianzen offers two answers: the first, a theory about why the Spirit is seldom directly referred to as god; the second, a series of passages in which the Spirit's divinity is inferred. A number of asides move through the oration, ones that do not weaken the presentation, but the argument formulated here returns to focus in sections 21 and 29. In the latter, the full force of the facts about the question are presented in a swarm of proof-texts from Scripture and thus the Neo-Arians, in Gregory's view, are refuted. The Spirit is not a strange God unknown in Scripture and tradition.

31.2 Being the powerful orator that he is, Nazianzen notices the particular problem the debate and more specifically this series of discourses present. Those exhausted and in his view battered by the conflict concerning the Son now turn all their energy to one last effort focused on the Spirit. Even the defenders of the faith are worn out by the previous exercises.

A second play on λόγος has troubled interpreters and translators alike. As before it seems appropriate to allow a series of meanings because it is difficult to exclude any one. The first use probably indicates both the "doctrine of" and the "discourse about" the Holy Spirit, ὁ περὶ Πνεύματος λόγος; the second use, as Wickham translates it, "discussions of the Son," τοῖς περὶ Υἱοῦ λόγοις, includes both meanings. Since the third use, ὁ λόγος, appears in a three fold series with "the Spirit" and "God," it must mean "The Word." Gregory purposely overloads important terms in an effort to meet the expectations of audiences accustomed to such richness. This poetic packing of individual expressions is common in orations from the ancient world and must be taken into account when interpreting various Fathers. They often do not restrict their writings to univocal meanings of words.

In order to meet the continued charge that his teaching about the Spirit is not to be found in the Bible (cf. sections 1, 3, 21 and 29), Gregory amasses a group of texts in paragraph 29, but here he forgoes what might be expected and only notices that others have made such investigations of Biblical passages. This stage in the argument heightens the audience's tension. Doubtless his opponents thought they had a proposition he could not confound.

The most significant historical insight in this section is the clear reference to his dependence upon the careful study of others and his contribution to their work. The fact that he mentions his own assistance of these "others" suggests that he is not referring to his reliance upon those like Origen who had passed from the scene. He did learn much from writers of previous centuries, but here he alludes to a circle of theologians that included Basil, Gregory of Nyssa, Amphilochius of Iconium and no doubt others to whom epistles are addressed. Although this tiny allusion to such a circle cannot become the basis of any large explanatory theory, it should be considered during discussions about the authorship of disputed letters and treatises. There is a striking similarity among the Cappadocians, one which finds some sense in this passage. It is also witnessed to by the *Philocalia* project, if we may accept the ambiguous reference in Gregory's Epistle 115 and the later manuscript evidence, which indicate that Basil and Nazianzen put that collection of texts together. Perhaps in other instances the circle divided up topics and shared the results. This allowed them to go on to further stages of discussion and not cover exactly the same ground.

Note also that the "systematic studies" they shared are described as ταῦτα πεφιλοσοφήκασιν, "things about which they had philosophical discussions." These "systematic studies" involved "careful, critical analysis," ἐξετάζειν καὶ διαιρεῖσθαι, common words from Aristotle for logical investigations. The focus of the investigation, however, was the sense of words in Scripture. For Nazianzen and his circle the philosophical, logical analysis of Christian doctrine involved philology and grammar as much as anything else, because those linguistic tools allowed the truth of Scripture to be uncovered. Throughout this treatise and the entire series, this understanding of philosophy, logic, rhetoric and grammar dominates Gregory's efforts and forms the context of his attack on Eunomian and now Pneumatomachian misunderstanding of *paideia*.

Ps. 148(147) has no fifteenth verse; thus it cannot be a Scriptural reference for 31.2.9.

31.3   The introduction of the difference between the letter and the spirit in Scripture suggests an undeveloped wordplay. What will the spirit of the text be without the Holy Spirit? Describing the love of the letter as "a cloak for irreligion," ἔνδυμα τῆς ἀσεβείας, might imply a love of allegorical interpretation of the texts. Nazianzen did respect and use Origen. Both individual passages and the *Philocalia*, traditionally ascribed to his and Basil's editing, indicate that influence. Yet it is improper on the basis of Origen's influence to expect that careful philological analysis of the texts will not be forthcoming. Origen's writings show that he gave much attention to the letter (cf. Neuschäfer, *Origenes als Philologe*, "Schweizerische Beiträge zur Altertumswissenschaft, 18'' [Basel, 1987]). The reference in section 2 of this oration to such critical analysis of word usages is to philological study. As has been seen in the previous orations, Gregory will attack the false logical principles which lie behind Eunomian interpretation of texts—as he sees them—but he will also argue the grammar of the texts themselves. His dialectical exegesis is much in evidence.

There is a hint of ascending the mount, a metaphor which appears in Oration 28.2, but here the emphasis is somewhat different. The ''lofty mountain,'' ὄρος ὑψηλόν, becomes the platform from which to proclaim his message, a place above the people, but the connection of both passages with the ascent and preaching of Moses is strong.

Again Nazianzen avoids the use of specific ontological concepts referring to the levels within the Trinity. Most of the time he juggles the relationships on the basis of what he finds in Biblical texts. Here he does not offer specific terms carefully restricted to each level. The distinctions are emphasized by threefold repetition of the verb ἦν, ''was,'' and the noun φῶς, ''light,'' connected by καί. The unity is emphasized by the phrase ἀλλ' ἓν ἦν, ''But a single reality was,'' that follows the verbal sequence and the clause ἀλλ' ἓν φῶς, καὶ εἷς Θεός, ''But the light is one, God is one,'' that conforms to the subjectival sequence.

Most translators find it difficult to make Gregory's meaning clear because he often leaves out the nouns. Yet the interpreter must be cautious about accepting imported substantive nouns as technical terms when the author did not include them. We should concede that this lack of nouns may indicate that the Theologian was not the type of philosopher, the metaphysician, which Gregory of Nyssa was, but as a philosophical rhetorician, one concerned with what he sees as the logical crudities of the later Arians, Nazianzen may have avoided metaphysical speculations for reasons different from a lack of philosophical skill. Perhaps, like theologians in other eras, he does not always opt for such definitions because he sees in them too much dependence upon metaphysical concepts. Perhaps he purposely restricts most of his ''philosophical'' comments to logic and lower-level epistemology and leaves the ontological definitions aside because the enigma of human existence and the mystery of divine reality surpass the ability to comprehend them, let alone express them (cf. sections 31-33 and Or. 28.4).

Gallay in 31.3.22 reads θεολογίαν with A, Q, B, W, V, T and S against the ὁμολογίαν of D, P and C. The evidence is difficult to assess. Gallay insists that family M, that is, S, D, P and C, is the better group of manuscripts. If that be true, perhaps the better reading is ὁμολογίαν. Nothing in the meaning of the two words, the grammatical structure of the sentence, or the immediate context demands that one be chosen over the other.

1 Cor. 3.6 has no relationship with 31.3.3. Rev. 22.11 has the form and the cadence of 31.3.22-23, but the words are from Isa. 21.2.

31.4 The bold threefold repetition of ἕν, "one," connected by καί represents a simple but forceful response to a form of the older Arian formula ἦν ὅτε οὐκ ἦν, "there was when he was not." Most translators supply the phrase "a time" in order to clarify the meaning, but at this stage in the argument Gregory does not include that clarification. Therefore, his point could be that if ever the Father was not, then it is proper to say that the Son was not. And if ever the Son was not, then it is appropriate to say that the Spirit was not. If, however, the one "was from beginning," ἦν ἀπ' ἀρχῆς—evidently a reference to John 1.1—then the three were also. Had he presented his case that way, Nazianzen would not be open to the later Arian charge that those whom we know as "orthodox" were all "chronists," people who misunderstood the later Arian claims as Aetius (*Syntagmation*, Intro.) indicates. The Eunomian position was not that there was a **time** when the Son and the Spirit were not. Before time began, the Father existed without the Son and the Spirit as Eunomius (*Apology* 10) says. Here Gregory insists that "from beginning," ἀπ' ἀρχῆς—the qualitative stress without the article—the three were together. Without a reference to time, his words would involve a stronger claim. From the beginning without concern for time, all three were present.

By introducing this section with the old Arian formula, Nazianzen makes specific reference to the Eunomian community, but by warning that if one of the Trinity is cast down, then the other two are in danger, he also returns to the second group of people who catch his attention, ones usually called Pneumatomachians or Macedonians. He mentioned them in section 1 as those who are basically sound in their teaching about the Son, but do not accept the divinity of the Spirit.

The Theologian's debate with the later Arians involves two levels. First, on the ontological level, i.e., within the Trinity itself, a claim that God is holy appears strange to Gregory if it does not acknowledge that the Holy Spirit is God. He also is pre-existent. Nazianzen's designation of "divinity," θεότης as "complete," τελεία indicates another aspect of his deep disagreement with the later Arians about ontological reality. For him, the Trinity is the complete divinity. Eunomians also would demand a perfect divinity, but they would restrict that to the Father. They have no difficulty envisioning the Son's nature as a God-like quality not shared by human creation, but for them, such a divinity is not complete. Thus they find it unthinkable to ascribe complete Godhead to a being of third rank like the Spirit.

Second, on the soteriological level, Gregory warns that if the Spirit is not from the beginning, then he must be of the same order as humans, even if he does have a small priority. Both the Spirit and human beings would then be separated from God "by time," χρόνῳ. A Holy Spirit of the same order as humans cannot make humans divine. In that way the basic economy of God would be destroyed.

Nazianzen's introduction of χρόνος, "time," is a major category mistake. It highlights the almost complete misunderstanding of each other that characterizes the two parties at this point. Most students of these debates now understand that the Arians did not place the beginning of the Son or the Spirit **in** time. They posited that dependence, that subordination, before time began. By not recognizing such a distinction Gregory missed an interesting chance. He might have sharpened his soteriological argument and noticed that if the Spirit is a third-order divinity, he could only make humans third-order divinities, not gods as Nazianzen's sense of salvation demanded. By speaking of "time," he has opened himself up to the Eunomian charge that he is a "chronist," a person too concerned with time and not enough aware of timelessness. Translators should not introduce the phrase into their renderings until this point so that the missed opportunity is clear. Gregory relied upon a soteriological argument similar to that found in Athanasius' refutation of the early Arians (*Against the Arians* 39). Perhaps Athanasius also employed the "time" argument from a source which had attempted to refute the old Arian formula.

1 Cor. 3.16 speaks of the indwelling Spirit; it does not use the language ἐμὲ ποιεῖ Θεόν found in 31.4.13. 2 Peter 1.4 is closer to the thought, γένησθε θείας κοινωνοὶ φύσεως, "you might become partakers of the divine nature," but it does not mention the Spirit.

31.5   For the historian of Christian doctrine this section is one of the most interesting paragraphs to appear in these orations. The contrast between the Sadducees' rejection of a Holy Spirit and some non-Christian theologians—philosophers with theological interests—who talked about the Spirit as "the mind of the universe," νοῦν τοῦ παντός, or "the external mind," τὸν θύραθεν νοῦν, is itself intriguing. The first phrase from the philosophers probably refers to the Platonic (*Phaedrus* 97C-D; *Philebus* 28C) or Platonist view of the world-soul, while the second appears to be a remembered reference from Aristotle (*De Generatione Animalium* 736B). Elias of Crete (p. 176; *PG* 36, 826) suggests not only Plato and Aristotle but also Anaxagoras and Hermotimus Clazomenus as sources for these views. This is one of a number of places in which Gregory makes his selective appreciation of Greek philosophers known.

The striking admission, however, is the amount of disagreement within the Christian community about the status of the Spirit. The Christian "experts," σόφοι—probably meant as a degrading, ironic reference—

have widely divergent views. The description Nazianzen offers is a bit confused in terms of determining exactly how many groups are involved, but according to his treatment of the various opinions, particularly in sections 10-14, there seem to be three major parties. The first is the later Arians. They do not confess a Trinity of equality, but a subordination of Son and Spirit. They can employ different terms to argue for that explanation. Gregory refers to some who call the Spirit an ἐνέργεια, an "active process," and others who call him a κτίσμα, "creature." Eunomius (*Apology* 25-26) refers to the Holy Spirit as an ἐνέργεια and a ποίημα, a "thing made." The latter term is synonymous with κτίσμα in Eunomius' vocabulary, for he uses both to describe the Son (*Apology* 17-18). Another view represented in this oration can be attributed to him. In section 25 of his *Apology* he argues for the position which Gregory terms "the rank inherent in the names," τὴν ἐν τοῖς ὀνόμασι τάξιν.

The second group is basically agnostic. They see no clear claim in Scripture that the Spirit is divine. Thus they do not offer the Spirit worship, but neither do they speak of him with any disrespect. In sections 10-14 this party is said to have worshipped the Son, but to have avoided worship of the Spirit. They are most likely the Pneumatomachians.

The third group views the Spirit as God, but is itself divided. Some are willing to confess in public that the Spirit is God; others prefer only to think the thought in silent prayer. These represent Nazianzen's party, specifically those like Gregory, who preach the doctrine boldly, and those like Basil, who never wrote that the Spirit was God. A.-M. Ritter (*Das Konzil von Konstantinople und Sein Symbol* [Göttingen, 1965], pp. 253-270) argues that Nazianzen was particularly dismayed by the third article of the creed adopted at the Council of Constantinople in 381. Ritter uses the *Carmen de vita sua* II, lines 1703-1765 (*PG* 37, 1148-1153) as part of his evidence. C. Jungck (*Gregor von Nazianz: De vita sua* [Heidelberg, 1974], pp. 220-225) finds Ritter's argument unconvincing, but it does seem that the Theologian's position over against those in his own party was hardened by the disappointment he felt at the council. By insisting thus far, particularly in section 3 of this oration, that the Holy Spirit is God, he already voices his own disagreement with Basil and those who followed the Caesarean.

The puzzle for the historian arises from the exact words of Gregory in this paragraph. Evidently there are a number of variations within what appear to be the three larger groups. Later Arians, Pneumatomachians and the "Orthodox" are represented, but there are subtle differences. Throughout this oration one senses the strain. Different groups of later Arians are given attention. Perhaps they were not a unified force within Constantinople. Eunomius (*Apology* 25) was frustrated by some who saw the Spirit as an ἐνέργεια, an ''activity'' of God, but still viewed the Spirit as of the same essence with the Father and the Son. Certainly Nazianzen's treatment of the Pneumatomachians appears odd to the modern reader. At times he seems to praise them for their stand concerning the Son and yet he attacks them so sharply because of their views of the Spirit that they well might have been angered by his words. He also does not handle the silent but prayerfully confessing ''Orthodox'' with care and patience. This oration reeks with the smell of live debate and intolerance, problems not yet clarified, parties not yet solidified.

31.6 Nazianzen leaves behind the Sadducees and the Greeks in order to attack the logic of his later Arian opponents. Their dialectical arguments, those with which he ''takes issue,'' διαλεξόμεθα, are primarily general ontological distinctions. If his antagonists are to be dialectically skillful and forceful, then they must solve in consistent fashion a number of conundrums. The form of Gregory's attack is the rhetorical enthymeme, but in this case as often earlier, the statements could take syllogistic form if necessary. Nazianzen includes the audience by leaving part of the syllogism for them to provide.

Much of the force of his points depends upon both accepted and contested definitions: an ἐνέργεια, ''activity,'' must be a συμβεβηκός, ''accident,'' since it could not be an οὐσία, a ''substance,'' say the Eunomians. Yet Gregory responds that their position cannot be true since Scripture speaks of the Holy Spirit as a subject, not merely as an activity done by a different subject.

Evidently the Theologian and his various opponents did agree that Godhead could not be ''composite,'' σύνθετος, but it is not clear that all those involved in this dispute would agree on specific definitions of ἐνέργεια, ''activity,'' συμβεβηκός, ''accident,'' and οὐσία, ''substance.'' Eunomius (*Apology* 25) calls the Spirit an ἐνέργεια, ''activity,'' of God who is something less than God's οὐσία, ''substance;'' he is troubled by those who can refer to the Spirit as an ''activity'' and still see his ''substance'' as one with the Father and the Son. In his case Gregory's definitions or enthymemes would fall on deaf ears. The force of Nazianzen's argument lies more in the Biblical quotations that view the Spirit as a subject. The question is how the later Arians would treat those texts. Could an ἐνέργεια be a subject, or be referred to as a subject?

The soteriological-liturgical argument concerning baptism into the Spirit has weight only if one stands in the theological tradition Gregory accepted. Why would later Arians be baptized in the Spirit, if they said he was a creature? Eunomius' preference (*Apology* 25) is for the word ποίημα, ''thing made,'' but the choice of this word implies some kind of creaturely status for the Spirit. Nazianzen knows his own soteriology will not allow precisely what the later Arians posit. In their view, second and third rank deities are possible. For them there is no clear choice that demands the Son or the Spirit be either of the same essence as the Father, or of the same essence as lowly creatures. Within hymnic passages in his *Confession* 3-4, Eunomius speaks about the Son and the Spirit neither as creatures exactly like humans nor as divinities exactly like the Father. Furthermore, the Eunomians had a different baptismal practice, a single immersion, that did not depend upon the Spirit to deify the participant.

The Theologian's ontological distinctions between essence / accident and God / creature with no possibility of intermediary levels between those extremes are not shared by his adversaries. Here the strict dialectical distinctions only become forceful if they are acceptable to or can be pressed upon the other side of the dispute. Gregory himself warns against either / or categories elsewhere in this oration, as in section 8 where he attacks the Eunomian insistence on no middle term between "ingeneracy" and "generacy." His attack here is not well formed. The Eunomians posit terms between an unbegotten God and a created humanity as he posits terms between "ingeneracy" and "generacy."

Mt. 12.20 and John 14.26 have no relationship to λέγει, "he speaks" in 31.6.11. The reference there should be Acts 13.2 which is correctly given for ἀφορίζει, "he decrees" in 31.6.12. For that word, Rom. 1.1 and Gal. 1.15 are incorrect. In 30.6.12 Job 4.9 has no connection with the passage.

31.7   Once more the Theologian invites dialectical, syllogistic combat. The quotation most likely comes from the Eunomians rather than the Pneumatomachians. Eunomius (*Apology* 25) argues that the Spirit is neither "unbegotten," ἀγέννητος, like the Father, nor a "begotten one," γέννημα, like the Son. He is third, both in "nature," φύσιν, and "rank," τάξιν. In his *Apology for the Apology* 1.4 (Jaeger 1.72; Vaggione, p. 102) Eunomius referred to the Spirit as a "third essence," οὔσης . . . τρίτης. Perhaps some within the Eunomian community set up a conundrum as Nazianzen states it in order to ridicule a Trinitarian doctrine. From the later Arian vantage point, "two unorginate beings," δύο ἄναρχα, is unthinkable.

The accusation that Gregory's party are those who "have such a penchant for corporeal ideas," φιλοσώματοι, is refuted by returning the favor. There is agreement among the disputants that being snagged in corporeal conceptions stops progress in theology, but each side finds the other in trouble. Each offers *reductio ad absurdum* responses. Nazianzen's are more interesting to modern readers since his indicate how odd it would be to think of the gender of nouns as designating sex. Both styles of argument, sophistically satisfying to those already convinced, fail to persuade and thus fail logically and rhetorically.

Two things should be noted here. First, Nazianzen has a strong sense that the later Arian position, with its second- and third-level deities that are not God and not human creatures, drags in the Graeco-Roman myths and the distrusted Christian Gnostic heresies. If the ontological distinctions of essence / accident and God / creature are excluded, then these descending, mediating beings must be injected. That wreaks havoc.

Second, Gregory does not accept the relationship between language and reality that the later Arians do. For him reality is not in the name. He shares one part of an Epicurean view of language which sees that the truth rests in the things that underlie the words, the πράγματα (*Or.* 29.13 and Epicurus, *Letter to Herodotus* 37 and 75). For Nazianzen language continues to be an approximation of the real, the first stage that Epicurus describes for words. Gregory, however, depends upon Aristotle's claim (*On Interpretation* 16A-B) that nouns signify things according to convention or arbitrary designation. His opponents meanwhile work from a different theory where names state the essence of the object in question, a theory supported by Philo (*Leg. All.* 2.14-15), Plato (*Cratylus* 430A-431E), Albinus (*Epit.* 6), Epicurus (*Letter to Herodotus* 75-76 [language's second stage], and Chrysippus (*SVF* II, 895). Basil (*Against Eunomius* 2.4) had rejected the later Arian view of language; Eunomius (*Apology* 16 and 18) defended it and (*Apology for the Apology* 1.6, Jaeger 1.345-346; Vaggione, pp. 107-108) attacked Basil's views as Epicurean and Aristotelian. Disagreement at that level makes discussion difficult and agreement almost impossible.

Gallay (pp. 288-289, n. 2) follows the witnesses he finds most reliable elsewhere—S, D, P and C—in suggesting that the name of Valentinus was added to the text in 31.7.23 as a correction, probably when the shift was made from uncial to minuscule transcription. Elias of Crete (p. 178) apparently had both names in his text. Gallay's case rests on a grammatical incongruity, rather than the absence of "Valentinus" in the other manuscripts. Τοῦ τοὺς καινοὺς αἰῶνας ἀνατυπώσαντος, "who pictured those outlandish aeons," is singular. A corrector well might have added "Valentinus" as the author of the pictures, particularly since Marcion's doctrine does not seem to have included the intermediary beings that are the focus of the debate at this point. This language is common fare in the debate. Eunomius (*Apology for the Apology* 1.7 and 2.19, Jaeger 1.356, 362 and 2.284; Vaggione, pp. 110-111 and 125) attacks Basil for bringing in the Valentinian aeons. E. Hardy, (*Christology of the Later Fathers*, "The Library of Christian Classics, III" [Philadelphia, 1954], p. 198, n. 11) ingeniously suggests that the Marcion reference may be a slip for the Gnostic Marcus mentioned by Irenaeus, *A.H.* 1.11. Moreschini (p. 167, n. 26) thinks that Nazianzen is confused about gnostic teachings, for he also mistakes Marcion for Marcus the Great in *Or.* 32.16.

31.8   As in earlier orations, Nazianzen does not accept the later Arian "dilemma," διαίρεσιν, another one of their "exclusive alternatives," διαιρέσεις. The logical division his opponents present as an A / non-A inclusive categorization fails because Jesus himself in John 15.26 said the Spirit "proceeds," ἐκπορεύεται, from the Father. Gregory posits that procession must be a "mean term," μέσος, between the alternatives of "ingeneracy," ἀγέννητος, and "generacy," γεννητός. If he is correct, the later Arian puzzle is itself a logical fallacy.

How then is "procession" to be explained? Here Nazianzen reintroduces arguments found in Oration 28. Because there are so many things near at hand that human intellect cannot explain, the category of mystery should not seem strange when it is applied to the depths of God. The later Arians are unable to define the "ingeneracy" of the Father; Gregory's inability to give a description of "procession" should be expected, particularly if God in himself is incomprehensible.

John 20.11 has no contextual relationship with 31.8.19.

31.9   The Eunomians insist that there "is something missing," λείπει, in the Spirit. Nazianzen knows that such "deficiency," ἔλλειψις, to them means grounds for "subordination in essence," τῆς κατὰ τὴν οὐσίαν ὑφέσεως. Gregory of Nyssa (*Against Eunomius* 1.19, Jaeger 1.92) says Eunomius taught subordination in essence. Aetius (*Syntagmation* 4ff.) made the "incomparability of essence," τὸ ἐν οὐσίᾳ ἀσύγκριτον, a centerpiece in his thought. Athanasius (*Against the Arians* 1.18) had found "deficiency" to be a teaching of the early Arians.

The Theologian counters with his own position. There is "difference," διάφορον, within the Trinity, but it is a difference "of manifestation," ἐκφάνσεως, of "relationship," σχέσεως. What must be safeguarded is "distinctness of the three persons within the single nature and quality of the Godhead," τὸ ἀσύγχυτον . . . τῶν τριῶν ὑποστάσεων ἐν τῇ μιᾷ φύσει τε καὶ ἀξίᾳ τῆς θεότητος. The unnamed opponents here are referred to as Sabellians (cf. section 30), those who collapse the distinctions in the Trinity and instead speak of something like different modes of a single actor. Eunomius (*Apology* 6) lumped his opponents with Sabellius, Marcellus of Ancyra and Photinus of Sirmium and (*Apology for the Apology* 2.16, Jaeger 2.246; Vaggione, p. 123) accused Basil of being a Sabellian. The Theologian, however, does not specifically refer to Marcellus or Photinus in these orations. He refers only in passing to "Galatians," followers of Marcellus, in 22.12 and Photinus in 33.16. Here he mentions "distinctness," τὸ ἀσύγχυτον, to avoid any sense of modalism, a position he evidently shares with his later Arian opponents.

Ἔκφανσις, "manifestation," appears to have no special technical or ontological sense in this section. It simply means that the persons of the Trinity can be distinguished. Plotinus (*Enneads* 3.5.9) employs the term in that way. The context here does not impose a precise meaning. In 29.16 Gregory makes his use of σχέσις, "relationship," clear by insisting that the name Father designates neither an "essence," οὐσία, nor an "action," ἐνέργεια, but a "relationship." Thus σχέσις as the explanation of "Father" also avoids ontological commitments like those entailed in οὐσία and ἐνέργεια. Eunomius (*Apology* 8, 18-19 and 23) insists that "unbegotten" was the name of God's essence and that other names like "Father" had to be equal to "unbegotten" to be names of God. The Son was an "action" of the Father. Throughout his work he emphasizes that names designate essences.

Gregory's statement of "three persons in one nature" provides nouns for his conceptions and thus represents what many see as a locus classicus for Cappadocian Trinitarian doctrine. Yet even here it is easier to specify what he intended to avoid than to state exactly what he wished to confess. Ὑπόστασις, "person," and φύσις, "nature," have long histories and can be traced in abundant secondary literature, but they do not have a strong context in Nazianzen's corpus. Here he does not define their meaning. What he rebukes (section 30) is a Sabellian collapse of the distinctions within the Godhead and a Eunomian division and subordination that in his eyes destroys the value, the "quality" of the Godhead.

This oration gives much more attention to the ontological questions involved in the Trinity than do the others in the series. Although Oration 29 discusses some of the same issues, it does not respond to metaphysical conundrums as this discourse does. The point of Oration 30 was to demonstrate that the later Arian proof-texts could be explained better under the rubric the Theologian brought to the Scripture, or as he would have said, read from it. He could interpret their texts by positing either a fully human subject or a divine subject limited by His incarnation. In Nazianzen's view, Eunomians did not explain properly the passages that spoke of a divine Son, equal in essence with the Father. In this oration more than the others, the ontological disagreements are mentioned, but they are as ever based in the understanding of language, in the relationship between names and essences, and are not given detailed explanation.

31.10 If section 9 is perhaps a locus classicus for Gregory's Trinitarian position, then this section is the same for his method. When pressed to indicate what he means, to give some "analogy," ὁμοίωσιν, for his views, he sets out his approach in clear and concise terms. He is not a crude fideist who would consider all queries concerning analogies to be out of court, but he does warn about the futility of such projects. In section 31 he will reiterate the impossibility of finding an "illustration," εἰκών, that depicts the Trinity. Here, however, he indicates that analogues are possible as a "support to argument," τῷ λόγῳ βοήθειαν.

Much as he did in Oration 28, he chides his opponents for not knowing what can be found in nature. They must not assume that only one way of producing offspring exists in this world. The later Arian charge at the beginning of the paragraph assumes that there are no analogies for Nazianzen's view and thus indicates to him a lack of scientific interest or knowledge among his adversaries. They have not looked at what examples appear in nature before they attack others as being unable to provide any support for a different understanding of the Godhead. Gregory does not go into detail, but he hints at what might be said to demonstrate the lack of learning among the Eunomians. Perhaps he has in mind some insights similar to those of Aristotle on animal history or on the generation of animals as Barbel (p. 237, n. 18) suggests. Elias of Crete (p. 181 and *PG* 36, 829) proposes that this section alludes to the phoenix legend, probably to show how narrow the sense of possibilities is among the Theologian's antagonists.

The disclaimers about human or natural analogies in the discussions of heavenly realities should not be passed over quickly. In most instances within these orations, the Theologian argues on philosophical / rhetorical grounds—primarily through the use of logic and grammar—that the positions taken by the later Arians do not hold together. In sections 9 and 10, however, he has posited certain ontological realities in order to counter their views: the Trinity is three persons in one nature. He seems willing to do that, but at the same time, is aware that analogies and words taken from this earth are inadequate. He knows sentences need nouns, but in describing the Godhead, all nouns fail to capture the truth (cf. section 31). Limited analogies may be employed, but they are used in an *ad hoc* fashion. They are neither systematic nor foundational.

He is not always careful, however, about the reductionistic danger involved in the inclusive use of opposing categories. In section 5 he employed "substance" and "accident" as mutually exclusive and yet inclusive of all possibilities. There he emphasized the implications of dismembering such categories, that is, the necessary introduction of aeons and middle terms. In paragraph 8 he attacked the Eunomian use of exclusive alternatives and developed his argument from implications, relationships and finally natural analogies.

Only when his orations are compared with the presentations of Chrysostom and Gregory of Nyssa for example does his method become clear. The debate forces him toward certain limited ontological claims, but he does not argue for metaphysical categories as Nyssa does with definitions and systematic schemes. Yet he is much more concerned with philosophy and logic in his attack than is Chrysostom. The best description of his work is that of a philosophical rhetorician who can use ontological categories, but who prefers to handle the debate on the level of logical, grammatical principles. Much of the time he points out the fallacies in his opponents' reductionistic definitions and offers only sketches of his own confessions. He does that because he believes God is incomprehensible in essence but at the same time knowable.

31.11 His analogy is telling because it is taken from Scripture, from the early narratives surrounding creation and the first human procreation. It must be possible for three individual beings to have the "same essence" if Adam, Eve and Seth are ὁμοούσιος. Being true to his own principles, Gregory immediately raises the disclaimers against the wrong uses of his analogy. "Molding," πλάσις, "division," τομή, and "anything bodily," σῶμα, do not apply to the heavenly realm. Those transitory aspects are always inappropriate when comparing earthly and heavenly realities.

The rephrased charge in this paragraph is answered by the points of the analogy he employs. A human-born child like Seth and the created humans like Adam and Eve did come from the same source, but the original charge from section 10 stands unanswered because Gregory does not explain why Seth, Adam and Eve are not to be considered primarily as three humans. The analogy can be pressed so that they become evidence for three gods rather than one God in Trinity.

Nazianzen's principle is all that saves him here. Even then his position is weak. Had he not insisted throughout these arguments that "it is impossible to track down a spotless picture of the whole truth," οὐδὲ γὰρ οἷόν τε τῶν εἰκαζομένων οὐδὲν πρὸς πᾶσαν ἐξικνεῖσθαι καθαρῶς τὴν ἀλήθειαν, his position would be untenable. The difficulty of using analogies at all is obvious. Which parts of them are to apply and which not?

Gen. 1.27 for 31.11.1 is a misprint for Gen. 2.7.

31.12 The questions raised in this section represent views of the later Arians, but they could also have come from the Pneumatomachians. Some members of that group accepted the divinity of the Son, but did not confess the Spirit as part of the Godhead. A form of this inquiry about the status of the Spirit in Scripture appeared in section 1 and will be handled in paragraphs 21ff. The concise responses from John, Rom. and 1 Cor. almost suggest that Gregory has tailored these questions to his answers rather than hearing them from his opponents, but that sense is false. The opponents are troubled by the way these New Testament passages might be employed to reproduce the polytheism of Graeco-Roman culture. Eunomius (*Apology* 25) uses John 4.24 to support his position. For him this verse shows that the Spirit and the Father are two different things, because the one worshipped and the one "in whom" he is worshipped are not identical. He also insists that since "the Saviour" himself said that "another," ἕτερον (cf. John 14.16, ἄλλον) would be sent, the Spirit is not identical with the Son.

Gregory's adversaries also claim that the Spirit must be a creature, because he is one of the things made by the Son. Eunomius (*Apology* 25) insists that the Spirit is a "thing made," ποίημα, but Nazianzen responds that John 1.2-3 has its own qualifier: The Son made all the things which were made. If the Spirit was not one of the things made, then this verse does not apply to him.

For Gregory a different danger is involved in these questions. While his main antagonists see the unity of God threatened, his oneness misinterpreted, even monotheism undermined (section 10 "God plus God"), Nazianzen sees the Trinity and thus the wholeness of the Godhead sacrificed by his adversaries. Again the soteriological motif underlies his position. If the Son and the Spirit are lowered to the level of creatures in order to give the Father some inordinate dignity, then those taking that position may be "banished from the Trinity," τῆς Τριάδος ἐκπέσῃς, "banished from the whole," τοῦ παντὸς ἐκπεπτωκώς. If the Spirit is a creature, if the Father is robbed of a Son and given a creature, then we human creatures will have forfeited the possibility of becoming gods. Only if the Son and the Spirit are of the essence of the Father can people be baptized in the name of the Son and the Spirit; only then can humans believe "in" them rather than "about" them (section 6). If the Trinity is lost because of this blasphemy, so is salvation.

31.13   In section 10, debate about the Spirit and the Father led to the question of two gods. But the ultimate query from his opponents is the possibility of three gods. Gregory of Nyssa's *That There Are Not Three Gods*, a piece probably written ten years after these discourses, indicates this problem persisted. In a rather interesting rebuttal of his own, Nazianzen divides his adversaries into two camps, Eunomians and Pneumatomachians, and plays them off against each other.

The repetition of the second person pronoun strongly suggests that Pneumatomachians were in his audience. Although he might be merely explaining in dramatic fashion what he would say to them, in a previous oration (27.1) he noted that the opponents were taking down notes on his presentation. There he also employed the second person pronoun in addressing them. Here Gregory's response hits the mark. The Pneumatomachian position of being a ditheist—from the standpoint of later Arians —or of arguing a sound case concerning the Son but a poor one about the Spirit – from the vantage point of Nazianzen – is weak considered from either the later Arian or the "orthodox" side. Yet Gregory's sharp attack on the Macedonians is difficult for a modern reader to understand. It gains debater's points for his supporters and himself. Whatever arguments these Pneumatomachians used to defend themselves from the charge of ditheism can be used by Nazianzen to defend himself against their charge of tritheism. The attack, however, only makes the Pneumatomachians look ridiculous. Perhaps Gregory was desperate or he found ridicule to be a motivating factor. The Biblical prophets used strong rebuke to make their points. It is possible that Nazianzen intended to embarrass the Pneumatomachians so that they might see their error. Some readers taught by more traditional European professors will have strong memories of that kind of motivation to learn. Yet the Theologian may have decided that the Pneumatomachians could not be won over to his side. They could be made to look stupid, but they could not be made to see his full position. Interestingly, Socrates (*H.E.* 7.7-9) notes that this group did join the discussion at the Council of Constantinople the next year, but eventually withdrew.

31.14   To take on both parties in this struggle, Gregory must return to the question of three gods. For him "the Godhead exists undivided in separate beings," ἀμέριστος ἐν μεμερισμένοις . . . ἡ θεότης. He hopes to make this paradoxical expression clearer by employing the figure of three interconnected suns from which comes a "single intermingled light," μία τοῦ φωτὸς σύγκρασις. Against attacks on the unity of the Godhead, he emphasizes the sameness of the light even though in section 12 he noted that the unity may be more meagerly represented in his view. That is probably true of this picture.

The metaphor itself is an older one that becomes part of the great credal tradition. Eunomius (*Apology* 19) understands its importance. He insists that the primary descriptive terms of the Father and Son are "unbegotten" and "begotten." Therefore, if there are references to "light," the light of the unbegotten must differ from that of the begotten since their natures are different. For the Son "light" is a homonym not a synonym.

Gregory confuses the issue by once again attempting to answer the question about πρώτη αἰτία, "primal cause." In previous sections of these orations he has gotten into philosophical difficulties by identifying the Father as the "primal cause" (esp. 29.15). That is a common problem, one which Basil (*On the Holy Spirit* 21 and 38) also discussed. Here Nazianzen changes ground and uses language that suggests a first cause outside the three: "But when we look at the three in whom the Godhead exists, who derive their timeless and equally glorious being from the primal cause, we have three objects of worship," ὅταν δὲ πρὸς τὰ ἐν οἷς ἡ θεότης, καὶ τὰ ἐκ τῆς πρώτης αἰτίας ἀχρόνως ἐκεῖθεν ὄντα καὶ ὁμοδόξως, τρία τὰ προσκυνούμενα. One difficulty for any Trinitarian theology that uses the concept of a "primal cause" is the placement of that cause within the scheme. The conundrum seems impossible to solve. If the primal cause is the Father, then the Father is different from the Son and the Spirit. But if that cause is outside or before the three, then part of the definition of God does not reside within the three. No matter which approach Gregory chooses, a puzzle remains. Meijering (*God Being History: Studies in Patristic Philosophy* [Amsterdam, 1975], pp. 111-113, esp. n. 43) insists Nazianzen's treatment is philosophically arbitrary while Meyendorff (*Byzantine Theology* 2nd rev. ed [New York, 1983] p. 183) notes the importance and creativity of the position within Eastern tradition. It is a Biblical puzzle that remains unsolved.

Nazianzen is neither consistent nor ontologically penetrating at these points. His attempt to provide a framework in which Biblical statements, theological and soteriological theory, and liturgical practice make the most sense has serious weaknesses. His philosophical power is most evident when he challenges the necessary conclusions of Eunomian syllogisms. When, however, he moves to ontological explanations, his presentation suffers. His case finally rests on the mystery of the Trinity. Its sense can be supported by the fullest arguments of Oration 28. Humans know so little about nature and themselves, they can hardly expect to comprehend God's nature. Yet the Theologian feels the pressure to provide analogies and at times ontological terms as partial explanations of his position. When he limits himself to carefully structured analogies he can be helpful, but occasionally he falters badly at the metaphysical level, such as here with the concept of a primal cause.

31.15 The Christian parties to this debate all recognize the larger context. Paganism surrounds them. The battle with polytheism persists. Thus Gregory's opponents introduce the analogy of a unified humanity with many individuals, evidently a picture that pagans employ to emphasize the unity of their polytheism. If the "orthodox" use such figures to explain their views, are they not in reality dreaded polytheists?

Nazianzen responds by pointing up the difference between his conception and those of the Greeks. Their view of the one Godhead is limited to "speculative thought," ἐπινοίᾳ θεωρητόν, alone. Humans / humanity is not analogous to Father, Son and Holy Spirit / God because humans are real, but "humanity" is a "speculative" concept. The differences are too great. The pagan analogy does not fit the Christian reality.

There is possibly a hidden argument in this paragraph, one directed against the later Arians. Eunomius (*Apology* 8) attacked the so-called "orthodox" positions as doing away with realities and leaving language only to be the "invention," ἐπίνοια, of men. By rejecting the concept of unity proposed by polytheism as a part of "speculative thought," ἐπινοίᾳ θεωρητόν, Gregory leaves the door open for an ἐπίνοια that is substantive. Both Basil (*Against Eunomius* 1.5-7) and Gregory of Nyssa (*Against Euno-*

mius 2.11-66, Jaeger 2.227-409) explained at length the substantive view of ἐπίνοια. For them not all "thoughts" are speculative or without reality.
31.16   The analogy between the Trinity and polytheism fails on other counts also. Within pagan pantheons, individual gods oppose each other. If the stories are explained as allegorical, the statement of Homer (*Iliad* 15) still demands plurality rather than unity: "All things are thrice divided," τριχθὰ δὲ πάντα δέδασται. The Christian Trinity, however, has an "identity of essence and power," τῷ ταὐτῷ τῆς οὐσίας καὶ τῆς δυνάμεως.

Gregory's closing lines suggest that he recognizes some weakness in his arguments. He hopes he has been persuasive, but if not, more might be expected. The oration is not quite half finished at this point.

One thing is perhaps clearer because of sections 15-16. Nazianzen has indicated how different his own view of the separation or division within the Trinity is from that of polytheistic Greeks. Neither an analogy of humanity nor an account of Greek gods is similar at crucial points to his view of the Godhead. The interesting undertone of these sections is that the positions of his opponents, however, do run such a risk. They have not predicated evil or mischievous attitudes and deeds of the Son or the Spirit, at least not on a par with the horrible pictures of deities in the Greek myths, but they have introduced differences of rank and distinctions of nature. That kind of variation is described in section 5 where gradations of power and essence are seen as basic to his antagonists' positions. For Gregory essence and power in the Godhead are identical. The danger of polytheism, with its distinctions of ranks and natures, lies with his adversaries.

In Homer (*Iliad* 14. 201) Oceanus and Tethys are referred to as the "gods before the gods." Orphic mythology gives a similar position to Phanes. Gallay (p. 307, n. 5) notices that Athenagoras (*The Supplication for Christians* 18-23) speaks of Oceanus, Tethys, Phanes and Kronos. The last is the god, here unnamed, who "gobbled up" the other gods and then "regurgitated" them.
31.17   An arithmetical puzzle appears here and occupies the next three sections. For the modern reader, part of the conundrum may be explained by remembering the old saw about mixing apples and oranges. The later Arians sense that they run no risk of three Gods since they insist that the Son and the Spirit are not like the Father. There is one apple, one orange and one peach; if all are apples, there must be three.

Eunomius (*Apology* 25) relies on an argument from numbering, but he does that in terms of "rank," τάξις, as first, second and third. A statement similar to that which Nazianzen reports does not seem to appear in the writings we still possess from Eunomius.

Gregory's wit comes through in this section, although the ridicule might have failed to persuade his adversaries. Ψόγος, "invective," primarily was employed to persuade supporters rather than opponents. Yet in Oration 29.21 the Theologian urged the Neo-Arians to be reconciled to God and thus probably hoped for their eventual change of heart.

31.18 From Nazianzen's vantage point, the problem is with the principle itself, for counting does not specify the nature of things. Arithmetic does not determine essence. There are numerous examples from Scripture in which things are listed in groups, that is, counted together, and yet their natures are different. In other instances, things of the same nature are counted separately and not included in a sum. If the antagonists are so attached to the word of Scripture, how is it that they have not seen these counter-examples which defy their principle?

This well-reasoned section wins the point. It is not the case that anything included in a sum must be of the same nature as all the units involved. No principle of grammar or logic is broken if one speaks of three in the group: one apple, one orange and one peach, or if one speaks of various things of the same nature but does not add them up. Mortley (II, pp. 172-173) notices that Gregory of Nyssa used this kind of argumentation in his refutation of Eunomius. He finds Nyssa's point an effective one because Eunomius did not consider alternative uses for number. The same applies to Nazianzen's argument. The later Arians are not wrong to see that numbers can involve ranking, but to restrict numbers to that function is to misunderstand mathematics. Once again their lack of education is evident.

Ex. 25.18 is a clearer reference for 31.18.16-17 than Ex. 37.8.

31.19 Gregory's opponents might try to clarify their point. For them the mistake of Nazianzen's party is not with apples and oranges, but with numerals and nouns. If there are "three apples" then there is no unity, only three distinct apples. The major error Gregory sees in his adversaries' position is a crucial one. They set out rules and foundational principles of language that do not cover the cases one actually finds in the use of language. They are not the purists and he the innovator. He follows ancient rules (cf. section 18). What the later Arians have done is to try to make language fulfill certain laws instead of looking at its usage, both by the general population and by the authoritative standard in theology, Scripture. Once again the similarity between his views and those held by modern linguistic analysts is striking.

1 John 5.8 fits his rebuttal, although the lack of a noun with "three who bear witness" somewhat complicates the argument. This Biblical text is a classical example of textual variation. Nazianzen's employment of it in this form suggests he had access to what is presently considered the best

text of the passage. Gallay (p. 24, n. 1) reports that Sablier, in an unpublished paper, analyzed the New Testament citations in Gregory's works. He concluded that usually Nazianzen followed a text similar to K or D. That is the case in this example.

Again the point of the argument is a matter of education, of *paideia*. Logic and grammar cannot be set up in a vacuum before language has been examined. A philosophical rhetorician like Gregory knows that many puzzles can be avoided if one looks at how language operates before one applies apparently logical rules. No matter which way the opponents employ their principle, it fails because it does not concentrate on usage. "If things of the same substance do not have to be counted together and things not of the same substance are counted together, and if in both cases nouns are used along with numerals, what is left of your school of thought?" Εἰ γὰρ μήτε τὰ ὁμοούσια πάντως συναριθμεῖται, καὶ συναριθμεῖται τὰ μὴ ὁμοούσια, ἥ τε τῶν ὀνομάτων συνεκφώνησις ἐπ᾽ ἀμφοῖν, τί σοι πλέον ὧν ἐδογμάτισας;

31.20   The argument about arithmetical ordering is concluded in this section. Gregory links it with previous discussions of the nature of language and reality. The Eunomians make numbered lists, "as if the realities depended upon the sequence of the names," ὥσπερ ἐν τῇ τάξει τῶν ὀνομάτων κειμένων τῶν πραγμάτων. Again the confusion of his antagonists comes from applying principles to Biblical texts that do not agree with what Scripture says.

At points the argument about numbers is difficult to follow, but it rests on the fact that addition, subtraction, or division can be applied to all numbers. If that is agreed, then it is impossible to make the nouns used with the numbers into categories that can only be added in one set and only be subtracted or divided in other sets. The same rules must apply both to the numbers and the nouns.

Later Arians evidently were satisfied to use lists of names to indicate the subordinate character of the realities' names. If they are Father, Son and Holy Spirit, then they are first, second and third rank. Eunomius (*Apology* 25) works with counting and does list the three in descending ontological order. Biblical lists of those names, however, are not consistently ordered; neither are prepositions employed in accordance with a descending rank.

The level of disagreement between Gregory and the later Arians becomes clearer in these kinds of exchanges. If he is representing them fairly—which in some instances can be established by correlation with Aetius' and Eunomius' writings and thus is usually accepted by scholars—then the issues stand out boldly. Nazianzen lives within a liturgical tradition that has been founded on certain soteriological demands. For those to function properly, both the Son and the Spirit must be divine. Salvation is at stake if they are not. At another level, however, the Theologian interprets Scripture on the basis of his education in philosophical rhetoric. He stands on Scriptural usage and common usage of language when he reads and explicates texts. He does not bring a metaphysical system to the texts, one based on a group of ontological commitments. He is not a foundational, systematic theologian like Aetius or Eunomius.

Yet he cannot be accused of being a crude fideist, an irrational, traditional theologian who offers no grounds for his positions. He has argued much as a contemporary linguistic analyst would in these last paragraphs and elsewhere. He does not deny metaphysical theories as some modern linguistic analysts have, but his rhetorical education makes him a keen observer of words and grammar, one who invokes few metaphysical or ontological principles.

For the modern reader his similarity to the linguistic analysts is significant. If linguistic analysis such as that practiced by Wittgenstein and his followers is to be regarded as a philosophical position, then Nazianzen is not to be repudiated as a mere rhetorician. His education included the study of some Stoic logic, Aristotelian logic and rhetoric as well as lengthy training in grammar; these led to a type of philosophical prowess. In sections 17-20 he successfully ridicules his opponents' misunderstanding of the relationship between number, name and reality.

31.21   Gregory returns to the charge with which he opened this oration, one voiced by both Eunomians and Pneumatomachians. In section 1, he noted that they find talk about the Spirit as God to be "unscriptural." In section 2, he indicated his reliance on other students of the Bible, probably including his own contemporaries, who had discussed the Biblical evidence at length. Here he concedes that the Spirit is not referred to as "God" clearly or very often as the Father is in the Old Testament and the Son in the New, but he insists that serious Biblical students have found grounds for calling the Spirit God.

In Orations 29 and 30 he did not utilize New Testament texts that might name the Son God. Perhaps his text of John 1.18 did not refer to the Son as God. He also does not punctuate Romans 9.5 in such a way that Christ is called God. His strongest "Scriptural" citation comes from Baruch and his New Testament arguments are based on what the texts attribute to the Son. Here he will follow the same procedure with the Spirit.

His words about those who "saw inside the written text to its inner meaning," διασχόντες τὸ γράμμα καὶ εἴσω παρακύψαντες, suggest a reliance on allegorical exegesis. His dependence upon the great allegorist, Origen, at various points is evident, but the emphasis here probably does not demand allegory. Gregory's exegesis is often grammatical and historical, as is his logic. His complaint about his opponents is that they do not penetrate to the point of the Biblical passages, to the meaning in the texts. They refuse to name the Spirit God because they do not find verses that explicitly make that statement. Nazianzen, however, first offers rules of interpretation and then examples that he and others have seen as evidence for the Spirit's divinity. The disagreement between the parties concerns "things and names," πράγματα καὶ ὀνόματα, the nature of reality and the nature of names.

John 20.11 is not contextually connected with 31.21.6–7. 2 Tim. 4.3 is also unrelated to 31.21.14–15.

31.22   The hermeneutical principles he employs here, similar to those in Origen's *On First Principles* 4.2.9, are crucial to his argument. They provide the structure of sections 22-24. Gregory finds them to be read from Scripture not brought to it and imposed upon it. 1) Some things that do not occur in reality are mentioned in Holy Writ. 2) Some things that occur are not mentioned. 3) Some things that do not occur are not mentioned. 4) Some things that occur are mentioned.

The Bible itself provides examples of these principles. A number of the anthropomorphic statements about God fit category (1). God neither has human emotions nor acts in human ways even though Scripture says he does. He has no body in any normal sense. Such human things are apparently ascribed to him, but they do not exist. In each of the many cases which Nazianzen discusses, it is the human need for mental pictures, for bodily analogies, that has led to this type of assertion. Although we know of Anthropomorphists in Egypt in the 390s who would disagree with this principle, Gregory expected his major antagonists, the later Arians and the Pneumatomachians, to agree with him.

The Theologian's Hellenistic education with its sense of the immaterial and the impassible aspects of divinity has made a deep impact upon this small paragraph. Gregory follows the lead of Origen in pressing for things material and passionate as not factual even though they are said of God. They are not true because God could not be that way. The Old Testament, however, speaks of a God with passions even though it depicts his nature as different from a human sense of things material.

Gen. 11.15 has no contextual relationship with 31.22.5. Ps. 10.12 is a misprint of Ps. 10(9).12(33) for 31.22.20-21.

31.23   The importance of the hermeneutical principles introduced in section 22 now becomes apparent. Category (2), things that exist but are not mentioned, applies to a number of words often employed to describe God. The later Arians prefer to talk about God the Father as ἀγέννητος, "ingenerate," and ἄναρχος, "unoriginate," while Gregory and his party use the word ἀθάνατος, "immortal." These are not descriptions that appear in Scripture, but they are real aspects of God. If the Eunomians will not grant this second hermeneutical principle, their own foundational concepts are disallowed. If they reject such inferences from Biblical passages as basic to theology, then they confound their own fundamental principles.

This argument counters the charge made by the Eunomians that Scripture never refers to the Spirit as God. Gregory concedes that it was seldom said and not particularly clear when stated, but he thinks that the inference from Holy Writ is necessary. Therefore, he mentions a group of texts he sees as the basis for the inference. His opponents contested his interpretation of such texts and the specific inference, but he has at least established on their grounds that some fundamental truths of the Christian faith are not mentioned often or clearly in Scripture. If the later Arians do not concede the point, their own position falls to the ground through the weight of their attacks on him.

Category (3) comes from imagination or inference. Principles and definitions from general education make up this category. Such things are not mentioned in Scripture, but any well-informed person would know that they do not exist. Once again Nazianzen's reliance on Greek *paideia*, on his education, is clear.

Category (4) is the obvious one: things that are true and are spoken about in Scripture.

Isa. 44.4 for 31.23.8 is a misprint of Isa. 44.6.

31.24 The adversaries, both Eunomians and Pneumatomachians (the former here in focus), are like Jewish literalists because they think the letter is the most important aspect of the text. They do not grasp that the fundamental meaning of any Biblical passage is the reality about which it speaks, τὰ νοούμενα, not the actual words in which it speaks, τὰ λεγόμενα. His unstated point is clear: although Scripture does not refer to the Spirit as God, scriptural description of the Spirit makes it impossible to refuse that name to the Spirit. Gregory's examples are telling. Correct inferences can lead to a name if the reality is described but not named. Once again he has brought his clear sense of the relationship between language and reality into play.

Yet more needs to be said about the Spirit who is seldom mentioned and often assumed. To advance the argument, it is important to look at reasons why the divinity of the Spirit is not one of the realities clearly mentioned. Why does it fit under the second category and not the fourth?

31.25 The next two sections contain some of the most often quoted paragraphs from Nazianzen. In giving the reason why the Holy Spirit's divinity is not specifically and repeatedly stated in Scripture, Gregory first introduces what he thinks to be the fundamental truth of God. God's activity is matched with the free will of human beings. God urges us, persuades us, to put our minds to his purpose.

A sovereign God who chooses to employ persuasion as the way he deals with the human beings to whom he gave free will is fundamental for Cappadocian theology. The progenitor of that position is Origen. This particular combination of basic theological principles fits well with a commitment to Greek *paideia* in terms of philosophical rhetoric. The first principle is persuasion. That is true of God; it also must be true of his messengers. One of the problems that bothers Gregory about his opponents is their assumption that syllogisms can force people to see particular views. There is proper logical force; enthymemes are related to syllogisms by Aristotle. Gregory has relied upon that relation throughout these orations, but the basic approach is always a larger understanding of persuasion since God himself chose that procedure.

In such a context of persuasion the reason for the two covenants stands out. God only revealed what humans could grasp. The process took much time and came in stages. He made concessions in each covenant so that humans could understand and grow.

31.26 Gregory's interpretation of the first covenant as emphasizing the Father and the second as stressing the Son is clear and true to the Old and New Testaments. He does not call the revelation of the Spirit to the disciples a third covenant, but he does view it as another aspect of revelation, this time one of addition not omission. The process is the same: ''in gradual states proportionate to their capacity to receive him,'' κατὰ μέρος ἐπιδημεῖ τῇ τῶν δεχομένων δυνάμει παραμετρούμενον.

This daring language has a pervasive influence in the history of Christian theology. Such doctrine is not taught specifically in Scripture. It is inferential and fits within the category of amassing texts under the hermeneutical principles listed in section 22. Its sense and power, if not compelling, are at least fascinating. Many ancient Christian theologians made similar statements about the relationship of the old and new covenants in terms of the actual agreements themselves and the Old and New Testaments. Few, however, expanded that understanding to see the fullest revelation of the Spirit outside the Scriptures as a necessary and fulfilling inference from what had gone before. Christian theologies that argue for tradition's role in adding to or completing what Scripture teaches see a precedent here. Basil's discussion within his *On the Spirit* of various practices from additional traditions suggested to some of his editors like Erasmus that the final chapters of the work were from forgers. Yet this sense of ''extra-Biblical'' tradition as part of the important gift to the contemporary church is genuinely Cappadocian. Yet Basil (*On the Spirit* 27) and Gregory would never view such traditions in a Protestant sense of "extra-Biblical." Christian tradition for them is formed of Scripture and church practice. On the other hand, no fair historian or theologian can question Cappadocian dependence upon Scripture. Even within this oration section 29 is intended to establish a biblical description of the Spirit that demands its place within the Trinity. And the entire debate with the Neo-Arians is an attempt to argue from the Bible and ecclesiastical practice against a competing view of the Bible and church life that the fullest understanding of Christianity is found in the Cappadocian view.

Indeed the Theologian sees himself on strong Scriptural grounds. He senses that he is only drawing out an inference from the way revelation is portrayed in the Bible. Yet his claim opens up the use of concepts, words and perhaps doctrines "not mentioned in Scripture." For him this process is correct as long as it is controlled. He attacks the Eunomians by noticing that their basic concepts are not in Scripture (section 23), by showing that his own are in the Bible (sections 21-30) and by demonstrating that the reality they talk about cannot be inferred from Scripture. Statements about things that exist but are not mentioned in the sacred text (sections 22-23) can be true, but later Arian inferences, which fit in that category, are wrongly drawn and thus false.

The Biblical passages Gregory uses in this section come primarily from John. He views them as supporting his teaching of the Trinity. "I will ask," "He will send," "I will send," and "He will come" mean for Gregory that the Spirit is one of the three within the Godhead. Eunomius, (*Apology* 25) however, sees John 14.26 as insisting upon differences in rank and essence.

31.27 Nazianzen stresses yet again the necessity of gradual revelation, but this time in new terms. He is not certain if others have claimed it, but for him the Spirit must teach its own Godhead in order to teach "all things." The Spirit must make clear what is understated in Scripture; he must draw the inferences that are sketched in the Biblical texts and teach the realities.

31.28 On the basis of these understandings Gregory again says that he worships the Father, Son and Holy Spirit: "three distinctions in personality, one Godhead undivided in glory, honor, substance, and sovereignty," τρεῖς ἰδιότητας, θεότητα μίαν, δόξῃ, καὶ τιμῇ, καὶ οὐσίᾳ, καὶ βασιλείᾳ μὴ μεριζομένην. The formula avoids the modalism of Sabellius. Marcellus of Ancyra and his pupil, Photinus of Sirmium, are seen together with Sabellius by Eunomius (*Apology* 6) as representing the pedigree of his opponents. In his *Apology for the Apology* 2.16 (Jaeger 2.246; Vaggione, p. 123) he accuses Basil of teaching Sabellian doctrines. Nazianzen's statement recognizes such a danger and also avoids the division of the Eunomians or the Pneumatomachians. But his words do not tell us if he had Marcellus and Photinus in mind.

Gregory cites this formula from someone he honors who had not been dead long. Elias of Crete (p. 199) says that the formula came from Gregory Thaumaturgus, a fellow Cappadocian who well might have had a deep influence upon Nazianzen. L. Abramowski, however, ("Das Bekenntnis des Gregor Thaumaturgus bei Gregor von Nyssa und das Problem seiner Echtheit," *ZKG* 87 [1976], pp. 149-151) argues that this passage in Nazianzen is too vague to mean that the confession attributed to Thaumaturgus is genuine. Elias may have been reading a forged document, but his report suggests that he had read a form of the confession in a text under Gregory Thaumaturgus' name, perhaps a text that we do not now possess. In any case the quotation once more indicates how much the Theologian senses that he is in the main stream of his tradition. Others are being borne along by the wave of the moment, senselessly floating with the times. As so often in these orations, Nazianzen does not define his own terms and thus buttress his argument in that way. Here he quotes an authority. His interests are not primarily metaphysical.

The Theologian's sense that great Christian leaders of the past taught Trinitarian doctrine gives him confidence, but he also relies on the soteriological understandings and the liturgical practice that Christians are baptized into the name of the Father, the Son **and** the Holy Spirit. Salvation for them is deification; its goal is to become God. If the Spirit is not divine, then he cannot deify Christians in baptism.

This appeal has much less force when one holds a different view of salvation and follows a different liturgical tradition. Later Arians had their own heritage of worship that evidently did not demand either trine immersion or perhaps the invocation of the Spirit or the Son at the time of baptism. Other aberrations from "orthodox" practice might also have been involved. As Kopecek (pp. 397-400) indicates, the later Arian tradition was considered by its opponents, even the Cyzican leaders who attacked Eunomius, as a recent innovation. Gregory, in order to make his case about the connection between baptism and the Holy Spirit, should have been more careful to attack Eunomian practice as a change in accepted customs.

These liturgical variations mark the later Arians as separate congregations. Although their debates with others often are based upon specific systematic and philosophical arguments, as in the writings of Aetius or Eunomius, they were a worshipping community. Their understanding of salvation did not include the soteriology that the Theologian finds compelling. It should remain a fascinating observation for any historian of Christian doctrine that soteriology as doctrine and liturgy as practice were not declared united or uniform by the early councils. In many instances differences in those areas kept the participants of debate from hearing each other.

Job 11.17 as a reference for 31.28.6 is a misprint of Job 3.9. 2 Peter 1.19 does not fit the context.

31.29 The arguments from sections 21-28 should, in Nazianzen's view, explain the reasons for any silence or unclarity in the Bible about the Spirit. Both according to what "he is able to do," δύναται, and what titles "he is given," προσαγορεύεται, the Spirit is God. On the basis of these Scriptural texts, he must be granted the status of being ὁμοούσιος, "consubstantial," with God.

The rhetorical technique of this passage is instructive. After spending most of the oration undermining any claim to logical prowess his adversaries might have made, Gregory now overwhelms his hearers with a "swarm of proof-texts," ὁ τῶν μαρτυριῶν ἑσμός. His opponents, who may have thought he had conceded their charge about a "strange, unscriptural God" (section 1), are now presented with verse after verse. The first set of parallels is most probably addressed to the Pneumatomachians. These five closely identify the Spirit with the Son. The second and third sets apply primarily to the Eunomians. The second catalogues the lofty titles of the Spirit and the third, the largest, lists what the Spirit is capable of doing and has already accomplished.

This collection of texts well may have come from the work of others to which he referred in section 2. The argument moves from title and function to nature. Even if Scripture does not often call the Spirit God, a point which is conceded, what he is called and what he does should make the inference plain. He must be God. Again deification and baptism are joined as crucial issues.

Gregory offers names for the levels in the Trinity: ἰδιότης for the "personality" and θεότης for the "Godhead." He can also speak of the "same essence," ὁμοούσιος, and thus claim the Nicene formula. Within these orations, he does not often employ the expected distinction between πρόσωπον, "person," and φύσις, "nature," even though it appears in the next section.

31.30 John 14.16, Mt. 12.31 and Acts 5.1–11 serve as the strongest evidence. If the Spirit is another Comforter, if the sin against him is unpardonable, if lying to him is lying to God, how can he not be called God?

Of course, there are other passages that raise the possibility of secondary status. The passives, the designations as grace or promise, etc., all these go back to the first cause as the Spirit's source and thus prevent polytheism. This section helps clarify Gregory's use of πρώτη αἰτία, "primal cause." As he sees it, unless there is one cause, there will be polytheism.

Yet as before, the problem is acute. If there is a cause that precedes the Father, Son and Spirit, what are they? And if the Father is the cause, what are the Son and the Spirit?

The Sabellian error of combining them into "one person," τῷ προσώπῳ, is for Nazianzen just as impious as the Arian error of separating them into different "natures," ταῖς φύσεσιν. Little is known specifically of Sabellius, but Marcellus of Ancyra and his disciple, Photinus of Sirmium, had been seen by some as modalists. Eunomius (*Apology* 6) names the three together and sees his opponents as representing their errors. It would thus be important in any discussion of Trinitarian doctrine for Gregory to respond to a charge of God in "one person" with the collapse of all distinctions between Father, Son and Holy Spirit just as he responds to the Arian separation. But again here he names neither Marcellus nor Photinus.

Stating those errors indicates what he wants to avoid, but it is not clear how he can teach what he does about the primal cause and not be involved in one of these impieties. Although he finds polytheism, Sabellianism and Arianism untenable, he does not provide a consistent solution. In 30.2 he insisted that anything tied to a cause within the life of Jesus must be attributed to the manhood and those things that were absolute and uncaused were to be referred to the Son. In 29.15, however, he referred the idea of cause to the Son with no apparent difficulty. Here he states the paradoxes and leaves them.

As noted above, his usual terms for the distinctive levels within the Trinity are ἰδιότης and θεότης, but his sense is always for the reality and not the specific names. That should be expected not merely for his polemic against the Eunomians, but also for his own confessions.

This is the only place within these orations in which Gregory uses the term "Arian," Ἀρειανῶς. Copyists and commentators have been secure in their insistence that the great foes in Constantinople during this period were the Eunomians, the later Arians. Evidently Nazianzen makes a connection between his immediate antagonists and the followers of Arius, but he does not rely on titles as much as he does on positions.

31.31 In concluding this discourse, Gregory returns to a point previously made. There is no clear "illustration," εἰκών, no absolute image, that can represent the divine nature. Each analogy only fits in some aspects, while it fails in others. This section offers support for his paradoxical statement of the problem in section 30. The insight is basic to his entire approach and is seen most clearly in Oration 28. If God is incomprehensible, we should not be shocked that we cannot explain everything about him. Because we have such difficulty understanding ourselves and nature around us, our inability to grasp God is not a set with one instance, a problem without analogue. Our minds have great difficulty penetrating many different puzzles. Without this sense of the issues, Nazianzen might be accused of a crude fideism that basically avoids rational argument. There is no doubt that even with Oration 28 and its restatement in the other orations within this group, Gregory's Eunomian opponents find him to be illogical.

Yet being an educated and skilled rhetorician, he has searched diligently for such "illustrations." One attractive possibility had been that of a source, a spring and a river. Gregory Thaumaturgus (*Ep. Philagrius*) had used ὀφθαλμός, πηγή and ποταμός in this way. He is probably one of the others to whom Nazianzen refers as having employed this illustration before him. Barbel (p. 274, n. 61) indicates that similar uses of this model can be found in Tertullian (*Against Praxeas* 8) and more importantly for Gregory in Athanasius (*To Serapion* 1.19) and Basil (*Against Eunomius* 5).

31.32 Another image Nazianzen had considered was that of the sun, a ray and the light. This one fails because it suggests "composition," σύνθεσις, and "non-being," τὸ μὴ εἶναι, in the Godhead and the possibility that the Son and the Spirit would be only "potentialities," δυνάμεις, rather than "individual beings," ὑπόστασεις. Importantly we get a glimpse here of Gregory's ontological understandings. He and his adversaries agree that "composition" and "non-being" are not possible in God, but both the Eunomians and the Pneumatomachians would balk at the description of the Spirit as an "individual being" within a unified Trinity. Gregory, however, offers no theoretical explanation of the terms or concepts he uses. In regard to ὑπόστασις, "individual being," it might be argued that he employs such language because both the Son and the Spirit can be subjects. Thus the noun itself is not necessarily loaded with great metaphysical meaning as much as it is meant to indicate a grammatical observation. In Scripture both the Son and the Spirit act.

A third illustration is a sunbeam reflected off water and then onto a wall. It is more appropriate than other images because it suggests both a "unity," ἕν, and a "manifold [character]," πολλά, a oneness and a plurality that change so quickly the observer cannot distinguish one from the other.

31.33 This third analogy fails, however, because it introduces a cause prior to the sunbeam and suggests attributes impossible for God: "composition, dispersion, and the lack of a fixed natural stability," συνθέσεως, χύσεως, ἀστάτου καὶ οὐ παγίας φύσεως. Here the ontological principles Gregory accepts are clear. These might be inferences from Scripture, but basically they are philosophical teachings taken over particularly from the Hellenistic world. He does not argue their necessity because his adversaries, both enlightened "pagans" and Christian "heretics," would in most cases have accepted them. The fact that here he rejects a cause prior to the sunbeam points up once again how much difficulty he had in placing the concept of "cause" within his understanding of the Trinity.

In each instance Nazianzen finds correct and incorrect features in his illustrations. His main point again is that all images or illustrations are tied to our human condition and thus are ever tainted. There is nothing in this world that can clearly depict the Trinity because it is not of this world.

Nazianzen, however, does not hesitate to provide analogies. When he uses them by pointing out both their ability to illustrate certain aspects and their inability to depict other features, they can be helpful. Yet part of his emphasis here is to warn his opponents that finally God's nature is incomprehensible. We cannot produce any analogies that in themselves explain fully the relationship of Father, Son and Holy Spirit. We cannot because we and all our conceptions are enmeshed in this world.

Barbel (pp. 274-275, n. 64) notices that in at least two other places, Oration 12.1 and Oration 23.11, Gregory employs the figure of νοῦς, λόγος and πνεῦμα, "mind," "word," and "spirit" for the Trinity. In those instances the Theologian includes a "psychological" model, although he does not develop it as Augustine did.

Phil. 4.3 has no contextual relationship with 31.33.15.

Nazianzen closes his fifth oration as he opened it, with a word about the worship of Father, Son and Holy Spirit. This last effort in the series fits his plan and method. Although it is not the only sequence given by the manuscripts, the 27-31 order of the SC edition, two pieces on the nature of theology, two on the Son and one on the Spirit, makes sense. The general rhetorical description of the approach to theology and then a specific defense of God's incomprehensibility provide a reasonable development of the argument. To defend his views he needed one oration on the Son to challenge the logic of the later Arian attacks and one to refute their interpretation of Biblical texts about the Son. He attempts to accomplish both tasks in a single discourse on the Spirit. Most of this final oration rehearses the charges of his major adversaries, both Eunomians and Pneumatomachians, and points out the illogical assumptions those charges entail. Once again his education as a philosophical rhetorician comes to the fore. He challenges their understanding of names and realities, their grasp of words and grammatical structures, and their absurd sense of counting and the nature of things counted. He rejects their understanding of the theologian's task and works within his own sense of calling.

The major weaknesses of his position and approach are three. First, he does not describe a relationship between primal cause and Trinity that withstands scrutiny. At the confessional level it is sound because it holds together a number of Biblical statements, but at the logical or philosophical level it appears to be arbitrary. At the least he should have given a richer explanation of his position. Second, he attacks his opponents for positing dual alternatives that exclude middle terms and yet employs the same procedure himself. To be persuasive, he would have to reformulate his attack in terms of specific concepts rather than employing a method he denies to his adversaries. Third, his appeal to a particular soteriological and liturgical tradition stumbles because his antagonists do not claim that tradition. He needs to offer more support for his understanding of θέωσις, "deification," and worship rather than simply affirm them.

Yet his efforts are not without force. The confession of God's incomprehensibility is weighty. God is not human. Gregory buttresses that confession by investigating various analogies in this oration. He finds helpful points and harmful ones in each picture. By looking carefully at each one known to him, yet confessing that each fails, he avoids the charge of crude fideism or irrationality while further explicating his view that faith gives fullness to reasoning. He argues persuasively from his philosophical rhetorical background that his opponents are not the dialectical wizards they make themselves out to be. Often he makes his case. He also only dabbles in ontological confessions and seldom if ever constructs explanations in terms of overarching metaphysical theories. His theology is basically confessional. It works from Scripture and tradition through a logic formed by the analysis of how language is used and does not attempt to create other foundations for its claims.

As an historical "victor" whose position was enforced by Theodosius, he has at times been perceived as homiletical and superficial. His own character was flawed and his arguments could be less than persuasive. Yet his title "The Theologian" is deserved. Many difficulties in theology could have been avoided if his views of the task and particularly his reliance upon philosophical rhetoric had become standards.

TRANSLATION

ORATION 27
AN INTRODUCTORY SERMON AGAINST THE EUNOMIANS

27.1 I shall address my words to those whose cleverness is in words. Let me begin from Scripture: "Lo, I am against you and your pride,"[1] also [your] education, hearing, and thought.

There are people, believe me, who not only have "itching ears:"[2] their tongues, also and now, I see, even their hands itch to attack my arguments. They delight in the "profane and vain babblings and contradictions of the Knowledge falsely so-called,"[3] and in "strife of words"[4] which lead to no useful result. "Strife of words"—that is the term given to all elaborate verbiage by Paul, who proclaims and confirms the "short and final account,"[5] Paul, the pupil and teacher of fishermen. These people I speak of have versatile tongues, and are resourceful in attacking doctrines nobler and worthier than their own. I only wish they would display comparable energy in their actions: then they might be something more than mere verbal tricksters, grotesque and preposterous word-gamesters—their derisory antics invite derisive description.

27.2 But in fact they have undermined every approach to true religion by their complete obsession with setting and solving conundrums. They are like the promoters of wrestling-bouts in the theaters, and not even the sort of bouts which are conducted in accordance with the rules of the sport and lead to the victory of one of the antagonists, but the sort which are stage-managed to give the uncritical spectators visual sensations and compel their applause. Every square in the city has to buzz with their arguments, every party must be made tedious by their boring nonsense. No feast, no funeral is free from them: their wranglings bring gloom and misery to the feasters, and console the mourners with the example of an affliction graver than death. Even women in the drawing-room, that sanctuary of innocence, are assailed, and the flower of modesty is despoiled by this rushing into controversy.

Such is the situation: this infection is unchecked and intolerable; "the great mystery"[6] of our faith is in danger of becoming a mere social accomplishment. I am moved with fatherly compassion, and as Jeremiah

---

[1] Jer. 50(27).31
[2] 2 Tim. 4.3
[3] 1 Tim. 6.20
[4] 1 Tim. 6.4
[5] Rom. 9.28; Isa. 10.23
[6] 1 Tim. 3.16

says, "my heart is torn within me."[7] Let these spies therefore be tolerant enough to hear patiently what I have to say on this matter, and to hold their tongues for a while—if, that is, they can—and listen to me. You can lose nothing by it, in any case: either I shall speak "to them that have ears to hear,"[8] and my words will bear fruit, and you will benefit (for, while he who sows the Word sows it in every kind of mind, it is only the good and productive kind which bears fruit);[9] or else, if you spit on this speech of mine as you have on others, when you go away you will take with you more material for your mockery and attacks on me, and you will then feast yourselves even better. But do not be surprised if what I say is contrary to your expectations and contrary to your ways, since you profess to know all and teach all—an attitude which is too naive and pretentious: I would not offend you by saying stupid and arrogant.

27.3 Discussion of theology is not for everyone, I tell you, not for everyone—it is no such inexpensive or effortless pursuit. Nor, I would add, is it for every occasion, or every audience; neither are all its aspects open to inquiry. It must be reserved for certain occasions, for certain audiences, and certain limits must be observed. It is not for all men, but only for those who have been tested and have found a sound footing in study, and, more importantly, have undergone, or at the very least are undergoing, purification of body and soul. For one who is not pure to lay hold of pure things is dangerous, just as it is for weak eyes to look at the sun's brightness.

What is the right time? Whenever we are free from the mire and noise without, and our commanding faculty is not confused by illusory, wandering images, leading us, as it were, to mix fine script with ugly scrawling, or sweet-smelling scent with slime. We need actually "to be still"[10] in order to know God, and when we receive the opportunity, "to judge uprightly"[11] in theology.

Who should listen to discussions of theology? Those for whom it is a serious undertaking, not just another subject like any other for entertaining small-talk, after the races, the theater, songs, food, and sex: for there are people who count chatter on theology and clever deployment of arguments as one of their amusements.

What aspects of theology should be investigated, and to what limit? Only aspects within our grasp, and only to the limit of the experience and

---

[7] Jer. 4.19
[8] Ecclus. 25.12(9)
[9] Mt. 13.3 and 23
[10] Ps. 46(45).10(11)
[11] Ps. 75(74).2(3)

capacity of our audience. Just as excess of sound or food injures the hearing or general health, or, if you prefer, as loads that are too heavy injure those who carry them, or as excessive rain harms the soil, we too must guard against the danger that the toughness, so to speak, of our discourses may so oppress and overtax our hearers as actually to impair the powers they had before.

27.4 Yet I am not maintaining that we ought not to be mindful of God at all times—my adversaries, every ready and quick to attack, need not pounce on me again. It is more important that we should remember God than that we should breathe: indeed, if one may say so, we should do nothing else besides. I am one of those who approve the precept that commands us to "meditate day and night,"[12] to tell of the Lord "evening, and morning, and at noon,"[13] and to "bless the Lord at all times,"[14] or in the words of Moses, "when we lie down, when we rise up, when we walk by the way,"[15] or when we do anything else whatever, and by this mindfulness be molded to purity. So it is not continual remembrance of God I seek to discourage, but continual discussion of theology. I am not opposed either to theology, as if it were a breach of piety, but only to its untimely practice, or to instruction in it, except when this goes to excess. Fullness and surfeit even of honey, for all its goodness, produces vomiting;[16] and "to everything there is a season,"[17] as Solomon and I think, and "what's well's not well if the hour be ill." A flower is completely out of season in winter, a man's clothing is out of place on a woman, a woman's on a man, immoderate laughter is unseemly during mourning, as are tears at a drinking party. Are we then to neglect "the due season" only in the discussion of theology, where observing the proper time is of such supreme importance?

27.5 Certainly not, friends and brethren—I still call you "brethren," though your attitude is not brotherly—do not let us accept such a view. We must not be like fiery, unruly horses, throwing Reason our rider and spitting out the bit of Discretion which so usefully restrains us, and running wide of the turning post. Let us conduct our debates within our frontiers, and not be carried away to Egypt or dragged off to Assyria. Let us not "sing the song of the Lord in a foreign land,"[18] by which I mean before any and every audience, heathen or Christian, friend or foe, sym-

---

[12] Ps. 1.2; Josh. 1.8
[13] Ps. 55(54).17(18)
[14] Ps. 34(33).1(2)
[15] Deut. 6.7
[16] cf. Prov. 25.16(27)
[17] Eccl. 3.1
[18] Ps. 137(136).4

pathetic or hostile: these keep all too close a watch on us, and they would wish that the spark of our dissensions might become a conflagration; they kindle it, they fan it, by means of its own draught they raise it to the skies, and without our knowing what they are up to, they make it higher than those flames at Babylon which blazed all around.[19] Having no strength in their own teaching, they hunt for it in our weakness, and for this reason like flies settling on wounds, they settle on our misfortunes—or should I say our mistakes? Let us be blind to our doings no longer, and let us not neglect the proprieties in these matters. If we cannot resolve our disputes outright, let us at least make this mutual concession, to utter spiritual truths with the restraint due to them, to discuss holy things in a holy manner, and not to broadcast to profane hearing what is not to be divulged. Do not let us prove that we are less reverent than those who worship demons and venerate obscene tales and objects; they would sooner give their blood than disclose certain words to non-initiates. We must recognize that as in dress, diet, laughter, and deportment there are certain standards of decency, the same is true of utterance and silence, particularly as we pay especial honor to "The Word" among the titles and properties of God. Let even our contentiousness be governed by rules.

27.6   Why do we allow audiences hostile to our subject-matter to listen to discussion of the "generation" and "creation" of God, or of God's "production from non-being," and such dissections, and distinctions, and analyses? Why do we appoint our accusers as our judges? Why do we put swords into our enemies' hands? How, I ask you, will such a discussion be interpreted by the man who subscribes to a creed of adulteries and infanticides, who worships the passions, who is incapable of conceiving anything higher than the body, who fabricated his own gods only the other day, and gods at that distinguished by their utter vileness? What sort of construction will **he** put on it? Is he not certain to take it in a crude, obscene, material sense, as is his wont? Will he not appropriate your theology to defend his own gods and passions? If we abuse these terms ourselves, it will be difficult indeed to persuade such people to accept our way of thinking; and if they have a natural inclination "to invent new kinds of evil,"[20] how could they resist the evil we offer them? This is what our civil war leads to. This is what we achieve by fighting for the Word with greater violence than is pleasing to the Word. We are in the same state as madmen who set fire to their own houses, tear their own children limb from limb, or reject their own parents, regarding them as strangers.

27.7   Once we have removed from our discussions all alien elements,

---

[19] cf. Dan. 3.20
[20] Rom. 1.30

and dispatched the great legion into the herd of swine to rush down into the abyss,[21] the next step—this we shall take—is to look at ourselves and to smooth the theologian in us, like a statue, into beauty. But first we must consider: what is this disorder of the tongue which leads us to compete in garrulity? What is this alarming disease, this appetite which can never be sated? Why do we keep our hands bound and our tongues armed?

Do we commend hospitality? Do we admire brotherly love, wifely affection, virginity, feeding the poor, singing psalms, nightlong vigils, penitence? Do we mortify the body[22] with fasting? Do we through prayer, take up our abode with God? Do we subordinate the inferior element in us to the better—I mean, the dust[23] to the spirit, as we should if we have returned the right verdict on the alloy of the two which is our nature? Do we make life a meditation of death? Do we establish our mastery over our passions, mindful of the nobility of our second birth? Do we tame our swollen and inflamed tempers? Or our pride which "comes before a fall,"[24] or our unreasonable grief, our crude pleasures, our dirty laughter, our undisciplined eyes, our greedy ears, our immoderate talk, our wandering thoughts, or anything in ourselves which the Evil One can take over from us and use against us, "bringing in death through the windows,"[25] as Scripture has it, meaning through the senses?

No. We do the very opposite: we offer freedom to the passions of others, like kings declaring an amnesty after a victory, on the sole condition that they give their assent to us—and thus rush against God more violently or more "piously" than before; for this discreditable purchase we pay them a dishonorable price, license in exchange for impiety.

27.8 However, since you are so fond of talking and of the dialectic method, I will address a few questions to you; and "you shall answer,"[26] as the voice speaking through the whirlwind and the clouds said to Job.

Are there "many mansions" in God's house,[27] as you are taught, or only one?

Many, you will of course concede, *and not merely one.*

Are all of them to be filled, or only some of them and not others, so that these will be empty and prepared in vain?

Yes, all of them; nothing which God does is without purpose.

Could you explain what you understand by this "mansion"? Is it that

---

[21] Mark 5.9-13; Luke 8.30-33
[22] 1 Cor. 9.27
[23] Gen. 2.7
[24] cf. Prov. 16.18; Luke 18.14
[25] Jer. 9.21(20)
[26] Job 38.3
[27] John 14.2

rest and glory reserved Yonder for the blessed, or is it something other than this?

No, that is exactly what it is.

Since we are agreed on this, let us examine a further question. Is there any meaning in the provision of these different mansions, as I maintain, or is there none?

Certainly there is.

What is it?

It is that there are different patterns of life and avocations, and as they lead to different places according to the proportions of faith,[28] *we call them "ways."*

Must we travel along all these ways, or only some of them?

Yes, all of them, if one individual is able; if not, as many as he can; failing that, some of them; if not even that is possible, it is a great thing, at least in my opinion, if a man follows one way excellently.

You have answered the questions correctly. Well now, when you read "there is one road and that a narrow one,"[29] what do the words seem to you to indicate?

"One," because it is the way of goodness: it is one way even though there are many branches. "Narrow" because of the effort it involves, and because it can be trodden only by few, compared with the numbers of our adversaries, or those who travel by the way of wickedness.

I agree. Well then, my friend, if this is so, why is it that people like you condemn our doctrine for its alleged "poverty," reject all the other ways, and rush, pushing and shoving, along one way only, the road you think is that of Reason and Study, as indeed you yourselves claim, but I say is of Gossip and Sensationalism? Accept the rebuke of Paul, who makes this bitter reproach when, after enumerating the gifts of the Spirit, he says: "Are all Apostles? Are all prophets?"[30] and so on.

27.9 Nevertheless, let us grant that you yourself have reached the heights, gone beyond them higher if you like than the clouds, that you have looked on things which are not to be seen, that you have heard "words human lips may not utter,"[31] that, a second Elijah, you have been raised up;[32] that, a second Moses, you have been judged worthy to see God;[33] that, a second Paul, you have been caught up into heaven.[34] Even so, why do you then try to mold other men into holiness overnight, appoint them theologians, and as it were, breathe learning into them, and

---

[28] Rom. 12.6
[29] Mt. 7.14
[30] 1 Cor. 12.29
[31] 2 Cor. 12.4
[32] 2(4) Kgs. 2.11
[33] Ex. 3.2; 19.20; 33.18-23
[34] 2 Cor. 12.2

thus produce ready-made any number of Councils of ignorant intellectuals? Why do you try to entangle your weaker brethren in your spiders' webs, as if this were some brilliant feat? Why do you stir up wasps' nests against the Faith? Why do you conjure up a crop of dialecticians to attack us, like the Earth-born warriors in the old stories? Why have you gathered together as though you were sweeping up rubbish into a gutter, all the weediest and most effeminate specimens of the male sex, softened them still further with flattery, and thus set up your revolutionary Profanity industry, a shrewd exploitation of their silliness?

Do you continue to speak even after these charges? Can it be that nothing else matters for you, but your tongue must always rule you, and you cannot hold back words which, once conceived, must be delivered? Well, there are plenty of other fields in which you can win fame. Direct your disease there, and you may do good.

27.10. Attack the silence of Pythagoras, or the Orphic beans, or the extraordinary pretentiousness of "Thus spake the Master." Attack Plato's Ideas, and the Re-embodiments and Cycles of our souls, and their Recollections, and those distasteful love-affairs where the soul was the object, but the beautiful body the route. Then there is Epicurus' atheism, or his atoms, or his ideal of Pleasure, unworthy of a philosopher; or Aristotle's mean conception of Providence, his artificial system, his mortal view of the soul, and the human-centered nature of his teaching. Or what about the superciliousness of the Stoics, the greed and vulgarity of the Cynics?

Attack "the Void"—which is full of nonsense, or all the mumbo-jumbo of gods and sacrifices, idols, demons beneficent or malignant, of soothsaying, summoning the gods or the spirits of the dead, and of the influences of the stars.

If, however, you reject these subjects as unworthy of your intellect, being petty and often refuted, and you wish to move in your own field, and fulfill your ambitions there: here also I will provide you with broad highways. Speculate about the Universe—or Universes, about Matter, the Soul, about Natures (good and evil) endowed with reason, about the Resurrection, the Judgment, Reward and Punishment, or about the Sufferings of Christ. In these questions to hit the mark is not useless, to miss it is not dangerous. But of God himself the knowledge we shall have in this life will be little, though soon after it will perhaps be more perfect, in the same Jesus Christ our Lord, to whom be glory for ever and ever.[35] Amen.

---

[35] Rev. 1.6

ORATION 28
ON THE DOCTRINE OF GOD

28.1 Last time we used theology to cleanse the theologian. We glanced at his character, his audience, the occasion and range of his theorizing. We saw that his character should be undimmed, making for a perception of light by light; that his audience should be serious-minded, to ensure that the word shall be no sterile sowing in sterile ground;[1] that the right occasion is when we own an inner stillness away from the outward whirl, avoiding all fitful checks to the spirit; and that the range should be that of our God-given capacity. These truths were established last time and so we broke up our fallow-soil with God's furrows, not wanting to sow on thorns;[2] we leveled off the face of the ground,[3] impressed and impressing it with Scripture's stamp. Well now let us go forward to discuss the doctrine of God, dedicating our sermon to our sermon's subjects, the Father, the Son, and the Holy Spirit, that the Father may approve, the Son aid, and the Holy Spirit inspire it—or rather that the single Godhead's single radiance, by mysterious paradox one in its distinctions and distinct in its connectedness may enlighten it.

28.2 I eagerly ascend the mount[4]—or, to speak truer, ascend in eager hope matched with anxiety for my frailty—that I may enter the cloud[5] and company with God (for such is God's bidding).[6] Is any an Aaron? He shall come up with me.[7] He shall stand hard by, should he be willing to wait, if need be, outside the cloud. Is any a Nadab, an Abihu, or an elder? He too shall ascend, but stand further off,[8] his place matching his purity. Is any of the crowd, unfit, as they are, for so sublime contemplation? Utterly unhallowed?—let him not come near, it is dangerous.[9] Duly prepared?—let him abide below. He shall hear but the voice and the trumpet, true religion's outer expressions; he shall see the mount in smoke with its lightning-flashes,[10] warning and wonder to those who cannot ascend it. Is any an evil, untamed beast, quite impervious to thoughts of

---

[1] Mt. 13.5-6; Mark 4.4-6; Luke 8.6-7
[2] Jer. 4.3
[3] Isa. 28.25
[4] Ex. 19.3 and 20; 24.9 and 15
[5] Ex. 24.18
[6] cf. Ex. 24.12
[7] Ex. 19.24
[8] Ex. 24.1-2, 9-10 and 14; cf. Lev. 10.1-3
[9] Ex. 19.12
[10] Ex. 19.16-20

contemplation and divinity? He shall not lurk in the woods, baneful and
harmful, to pounce out on some truth or utterance and rend "wholesome
thoughts"[11] with his abuse. No, he shall stand still further off. He shall
quit the mount or "be stoned"[12] and "crushed"[13]—an evil death for an
evil man,[14] seeing that the brutish find real and solid arguments to be
stones. Is he a leopard? He shall die spots and all.[15] A predatory, roaring
lion, seeking our souls[16] or our phrases for meat? A swine, trampling
truth's fair, clear pearls?[17] A wolf, Arabian[18] and foreign, or even sharp-
er than these are at chop-logic? A fox, a shifty, treacherous soul, matching
its form to the hour's need, fed off stinking corpses, or avoiding the big,
off little vineyards?[19] Some other carnivore, rejected by the Law, un-
clean, useless as food?[20] Our sermon leaves these behind, meaning to be
engraved on solid tables of stone[21] and on both sides of these because the
Law has an obvious and hidden aspect. The obvious belongs to the crowd
waiting below, the hidden to the few who attain the height.

28.3   What experience of this have I had, you friends of truth, her initiates, her lovers as I am? I was running with a mind to see God and so it
was that I ascended the mount. I penetrated the cloud, became enclosed
in it, detached from matter and material things and concentrated, so far
as might be, in myself. But when I directed my gaze I scarcely saw the
averted figure of God, and this whilst sheltering in the rock,[22] God the
word incarnate for us.[23] Peering in I saw not the nature prime, self-
apprehended (by "self" I mean the Trinity), the nature as it abides within
the first veil and is hidden by the Cherubim,[24] but as it reaches us at its
furthest remove from God, being, so far as I can understand, the grandeur, or as divine David calls it the "majesty"[25] inherent in the created
things he has brought forth and governs. All these indications of himself
which he has left behind him are God's "averted figure."[26] They are, as

---

[11] Titus 2.8
[12] Ex. 19.13
[13] Lev. 11.33
[14] Mt. 21.41
[15] Jer. 13.23
[16] 1 Pet. 5.8
[17] Mt. 7.6
[18] Hab. 1.8 [LXX]
[19] Cant. 2.15
[20] Gen. 7.2, 3 and 8; Lev. 11; Deut. 14.3-20
[21] Ex. 31.18
[22] Ex. 33.21-23
[23] 1 Cor. 10.4; John 1.14
[24] Ex. 26.31-33; 36.35-36
[25] Ps. 8.1(2); 111(110).3; 145(144).5 and 12
[26] Ex. 33.22-23

it were, shadowy reflections of the Sun in water, reflections which display to eyes too weak, because too important to gaze at it, the Sun overmastering perception in the purity of its light. Thus and thus only, can you speak of God, be you Moses and Pharaoh's "God,"[27] had you reached, like Paul the third heaven and heard ineffable mysteries,[28] had you even transcended it, deemed worthy of an angel's or an archangel's station and rank. For were a thing all heavenly, all super-celestial even, far more sublime in nature than ourselves, far nearer God, its remoteness from him and from his perfect apprehension is much greater than its superiority to our low, heavy compound.

28.4   So we must begin again with this in mind. To know God is hard, to describe him impossible, as a pagan philosopher taught—subtly suggesting, I think, by the word "difficult" his own apprehension, yet avoiding our test of it by claiming it was impossible to describe. No—to tell of God is not possible, so my argument runs, but to know him is even less possible. For language may show the known if not adequately, at least faintly, to a person not totally deaf and dull of mind. But mentally to grasp so great a matter is utterly beyond real possibility even so far as the very elevated and devout are concerned, never mind slack and sinking souls. This truth applies to every creature born, to all beings whose view of reality is blocked by this gloom, this gross portion of flesh. Whether higher, incorporeal natures can grasp it, I do not know. They may, perhaps, through their proximity to God and their illumination by light in its fullness know God if not with total clarity, at least more completely, more distinctly than we do, their degree of clarity varying proportionately with their rank.

28.5   But enough of this! For our part, not only does God's peace pass all thought and understanding[29] with all the things stored up in promise for the righteous—things unseen by the eye, unheard by the ear,[30] unthought, or at least but glimpsed by the mind—but so does exact knowledge of the creation as well. You can be sure that we possess but the bare outline of the creation when you hear the words: "I shall see the heavens, the works of thy fingers, the Moon and the Stars"[31] and the fixed order they contain. He does not see them now, but there is a time when he shall see them. Yes, far before these things does their transcendent cause, the incomprehensible and boundless nature pass understanding. I mean understanding what that nature is, not understanding that it

---

[27] Ex. 7.1
[28] 2 Cor. 12.2-4
[29] Phil. 4.7
[30] 1 Cor. 2.9
[31] Ps. 8.3(4)

exists. Our preaching is not vain, our faith empty;[32] it is not **that** doctrine we are propounding. Do not take our frankness as ground for atheistic caviling and exalt yourselves over against us for acknowledging our ignorance. Conviction, you see, of a thing's existence is quite different from knowledge of what it may be.

28.6 That God, the creative and sustaining cause of all, exists, sight and instinctive law inform us—sight, which lights upon things seen as nobly fixed in their courses, borne along in, so to say, motionless movement; instinctive law, which infers their author through the things seen in their orderliness. How could this universe have had foundation or constitution, unless God gave all things being and sustains them? No one seeing a beautifully elaborated lyre with its harmonious, orderly arrangement, and hearing the lyre's music will fail to form a notion of its craftsman-player, to recur to him in thought though ignorant of him by sight. So to us the creative power, which moves and safeguards its objects, shows clear, though it be not grasped by the understanding. Anyone who refuses to progress this far in following instinctive proofs must be very wanting in judgment. But still, whatever we imagined or figured to ourselves or reason delineated is not the reality of God. If anyone ever did compass this in any degree of thought, where is the proof? Who was it who reached this ultimate in wisdom? Who was it who was sometime counted worthy of so great a gift? Who was it who thus opened his mind's mouth[33] and drew in the Spirit, that by the Spirit which searches out and knows God's depths[34] he might comprehend God, might stand in no need of further progress as owning already the ultimate object of desire towards which speeds all a lofty soul's thought and conduct?

28.7 What can your conception of the divine be, if you rely on all the methods of deductive argument? To what conclusion will closely-scrutinized argument bring you, you most rational of theologians, who boast over infinity? Is it corporeal? How then can it be boundless, limitless, formless, impalpable, invisible? Can bodies be such? The arrogance of it! This is not the nature of bodies. Or is it corporeal but without these properties? The grossness of it, to say that deity has no properties superior to ours! How could it be worth worship were it bounded? How could it escape elemental composition and disintegration or even total dissolution? For composition is cause of conflict, conflict of division, division of dissolution. But dissolution is utterly alien to God the prime nature. So no dissolution means no division; no division means no conflict; no conflict

---

[32] 1 Cor. 15.14 and 17
[33] Ps. 119(118).131
[34] 1 Cor. 2.10

means no composition, and hence no body involving composition. The reasonings stand so, mounting from consequences to first conditions.

28.8   How, again, can justice be done to the Scriptural fact that God pervades and fills the universe ("'Do not I fill heaven and earth?' saith the Lord,"[35] and, "The spirit of the Lord filleth the world"[36]) if part of it limits him and part of it is limited by him? It cannot, for he must either occupy a complete vacuum and our universe vanish—involving the blasphemy that God has been made corporeal and does not possess the universe he made; or his body must be contained by bodies—which is impossible; or he must be knit through them as a contrasted strand, like liquids in mixture, parting some, parted by others—which is a more absurd old wives' tale[37] than even Epicurus' atoms. It follows, then, that talk of God's body has no solid body to it and must collapse. What if we call God "immaterial," the fifth element envisaged by some, borne along the circular drift? Let us assume that he is some immaterial, fifth body, incorporeal, if they want it so to suit their free-drifting, self-constructing argument—I will not quarrel over the point. What place will he have in the moving drift of things—leaving out of account the blasphemy of identifying the creatures' motion with their creator's, the mover's (if they will concede the term) with that of the moved? What moves this fifth element? What moves the whole? What moves that which moves the whole? and so on *ad infinitum*. Must not this moving fifth element be in space? Suppose that they call it something other than the fifth element, an angelic body, say. What grounds have they for asserting angels are bodies? What are these bodies? How far will God transcend angels who are his ministers?[38] If supra-angelic, a countless swarm of bodies will be fetched in, an abyss of nonsense with no halting place.

28.9   So we have proved that God is not a body. No inspired[39] teacher has asserted or accepted that idea; the verdict of our fold[40] is against it. He can only be incorporeal. But the term "incorporeal," though granted, does not give an all-embracing revelation of God's essential being. The same is true of "ingenerate," "unoriginate," "immutable," and "immortal," indeed of all attributes applied, or referred, to God. For what has the fact of owning no beginning, of freedom from change, from limitation, to do with his real, fundamental nature? No, the full reality is left to be grasped, philosophically treated, and scrutinized by a more ad-

---

[35] Jer. 23.24
[36] Wis. 1.7
[37] 1 Tim. 4.7
[38] cf. Heb. 1.4 and 14
[39] 2 Tim. 3.16
[40] John 10.16

vanced theorist of God. Just as predicating "is body" or "is begotten" of something or other where these predicates are applicable is not enough clearly to set out the thing but you must also, if an object of knowledge is to be displayed with adequate clarity, give the predicates their subject; (men, cows, and horses, you see are "corporeal," "begotten," and "mortal") so, in the same way, an inquirer into the nature of a real being cannot stop short at saying what it is **not** but must add to his denials a positive affirmation (and how much easier it is to take in a single thing than to run the full gamut of particular negations!). The point of this is that comprehension of the object of knowledge should be effected both by negation of what the thing is not and also by positive assertion of what it is. A person who tells you what God is not but fails to tell you what he is, is rather like someone who, asked what twice five are, answers "not two, not three, not four, not five, not twenty, not thirty, no number, in short, under ten or over ten." He does not deny it **is** ten, but he is also not settling the questioner's mind with a firm answer. It is much simpler, much briefer, to indicate all that something is **not** by indicating what it **is**, than to reveal what it **is** by denying what it is **not**.

This is all common sense, surely, (**28.10.**) but now that we have proved deity incorporeal, we shall take the examination a stage further. The problem is this: is deity located in space or not? If it is not, then your shrewd critic might ask how it can even exist at all. Granted that what does not exist has no spatial location, it may well be the case that what has no spatial location does not exist. But if deity is spatially located there are two possible consequences: either the universe contains it, or it is located above the universe. Taking the first alternative then, it is either contained in a part of the universe or the whole of it. Supposing deity is contained in a part of the universe, it will be delimited by something relatively small; if in the whole, by something relatively large, indeed the largest there is—relatively, I mean, as between deity inside and the surrounding universe—granted the universe is going to be contained by the universe and all spatial location to have its bounding line. These consequences follow the hypothesis that the universe contains God. Again, where was it before the universe was created? This produces a considerable problem, you see. If, on the other hand, deity is located above the universe, what is the dividing line between it and the universe? Where is this higher place? How are higher and lower levels to be recognized, where there is no dividing line between to separate them? There will have, surely, to be something in heaven, something to bound the universe off from what lies above it. In that case this something in between must have the very spatial location we rejected. I do not now insist upon the fact that deity must be

delimited if it be mentally comprehended, for comprehension is one form
of delimitation.

28.11   Why have I made this digression, too labored, I daresay, for the
general ear but in tune with the prevalent fashion in sermons, a fashion
which despises noble simplicity and substitutes tortuous conundrums? I
did it to make the tree known by its fruits,[41] to make the darkness which
activated dogmas like these, I mean, known by the obscurity of their expression. I did not do it to gain a reputation for startling oratory or extraordinary wisdom as a marvelous Daniel for "showing hard sentences and dis-
solving doubts."[42] No, I wanted to make plain the point my sermon
began with, which was this: the incomprehensibility of deity to the human
mind and its totally unimaginable grandeur. Not that deity resents our
knowledge – resentment is a far cry from the divine nature, serene as it
is, uniquely and properly "good," especially resentment of its most prized
creation. What can mean more to the Word than thinking beings, since
their very existence is an act of supreme goodness? It is not that he treasures
his own fullness of glory, keeping his majesty costly by inaccessibility. It
would be utterly dishonest, utterly out of character not merely for God but
for an ordinary good man with anything of a proper conscience about him
to get the top place by keeping others out.

28.12   There may be other reasons known to those nearer God, "eye-
witnesses and spectators of his unsearchable judgments,"[43] beings, if
such there are, of such high excellence that they walk, as Scripture has it,
"in the footsteps of the abyss."[44] Yet so far as we have understood it, we
with our limited gifts for hard speculation, a possible reason is to avoid
a too ready loss of the lightly gained. What is gained by effort is usually
kept; what is lightly gained is quickly spurned because it can be gained
anew. So for men of sense at least, the scarceness of some benefit is itself
of benefit, saving us, perhaps, from sharing Lucifer's fate of falling[45] into
stubborn disobedience against the Lord Almighty[46] as a result of taking
in the light in its fullness (the wretchedest of all falls which pride precedes!)[47] and perhaps so that those who have in this world been cleansed,
yearning yet patient, may have in the world to come some greater prize
for the brilliant labors of their lives. That may be the reason this corporeal
gloom stands barrier between us and God like the cloud of old time be-

---

[41] Mt. 7.19-20
[42] Dan. 5.12
[43] Rom. 11.33
[44] Job 38.16 [LXX]
[45] Isa. 14.12
[46] Job 15.25
[47] cf. Prov. 16.18; Luke 18.14

tween Hebrews and Egyptians,[48] being, it may be, too, the "darkness which he made his hiding-place,"[49] meaning our grossness, through which few but briefly peer. Let those whose business it is discuss the matter, let them take their investigation as high as they can. Yet we "prisoners of the earth,"[50] in divine Jeremiah's phrase, pent in this gross portion of flesh, know this: you cannot cross your own shadow however much you haste—it is always exactly ahead of your grasp. Sight cannot approach its objects without the medium of light and atmosphere; fish cannot swim out of water; and no more can embodied beings keep incorporeal company with things ideal. Some corporeal factor of ours will always intrude itself, even if the mind be most fully detached from the visible world, and at its most recollected when it attempts to engage with its invisible kin. Here is your proof.

28.13 "Spirit,"[51] "fire,"[52] and "light,"[53] "love,"[54] "wisdom,"[55] and "righteousness,"[56] "mind,"[57] and "reason"[58] and so forth, are titles of the prime reality, are they not? Can you think of wind without movement and dispersal? Of fire without matter, with no rising motion, no color and shape of its own? Or light unmixed with atmosphere, detached from what shines to give it birth, so to say. What of mind? Something else contains it, surely; its thoughts, silent or uttered, are movements. How can you think of reason other than as our inner discourse, unspoken or expressed—I shrink from saying "dissolved"? As for wisdom, how can you think of it except as a state involved in investigations human or divine? Justice and love are commended dispositions, surely, the opposites of injustice and hate, now intense, now slack, now present, now absent; in short they make us and change us, as complexions do our bodies? Or must we abstract, using the words to take, if we can, a view of deity in the absolute, making the images yield some picture in mosaic? Then what scheme will the pieces yield, which is not just the pieces? How can the simple, unpicturable reality be all these images and each in its entirety? This way our mind tires of getting past bodily conditions and companying with things sheerly incorporeal, and meanwhile it gazes in impotence at what lies beyond its powers. Because though every thinking being

---

[48] Ex. 14.19-20
[49] Ps. 18(17).11(12)
[50] Lam. 3.34
[51] John 4.24
[52] Deut. 4.24
[53] 1 John 1.5
[54] 1 John 4.16
[55] Job 12.13
[56] Ps. 103(102).17; 97(96).2
[57] Isa. 40.13
[58] cf. John 1.1

longs for God, the first cause, it is powerless, for the reasons I have given, to grasp him. Tired with the yearning it chafes at the bit and, careless of the cost, it tries a second tack. Either it looks at things visible and makes of these a god—a gross mistake, for what visible thing is more sublime, more godlike, than its observer, and to what degree, that it should be the object, be the subject, of worship?—or else it discovers God through the beauty and order of things seen, using sight as a guide to what transcends sight without losing God through the grandeur of what it sees.

28.14   So it comes about that some men have reverenced the Sun, others the Moon, others the host of stars, others again include the heaven itself. To these they ascribe a universal sway in virtue of their speed and type of motion. Some men have worshipped the elements—earth, water, air, and fire—because of their necessity to the maintenance of human life. Others again have taken as patronal deities whatever objects of special beauty happened to strike their sight. There are yet others, more emotional, more sensual, who have paid divine reverence to pictures and statues. At first these were of their kin; men honored the departed with memorials. Later they were of strangers too. Men remote from these strangers in time and space and ignorant of the primal nature, followed the traditional rule of honoring them. They took that honoring for right and essential, when the practice had been hardened by time into an established law. Flatterers of power too, surely, who praised and admired physical strength and beauty, in course of time made a god of the man honored, fastening on some tale to aid the deception.

28.15   Men of worse passions even made gods of their emotions, or gave divine honors to anger, murder, lust, drunkenness, and I know not what else of the same kind. They found here no fair, no just excuse for their own sins. Some gods they unleashed in the world, others they hid underground (their only wise act!) and yet others they took up to heaven. What a ludicrous allocation of territory! Next, error took its own sweet way and they gave each counterfeit god or devil a name. They put up statues whose very costliness made them bait, and periodically saw fit to honor them with reeking blood and with vile acts of frenzied human slaughter. Such honors suited such gods. They insulted themselves; they took God's glory and attached it to monstrous animals, four-footed beasts and reptiles,[59] the vilest and most ludicrous of their kind. They make it hard to tell which was the more contemptible, the worshippers or the worshipped; perhaps the worshippers by far, since they as rational beings, recipients of God's grace, chose their inferior for patron and better. This was the Evil One's

---

[59] Rom. 1.23

trick, to use good for a bad end, as so many of his schemes do. He caught at their unguided longing to search for God, meaning to divert power to himself and cheat that desire of theirs—it was like taking a blind man's hand when he is eager to find the road. He pushed them headlong down a variety of cliffs but the pieces he had made of them went into just one pit of death and destruction.

28.16 This was their fate. But reason took us up in our desire for God, in our refusal to travel without guide or helmsman. Reason looked on the visible world, lighted on things primeval yet did not make us stop at these (for reason will grant no superiority to things as much objects of sense as we are) but leads us on through them to what transcends them, the very means of their continued existence. For what gave order to things heavenly and earthly and to all that pass through air and live under water, and more than that to what came before them—I mean heaven, earth, air, and the element of water themselves? Who combined these elements and divided them out? What common factors have they of nature and purpose? I commend the man, non-Christian though he was, who asked: "What set these elements in motion and leads their ceaseless, unimpeded flow?" It was surely their designer, who implants in all things reason whereby the universe is conducted and carried along. And who is their designer? Surely he who made them and brought them into existence. Great power like this cannot be ascribed to chance. Supposing chance created them, what gave them order? Granting this possibility too, if you like, to chance, what preserves and guards them in the conditions of their first constitution? Chance again, or something else? Clearly something beyond chance. What can this 'something' be if not God? Thus God-derived reason, bound up, connected, with the whole of nature, man's most ancient law, has led us up from things of sight to God. Let us make a fresh start here.

28.17 No one has yet discovered or ever shall discover what God is in his nature and essence. As for a discovery some time in the future, let those who have a mind to it research and speculate. The discovery will take place, so my reason tells me, when this God-like, divine thing, I mean our mind and reason, mingles with its kin, when the copy returns to the pattern it now longs after. This seems to me to be the meaning of the great dictum that we shall, in time to come, "know even as we are known."[60] But for the present what reaches us is a scant emanation, as it were a small beam from a great light[61]—which means that anyone who has "known"

---

[60] 1 Cor. 13.12
[61] Wis. 7.26

God or whose "knowledge" of him has been attested in the Bible, had a manifestly more brilliant knowledge than others not equally illuminated. This superiority was reckoned knowledge in the full sense, not because it really was so, but by the contrast of relative strengths.

28.18   It is for this reason that Enoch "hoped to invoke the Lord."[62] His accomplishment consisted in hoping not, mark you, for knowledge but invocation of the Lord. Enoch was "transferred"[63]—yes, but it is quite unclear whether this was a consequence or a pre-condition of his comprehending God's nature. Noah's distinction lay in his being "well-pleasing" to God,[64] and to him was entrusted the task of rescuing the whole world, or rather the world's elements, from the waters, when he escaped the deluge in a small boat.[65] Abraham, mighty patriarch that he was, was "justified by faith."[66] The sacrifice he offered was unusual in its foreshadowing of the great one to come.[67] Yet he did not see God directly. No, he gave him food as man and was commended because his awe matched his comprehension.[68] Jacob dreamed of a lofty ladder and of angels ascending it.[69] His anointing a pillar had a hidden meaning perhaps,[70] a revelation of the rock anointed for our sakes.[71] He gave a place the name "vision of God" in honor of what he dreamed.[72] He wrestled as man with God[73]—whatever "wrestling" between God and man may be (the comparison of human excellence with God, perhaps?)—and bore on his body the tokens of the wrestling, tokens which displayed a worsting of the created nature. As prize for his true religion he earned a change of name. From being called "Jacob" he was called by the great and precious title "Israel."[74] Yet neither he, nor any other after him to this day from the twelve tribes, whose Father he was, could boast this: that he had taken in the nature, the total vision, of God.

28.19   For Elijah, so the narrative tells us, it was not the mighty wind or the earthquake but a light breeze which gave outline to the presence, but not the nature, of God.[75] Elijah? Yes, the man whose more than hu-

---

[62] Gen. 4.26 [LXX]
[63] Gen. 5.24
[64] Gen. 6.9 [LXX]
[65] Gen. 6.13-19
[66] Gen. 15.6; Rom. 4.3
[67] Gen. 22.2-14
[68] Gen. 18.1-15
[69] Gen. 28.12
[70] Gen. 28.18; 35.14
[71] cf. Mt. 21.42
[72] Gen. 32.30-31
[73] Gen. 32.24-30
[74] Gen. 32.28-30
[75] 1(3) Kgs. 19.11-12

man devotion to duty was manifested by a chariot of fire bearing him up to heaven.[76] Must you not show respect for Manoah, the Old Testament judge, and Peter, the New Testament disciple: Manoah was overwhelmed by the sight of God in a vision. "Wife," he said, "we are lost, we have seen God"[77]—meaning by this that even a vision of God is too much for men let alone God's nature. Peter would not let the apparition of Christ on board the boat and so bade him depart,[78] despite the fact that Peter was more fervent than the rest for knowledge of Christ. For this fervor he was blessed, and entrusted with the greatest powers.[79] What will you say of Isaiah, or Ezekiel, eyewitness of things most mighty, and of the rest of the prophets? Isaiah saw the Lord Sabaoth seated on his throne of glory, surrounded, enveloped, by six-winged seraphim praising him. Isaiah himself was purged by the coal and equipped for his prophetic function.[80] Ezekiel describes God's chariot of cherubim, the throne above them, and beyond the throne the firmament. He describes the visionary figure he saw in the firmament, certain sounds, movements, and actions too.[81] Was this a day-time appearance, the kind seen only by saints? A veridical vision of the night? An impression upon the reasoning mind of company-ing with future, as though they were present, realities? Some other form of prophecy? I cannot say. The God of the prophets—he knows; so do the prophetically inspired. But none of those I talk of, nor any other of their sort, stood within the essential "basis," as Scripture has it, "of the Lord."[82] None saw, none told, of God's nature.

28.20 Had Paul been able to express the experiences gained from the third heaven,[83] and his progress, ascent, or assumption to it, we should, perhaps, have known more about God—if this really was the secret mean-ing of his rapture. But since they were ineffable, let them have the tribute of our silence. Let us give this much attention to Paul when he says: "We know in part and we prophesy in part."[84] This and the like is the confes-sion of one who is no mere layman in knowledge, of one who threatens to give proof of Christ speaking in him,[85] of a great champion and teacher of truth. Yet he counts all knowledge in this world as nothing more

---

76 2(4) Kgs. 2.11
77 Judg. 13.22
78 cf. Mark 6.49; Luke 5.8
79 Mt. 16.17-19
80 Isa. 6.1-8
81 Ezek. 1.4-28
82 Jer. 23.18 [LXX]
83 2 Cor. 12.2-4
84 1 Cor. 13.9
85 2 Cor. 13.2-3

than "puzzling reflections in mirrors,"[86] because it has its basis in small-scale images of reality. I hope I may not seem to some of you to be laboring the matter if I say that it may be this that the Word himself was hinting at, when he said that some things, which could not be borne, would at some future time, be borne and made plain.[87] Perhaps it is those things which John, the Word's messenger and great voice of truth, affirmed to be beyond the present world's power to contain.[88]

28.21   All truth, all philosophy, to be sure, is obscure, hard to trace out. It is like employing a small tool on big constructions, if we use human wisdom in the hunt for knowledge of reality. We do not abandon the senses, they go with us, when we look at supra-sensible realities. But by these same senses we are perplexed and led astray. We cannot get nearer the truth by meeting things in their naked reality with naked intellect. Our minds cannot receive direct and sure impressions. Now theology is fuller, and so harder, with more counter-arguments, tougher solutions, than other philosophy. Every slightest objection bars, hinders, the course of the argument, and checks its progress. It is like applying the reins suddenly to galloping horses, making them veer round with the surprise of the shock. So it was with Solomon, the superior of his predecessors and contemporaries in education,[89] gifted by God with breadth of heart and an expanse of vision ampler than the sand.[90] The more he entered into profundities, the more his mind reeled. He made it a goal of his wisdom to discover just how far off it was.[91] Paul tried to get there—I do not mean to God's nature (that he knew to be quite impossible) but only to God's judgments. Paul found no way through, no stopping-place in his climb, since intellectual curiosity has no clear limit and there is always some truth left to dawn on us. The marvel of all—I share his feelings as he closes his argument with impassioned wonder at the sort of things he calls "the wealth and depth of God"[92] in acknowledgement of the incomprehensibility of God's judgments. His language is almost the same as David used. David at one point calls God's judgments a "great abyss" fathomless by sense;[93] at another point he says that the knowledge even of his own make-up was "too wonderful" for him, "too excellent" for him "to be able to grasp."[94]

---

[86] 1 Cor. 13.12
[87] John 16.12-13
[88] John 21.25
[89] 1(3) Kgs. 3.12; 2 Chr. 1.12
[90] 1(3) Kgs. 4(5).29(9)
[91] Eccl. 7.23-25; 8.17
[92] Rom. 11.33
[93] Ps. 36(35).6(7)
[94] Ps. 139(138).6

28.22 If he says—I discount the rest—to look at myself, the whole of my nature and construction as a man, I ask what combination of forces sets us going.[95] In what way was the immortal mixed in with the mortal? How do I drift down, yet am borne up? What causes the soul's confinement? Why does the soul give life, yet have its share of pain? What makes the mind both confined and boundless, both at home in us and touring the universe in rapid, flowing course? In what way is mind conveyed and communicated by speech? How does it go through the air and enter along with objects? What makes it share in sense-perception, whilst isolating itself from sense-perception? There are questions still more basic than these. What was the first stage in the process of molding and bringing us together in nature's workshop? What is the final stage of formative development? What is the urge to get and provide food? What is the instinct which brings us to the first springs and materials of life? What makes food nourishment for the body and speech for the soul? What is nature's spell, binding parents and children together? What goes to make stable variations of appearance, when an infinitely large number of special factors is involved? How does it come about that the same living thing is both mortal and immortal? Changing its state, it dies; giving birth makes it immortal. Now it goes away, now it comes back in again, channeled like a constant, flowing river. There are many more aspects you can reflect on, facts about our limbs and parts, about their mutual adaptation, about how they are co-ordinated and differentiated with a view to practical utility combined with beauty, about how they are dove-tailed together, how they are parted yet function as one, how some act as containers of others—and all this by an in-built condition of their nature. There are many facts about speech and hearing, how sounds are produced through the vocal organs and received by the ears, how sounds and ears are knit together by the imprinted impulse transmitted by the intervening air. There are many facts about sight and its mysterious communion with objects. It is set going along with, and only by, the will. Sight is in the same case with mind, for it joins its objects with just the same speed as does the mind its thoughts. There are many facts about the rest of the senses, which act as receivers of external impressions unseen by the eye of reason. There are many facts about rest in sleep, about our imagination at work in dreams, about memory and recollection, about calculation, anger and desire—to be brief, about all that runs the affairs of this little world called Man.

28.23 Would you like me to enumerate the points at which animals differ from us and from one another, differences in natural constitution, production and diet, differences in habitat, behavior and social structure,

---

[95] Ps. 139(138).13-16

so to say? What makes some animals gregarious, others solitary? Some eat grass, others eat flesh. Some are fierce, others gentle. Some are friendly and domesticated, others wild and free. Some come quite close to what one might call reason and learning-ability, others are totally devoid of these capacities. They vary in the number of their senses, in their powers of movement. Some are very swift, others very gross. Some have a superiority in size and beauty or in one of these qualities; others are minute or hideous or both at once. Some have strength, others are weak. Some make a quick response to attack, others are treacherous and not to be trusted. Some you must watch out for, others you need not. Some like work and can cope, others are lazy and do not look ahead. Why should all this be? And there are questions prior to these. What makes some animals crawl and others go upright? Why are some attached to a habitat, others amphibious? Why do some take pride in their appearance, others shun adornment? Why do some have mates, others not? Why are some in control of their appetites, others not? What makes some animals fertile, others have few offspring? Why are some long-lived, others short-lived? To argue it through in detail would tire us out.

28.24 Look at fish too. They glide through the water, flying, you might say, under the liquid element. They absorb in water their own special atmosphere, dangerous to us as ours is to them. In behavior and temperament, in the way they couple and produce offspring, in their range of size and beauty, in the way they congregate in particular habitats and roam in migration, here they have almost as many special characteristics as land animals. With these they have many features in common, as well as opposed characteristics of their own, both in their appearance and in their names. Look, again, at the types of birds, with the manifold varieties of design and color all of them, including song-birds, possess. How are we to account for their music, and where did they get it? Who puts a sounding-board in the cicada's chest with the chirping songs it makes in the branches? Whenever the sun sets them going they make mid-day music, stirring the groves and giving the traveler an escort of sound. Who wove the web of song for the swan, when it spreads out its wings to the breeze, turning its hissing into melody? I forebear to speak of all the unreal and artificially induced vocal noises. How comes it that the pretentious Median peacock is so proud, so fond of admiration for his conscious beauty, that he shows off to his hens or on sight of an approaching male? He lifts up his neck, fans out his plumage and gives his admirers a stage-show of beauty as he struts about. Then again Holy Scripture shows admiration for feminine skill at weaving cloth. "Who," it says, "gave to women skill at weaving cloth and knowledge of embroidery?"[96] This faculty

---

[96] Job 38.36 [LXX]

belongs to a living, thinking being, one with more wisdom than any other and on the way to being something heavenly.

28.25   But, I beg you, admire the instinctive intelligence of unthinking beings and present your explanations. How is it that birds make rocks, trees and roofs their bowers, equipped to be secure and handsome as the nurslings require? Where do bees and spiders get the ingenious industry that makes bees devise honeycombs which hold together with hexagonal, matching cavities, made elaborately firm by a partition and by the subtlety of alternate straight lines and angles, in hives too dark for them to see the structure of the comb? How are spiders able to weave complex webs with such light and almost etherial threads of manifold extension, threads you cannot see the ends of, to make precious homes as well as hunting-grounds for weaker prey? Could any Euclid copy these threads, investigating them with non-existent lines and flagging in his proofs? Could a Palamedes have produced the tactical movements and formations of cranes, which move, so we are told, through the same drills without breaking rank, in intricate flight-patterns? Did they have any kind of Phidias, Zeuxis, or Polygnotus, any Parrhasius or Aglaophon with science enough to draw or sculpt their extravagance of beauty? Did they have their Daedalus with that superbly beautiful bridal-gift he wrought, his "Chorus of Knossus," or his Cretan labyrinth "so hard to travel, so hard to unravel," to use the poetic phrase, and cunningly devised to run so frequently into itself? I forebear mentioning ants with their stores and stewards, their treasures of good in match with the season, and all the rest we know to be on record as to their routes, their leaders, and the orderliness found in their works.

28.26   If you have understood the intelligence at work here and can explain it, turn your attention to the different kinds of plants, to the artistry displayed in their foliage, affording at once the maximum of pleasure to the eyes and of advantage to their fruit. Consider too the rich variety, the lavish abundance of fruits, the special beauty of the particularly important kinds. Examine the potentialities the juices of their roots and the scents their flowers have, not just the pleasant but the medically useful ones too, with their charming qualities of color. Their value shines through clearer than gems, since nature has made a sort of open banquet and served you with all you need to live and enjoy life. The purpose of this is to make you recognize God at least from the benefits you receive, and more conscious of your position if you lack them. Leave here and range over mother earth's length and breadth, her bosom of sea bound round by land, her noble groves and rivers. Traverse her abundant, overflowing fountains of cool drinking-water above ground, besides all those which flow underground. Under caverns these flow, till forced out by the pressure of the wind, their temperature raised in the vehemence of the struggling-match, they burst out at slight opportunity. This way they provide us all over the world with the hot baths we need, and, through the force of the contrast they make, with a free, natural corrective. Tell me the cause of all this, explain the nature of this spontaneous fabric, as commendable in its details as in their relationship. What makes the world stand steadfast? What does it ride on, what actually supports it and what does that support rest on? Reason has no explanation of what upholds the world except the will of God. And again, how comes it that part of the earth has been elevated to make mountain peaks, part settled into plains, in this variety of shapes? What causes it to have its gradual alternations, which make for more unstinting usefulness and render it pleasanter by variety? Part of the earth is apportioned for habitation, part—the whole area consecrated as mountain heights—is unoccupied, and sundered from one another they come to different boundaries. Is not this the clearest mark of God's mighty hand at work?

28.27 As for the sea, if I had felt no wonder at its size, I should have felt it for its stillness, at the way it stands free within its proper limits.[97] If its stillness had not moved my admiration, its size must have done. Since both aspects move me, I shall praise the power involved in both. What binding force brought the sea together? What causes it to swell yet stay in position, as if in awe of the land its neighbor? How can it take in all rivers and stay the same through sheer excess of quantity—I know no other explanation?[98] Why does so great an element have sand as its frontier?[99] Can natural philosophers, with their futile cleverness, give any account of it, when they actually take the sea's vast measurements with pint-pots of their own ideas? Or shall I give you the short answer from Scripture, the one more credible, more real, than their long arguments? "He made his command a fence for the face of the waters."[100] This command is what binds the elemental water. What makes it carry the sailorman in his little boat with a little wind—do you not find it a marvelous sight, does not your mind stand amazed at it?—to bind land and sea with business and commerce and unify for man such very different things? What springs do the first springs have? Look for them and see if you, a man, can discover or track one down. Who parted plains and hills with rivers and gave them free course? How do we get a miracle from opposites—from a sea that does not get out and rivers that do not stand still?[101] What feeds the

---

[97] cf. Job 38.8-11
[98] cf. Eccl. 1.7
[99] Jer. 5.22
[100] Job 26.10 LXX
[101] cf. Eccl. 1.7

waters, what different kinds of food do they get? Some are nourished with rain, others drink with their roots—if I may use a rich metaphor to describe the richness of God.[102]

28.28 But now leave earth and earthly themes, soar up into the air on the wings of your mind, letting the argument move forward on its path. From here I shall bear you up and on to themes heavenly, heaven itself and what lies above heaven. As for the further stage beyond, words shrink from approaching it; yet approach it they will, so far as they can. Who poured out the air so unstintingly? Its vast riches are not counted out by rank or fortune; they have no frontiers to hold them in; their distribution takes no account of age. No, like the division of the manna, there is enough to go round and all shares are equal.[103] Winged creatures ride on it, the winds have it for their throne. It gives the seasons their timeliness and life to animals—or rather preserves the life in their bodies. It contains our bodies. Speech takes place with its aid. Light and what light makes known are found in it and through it flows the current of sight. Yet see what comes next after air—I cannot yield to air entire dominion over all it is reckoned as owning. What of the "storehouses of the winds,"[104] of the "treasuries of the snow"?[105] Who "gave birth," as Scripture has it, "to the dewdrops"?[106] From whose "womb does the ice come forth"?[107] Who "binds up the water in the clouds"?[108] The miracle of it—that he sets something, whose nature it is to flow, on clouds, that he fixes it there by his word! Yet he pours out some of it on the face of the whole earth, sprinkling it to all alike in due season.[109] He does not unleash the entire stock of water—the cleansing of Noah's era was enough, and God most true does not forget his own covenant.[110] He does not hold back, making us need a second Elijah to end the drought.[111] "If he closes heaven," Scripture says, "who will open it?"[112] If he opens the sluices,[113] who will shut them? Who could endure extremes of drought and deluge, should God fail to control the whole universe by his checks and balances?[114] You

---

[102] Ezek. 31.9 [LXX]
[103] Ex. 16.14-18
[104] Ps. 135(134).7
[105] Job 38.22
[106] Job 38.28
[107] Job 38.29
[108] Job 26.8
[109] cf. Mt. 5.45
[110] Gen. 9.8-17
[111] 1(3) Kgs. 17.1-18.45
[112] Job. 12.14; 2 Chr. 7.13
[113] Mal. 3.10. Gregory deletes the μή, "not," from the reference to fit his positive statement. He probably did that from memory, not from a conscious decision.
[114] Job 28.25

philosopher, you thunder from the ground, you lack even the shine a few sparks of truth might give you. What explanation will you give me of lightning and thunder? Will you allege that vapors from the ground make the mass of clouds or that these clouds are made by condensation of air? Will you ascribe the cause of thunder and lightning to the friction and explosion into one another of fine-spun masses of cloud, friction being your cause of lightning, explosion your cause of thunder? But how could moving air be bottled up so as to explode and produce lightning under the pressure of friction? If you have traversed the air and reckoned up all it involves, come now with me, touch heaven and things celestial. Faith rather than reason shall lead us, if that is, you have learned the feebleness of reason to deal with matters quite close at hand, and have acquired enough knowledge of reason to recognize things which surpass reason. If so, it follows that you will not be a wholly earthbound thinker, ignorant of your very ignorance.

28.29   Who made heaven rotate and set the stars in order? Can you tell me what heaven and the stars are? You are so high up in the air yet so ignorant of what lies at your feet, so very busy with gaping at the immeasurable realities above you yet so incapable of taking your own measure. Granted you have a grasp of revolutions and orbits, conjunctions and separations, settings and risings, the finer points of degrees (as they are called) and all the other subjects you take such inordinate pride in knowing, this is not a real grasp of the actual things by any means. No, observation of a certain movement is confirmed by further exercise and unifies the observations made by many others. It then thinks out a rule and gets the title "knowledge." This "knowledge" is just like the common awareness of lunar change, in taking its start from visual experience. But if you are very knowledgeable on these subjects and are on the look-out for proper respect, explain the cause of the order and movement. What makes the Sun a beacon for the whole world to look at, a chorus-leader, as it were, who puts the other stars in the shade by his superior brilliance, outdoing them more than any of them can outdo the others? They vie with him, but he outshines them all, not even allowing their rising with him to be noticed. I have a proof-text here—"handsome as a bridegroom, swift and mighty as a giant."[115] I do not, you see, allow his praises to be sung except by Scripture. So great is the Sun's power that its heat reaches from one end of the world to the other. Nothing can avoid experiencing the Sun; every eye is filled with its light, each body with its heat. The mild temperature and ordered movement of it give warmth without burning. Present to all, it embraces all alike.

---

[115] cf. Ps. 19(18).5(6)

28.30 I wonder if you have noticed the important truth that, as a non-Christian writer puts its, "the Sun has the same place in things of sense as God has in things ideal." It gives light to the eyes, just as he does to the mind. The Sun is the noblest thing we can see, God the noblest we can know by thought. But what power set the Sun in motion to start with? What force keeps him moving in orbit by a fixed immovable law? Poets speak reasoned truth not metaphor, when their hymns call the Sun "unflagging," "bringer of life," "life-begetting" and the rest—the Sun, unhalting in its course and its kindnesses. How, above earth, does he fashion day, below it, night—or whatever the right words are to describe how the Sun looks to us? What makes the even imbalance, to use a rather paradoxical phrase, of night and day with their gain and loss? How does he create the orderly arrival, and assign the disciplined departure of the seasons? Love rules that they embrace, seemly discipline that they part, like dancers; they gradually mingle, stealthily closing in exactly as do days and nights, to avoid giving pain by their novelty. But let the Sun go its way now. Have you knowledge of the Moon's nature, its changes, the measures of its light, its course? Do you know why it presides over night, whilst the Sun rules day: why the Moon gives wild animals boldness, whilst the Sun gets man up for work,[116] doing the most effective service whether high or low in the sky? Do you know what binds the Pleiades or what fences Orion in,[117] as God does who "counts the number of the stars and calls them all by their names"?[118] Do you understand the "different glory"[119] of each and the order of their motion, that I may have grounds to trust you when you use the stars to scheme human schemes and arm the creature against his creator?

28.31 What do you think? Shall we stop our preaching here at matter and objects of sight? Or, since Scripture recognizes the tabernacle of Moses as a symbol for the whole world[120] (the world I mean, of things "visible and invisible")[121] shall we pass through the first veil,[122] transcending sense, to bend our gaze on holy things,[123] on ideal and heavenly reality? But not even this can we see as something free of body, even if it actually be so, since it has "fire" and "wind" for its name or created being. "He makes his angels winds," it says, "and his ministers a flame

---

[116] cf. Ps. 104(103).22-23
[117] Job 38.31
[118] Ps. 147(146).4
[119] 1 Cor. 15.41
[120] cf. Heb. 9.1-2 and 24
[121] Col. 1.16
[122] cf. Ex. 26.31
[123] cf. Heb. 9.24

of fire,"[124] Unless "makes" here means "preserves with the state they were created in" and "wind" and "fire" have the sense of being what is "ideal" and "purifies"—since I am aware that these same epithets are applied to the primal being of God as well. However, so far as we are concerned, angels must be incorporeal or very near it. You see how we become dizzy with the theme and can get no further than the stage of being aware of angels[125] and archangels,[126] thrones, dominions, princedoms, powers,[127] of glowing lights, ascents, intellectual powers or minds, beings of nature pure and unalloyed. Fixed, almost incapable of changing for the worse, they encircle God, the first cause, in their dance. What words can one use to hymn them? He makes them shine with purest brilliance or each with a different brilliance to match his nature's rank. So strongly do they bear the shape and imprint of God's beauty, that they become in their turn lights, able to give light to others by transmitting the stream which flows from the primal light of God. As ministers of the divine will, powerful with inborn and acquired strength, they range over the universe. They are quickly at hand to all in any place, so eager are they to serve, so agile is their being. Each has under him a different part of the Earth or the universe, which God alone, who defined their ranks, knows. They unify the whole, making all things obey the beck and call of him alone who fashioned them. They hymn God's majesty in everlasting contemplation of everlasting glory, meaning, not to make God glorious— God, whose fullness supplies all else with excellence, cannot be added to—but to leave beings supreme after God with no kindness unshown them. If our hymn has been worthy of its theme, it is the grace of the Trinity, of the Godhead one in three; if desire remains incompletely satisfied, that way too my argument can claim success. For it has been engaged in a struggle to prove that even the nature of beings on the second level is too much for our minds, let alone God's primal and unique, not to say all-transcending, nature.

---

[125] cf. Rom. 8.38
[126] cf. 1 Thess. 4.16
[127] Col. 1.16

ORATION 29
ON THE SON

29.1 Yes, these are the replies one can use to put a brake upon this hasty argumentativeness, a hastiness which is dangerous in all matters, but especially in theological topics. To censure, of course, is a trivial task—anyone so minded can do it quite easily. But to substitute one's own view takes a man of true religion and sound sense. So, come now, let us put our confidence in the Holy Spirit **they** dishonor but **we** worship. Let us bring our convictions about the Godhead—convictions of some significance and standing—into broad daylight, like an offspring of good stock ripe for birth. Not that we have held our peace at other times—here is the one point we become brash and arrogant on—but now we express the truth even more outspokenly, in order that, as Scripture puts it, we may not suffer the condemnation of God's disfavor by balking the issue.[1]

Every speech has two parts to it. One part aims at establishing one's own position; the other refutes the opposing case. This is the method we shall try, expounding our own, before refuting our opponents' arguments. Both parts will be as brief as possible, so that there may be as good a conspectus of our views as the introductory treatise they have invented for the deception of simpler or more gullible souls provides. Besides which we do not want our thoughts to be dissipated through the length of discussion, like water, without a channel to hold it in, running to waste over flat ground.

29.2 The opinions about Deity which hold pride of place are three in number: atheism, polytheism, and monotheism. With the first two the children of Greece amused themselves. Let the game go on! Atheism with its lack of a governing principle involves disorder. Polytheism, with a plurality of such principles, involves faction and hence the absence of a governing principle and this involves disorder again. Both lead to an identical result—lack of order, which, in turn, leads to disintegration, disorder being the prelude to disintegration. Monotheism, with its single governing principle, is what **we** value—not monotheism defined as the sovereignty of a single person (after all, self-discordant unity can become a plurality) but the single rule produced by equality of nature, harmony of will, identity of action, and the convergence towards their source of what springs from unity—none of which is possible in the case of created nature. The result is that though there is numerical distinction, there is

---

[1] cf. Heb. 10.38-39

no division in the being. For this reason, a one eternally[2] changes to a two and stops at three—meaning the Father, the Son, and the Holy Spirit. In a serene, non-temporal, incorporeal way, the Father is parent of the "offspring" and originator of the "emanation"—or whatever name one can apply when one has isolated them from things visible. We shall not venture, as a non-Christian philosopher rashly did, to talk of an "over-flowing of goodness," "as though a bowl had overflowed"—these were the plain terms he used in his disquisition on primary and secondary causes. We ought never to introduce the notion of involuntary generation (in the sense of some sort of unrestrained natural secretion) notions which are completely out of keeping with ideas about the Godhead. This is why we limit ourselves to Christian terms and speak of "the Ingenerate," "the Begotten," and (as God the Word himself does in one passage) "what Proceeds from the Father."[3]

29.3 *So when did these last two originate?*

They transcend "whenness," but if I **must** give a naive answer —when the Father did.

When was that?

There has not been [a time] when the Father has not been in existence. This, then, is true of the Son and of the Holy Spirit. Put another question and I will answer it.

Since when has the Son been begotten?

Since as long as the Father has **not** been begotten.

Since when has the Spirit been proceeding?

Since as long as the Son has **not** been proceeding but being begotten in a non-temporal way that transcends explanation. We cannot, though, explain the meaning of "supra-temporal" **and** deliberately keep clear of any suggestion of time. Expressions like "when," "before x," "after y," and "from the beginning" are not free from temporal implications however much we try to wrest them. No, we cannot explain it, except possibly by taking the world-era as the period coinciding with eternal things, being a period which is not, as "time" is, measured and fragmented by the Sun's motion.

How is it, then that these latter are not like the Father in having no origin, if they are co-eternal with him?

Because they are **from** him, though not **after** him. "Being unoriginate" necessarily implies "being eternal," but "being eternal" does not entail "being unoriginate," so long as the origin referred to is the Father. So because they have a cause they are not unoriginate. But clearly

---

[2] 1 John 1.1; John 1.1
[3] John 15.26

a cause is not necessarily prior to its effects—the Sun is not prior to its light. Because time is not involved, they are to that extent **unoriginate**—even if you do scare simple souls with the bogey-word; for things which produce Time are beyond time.

29.4 *How, then can the process of begetting not involve subjection to change?*

Because a body is not involved. If corporeal begetting implies subjection to change, an incorporeal one must be free of it. Let me put a question to you in return: how can he be God, if he is a creature? What is created is not God. Not to mention the fact that if "creating" is given a corporeal interpretation, emotion and change are to be found here as well—for instance, time, desire, imagination, thought, hope, distress, risk, failure, and success. All these factors, and more besides, as everybody knows, are involved in creating. I wonder why you do not go the full length of envisaging mating, periods of gestation and risks of miscarriage as necessarily involved if he were to beget at all, or why you do not list the ways in which birds, beasts, and fish produce offspring and put the divine and unutterable generation down on one of these, or else use your new-fangled scheme to get rid of the Son. You are incapable of understanding that one who has a distinctive fleshly birth—what other case of a Virgin Mother of God do you know?—has a different spiritual birth, or rather, one whose being is not the same as ours has a different way of begetting as well.

29.5 *Can anyone be a "father," without beginning to be one?*

Yes, one who did not begin his existence. What begins to exist begins to be a father. **He** did not begin to be Father—he did not begin at all. He is "Father" in the true sense, because he is not a son as well. In our case, the word "father" cannot be truly appropriate, because we must be fathers **and** sons—the terms carry equal weight. We also stem from a pair, not a single being, making us be divided and become human beings gradually, and maybe not even human beings of the kind we are intended to be. The ties are dissolved by one side or the other, so that only the relationships remain, bereft of the realities.

But, it may be said, "*he begat*" and "*he has been begotten*" *can and must bring in the idea of a beginning of this process of generation.*

Why not say then instead, "he has existed as begotten from the beginning," and so avoid your labored objections with their penchant for time? Will you accuse us of falsifying a Scriptural truth? Is it not clear to everybody that there are plenty of examples of tenses being employed in an opposite sense, especially in Biblical usage? This is true not only of the past tense, but of the present and the future as well. For example: "Why did the heathen rage?"[4]—the raging had not yet occurred; and, "They will

---

[4] Ps. 2.1

cross the river on foot''⁵—which means, ''they **have** gone through it.'' It would be a long task to list all the expressions of this kind on which scholars have bestowed their attention.

29.6 So much for that objection! This next one of theirs is like it in being outrageously provocative.

Has the Father, they ask, *begotten the Son voluntarily, or involuntarily?*

They now bind us round with what they think are strong cords, but are really feeble ones.

If, they say, *it was involuntary, he was in someone's power. Who exercised the power? How could God be under someone's power? But if it was voluntary, the Son is son to a will; so how can he stem from the Father?*

They make the will into a new kind of mother in place of the Father.

First, it is certainly a point in their favor if they say this. It means that they are deserting passivity to take refuge in the will. Volition is not, after all, a passive experience. Secondly, let us take a look at what they put as their strong point. They had best now be grappled with at closer quarters. You who coolly assert what you will, did **you** come into existence as a result of your father's willing it, or without his will? If without his will, he must have been in someone's power. What an act of violence! And who exercised that power over him? You cannot answer, ''Nature''—nature is also capable of self-control. If it was voluntary, a few syllables have lost you your father—you are evidently a son of his will, not of your father. Let me pass on to the subject of God and creatures, and address this question of yours to your own intelligence. Did he create the universe voluntarily or under compulsion? If it was under compulsion, then external domination and a dominator are involved. If voluntarily, then creatures have been deprived of their God, and you most of all who invent sophistries of this kind. God is walled off from his creation by his will. No, if we are sober, we make a distinction, I think, between ''willing'' and ''a will,'' between ''begetting'' (as a participle) and ''begetting'' (as a noun) between ''speaking'' and ''speech.'' The participles refer to a subject of motion, the nouns designate the motion itself. What is willed does not **belong** to a will—it is not a necessary concomitant of it. Nor does what is begotten **belong** to a begetting, nor what is heard to an act of speech. They belong instead to the subject who willed, who begat, who speaks. What belongs to God transcends all these cases even. For him begetting may well just be the will to beget—but without any superiority of begetting to willing either. If we accept this last proposition without reservation, nothing will intervene.

29.7 Do you want me to take the game on to the Father? You make me

---

⁵ Ps. 66(65).6

do rash things like that! The Father is God either voluntarily or involuntarily. Now (if you do not want to be trapped by your own expertise) when, if it was involuntary, did he begin to will it? Not, of course, before he actually was God—there being nothing prior to that. Or is he partly the subject, partly the object of an act of will? In that case, he must be divided. According to you, there is a problem how he can avoid belonging to a will. But if it was involuntary, what forced him into being God? How can he be God, if he is forced, forced into nothing less than being God?

How, then, has the Son been begotten?

How has he been created, if, as you say, created he has been? Indeed this is part of the same puzzle.

Perhaps you will answer: *by his will and his reason.*

But your explanation is so far incomplete, for how will and reason can have the power to effect anything remains unexplained—in the case of human beings, after all, they do not.

29.8 How, then has he been begotten? This begetting would be a triviality if it could be understood by you, who have no knowledge of how you yourself procreate and are ashamed to explain in full the limited understanding you have. Do you really think you know it all? It will cost you much effort before you discover the principles involved from conception through formation to delivery, and the linking of soul to body, of intellect to soul and of reason to intellect, and can explain the rest of your make-up—movement, growth, assimilation of food, perception, memory, and recollection and what belongs jointly to soul and body, what separately to one and what involves their interplay. Faculties, after all, whose maturity belongs to a later stage, have principles which accompany the procreative process. Explain these, and even then you are not able to treat of God's begetting. That would be risky. For if you know your own, it by no means follows that you know God's; and unless you know your own, how could you know God's? The heavenly begetting is more incomprehensible than your own, to the same extent that God is harder to trace out than Man. If you make its incomprehensibility a ground for denying the fact, it is high time you ruled out as non-existent a good number of things you do not understand, the chief of which is God himself. However audacious, however enthusiastic you are, you cannot explain what **he** is at all. Drop your ideas of flux, division and cleavage, drop the habit of treating the incorporeal nature as if it were a body and you might well get a worthy notion of God's begetting. How has he been begotten?—I re-utter the question with loathing. God's begetting ought to have the tribute of our reverent silence. The important point is for you to learn that he has been begotten. As to the way it happens, we shall not concede that even angels, much less you, know that. Shall **I** tell you the way? It is a way known only to the begetting Father and the begotten Son. Anything beyond this fact is hidden by a cloud and escapes your dull vision.

29.9. *Well then, he either existed or did not exist when the Father begat him?*

What drivel! That dilemma might have relevance to you and me. Like Levi in Abraham's loins[6] we did have some sort of being, and yet we have **come** into being as well, so that, in a certain fashion, our condition is a product of being and non-being. This is the opposite of primeval matter, which obviously came into existence from non-being, despite the fact that some people imagine it to be uncreated. In the present case, being begotten coincides with existence, and is from all eternity;[7] so where are you going to put this cleft stick of a question? What point is there prior to eternity to fix the existence or non-existence of the Son? Either way the notion of eternity will be destroyed. Unless, when we put the question whether the Father comes from being or non-being, you risk the answers **either** that he has a double being, partly existing, partly pre-existing, **or** that he is in the same case with the Son, being a product of non-being. This is what your puerile conundrums lead to. Sandcastles, they cannot stand a puff of wind.

No, I allow neither supposition. I say that the question presents an absurdity, not the answer a difficulty. If you follow your logical presuppositions and hold that in every case one of the pair of alternatives must be true, then I shall put you a little question. Is Time **in** Time, or not? If it is, what is the Time it is in? What is the difference between them? How does one contain the other? If Time is not in Time, how acute your wits are to get us non-temporal Time! What about the proposition: "I am now making a false statement"? You must concede one of the alternatives, it is either true or false—we cannot allow both. But that is impossible. If the statement is false, it will be true and if it is true, it will be false, by logical necessity. Is there anything remarkable then in the fact that two contradictories can both be true in the case under discussion, just as they are both false here, and thus your sophistry will be shown up for the silliness it is? Here is another teaser for you to solve: were you present to yourself when you were being begotten and are you present to yourself now, or are both propositions false? If you were and are present, who is present to whom? How did the pair of you come to be a single whole? If both alternatives are false, how is it that you came to be parted from yourself and what caused the separation? No, it is stupid to stir up a dust about whether a thing is present to itself or not. The expression "is present" is used to imply a relationship with other things not with itself. You must appreciate

---

[6] Heb. 7.9-10
[7] 1 John 1.1; John 1.1

that it is even stupider to be correcting people on the subject of whether or not what has been begotten from eternity[8] existed prior to its begetting. That question only arises in connection with temporally determined beings.

29.10 *But*, it may be said, *the ingenerate and the generate are not the same thing. If that is the case, the Father and the Son cannot be the same thing.*

It goes without saying that this argument excludes either the Father or the Son from the Godhead—if ingeneracy is the essence of God, generacy is not his essence and *vice versa*. There is no gainsaying this, is there? Make your choice of the alternative blasphemies, you empty-headed theologian, if you are fully intent on blaspheming. Still, what are your grounds for denying that ingenerate and generate are the same? If you had said uncreated and created, I should agree—what has no origin and what is created cannot be identical in nature. But if you are talking about begetter and begotten, this is a false statement—these must be the same; it is in the nature of an offspring to have a nature identical with its parent's. Here is another objection: what do you mean by "the ingenerate" and "the generate"? If you mean ingenerateness and generateness—no, these are not the same thing; but if you mean the things which have these properties in them why should they not be the same? Lack of intelligence and intelligence are not identical, but they can be predicated of the same thing, a man. They do not mark out separate beings, they are separate qualities of the same being. Do immortality, purity, and immutability each constitute God's being? No, if that were so, there would be a plurality of "beings" of God, not a single being. Or is Deity a composite resulting from these?—if these are "beings" or substances, there would have to be composition.

29.11 They do not hold that view, because these are properties of other beings besides God. The substance of God is what belongs to him particularly and uniquely. The people who allege that "matter" and "form" are ingenerate would not agree that ingeneracy is uniquely a property of God—we will put the Manichaean darkness in the further background. But suppose it does belong uniquely to God, what was Adam? Was he not uniquely a creation formed by God?

Yes, you will say.

Was he a unique human being as well?

Of course not.

Why?

Because manhood does not consist of being formed by God; what has parentage is also man.

---

[8] Ibid.

In the same way, it is not the case that the ingenerate and only the ingenerate is God (though only the Father is ingenerate) but you must allow that the Begotten too is God. The Begotten stems from God, however fond you are of unbegottenness. Next, how are you to talk of the being of God, when what is said about that being is not a positive assertion but a negation? "Unbegotten" means that he has no parent. It does not state his nature, but simply the fact that he was not begotten.

So what is the being of God?

You must be mad to ask the question, making such a fuss about begottenness! We count it a high thing that we may perhaps learn what it is in the time to come, when we are free of this dense gloom. That is the promise of one who cannot lie.[9] Yes, this is what men, who purify themselves for it, must think of and hope for. As for us, we can confidently affirm that if it is a high thing for the Father to have no origin, it is no lesser thing for the Son to stem from such a Father. He must share in the glory of the uncaused, because he stems from the uncaused. That he has been begotten is a further fact about him, as significant as it is august, for men whose minds are not totally earthbound and materialistic.

29.12 *But,* they say, *if the Son is the same in substance as the Father, and the Father is unbegotten, then the Son must be unbegotten too.*

True—provided that ingeneracy constitutes God's being. That would give us an outlandish mix-up—an unbegotten-begotten. But supposing the difference lies outside the substance of God, what validity has your argument got? Must you be your father's father, if you are to avoid missing anything he has, when you are the same in being as he? Surely it is clear that when we are looking, if look we can, for what God's being consists in, a personal characteristic must be left out of account. This is the way to find out that God and ingeneracy are not identical. If they were identical, both "God" and "ingenerate" would have to be relational terms, or, since "ingenerate" is an absolute term, "God" would have to be one too, seeing that logical equivalents can be used interchangeably. But what does "ingenerate" relate itself to, what is it the ingenerate **of**? God has such terms—he is God **of** all. So how can "God" and "ingenerate" be identical? And again since ingeneracy and begotten-ness are mutually opposed, as condition and privation, it follows that mutually opposed beings or substances have been brought in—which is impossible. Or again, since conditions are prior to privations, and privations take away conditions, not only must the Father's substance be prior to the Son's but it must also be in process of destruction by the Father on your presuppositions.

---

[9] Titus 1.2

29.13   What is left of their invincible arguments? Perhaps they will take a last refuge in this argument:

Unless God has ceased to beget, the begetting must be unfinished and at some time stop; but if it has stopped, it must have started.

Here again we have crude, bodily ideas, from crude, bodily people. For my own part I am not committing myself to saying whether or not the process of being begotten is eternal, until I have made a close examination of the text: "Before all the hills, he begets me."[10] But I see no necessity in their argument.

If, as they say, *what is going to stop must have started, what is not going to stop cannot have started.*

What, on that showing, will the soul or angels be? If they have a beginning, they must cease, but if they are not going to end, obviously, according to these people, they have no beginning either. But in fact they did begin and they will not end. Their argument then, that something which is going to end requires a beginning, is untrue. Our position, of course, is that horses, man, oxen, and each item that comes under the same species have a single concept. Whatever shares in the concept is rightly called by that name, and whatever does not share in it is not properly called by the name. Thus in the same way there is a single being, nature, and name of God, even though the titles are distinguished along with the distinct ideas about him. Whatever is properly called "God" **is** God and whatever he is in his nature is a true name for him—granted that real truth is contained in facts, not in names. These people, though, act as if they were afraid of leaving any opposition to the truth untried. They acknowledge the Son as "God," when forced by reason and proof-texts to do so, but only in an equivocal sense. He shares the name and the name alone!

29.14   When we make them the rejoinder, 'Well, do you really mean that the Son is not 'God' in the proper sense of the word, in the same way that a picture of an animal is not an animal? In that case, how can he be God, supposing he is not 'God' in the proper sense?'' they answer,

Why should not the names be the same and used in the proper sense in either case?

They instance the Greek word for "dog," which can be used in the proper sense to mean both a dog and a shark (there being this sort of case of equivocal terms) and any other case where something bears the same title it shares equally with something else of a different nature.

In these instances, dear fellow, you are putting two natures under the same name, not making one superior to, or prior to, the other, or one more true to its name than the other. There is nothing attached to the names to force that conclusion—the animal and the fish are equally en-

---

[10] Prov. 8.25

titled to the same Greek name, "dog"—and why not? No, things of the
same and things of differing status can have the same name. Yet when it
comes to God, you attach an awe-inspiring solemnity to him, a transcendence of every essence and nature which constitutes the unique nature of
God's deity, so to say. You ascribe this to the Father but then rob the Son
of it and make him subordinate. You give the Son second place in reverence and worship. Even if you endow him with the syllables which make
up the word "**similar**," you in fact truncate his godhead, and make a mischievous transition from parity to disparity in the usage of a common
name. The result is that a pictured and a living man are apter illustrations
for you of the Godhead of Father and Son than the dog and shark you
used. Alternatively, you must concede that the fact that they have a common name puts their natures on the same level, even if you are making
out that they are different; in that case, you have ruined your "dog" example, which you hit on to illustrate a disparity of natures. What does it
matter that the animals you distinguish have the same name, "dog," if
they are on the same level? The point, after all, of having recourse to
"dogs" and ambiguous names was to prove disparity, not parity. How
could anyone stand more clearly convicted of self-confuting blasphemy?
29.15 If we say that the Father is **qua** cause superior to the Son, they
add the minor premise,

> *but he is cause by nature* and hence conclude that *he is superior by nature.*

I do not know whom the fallacy misleads—themselves or their opponents. For it is not the case that all the predicates affirmed of some particular being can be affirmed without further qualification of his basic substance. No, plainly they are affirmed of some particular thing, in some
particular respect. Is there anything to stop me also taking as my minor
premise, "but 'being superior by nature' does not entail 'being Father,'"
and then concluding either that "being superior" does not entail "being
superior" or that "being the Father" does not entail "being Father." Or
take another example: God is being, but being is not necessarily God.
Draw the conclusion for yourself—God is not necessarily God. No, the
fallacy here arises from arguing, as the logicians call it, "from the particular to the general." We concede, of course, that it belongs to the nature
of the cause to be superior, but they infer that the superiority belongs to
the nature—which is like our saying "X is a dead man" and their drawing
the inference that "Man," without qualification, is dead.
29.16 How could we by-pass this next point of theirs, which is quite as
dumbfounding as the rest of what they say?

> *"Father,"* they say, *is a designation either of the substance or the activity; is it
> not?*

They intend to impale us on a dilemma, for if we say that it names the substance we shall then be agreeing that the Son is of a different substance, there being a single substance and that one, according to them, pre-empted by the Father. But if we say that the term designates the activity, we shall clearly be admitting that the Son is a creation not an offspring. If there is an active producer, there must be a production and they will declare themselves surprised at the idea of an identity between creator and created. I should have felt some awe myself at your dilemma, had it been necessary to accept one of the alternatives and impossible to avoid them by stating a third, and truer possibility. My expert friends, it is this: ''Father'' designates neither the substance nor the activity, but the relationship, the manner of being, which holds good between the Father and the Son. Just as with us these names indicate kindred and affinity, so here too they designate the sameness of stock, of parent and offspring. But to please you, let it be granted that ''the Father'' names a substance. That idea will bring in the Son along with it, not alienate him, if we follow common sense and the meaning of terms. Suppose, if you like, it stands for his activity; you will not catch us out that way either. He will actively have produced that very consubstantiality, even if the assumption of active production's being involved here is decidedly odd.

You see how we get clear of your twists and turns, even though you mean to fight foul. Now that we know just how invincible you are in logical twists, let us see what strength you can muster from Holy Scriptures. Perhaps you may undertake to win us over with them.

29.17 We, after all, understand and preach the Son's Godhead on the basis of their grand and sublime language. What do we mean here? Expressions like ''God,'' ''Word,'' ''he who is in the beginning,'' who was ''with the beginning,'' who was ''the beginning,'' ''In the beginning was the Word and the Word was with God and the Word was God''[11] and ''with thee is the beginning''[12] and ''who calls it the beginning from the generations of old.''[13] Then he is the Only-begotten Son: ''The Only-begotten Son, who is in the bosom of the Father, he has declared him.''[14] He is ''way,'' ''truth,'' ''life,'' and ''light:'' ''I am the way, the truth, and the life''[15] and ''I am the light of the world.''[16] He is ''wisdom'' and ''power:'' ''Christ the power of God and the wisdom of God.''[17] He is the ''effulgence,'' ''stamp,'' ''image,'' and ''seal:'' ''Who being the ef-

---

[11] John 1.1
[12] Ps. 109.3 [LXX]
[13] Isa. 41.4
[14] John 1.18
[15] John 14.6
[16] John 8.12
[17] 1 Cor. 1.24

fulgence of his glory and the stamp of his person"[18] and "image of
goodness"[19] and "for him did God the Father seal."[20] He is "Lord,"
"King," "he who is," and "almighty:" "The Lord rained down fire
from the Lord"[21] and "A scepter of righteousness is the scepter of thy
kingdom"[22] and "who is and was and is to come and the almighty."[23]
Plainly these, and all the expressions synonymous with these, refer to the
Son. None of them is a later acquisition, none became attached at a later
stage to the Son or to the Spirit any more than to the Father, for perfection
does not result from additions. There never was [a time] when he was
without his word, when he was not Father, when he was not true, or when
he was without wisdom and power, or when he lacked life, splendor or
goodness.

29.18 Count up the phrases which in your ignorance you set over
against these—"My God and your God,"[24] "greater,"[25] "he created,"[26] "he made,"[27] and "he sanctified."[28] Reckon in, if you like,
"slave,"[29] and "obedient,"[30] "he gave,"[31] "he learned,"[32] "he was
commanded,"[33] "he was sent,"[34] "he could do nothing,"[35] "speak
nothing,"[36] "judge nothing,"[37] "give nothing,"[38] "will nothing of himself."[39] You may add these: his "ignorance,"[40] his "subjection,"[41] his
"praying,"[42] his "asking,"[43] his "progress,"[44] and "growing up."[45]

---

[18] Heb. 1.3
[19] Wis. 7.26
[20] John 6.27
[21] Gen. 19.24
[22] Ps. 45(44).6(7)
[23] Rev. 1.8
[24] John 20.17
[25] John 14.28
[26] Prov. 8.22
[27] Acts 2.36
[28] John 10.36
[29] Phil. 2.7
[30] Phil. 2.8
[31] John 18.9
[32] Heb. 5.8
[33] John 15.10; 10.18
[34] John 5.36, 20.21
[35] John 5.19, 30; 8.28
[36] John 12.49
[37] John 8.15-16
[38] Mark 10.40
[39] John 5.19, 30; 8.28
[40] Mt. 24.36
[41] Luke 2.51
[42] e.g. Luke 3.21; 6.12
[43] e.g. John 11.34; Luke 2.46
[44] Luke 2.52
[45] ibid.

Put in, if you like all the even lowlier expressions used about him—the fact
that he "slept,"[46] "was hungry,"[47] "got tired,"[48] "wept,"[49] "was in
agony,"[50] was subject to things.[51] Maybe you reproach him for his cross
and death—I expect you will let his Resurrection and Ascension go free,
seeing that here there is something on our side. You can pick up many
more scraps besides these, if you mean to go on fabricating this intruder
of yours, this namesake of God. For us he is true God, and on the same
level as the Father. Yes, one could easily go through each of these expressions in detail and give you the truly religious interpretation. It is not a
hard task to clear away the stumbling-block which the literal text of Scripture contains—that is, if your stumbling is real and not just willful malice.
In sum: you must predicate the more sublime expressions of the Godhead,
of the nature which transcends bodily experiences, and the lowlier ones
of the compound, of him who because of you was emptied, became incarnate and (to use equally valid language) was "made man."[52] Then next
he was exalted, in order that you might have done with the earthbound
carnality of your opinions and might learn to be nobler, to ascend with
the Godhead and not linger on in things visible but rise up to spiritual realities, and that you might know what belongs to his nature and what to
God's plan of salvation.

29.19 He whom presently you scorn, was once transcendent over even
you. He who is presently human was incomposite. He remained what he
was; what he was not, he assumed. No "because" is required for his existence in the beginning,[53] for what could account for the existence of
God? But later he came into being because of something, namely your
salvation, yours who insult him and despise his Godhead for that very reason, because he took on your thick corporeality. Through the medium of
the mind he had dealings with the flesh, being made that God on earth
which is Man. Man and God blended; they became a single whole, the
stronger side predominating, in order that I might be made God to the
same extent that he was made man. He was begotten[54]—yet he was already begotten[55]—of a woman.[56] And yet she was a virgin.[57] That it was

[46] Mt. 8.24
[47] Mt. 4.2
[48] John 4.6
[49] John 11.35
[50] Luke 22.44
[51] cf. 1 Cor. 15.28
[52] cf. Phil. 2.7
[53] John 1.1
[54] Mt. 1.16
[55] Ps. 2.7; Acts 13.33; Heb. 1.5, 5.5
[56] Gal. 4.4
[57] Mt. 1.23; Isa. 7.14; cf. Luke 1.34-35; Mt. 1.20

from a woman makes it human, that she was a virgin makes it divine. On earth he has no father,[58] but in heaven no mother.[59] All this is part of his Godhead. He was carried in the womb,[60] but acknowledged by a prophet as yet unborn himself, who leaped for joy at the presence of the Word for whose sake he had been created.[61] He was wrapped in swaddling bands,[62] but at the Resurrection he unloosed the swaddling bands of the grave.[63] He was laid in a manger,[64] but was extolled by angels, disclosed by a star and adored by Magi.[65] Why do you take offense at what you see, instead of attending to its spiritual significance? He was exiled into Egypt,[66] but he banished the Egyptian idols.[67] He had "no form or beauty"[68] for the Jews, but for David he was "fairer than the children of men"[69] and on the mount he shines forth, becoming more luminous than the Sun,[70] to reveal the future mystery.

29.20   As man he was baptized,[71] but he absolved sins as God;[72] he needed no purifying rites himself—his purpose was to hallow water. As man he was put to the test, but as God he came through victorious[73]—yes, bids us be of good cheer, because he has conquered the world.[74] He hungered[75]—yet he fed thousands.[76] He is indeed "living, heavenly bread."[77] He thirsted[78]—yet he exclaimed: "Whosoever thirsts, let him come to me and drink."[79] Indeed he promised that believers would become fountains.[80] He was tired[81]—yet he is the "rest" of

---

[58] Mt. 1.20
[59] cf. Ps. 2.7
[60] cf. Luke 1.31
[61] Luke 1.41
[62] Luke 2.7 and 12
[63] cf. John 20.6-7
[64] Luke 2.7 and 16
[65] Mt. 2.2, 7 and 9-11
[66] Mt. 2.13-14
[67] cf. Pseudo-Mt. 23ff, Hennecke-Schneemelcher, *New Testament Apocrypha*, Vol. 1, p. 308 and Barbel, p. 164, n. 46
[68] Isa. 53.2
[69] Ps. 45(44).2(3)
[70] Mt. 17.2
[71] Mt. 3.16; Luke 3.21
[72] John 1.29; Mt. 9.2
[73] Mt. 4.1-11; Luke 4.1-13
[74] John 16.33
[75] Mt. 4.2; Luke 4.2
[76] Mt. 14.20-21; 15.37-38; Mark 6.42-44, 8.9
[77] John 6.51
[78] John 19.28
[79] John 7.37
[80] cf. John 7.38
[81] John 4.6

the weary and the burdened.[82] He was overcome by heavy sleep[83]—yet he goes lightly over the sea, rebukes winds, and relieves the drowning Peter.[84] He pays tax—yet he uses a fish to do it;[85] indeed he is emperor over those who demand the tax. He is called a "Samaritan, demonically possessed"[86]—but he rescues the man who came down from Jerusalem and fell among thieves.[87] Yes, he is recognized by demons,[88] drives out demons,[89] drowns deep a legion of spirits[90] and sees the prince of demons falling like lightning.[91] He is stoned, yet not hit;[92] he prays yet he hears prayer.[93] He weeps,[94] yet he puts an end to weeping.[95] He asks where Lazarus is[96]—he was man; yet he raises Lazarus[97]—he was God. He is sold, and cheap was the price—thirty pieces of silver;[98] yet he buys back the world at the mighty cost of his own blood.[99] A sheep, he is led to the slaughter[100]—yet he shepherds Israel[101] and now the whole world as well.[102] A lamb, he is dumb[103]—yet he is "word,"[104] proclaimed by "the voice of one crying in the wilderness."[105] He is weakened, wounded[106]—yet he cures every disease and every weakness.[107] He is brought up to the tree[108] and nailed to it[109]—yet by the tree of life he restores us.[110] Yes, he saves even a thief crucified with him;[111] he wraps all

---

82 Mt. 11.28
83 cf. Mt. 8.24; Mark 4.38
84 Mt. 14.25-32; Mark 6.48-51; John 6.19-21; Mt. 8.26; Mark 4.39; Luke 8.24
85 Mt. 17.24-27
86 John. 8.48
87 cf. Luke 10.30
88 Luke 4.33-34; Mark 1.23-24
89 cf. Mt. 8.16
90 Mark 5.9 and 13; Luke 8.30 and 33.
91 cf. Luke 10.18
92 cf. John 8.59; 10.31 and 39
93 e.g. Mark 1.35; Mt. 8.13
94 John 11.35
95 cf. Luke 7.13; 8.52; 23.28
96 John 11.34
97 John 11.43-44
98 Mt. 26.15
99 cf. 1 Cor. 6.20; 1 Pet. 1.19
100 Acts 8.32; Isa. 53.7
101 Ps. 80(79).1(2)
102 cf. John 10.11 and 16
103 Isa. 53.7
104 John 1.1
105 John 1.23
106 Isa. 53.5
107 Mt. 9.35
108 1 Pet. 2.24
109 cf. John 19.17
110 cf. Gen. 2.9, 3.2; Rev. 2.7
111 Luke 23.43

the visible world in darkness.[112] He is given vinegar to drink,[113] gall to eat[114]—and who is he? Why, one who turned water into wine,[115] who took away the taste of bitterness,[116] who is all sweetness and desire.[117] He surrenders his life, yet he has power to take it again.[118] Yes, the veil is rent, for things of heaven are being revealed, rocks split, and dead men have an earlier awakening.[119] He dies,[120] but he vivifies[121] and by death destroys death.[122] He is buried,[123] yet he rises again.[124] He goes down to Hades, yet he leads souls up,[125] ascends to heaven,[126] and will come to judge quick and dead,[127] and to probe discussions like these. If the first set of expressions starts you going astray, the second set takes your error away.

29.21 This is the answer we make perforce to these posers of puzzles. Perforce—because Christian people find long-winded controversy disagreeable and one Adversary[128] enough for them. Yet our attackers made it essential, since remedies too must be made for diseases, if they are to learn that their wisdom is not complete and that they are not invincible in their lavish attempts to nullify the Gospel. For when we abandon faith to take the power of reason as our shield, when we use philosophical enquiry to destroy the credibility of the Spirit, then reason gives way in the face of the vastness of the realities. Give way it must, set going, as it is, by the frail organ of human understanding. What happens then? The frailty of our reasoning looks like a frailty in our creed. Thus it is that, as Paul too judges, smartness of argument is revealed as a nullifying of the Cross.[129] Faith, in fact, is what gives fullness to our reasoning.

But may he who "expounds hard questions and solves difficulties,"[130] who puts it into our minds to untie the twisted knots of their strained dog-

---

[112] cf. Mt. 27.45; Mark 15.33; Luke 23.44
[113] Mt. 27.48
[114] Mt. 27.34
[115] John 2.7-9
[116] cf. Ex. 15.25
[117] Cant. 5.16 [LXX]
[118] John 10.17-18
[119] Mt. 27.51-52
[120] Mt. 27.50; Mark 15.37; Luke 23.46; John 19.30
[121] John 5.21
[122] 2 Tim. 1.10; Heb. 2.14
[123] Mt. 27.60; Mark 15.46; Luke 23.53; John 19.41-42; 1 Cor. 15.4
[124] John 20.8-9; Mt. 28.6; Mark 16.6; Luke 24.6; 1 Cor. 15.4
[125] cf. Eph. 4.8-9; Ps. 68(67).18(19)
[126] Mark 16.19; Luke 24.51; Acts 1.10-11
[127] 2 Tim. 4.1; 1 Pet. 4.5
[128] cf. 1 Pet. 5.8
[129] 1 Cor. 1.17
[130] cf. Dan. 5.12

mas, may he, above all, change these men and make them believers instead of logicians, Christians instead of what they are currently called. Indeed this is our entreaty. ''We beseech you, for Christ's sake; be reconciled to God and quench not the Spirit''[131]—or rather let Christ be
reconciled with you and may the Spirit at long last illuminate you. Bent
on quarrel though you may be, yet we have the Trinity in our safekeeping
and by the Trinity can be saved, abiding pure and blameless[132] until the
more complete revelation of what we long for in Christ himself, our Lord,
to whom be glory for ever and ever.[133] Amen.

---

[131] 2 Cor. 5.20; 1 Thess. 5.19
[132] Phil. 1.10
[133] Rev. 1.6

ORATION 30
ON THE SON

30.1 Last time, by the power of the Spirit, we made havoc enough for you of the subtly calculated dodges, the objections and counter-arguments from the side of sacred Scripture, which these textual vandals use to rob the written words of their sense, get the people on their side, and throw the way of truth into disorder. We have now established a general, and I believe, clear solution, satisfactory to people of sound sense—the solution, I mean, of allocating the more elevated, the more distinctly divine expressions of Scripture to the Godhead, the humbler and more human to the New Adam,[1] God passible for our sake over against sin. The pressure of the argument did not allow us to treat of the passages individually. You want brief explanations here to avoid being swept away by their plausible arguments, and we shall group these explanations in numbered sections to aid the memory.

30.2 This is one passage they have very ready at hand:

"The Lord created me as the beginning of his ways for his works."[2]

How are we to treat it? Are we not to denounce Solomon? Shall we not cancel his earlier words because of his later lapse?[3] Must we not take the statement as that of Wisdom herself in the poetical sense of the skill, the systematic principle on which the universe is composed.[4] Scripture consciously personifies many inanimate objects; for example "The Sea said such and such,"[5] "The Deep said, 'It is not in me,'"[6] and "The Heavens declare the glory of God."[7] A sword, to continue the examples, is given an order;[8] mountains and hills are asked why they skip.[9] We adopt none of these approaches, though they have been taken as forceful by some of our predecessors. No, let the statement stand as that of the Saviour himself, the true Wisdom.[10] Let us look at it together for a moment. What reality has no cause? Godhead—no one can talk of the "cause of God," otherwise it would be prior to God. But what is the cause of man-

---

[1] cf. 1 Cor. 15.45
[2] Prov. 8.22
[3] 1(3) Kgs. 11.1-13
[4] Col. 1.17
[5] Job 28.14
[6] ibid.
[7] Ps. 19(18).1(2)
[8] Zech. 13.7
[9] Ps. 114(113).6
[10] cf. 1 Cor. 1.24

hood, which God submitted to for us? Our salvation, of course, what else could it be? The statement is not free of complication, seeing that we find here clearly both expressions "created" and "begets me."[11] Whatever we come across with a causal implication we will attribute to the humanity; what is absolute and free of cause we will reckon to the Godhead. "Created" has a causal implication, has it not? The text in fact runs: "He created me as the beginning of his ways **for his works**."[12] "The works of his hands are truth and judgment,"[13] and for the sake of these works he was anointed with deity—the humanity being the object of this anointing. But the expression, "begets me," has no causal implication—indicate, if you can, some qualifying term for it. What objection will there be, then to Wisdom's being called "creature" in respect to earthly generation, but "offspring" with regard to the primal and less comprehensible one?

30.3 His being called a "slave" rendering good service to "many,"[14] his being given the grand title "Child of God"[15] coheres with this. He was actually subject as a slave to flesh, to birth, and to our human experiences; for our liberation, held captive as we are by sin, he was subject to all that he saved. What does the lowliness of Man possess higher than involvement with God, than being **made** God as a result of this intermingling, than being so "visited by the dayspring from on high" that "the holy thing which is born" has been called "Son of the most high"[16] and that there has been "bestowed on it the name which is above every name"?[17] What could it be but God? What of the "bowing of every knee" to one who "was made empty on our account," who blended the "divine image" with a "slave's form"?[18] What of the "acknowledgement by all the house of Israel that God made him both Lord and Christ"?[19] Yes, these things were brought about by the action of the offspring and the favor of his parent.

30.4 What is the second of their grand, irresistible arguments?

"He must reign until"[20] so and so, must be *"received by heaven **until** the times of restoration,"*[21] must *"possess the throne on the right hand **until** the overpowering of his enemies."*[22]

---

[11] Prov. 8.22 and 25
[12] Prov. 8.22
[13] Ps. 111(110).7
[14] cf. Isa. 49.3 and 5, 53.11 [LXX]
[15] cf. Isa. 49.6 [LXX]
[16] Luke 1.78, 35, 32
[17] Phil. 2.9
[18] Phil. 2.5-11; 2 Cor. 4.4; Col. 1.15
[19] Acts 2.36
[20] 1 Cor. 15.25
[21] Acts 3.21
[22] Ps. 110(109).1

What is to happen afterwards? Will he stop ruling as king or be thrust out of heaven? Who is to make him stop or what grounds would he have for doing so? What a bold expositor you are, how very independent of royal government! And yet you hear that "there is no end of his royal rule."[23] No, you are in this sorry case thanks to your failure to recognize that "until" is by no means the logical contrary of what lies in the future; it states the point up to which something happens, but does not deny what goes beyond that point. To cite but one example: how are you to take the statement, "I shall be with you till the end of the world"?[24] As meaning that he will not be with us afterwards? Why should he say that? Besides, you also fail to distinguish meanings. The word "rule" is used in one sense of him as being King Almighty, with or without our consent; but it has another sense of actively producing our submission, of setting us under his royal rule in free acceptance of our being ruled. Of his royal rule in the first sense there will be no end. Will it have an end in the second sense? Yes, when he takes us in safety under his control. Why need he go on producing submission in those who have yielded it? After that submission he rises up in judgment of the earth,[25] dividing saved and lost.[26] After that submission "God stands in the midst of the gods"[27] (meaning "the saved") appointing to each the particular honor, the special mansion,[28] of which he is worthy.

30.5   You must connect with this your subordination of the Son to the Father.[29]

Why? you will say. *Is he not subordinate now? If he is God, does he need at all to be made subordinate to God? You are talking as if he were a bandit or an opponent of God!*

No—look at this fact: the one who releases me from the curse was called "curse"[30] because of me; "the one who takes away the world's sin" was called "sin"[31] and is made a new Adam to replace the old.[32] In just this way too, as head of the whole body,[33] he appropriates my want of submission. So long as I am an insubordinate rebel with passions which deny God, my lack of submission will be referred to Christ. But when all things

---

[23] Luke 1.33
[24] Mt. 28.20
[25] Ps. 94(93).2
[26] cf. Mt. 25.32-33
[27] Ps. 82(81).1
[28] John 14.2
[29] cf. 1 Cor. 15.25
[30] Gal. 3.13
[31] John 1.29; 2 Cor. 5.21
[32] cf. 1 Cor. 15.22 and 45
[33] Col. 1.18; Eph. 5.23

are put in submission under him,[34] when transformed they obediently acknowledge him, then will Christ bring me forward, me who has been saved, and make his subjection complete. In my view Christ's submission is the fulfillment of the Father's will. As we said before, the Son actively produces submission to the Father, while the Father wills and approves submission to the Son. Thus it is that he effects our submission, makes it his own and presents it to God.[35] "My God, My God, look upon me, why didst thou forsake me?"[36] seems to me to have the same kind of meaning. He is not forsaken either by the Father or, as some think, by his own Godhead, which closes up, afraid of suffering, and abandons the sufferer. Who applies that argument either to his birth in this world in the first place or to his ascent of the cross? No, in himself, as I have said, he expresses our condition. We had once been the forsaken and disregarded; then we were taken and now are saved by the sufferings of the impassible. He made our thoughtlessness and waywardness his own, just as the psalm, in its subsequent course, says[37]—since the 21st Psalm clearly refers to Christ.

30.6 Connected with this general view are the facts that he "learned obedience by the things which he suffered," his "strong crying" and "tears," the fact that he "entreated," that he "was heard" and that he was "God-fearing."[38] These things are a marvelously constructed drama dealing with us. As Word he was neither obedient nor disobedient—the terms apply to amenable subordinates or inferiors who deserve punishment. But as the "form of a slave"[39] he comes down to the same level as his fellow-slaves; receiving an alien "form" he bears the whole of me, along with all that is mine, in himself, so that he may consume within himself the meaner element, as fire consumes wax or the Sun ground-mist, and so that I may share in what is his through the intermingling. For this reason he honors obedience in practice and puts it to the proof by suffering. Just as in our case, the disposition is an unsatisfactory thing unless we give it practical effect—deeds show dispositions. We may also make the not invalid assumption that he tests our obedience and measures all our sufferings by his own, so that he can with generous humanity take frailty into account along with suffering, knowing the extent of the demand made on us by the one and how much we are excused by the other. If his Light "shining in the darkness"[40] of this present life was hunted by

---

[34] 1 Cor. 15.28
[35] cf. 1 Cor. 15.28
[36] Ps. 21.1 [LXX]; cf. Mt. 27.46
[37] Ps. 22(21).1-3
[38] cf. Heb. 5.7-8
[39] Phil. 2.7
[40] John 1.5

the other darkness (the evil one,[41] the tempter,[42] I mean) because it had a shade over it, how hotly will our shadows be hunted, seeing they have less power than the light? Is it to be wondered at, if, while he entirely escaped, we should to some degree be overcome? With those who keep a true score of these things his pursuit is a greater miracle than our capture. Let me add here to those I have mentioned this further text, which I judge has clearly the same meaning: "For because he himself has suffered and been tempted, he is able to help those who are tempted."[43]

"God will be all in all"[44] at the time of restoration[45]—"God," not "the Father." The Son will not revert to disappear completely in the Father, like a torch temporarily withdrawn from a great flame and then joined up again with it—Sabellians must not wrest this text. No, God will be "all in all" when we are no longer what we are now, a multiplicity of impulses and emotions, with little or nothing of God in us, but are fully like God,[46] with room for God and God alone. This is the "maturity"[47] towards which we speed. Paul himself is a special witness here. What he predicates of "God" without further specification in this passage, he elsewhere assigns clearly to Christ. I quote: "Where there is neither Greek nor Jew, circumcision nor uncircumcision, Barbarian, Scythian, bond nor free; but Christ is all in all."[48]

30.7 Take as third the expression,

"*greater;*"[49]

as fourth, the phrase,

"*my God and your God.*"[50]

Certainly, supposing the Father were called "greater" with no mention of the Son's being "equal,"[51] they might have a point here. But if it is clear that we find both, what strength does their case have? How can there be harmony between incompatible terms? It is impossible for the same thing to be, in a like respect, greater than and equal to the same thing. Is it not clear that the superiority belongs to the cause and the equality to the nature? **We** admit this with a good grace. But someone else might persist with our argument and say that derivation from the uncaused does not mean inferiority to the uncaused. He will share in the glory of the unori-

---

[41] cf. 1 John 5.18
[42] Mt. 4.3
[43] Heb. 2.18
[44] 1 Cor. 15.28
[45] cf. Acts 3.21
[46] cf. 1 John 3.2; 2 Peter 1.4
[47] cf. Col. 1.28
[48] Col. 3.11
[49] John 14.28
[50] John 20.17
[51] Phil. 2.6

ginate because he derives from the unoriginate; for men of sense, his generation is a further fact, as significant and as august, about him. Of course, the explanation that the Father is greater than the Son considered as man, is true but trivial. Is there anything remarkable about God's being greater than man? Certainly this must be our answer to those who vaunt "superiority."

30.8 On the other hand, God is not called the Word's "God" (how could God, in the proper sense of the term, have a "God"?) but God of the one men saw, in the same way as God is "Father," not of the one men saw but of the Word. In fact, there was a duality about him, with the result that in both cases the reverse of what does or does not properly apply to us holds good of him. In the proper sense of the term, God is our "God" but not our "Father." What leads heretics astray is the coupling together of titles, titles which, because of the intermingling, overlap. Which means that when the natures are distinguished, the titles are differentiated along with the ideas. Listen to Paul's words: "that the God of our Lord Jesus Christ, the Father of Glory . . ."[52] "God" goes with "Christ," "Father" with "Glory." Although both together make a single whole, it is by combination not by nature. What could be more straightforward?

30.9 The fifth point to be mentioned is that

he receives "life,"[53] "judgment,"[54] "inheritance of the Gentiles,"[55] "power over all flesh,"[56] "glory,"[57] "disciples,"[58]—everything.

This "receiving" belongs to his manhood. Yet it would not be absurd to ascribe it to the Deity. You will not be ascribing him acquired properties, but properties which have existed with him from the outset, not by a principle of grace but by a condition of his nature.

30.10 In the sixth place comes the fact that

"the Son can do nothing of himself but only what he sees the Father doing."[59]

The explanation here is along these lines: "can" and "cannot" have many meanings, not just one. One meaning of "cannot" is want of capacity at a certain time with respect to some object. A child "cannot" take part in the games, a young hound "cannot" see or "cannot" be a match for some other young hound, in this sense. A time will come perhaps when the child does take part in the games, when the young hound does see and

---

[52] Eph. 1.17
[53] John 5.26
[54] John 5.22 and 27
[55] Ps. 2.8
[56] John 17.2
[57] Rev. 5.12
[58] John 17.6
[59] John 5.19

is a match for that other young hound though it cannot take on a different one. Another meaning of ''cannot'' implies a general rule, for example: ''A city set on a hill cannot be hidden.''[60] It would be hidden were there something larger in the way. Another meaning involves moral unsuitability, for example: ''The sons of the bridechamber cannot fast as long as the bridegroom remains with them.''[61] We can take this either of the bridegroom in his visible body (his stay here was not a time for misery but festivity) or of the bridegroom known spiritually to us as the Word—why need the spiritually cleansed make a bodily fast? Another sense of ''cannot'' is of refusal by the will. Take, for example, Christ's inability to do any signs in that area because of unbelief on the part of the recipients.[62] Something essential for cures was required on both sides—faith on the part of the patients, power on that of the healer. So one side without its counterpart could not perform them. I am not sure whether this does not count as a case involving moral unsuitability as well—medical cure is out of place with people who are going to be damaged as a result of unbelief. In this same category refusal by the will come: ''The world cannot not hate you''[63] and ''How can you speak good, being evil?''[64] Impossibility here must mean refusal by the will, surely. A similar sort of case occurs with those passages which mention what is impossible for Nature but possible for God if he so chose. For example, the same man ''cannot'' be born a second time[65] and a needle's eye ''cannot'' let a camel through.[66] What could stop these events happening if God willed them?

30.11   Besides all these there is, as in the case we are presently considering, ''cannot'' in the sense of the totally inconceivable. Just as we affirm that God cannot be evil or fail to exist (''can'' would mean impotence in God here, not power) that the unreal cannot exist or twice two be both four and ten, so here it cannot be the case that the Son does anything which the Father does not do. For all that the Father has, is the Son's and *vice versa*.[67] Nothing belongs only to one, because all things belong to both; even existence *per se*, though it comes to the Son from the Father, belongs to both and both alike. The statement: ''I live because of the Father,''[68] corresponds with this fact—meaning **not** that his living and being are restricted by the Father, but that he exists outside time and abso-

[60] Mt. 5.14
[61] Mt. 9.15; Mark 2.19; Luke 5.34
[62] Mt. 13.58; Mark 6.5
[63] cf. John 7.7
[64] Mt. 12.34
[65] John 3.4
[66] Mt. 19.24
[67] John 16.15; 17.10
[68] John 6.57

lutely, in dependence on the Father. In what sense does he see the Father doing something and does it himself?[69] Is it the way people draw the shapes of letters, keeping their eyes on the copy-book and guided by it because otherwise they cannot get to the real thing? How could Wisdom possibly need a teacher or be incapable of doing something without instruction? Again, in what sense does the Father "do" something whether now or in the past? Did he establish another, corresponding world before this one and is he going to bring a future world into existence—the idea being that the Son kept his eyes on these and brought the present world into existence and will do the same for the future one? This argument gets us four worlds—one lot created by the Father, the other by the Son. The thing is absurd! He cleanses lepers,[70] releases men from demons and diseases,[71] he restores dead men to life,[72] walks on the sea,[73] does all the other things he did—how or when did the Father perform these actions before the Son? Clearly the Father indicates the outline, whilst the Word makes a finished product, of the same facts. He acts not like an ignorant slave but with a master's knowledge—to put it more appropriately, like the Father. This is how I take the statement that the Son does whatever is effected by the Father, in the same way.[74] It is not a question of similarity between their creatures, but of having equal authority over their creation. This will be the meaning too of "the Father's working up till now and the Son also."[75] It is a question not only of creating but of governing and preserving the creatures. The fact that "his angels are **being** made winds"[76] proves the point. So does the fact that "the earth is **being** established on its sure foundation."[77] Yet these things were securely created, once for all. So does the "compacting" of the thunder and the "founding of the wind."[78] Their principle was laid down once for all, but their activity is present and continuous.

30.12 Seventhly must be mentioned:

the Son's *"coming down from heaven not to do his own will, but the will of him who sent him."*[79]

Certainly had these words not been spoken by the very one who "came

---

[69] John 5.19
[70] e.g. Mt. 8.2-3; Mark 1.40; Luke 5.13; 17.12-14
[71] Mark 1.34; Mt. 8.16
[72] e.g. Mt. 9.23-25; John 11.43-44
[73] Mt. 14.25; Mark 6.48; John 6.19
[74] John 5.19
[75] John 5.17
[76] Ps. 104(103).4
[77] Ps. 104(103).5
[78] Amos 4.13
[79] John 6.38

down'' we should have said the language bore the stamp of a mere man like us, not that of the Saviour we know. **His** will is not in the least degree opposed to God, is totally dependent upon God. Our merely human will does not always follow the divine; it often resists and struggles against it. This is the way we interpret ''Father, if it be possible let this cup pass from me, but not what I will—let thy will prevail.''[80] The alternative suppositions—either he was ignorant of the thing's possibility, or, he was opposing the Father's will—are both implausible. No, given that the words come from the one who assumed, that is to say, what ''came down,'' not from what was assumed, we must meet this problem in the same way as the one before. The words there mean not that the Son has, but that he has **not**, an individual will alongside the Father's. This would give the sense: '' 'Not to do my own will,'[81] for what is mine is not distinct from what is thine but belongs to both thee and me, who have one will as we have one Godhead.'' There are many statements of this kind, which make a general negation and no affirmation. For example, ''God does not give the Spirit by measure.''[82] He does not ''give'' it, nor is it ''measured'' out—God is not measured out by God. Take another case: ''Neither was it for my iniquity or for my sin.''[83] These words mean not that he did, but that he did not, have iniquity and sin. Again, take the phrase: ''Not for the righteousnesses we have done''[84]—no, we did none. This is the clear meaning contained in the subsequent words of the passage. He says what the Father's will is: that every believer in the Son should be saved and should obtain resurrection on the last day.[85] Is this the Father's will, but not the Son's at all? Is he unwilling to be preached about or believed in? Who would credit that idea, when the statement that the word which is heard is not the Son's but the Father's[86] has the same source? Though I have often looked into the matter, I cannot understand how what belongs to two things could be the particular property of one of them alone. Nor, I think, can anyone else. If you take this view of the Son's will, you take a sound and truly religious view. Every man of good judgment will, I believe, say so too.

30.13   Eighth, they have the passages:

''*That they may know thee, the sole, true God, and Jesus Christ whom thou hast sent,*''[87] and ''*None is good save only one, God.*''[88]

---

[80] Mt. 26.39
[81] John 6.38
[82] John 3.34
[83] Ps. 59(58).3(4)
[84] Dan. 9.18
[85] John 6.40
[86] John 14.24
[87] John 17.3
[88] Mark 10.18; Luke 18.19

The explanation here seems to me quite straightforward. If you attribute "sole, true" to the Father, to what will you attribute Truth *per se*? In fact, if you understand "the sole, wise God"[89] or "who alone possesses immortality, dwelling in light unapproachable"[90] or "King of the ages, incorruptible, invisible, sole wise God"[91] in this way, you will lose the Son altogether. He will have been condemned to death or darkness, judged not wise, not a King, not invisible, **not**—and this is the main point—God at all. How can he help losing the goodness, which in a special way belongs to God alone, along with the rest? No—I think the words, "That they may know thee, the sole, true God," are meant as a denial of the non-existent, so-called "gods." The passage could not go on, "And Jesus Christ whom thou hast sent"[92] if "sole, true" excluded him, and the category of deity was unshared. The words, "None is good"[93] are a reply to the lawyer who was testing him and had borne witness to his goodness as man. Consummate goodness, he meant, belongs to God alone, though the word "good" can be applied to man. Take for example, "The good man out of his good treasure brings forth good,"[94] and "I will give the kingdom to one more good than you"[95] (God is speaking to Saul about David) and "Do good, Lord, to the good"[96]—and all the other passages of a similar character about praiseworthy men touched by what flows from the primal Beauty to their secondary level. If we gain your conviction on this point, that is excellent! If we fail, how are you going to answer those who take the other view that on your premises the Son alone is called "God"? Where? In the following words: "This is your God; no other can be reckoned with him!"[97] and a little later, "Afterwards he was seen on earth and lived among men."[98]

The addition makes it quite clear that the words do not apply to the Father, but to the Son. He it was who had dealings in the body with us and was made companion of those here below. Supposing an attribution to the Father, not the alleged "gods," wins here, we shall have lost the day so far as the Father is concerned in the process of directing our efforts against the Son. Could there be a wretcheder, costlier victory than that?

30.14 The ninth point they will make is the phrase

---

[89] Rom. 16.27
[90] 1 Tim. 6.16
[91] 1 Tim. 1.17
[92] John 17.3
[93] Luke 18.19
[94] Mt. 12.35
[95] 1 Sam.(1 Kgs.) 15.28
[96] Ps. 125(124).4
[97] Bar. 3.36
[98] Bar. 3.38

"Ever living to make petition for us."[99]

Yes indeed—what deep significance and humanity it expresses! Petition does not imply here, as it does in popular parlance, a desire for legal satisfaction—there is something humiliating in the idea. No, it means interceding for us in his role of mediator, in the way that the Spirit too is spoken of as "making petition" on our behalf.[100] "For there is one God, and one mediator between God and men, the man, Jesus Christ."[101] Even at this moment he is, as man, interceding for my salvation, until he makes me divine by the power of his incarnate manhood. "As man" I say, because he still has with him the body he assumed, though he is no longer "regarded as flesh"[102]—meaning the bodily experiences, which, sin aside, are ours and his. This is the "Advocate"[103] we have in Jesus—not a slave who falls prostrate before the Father on our behalf. Get rid of what is really a slavish suspicion, unworthy of the Spirit. It is not in God to make that demand nor in the Son to submit to it; the thought is unjust to God. No, it is by what he suffered as man that he persuades us, as Word and Encourager, to endure. That, for me, is the meaning of his "advocacy."

30.15   Their tenth point is his ignorance, the fact that

no one except the Father knows the last day or hour, not even the Son himself.[104]

Yet how can any fact be unknown to Wisdom,[105] the worlds' maker,[106] who perfects,[107] transforms,[108] and limits[109] things created, who knows the things of God just as man's spirit knows the things in man?[110] What knowledge could be more perfect than that? How can he know distinctly what precedes the hour of the world's end, what, so to say, lies on its surface, and yet not know the hour itself? The thing is like a riddle—like saying a person has a distinct knowledge of what is in front of a wall, but does not know the wall itself, or, that he distinctly knows the end of the day, but does not know the beginning of night. Knowledge of one thing here necessarily involves knowledge of the other. Surely everyone will see that if you separate the real from the apparent meaning of the passage it is saying that he does know as God, but that, as man, he does not. The absolute

---

[99] Heb. 7.25
[100] Rom. 8.26
[101] 1 Tim. 2.5
[102] 2 Cor. 5.16
[103] 1 John 2.1
[104] Mark 13.32
[105] 1 Cor. 1.30
[106] Heb. 1.2
[107] Heb. 12.2
[108] cf. Rev. 21.5
[109] Rev. 1.8; 22.13
[110] 1 Cor. 2.11

use of the title, "Son," here, without any relational qualification of the term telling you **whose** son, provides us with a deeper meaning, so that we interpret this ignorance in the most truly religious way by ascribing it not to the divine but to the human.

30.16 If this is an adequate explanation, we should stop and nothing further ought to be demanded of us. If not, a second explanation is required. Let us, as in every other case, pay honor here to the parent by referring knowledge of the highest things also to him as cause. I think that even if one reads the text in a different way from our scholars one would have some idea of the fact that even the Son's knowledge of the day or hour is none other than his knowledge that the Father knows them. What conclusion do we draw? Since the Son's knowledge is grounded in the Father's, the obvious conclusion that here we have what can be known and understood by none but the primal nature.

It would remain for us to discuss the fact that he "received commandments"[111] and "kept" them,[112] and at all times did what was pleasing to the Father.[113] There would still be the questions of his "perfecting,"[114] and "exaltation,"[115] his "learning obedience as the result of what he suffered,"[116] his "high-priesthood"[117] and "offering,"[118] his "surrender,"[119] his "prayer to the one who could save him from death,"[120] his "agony,"[121] his "bloody sweat,"[122] his "prayer,"[123] and everything else of the same character. Yes there would, were it not clear to everybody that expressions like these refer to the passible element not the immutable nature transcending suffering.

The explanations given so far in reply to objections are certainly only a rough draft, a basis on which closer critics can work out something fuller. An appropriate sequel to our previous discussions would be the explanation of the deep significance of each of the titles applied to the Son. We ought not to pass them by unlooked at because of their number and the multiplicity of aspects they refer to.

30.17 Our starting-point must be the fact that God cannot be named.

---

[111] cf. John 10.18; 12.49
[112] John 15.10
[113] John 8.29
[114] Heb. 5.9
[115] Acts 2.33; cf. Phil. 2.9
[116] Heb. 5.8
[117] Heb. 5.10; 7.1; 8.1
[118] Heb. 9.7; Eph. 5.2
[119] Gal. 2.20
[120] Heb. 5.7
[121] Luke 22.44
[122] ibid.
[123] ibid.

Not only will deductive arguments prove it, but the wisest Hebrews of antiquity, so far as can be gathered, will too. The ancient Hebrews used special symbols to venerate the divine and did not allow anything inferior to God to be written with the same letters as the word "God," on the ground that the divine should not be put on even this much of a level with things human. Would they ever have accepted the idea that the uniquely indissoluble nature could be expressed by evanescent speech? No man has yet breathed all the air; no mind has yet contained or language embraced God's essence in its fullness. No, we use facts connected with him to outline qualities which correspond with him, collecting a faint and feeble mental image from various quarters. Our noblest theologian is not one who has discovered the whole—our earthly shackles do not permit us the whole—but one whose mental image is by comparison fuller, who has gathered in his mind a richer picture, outline, or whatever we call it, of the truth.

30.18 So far as we can get to them, then, "He who is" and "God" are in some special way names of his essence. "He who is" has the superiority here. He used it of himself, in delivering his oracles to Moses on the mountain, telling Moses, who asked what he should be called, to say to the people: "He who is has sent me."[124] But this is not the only reason; we also find it to be a more distinctively personal name. "God," according to bright students of Greek etymology, is derived from words meaning "to run" or "to burn"—the idea being continuous movement and consuming of evil qualities hence, certainly, God is called a "consuming fire."[125] Nevertheless, it is a relational, not an absolute term. The same thing applies to the word "Lord" which is also used as a name of God. "I am the Lord thy God," he says, "this is my name."[126] and, "The Lord is his name."[127] But we are making deeper enquiries into a nature which has absolute existence, independent of anything else. The actual, personal being of God in its fullness is neither limited nor cut short by any prior or any subsequent reality—so it was and so it will be.

30.19 God's other titles fall into two distinct groups. The first group belongs to his power, the second to his providential ordering of the world, a two-fold providential ordering—involving, and not involving, incarnation. Clear cases of titles which belong to his power are "Almighty"[128] and "King"—be it of "glory,"[129] "the ages,"[130] "of the forces,"[131] or

---

[124] Ex. 3.14
[125] Deut. 4.24
[126] Isa. 42.8
[127] Ex. 15.3
[128] Amos 3.13; Rev. 4.8
[129] Ps. 24(23).10
[130] 1 Tim. 1.17
[131] Ps. 68(67).13

"of the Beloved,"[132] or "rulers"[133]—"Lord Sabaoth,"[134] which means "Lord of the armies," "forces,"[135] or "masters."[136] To his providential ordering belong: "God"—be it "of salvation,"[137] "retribution,"[138] "peace,"[139] "righteousness,"[140] or "of Abraham, Isaac, and Jacob,"[141] or of all the spiritual "Israel,"[142] which has the vision of God.[143] For since we are controlled by three conditions—fear of punishment, hope for salvation and glory too, and the practice of the virtues which results in these last—the name which mentions retribution deals with fear, the one which mentions salvation with hope and that which refers to virtues disciplines us to practice them. The intention is that by, as it were, carrying God inside him,[144] a man may have some success here and press on all the harder to perfection, towards that affinity with God which comes from the virtues.

These names of deity are shared. The personal name of the unoriginate is "Father;" of the eternally begotten, "Son;" of what has issued, or proceeds, without generation, "the Holy Spirit."

Let us turn now to the main point of our discussion—the Son's titles. **30.20** I take the view that he is called "Son" because he is not simply identical in essence with the Father, but stems from him. He is "Only-begotten"[145] not just because he alone stems uniquely from what is unique, but because he does so in a unique fashion unlike things corporeal. He is "Word,"[146] because he is related to the Father as word is to mind, not only by reason of the undisturbed character of his birth, but also through the connection and declaratory function involved in the relationship. One could say too, perhaps, that his relationship is that of definition to term defined, since "word" has the meaning in Greek of "definition." He who has known the Son ("seen" means "known" in that context) has known the Father.[147] The Son is the concise and simple

---

132 Ps. 67.13 [LXX]
133 1 Tim. 6.15
134 Isa. 1.9; Rom. 9.29
135 Ps. 24(23).10
136 1 Tim 6.15; cf. Deut. 10.17
137 Ps. 68(67).20(21)
138 Ps. 94(93).1
139 Rom. 15.33
140 Ps. 4.1(2)
141 Ex. 3.6
142 cf. Rom. 9.6-8; 11.26; Gal. 6.16
143 cf. Gen. 32.30(31)
144 cf. 1 Cor. 6.19-20
145 John 1.18
146 John 1.1
147 John 14.9; cf. Mt. 11.27

revelation of the Father's nature—everything born is a tacit definition of its parent. You would not be wrong, were you to explain the name from the fact that he exists inherently in real things. Is there anything whose being is not held together[148] by reason? He is called "wisdom"[149] as being the knowledge of matters divine and human. How could the maker[150] be ignorant of the principles involved in his works? He is "Power,"[151] because he is what sustains his creatures[152] and furnishes them with the power to maintain themselves. He is "Truth,"[153] because truth is a single whole, whilst falsehood is a splintered complex, and because he is the unstained seal,[154] the utterly faithful impress[155] of the Father. He is called "Image"[156] because he is of one substance with the Father; he stems from the Father and not the Father from him, it being the nature of an image to copy the original and be called after it. But there is more to it than this. The ordinary image is a motionless copy of a moving being. Here we have a living image of a living being, indistinguishable from its original to a higher degree than Seth from Adam[157] and any earthly offspring from its parent. Beings with no complexity to their nature have no points of likeness or unlikeness. They are exact replicas, identical rather than like. He is called "Light,"[158] because he is the brilliance of souls pure in mind and life. He is "Life,"[159] because he is "Light," constituting and giving reality to every thinking being. "For in him we live, move, and exist"[160] and there is a two-fold sense in which he breathes into us;[161] we are filled, all of us, with his breath, and those who are capable of it, all those who open their mind's mouth wide enough, with his Holy Spirit.[162] He is called "Righteousness,"[163] because he decides in accordance with merit;[164] he makes a fair assessment of the competing claims of the body under the Law and the soul under Grace[165] so that one side

---

[148] Col. 1.17
[149] 1 Cor. 1.30
[150] Col. 1.17
[151] cf. Rom. 1.4; Col. 1.15-19
[152] cf. John 1.3
[153] John 14.6
[154] John 6.27
[155] Heb.1.3
[156] Col. 1.15
[157] cf. Gen. 4.25
[158] John 8.12; 9.5
[159] John 14.6
[160] Acts 17.28
[161] cf. Gen. 2.7; John 20.22
[162] Ps. 118.131 [LXX]
[163] 1 Cor. 1.30
[164] cf. Mt. 16.27; Rom. 2.6
[165] Rom. 6.14

has the supremacy over the other, the better rules the inferior and the baser cannot rebel against the superior. He is called "Sanctification,"[166] because he is purity, so that what is pure may be filled with his pureness. He is "Redemption,"[167] because he sets us free from the bonds of sin and gives himself in exchange for us as a ransom sufficient to cleanse the world. He is "Resurrection,"[168] because he raises us up from this world and leads us on to life,[169] done to death, though we were, by tasting [the forbidden tree].[170]

30.21 These titles so far, of course, belong to him on both levels, the transcendent and the human. Those which are distinctively human and belong to what he assumed from us men are, first, "Man."[171] He bears the title, "Man" not just with a view to being accessible through his body to corporeal things—being in all other respects inaccessible, owing to the incomprehensibility of his nature—but with the aim of hallowing Man through Himself, by becoming a sort of yeast for the whole lump. He has united with himself all that lay under condemnation, in order to release it from condemnation. For all our sakes he became all that we are, sin apart—body, soul, mind, all that death pervades. The result is a man who, at the same time, is seen visibly, because spiritually discerned, as God. He is "Son of Man"[172] through Adam and through the Virgin, from whom he was descended—from Adam his forefather, from the Virgin by the law of motherhood, not by that of fatherhood. He is "Christ,"[173] because of his Godhead. This unction belongs to his manhood. Unlike all other anointed men,[174] it does not hallow him by its action, but by the presence of the anointer in fullness. (The effect here is to give what anoints the title, "Man," and to make what receives the unction God.) He is "the Way,"[175] because he takes us along him. He is "the Door,"[176] because he leads us in. He is "Shepherd,"[177] because he settles us in green pastures, nurtures us by still waters,[178] leading us hence[179] and defending us against wild beasts.[180] The straying he turns

---

[166] 1 Cor. 1.30
[167] ibid.
[168] John 11.25
[169] cf. Tob. 13.2; Wis. 16.13; Deut. 32.39; 1 Sam. (1 Kgs.) 2.6
[170] Gen. 3.1-24
[171] John 9.11
[172] Mt. 9.6
[173] Mt. 1.16
[174] cf. Ex. 30.30; 1 Sam.(1 Kgs.)10.1
[175] John 14.6
[176] John 10.9
[177] John 10.11
[178] Ps. 23(22).2
[179] cf. John 10.4
[180] cf. Ezek. 34.25

back, the lost he recovers; what is broken he binds up, what is strong he watches.[181] Using the principles of pastoral science, he gathers us into his heavenly fold.[182] He is called "Sheep,"[183] because he was sacrificed, a "Lamb,"[184] because he was without blemish.[185] He is the "High Priest,"[186] because he presented the offering, "Melchizedek,"[187] because on the transcendent level he had no mother, on the human level no father, and his high estate is without genealogy.[188] "Who," it says, "can recount his generation?"[189] He is "Melchizedek" too, as King of Salem or Peace, as King of Righteousness, and because he tithes the Patriarchs who prevailed over evil powers.[190]

There you have the Son's titles. Walk like God through all that are sublime, and with a fellow-feeling through all that involve the body; but better, treat all as God does, so that you may ascend from below to become God, because he came down from above for us. Above all, keep hold of this truth and apply it to all the loftier and lowlier names and you will never fail: Jesus Christ in body and spirit the same, yesterday, today, and forever.[191] Amen.

---

[181] Ezek. 34.16
[182] Isa. 40.11
[183] Isa. 53.7
[184] ibid.
[185] Ex. 12.5
[186] Heb. 6.20
[187] ibid., 7.1
[188] Heb. 7.3
[189] Isa. 53.8
[190] Heb. 7.1-2
[191] Heb. 13.8

ORATION 31
ON THE HOLY SPIRIT

31.1   So stands the doctrine of the Son. It has passed through the midst of its adversaries unscathed by their stones.[1] The Word cannot be stoned. The Word, if you like, flings stones, striking the wild beasts, the arguments, which mischievously approach the mount.

But what do you say, they ask, *about the Holy Spirit? Where did you get this strange, unscriptural ''God'' you are bringing in?*

This is the view of people fairly sound so far as the Son is concerned. You find roads and rivers will divide and join up again, and the same things occurs here because there is such a wealth of irreligion. People elsewhere divided concur on some points and the result is that it is impossible to get a clear idea of what they agree, and what they disagree, on.

31.2   Of course there is something specially difficult in the doctrine of the Holy Spirit. It is not just that men exhausted by discussions of the Son are more eager to take on the Spirit—they must have something to blaspheme or life would be unlivable—but also that we too become worn by the quantity of the issues. We are in the same condition as men who lose their appetite for all food regardless of what it is, after being disgusted with some particular dish; we take an equal dislike to all doctrinal discussion. All the same, let the Spirit aid us, and the Word will have its course and God be glorified. We leave to others a careful, critical analysis of the many different senses in which ''spirit'' and ''holy'' are used in Scripture, with the texts that bear upon the enquiry. We leave too the additional problem of the particular sense resulting from the combination of the terms—I mean ''Holy Spirit.'' Others have benefited themselves and us, as we too have benefited them, by systematic studies here. We, though, shall now turn to a further stage in the discussion.

31.3   Yes, some people, very eager to defend the letter, are angry with us for introducing a God, the Holy Spirit, who is a stranger and an intruder. They must understand that ''they are afraid where no fear is.''[2] They must recognize clearly that their love for the letter is a cloak[3] for irreligion, as shall be proved presently when we refute their objections. For our part we have such confidence in the Godhead of the Spirit, that, rash though some may find it, we shall begin our theological exposition by ap-

---

[1]   cf. John 8.59; Luke 4.30
[2]   Ps. 13.5 [LXX]; 53(52).5(6)
[3]   cf. Mt. 7.15

plying identical expressions to the Three. "He was the true light that lightens every man coming into the world"[4]—yes, the Father. "He was the true light that lightens every man coming into the world"—yes, the Son. "He was the true light that lightens every man coming into the world"—yes, the Comforter.[5] These are three subjects and three verbs—he was and he was and he was. But a single reality **was**. There are three predicates—light and light and light. But the light is one, God is one. This is the meaning of David's prophetic vision: "In thy light we shall see light."[6] We receive the Son's light from the Father's light[7] in the light of the Spirit: that is what we ourselves have seen and what we now proclaim—it is the plain and simple explanation of the Trinity. Let the treacherous deal treacherously, let the transgressor transgress[8]—**we** shall preach what we know. We shall climb a lofty mountain and shout it out, if we are not given a hearing below. We shall extol the Spirit; we shall not be afraid.[9] If we do have fear, it will be of silence not of preaching.

31.4 If there was [a time] when the Father did not exist, there was [a time] when the Son did not exist. If there was [a time] when the Son did not exist, there was [a time] when the Holy Spirit did not exist. If one existed from the beginning,[10] so did all three. If you cast one down, I make bold to tell you not to exalt the other two. What use is incomplete deity? Or rather what **is** deity if it is incomplete? Something **is** missing if it does not have Holiness, and how could it have Holiness without having the Holy Spirit? Either God's Holiness is independent of the Holy Spirit (and in that case I should like to be told what it is supposed to be) or if it is identical with the Holy Spirit, how, I ask, could it fail to be from the beginning[11]—as if it had at one time been to God's advantage to be incomplete and without his Spirit. If he did not exist from the beginning,[12] he has the same rank as I have, though with a slight priority—we are both separated from God by time. If he has the same rank as I have, how can he make me God,[13] how can he link me with deity?

31.5 But I will now take the investigation a stage further back for you— we have discussed the Trinity earlier. The Sadducees alleged that the

---

4 John 1.9
5 John 14.16 and 26
6 Ps. 36(35).9(10)
7 cf. John 1.5
8 cf. Isa. 21.2
9 Isa. 40.9
10 1 John 1.1
11 ibid.
12 ibid.
13 cf. 2 Pet. 1.4, Mt. 28.19

Holy Spirit does not exist at all and that there are no angels and no resurrection. I do not know what grounds they had for their scornful rejection of so many important proof-texts in the Old Testament. Amongst non-Christians, on the other hand, the more theologically-minded, with views nearer our own, had, I think, some mental picture of him. They were divided, though, as to his name; "mind of the universe," "external mind" and such like were the titles they gave him. Amongst our own experts, some took the Holy Spirit as an active process, some as a creature, some as God. Others were agnostic on this point

out of reverence, as they put it, *for Scripture, which has given no clear revelation either way.*

On these grounds they offer him neither worship nor disrespect; they take up a sort of half-way (or should I say "a thoroughly pitiful"?) position about him. Amongst those who take him as God, some keep their devotion to their own minds, others venture to express it with their lips as well. I understand that there are others besides, even more expert at measuring out Godhead. These acknowledge as we do that it is three beings which are spiritually discerned, but they put a vast distance between them. One is infinite in essence and power; one is infinite in power but not in essence, and one is finite on both counts. These people copy, if in a slightly different form, those who use the names "Creator," "Co-worker," and "Minister," alleging that the rank inherent in the names coincides with the quality of the realities.

31.6 We shall not argue with those who deny the Holy Spirit's existence or with pagan chit-chat—we must forgo the luxury of the "oil of sinners"[14] and get on with the sermon. With the rest though we shall take issue. The Holy Spirit must be presumed to be either an independently existing being or an inherent property of something else—what the subtle here call a "substance" or an "accident" respectively. If "accident" applies here, the Holy Spirit must be an activity of God. What otherwise, whose otherwise, could it be? The Holy Spirit has, after all, a certain superiority and is unscathed by composition. If he is an activity, clearly he must be put in operation, because he has no active power and ceases with the cessation of his production—that is the kind of thing an activity is. How comes it then that he **does** act?[15] He says things,[16] he decrees,[17] he is grieved,[18] he is vexed[19]—all of which belong to a being

---

[14] Ps. 141(140).5
[15] 1 Cor. 12.11
[16] Acts 13.2
[17] Ibid.
[18] Eph. 4.30
[19] Isa. 63.10

with motion, not to the process of motion. If he is a substance, not the attribute of a substance, he must be taken either as a creature or as God. Not even the inventors of fabulous goat-stags could envisage a half-way being here, or anything that belonged to, or was composed out of, both sides. But if he is a creature why do you believe in him, why are we baptized in him? "Believing **in**" is not the same thing as "believing a fact **about**." The first applies to God, the second to everything. If he is God, then he is not a "creature," or a "product" or a "fellow-slave"—none of these lowly names belongs to him at all.

31.7   Now for your say! Let the slings fly and the subtle inferences be drawn!

The Holy Spirit must either be ingenerate or begotten. If he is ingenerate, there are two unoriginate beings. If he is begotten, we again have alternatives: either begotten from the Father or from the Son. If from the Father, there will be two sons who are brothers.

Make them twins if you like, or one older than the other, since you have a penchant for corporeal ideas. If he is begotten from the Son, our God apparently has a grandson, and what could be odder than that? We certainly have here the arguments of people "wise to do evil, but unwilling to write what is good."[20] For my part, if I saw the necessity for the alternatives, I should accept the realities without being put off by the names. But because the Son is "Son" in a more elevated sense of the word, and since we have no other term to express his consubstantial derivation from God, it does not follow that we ought to think it essential to transfer wholesale to the divine sphere the earthly names of human family ties. Do you take it, by the same token, that our God is a male, because of the masculine nouns "God" and "Father"? Is the Godhead a female, because in Greek the word is feminine? Is the word "Spirit" neuter, because the Spirit is sterile? If you want to take the joke further you could say, as the trashy myths of old did, that God coupled with his own will and fathered the Son. We should then be faced with the bisexual God of Marcion, who pictured those outlandish aeons.

31.8   But since we do not admit your first pompous dilemma with its assumption that there is no midway term between ingeneracy and generacy, away go your "brothers" and "grandsons" at once along with it, beating a retreat from theology, dissolved, so to say, along with the dissolution of the first link in the complex chain. Explain to me where you are going to put "procession" which is evidently a mean term between alternatives and was introduced by a better theologian than you, our Saviour? I take it that you have not composed a new New Testament and on the strength

[20] Jer. 4.22

of it removed the phrase: "The Holy Spirit which proceeds from the Father."[21] In so far as he proceeds from the Father, he is no creature; in as much as he is not begotten, he is not Son; and to the extent that procession is the mean between ingeneracy and generacy, he is God. Thus God escapes your syllogistic toils and shows himself stronger than your exclusive alternatives. What, then, is "proceeding"? You explain the ingeneracy of the Father and I will give you a biological account of the Son's begetting and the Spirit's proceeding—and let us go mad the pair of us for prying into God's secrets. What competence have we here? We cannot understand what lies under our feet, cannot count the sand in the sea, "the drops of rain or the days of this world,"[22] much less enter into the "depths of God"[23] and render a verbal account of a nature so mysterious, so much beyond words.

31.9 *In what particular, then*, it may be asked, *does the Spirit fall short of being Son? If there were not something missing, he would be Son.*

We say there is no deficiency—God lacks nothing. It is their difference in, so to say, "manifestation" or mutual relationship, which has caused the difference in names. The Son does not fall short in some particular of being Father. Sonship is no defect, yet that does not mean he **is** Father. By the same token, the Father would fall short of being Son—the Father is **not** Son. No, the language here gives no grounds for any deficiency, for any subordination in essence. The very fact of not being begotten, of being begotten and of proceeding, gives them whatever names are applied to them—Father, Son, and Holy Spirit respectively. The aim is to safeguard the distinctness of the three persons within the single nature and quality of the Godhead. The Son is not Father; there is **one** Father. Yet he is whatever the Father is. The Spirit is not Son because he is from God; there is **one** Only-begotten.[24] Yet whatever the Son is, he is. The three are a single whole in their Godhead and the single whole is three in its individual distinctions. Thus there will be no Sabellian "One," no three to be mischievously divided by our contemporaries.

31.10 *What, then? Is the Spirit God?*

Certainly.

Is he of the same substance?

Yes, if he is God.

Present me then, someone may say, *with two things from the same source, one a Son, the other not as Son but, despite that, of the same substance, and I get God plus God.*

---

[21] John 15.26
[22] Sir. 1.2
[23] 1 Cor. 2.10
[24] John 1.14

Yes, and you give me one more "God" and grant me God's nature, and I will present you with the same Trinity along with the same names and realities. If there is one God, one supreme nature, where can I find an analogy to show you? Are you looking for one from your environment here in this world? It is a singularly graceless, and not just graceless but a pretty well futile notion, to get a picture of things heavenly from things of earth, of things fixed immutably from this transitory element. As Isaiah says, it is "seeking the living among the dead."[25] All the same, to oblige you, I shall try to get a picture even from this source to give my argument some support. There are, of course, many illustrations I could give (all of which I have resolved to leave out) drawn from natural history, about nature's devices for the production of living things. Some of the facts are known to us all, others only to a few. For example, it is asserted that not only do we have identity and difference in the parents reflected exactly in the offspring, but identical offspring can also result from different parents and *vice versa*. If the story is at all reliable, there is a further kind of parentage when a thing is spontaneously consumed and reproduced. There are, in addition, things which, through nature's munificence stop being themselves and change, transformed from one living thing into another. Indeed two things of the same substance, one an offspring, the other not an offspring, can be from the same source—an example which is rather more to the point at issue. I will mention one case, well known to everybody, from human history, before passing on to another subject.

31.11   What was Adam? Something molded by God.[26] What was Eve? A portion of that molded creation.[27] Seth? He was the offspring of the pair.[28] Are they not, in your view, the same thing—the molded creation, the portion, and the offspring? Yes, of course they are. Were they of the same substance? Yes, of course they were. It is agreed, then, that things with a different individual being can be of the same substance. I say this without implying molding or division or anything bodily as regards the Godhead—no quibbler shall get a grip on me again here—but by way of contemplating spiritual realities, stages as it were, in these things. It is impossible, you see, to track down a spotless picture of the whole truth.

What does this amount to? people will say. *There cannot be two things, one an offspring and the other something else, coming from the single source.*

Why not? Were not Eve and Seth of the same Adam, who else? Were they both offspring? Certainly not. Why?—because one was a portion of Adam, the other an offspring. Yet they had a mutual identity—they were

---

[25] Isa. 8.19
[26] Gen. 2.7
[27] Gen. 2.21-23
[28] Gen. 4.25

both human beings, nobody can gainsay that. You have grasped the possibility of our position by means of human illustrations, so will you stop fighting desperately against the Spirit for your view that he must either be an offspring or not consubstantial and not God? I think it would be as well for you if you did, unless you are extremely determined to argue and fight plain facts.

31.12 *But who worships the Spirit?* it might be asked. *Is there any ancient or modern example? Who prays to the Spirit? Where is the Scriptural authority for worshipping or praying to him, where did you get the idea from?*

We shall give fuller grounds when we discuss the question of what is not in the Bible, but for the present it will be sufficient for us to say just this: it is the Spirit in whom we worship and through whom we pray. "God," it says, "is Spirit, and they who worship him must worship him in Spirit and in Truth."[29] And again: "We do not know how to pray as we ought, but the Spirit himself intercedes for us with sighs too deep for words."[30] And again: "I will pray with the Spirit and I will pray with the mind also"[31]—meaning, in mind and spirit. Worshipping, then, and praying in the Spirit seem to me to be simply the Spirit presenting prayer and worship to himself. Could any inspired man, with full awareness of the facts, disapprove, seeing that the worship of one is the worship of all three, in virtue of the equal rank and equal deity inherent in all three. Moreover, I shall not be put off by the argument that all things were, according to Scripture, made by the Son,[32] the Spirit being one of the things included in the "all." What Scripture says is that all things **which were made**,[33] were made by the Son, not all things without further qualification— neither the Father nor all things unmade are included. Prove that the Spirit was made before assigning him to the Son, and grouping him along with creatures. Until you can do that, the inclusive phrase offers your irreligion no comfort. If he was made, he must have been made through Christ—I shall not deny it. But he was **not** made, how could he be included in the "all," or have been made through Christ? Stop giving a false dignity to the Father at the expense of the Only-begotten (it is a poor kind of honor, giving him a creature by robbing him of that nobler thing, a Son!) and to the Son at the expense of the Spirit. He is no creator of a fellow-slave like us, but is glorified with an equal honor. Do not put yourself alongside the Trinity, lest you be banished from the Trinity. Do not truncate the single and equally august nature at any point. Because

---

[29] John 4.24
[30] Rom. 8.26
[31] 1 Cor. 14.15
[32] John 1.3
[33] ibid.

whichever of the Trinity you destroy, you will have destroyed the whole—or rather, you will have been banished from the whole. It is better to have a meager idea of the union than to venture on total blasphemy. **31.13** Our sermon has reached the fundamental point. Though I lament the re-opening now of a long dead enquiry which had yielded to faith, we must nonetheless make a stand against babblers and not allow the case to go by default. The Word is on our side as we plead the Spirit's case.

If, it is asserted, *we use the word "God" three times, must there not be three Gods"? How can the object of glorification fail to be a plurality of powers?*

Who are the spokesmen here? Is it the thorough-going in irreligion or is it also those of the second class, meaning people fairly sound on the Son? My argument applies to both, but is specially directed to the latter. This is indeed the approach I would adopt towards them. "Though," I should say, "you are in revolt from the Spirit, you worship the Son. What right have you to accuse us of tritheism—are you not ditheists? If you deny the worship of the Only-begotten as well, you align yourselves with our opponents. Why should we deal tenderly with you, as though you were not utterly dead? But if you do revere the Son, if you have that much disposition towards salvation, we shall put a question to you: what defense would you make here, were you charged with ditheism? If you have any words of wisdom, give us an answer and provide us with a way to reply. The very arguments you can use to rebut the accusation of ditheism will suffice for us against the charge of tritheism." Thus we win our case by using the prosecution to plead our cause. Could there be a nobler triumph than that?

31.14 But what is our case, our battle, against both parties alike? We have one god, because there is a single Godhead. Though there are three objects of belief, they derive from the single whole and have reference to it. They do not have degrees of being God or degrees of priority over against one another. They are not sundered in will or divided in power. You cannot find there any of the properties inherent in things divisible. In a nutshell, the Godhead exists undivided in separate beings. It is as if there were a single intermingling of light, which existed in three mutually connected Suns. When we look at the Godhead, the primal cause, the sole sovereignty, we have a mental picture of the single whole, certainly. But when we look at the three in whom the Godhead exists, who derive their timeless and equally glorious being from the primal cause, we have three objects of worship.

31.15 *But what does that amount to?*, they might say. *Do not non-Christians too, according to their more expert theoreticians, hold to a single Godhead, and do not we also hold to a single humanity, the whole human race? Nonetheless they think that* *there is a plurality of gods and not just one, in the way that there is a plurality of men.*

Yes, but in these cases the universal is only a unity for speculative thought. The individuals are widely separated from one another by time, temperament, and capacity. We human beings are not merely composite; we are mutually opposed and inconsistent even with ourselves. We do not stay exactly the same for one day, let alone a lifetime. In our bodies and in our souls we are ever fluctuating, ever changing. I do not know whether this is true of angels and of all that exalted nature which comes next after the Trinity, or not. They, though, are not composite, and by their nearness to the crown of beauty are more firmly fixed in their relation to beauty than we are.

31.16 The "gods" and (as they themselves style them) "demons" worshipped by the pagans have no need of **us** to accuse them. They stand convicted by their own theologians of being affected by evil emotions, of being quarrelsome, of being brimful of mischief in all its varieties. They are opposed not simply to one another but also to their first causes, who are called Ocean, Tethys, Phanes, and I do not know what else. To cap it all, one god (according to these theologians) had such a lust for power that he hated his children and so insatiable was his desire to be the father of gods and men alike that he gobbled all the rest of the gods up; the ill-starred meal was then regurgitated. If these are mythical, allegorical tales (as those theologians, trying to avoid the ugly character these stories have, aver) how can they explain the phrase, "All things are thrice divided," the fact that different gods preside over different things and that they have distinct elements under them and different grades?

But this is not the kind of thing we believe. "This portion does not belong to Jacob,"[34] says my theologian. No, each of the Trinity is in entire unity as much with himself as with the partnership, by identity of essence and power. This is how we explain the unity to the best of our ability to understand it. If the explanation here is convincing, we ought to thank God for the insight. If not, we should look for a better one.

31.17 I do not know whether we are to take jokingly or seriously the arguments you are using to undermine our account of the unity. Indeed, what **is** the argument?

Things of one substance, it goes, *are counted together*

—meaning by "counting together," "adding together to produce an arithmetical sum."

Things which do not have the same substance are not counted together. The result is that by your present argument you cannot avoid mentioning three Gods. We run no risk here, since we deny that they are of one substance.

---

[34] Jer. 10.16

Yes, you have relieved yourself of trouble by a single word. Yet you gain a poor kind of victory—it is rather like people hanging themselves because they are afraid of death. To save yourself the exertion of defending monotheism, you have denied the Godhead and surrendered the point at issue to the enemy. For my part, I will not give up the things we worship, even if it means some hard work. But I do not see what the labor involved **is**.

31.18 *Things of one substance,* you say, *are counted together, but things not of one substance can only be indicated singly.*

What school of mythology did you get that idea from? Do you not know that every number indicates an amount of objects, not their nature? I am old-fashioned enough, or rather, uncouth enough, to use the word ''three'' of things that amount to three, even if they differ in nature. I use the word ''one'' three times, at all events where that quantity of units is involved, even if the things in question are linked together in their essence. In doing so I am not attending to things, so much as to the **amount** of things referred to in counting them. Since you have such a strong attachment to the written word, despite the fact indeed that you are doing battle with the written word, you shall have my proofs from it. In the book of Proverbs there are three things which travel easily—a lion, a goat, and a cock; and fourthly, there is a king making a speech amongst his people.[35] I forbear to mention all the other sets of four things listed there, which are different in nature. In addition, I find two cherubim counted singly by Moses.[36] How, according to your system, could those things in the book of Proverbs, which are utterly different in their nature, be ''three''? How could the cherubim, which are of the same stock and closely connected, be counted singly? Were I to mention two masters, God and Mammon,[37] counted as one group despite their remoteness from each other, I might well be laughed at even more for my way of counting things together.

31.19 *But,* someone may say, *what I am talking about is things of the same substance being counted together which have nouns, that are mentioned as well, to match them. For example: Three* **men***, three* **gods***—not three odds and ends.*

What answer are we to make? This is the behavior of a man who lays down the law for words, not one who uses them to speak the truth. I say this, since, for my part, Peter, Paul, and John are not going to be three or of one substance, so long as three Pauls, three Peters, and as many Johns cannot be spoken of. We shall demand that you apply to more

---

[35] cf. Prov. 30.29-31
[36] Ex. 25.18
[37] Mt. 6.24

specific nouns the new-fangled rule you have kept to in the case of the more generic ones. Or will you break the rule by not conceding whatever rights you have assumed? Why does John in the Catholic Epistles say that there are "three who bear witness, the Spirit, the water, and the blood?"[38] Is he not talking nonsense in your opinion? First, because he has been rash enough to count together things which are not of the same substance—and that right you only allow to things which **are** of the same substance. Who could call these "of one substance"? Secondly, because he has appeared without getting his grammatical agreement right. He puts the word "three" in the masculine and then tacks on three words in the neuter, in defiance of your definitive rules of grammar. Yet what is the difference between putting "three" in the masculine and tacking on single things in the neuter, and using "one" thrice in the masculine without calling them "three" in the masculine but instead "three" in the neuter? This is the very proposition you reject in the case of the Godhead!

What do we make of the fact that the same Greek word can mean the animal a crab, a pair of tongs, or the sign of the zodiac, Cancer? What about the word which can denote a dog, a dog-fish, or the dog-star in the sky? Do you not agree that people talk about "three crabs" or "three dogs"? Of course you do. Does that mean that they are of the same substance? What man in his senses would assert that? You see how your argument about counting things together has collapsed under the weight of so many proofs to the contrary. If things of the same substance do not have to be counted together and things of the same substance are counted together, and if in both cases nouns are used along with the numerals, what is left of your school of thought?

31.20 Let us look at an additional point which lies, I take it, within the present area of discussion. One plus one makes two, and two divides into one plus one? Yes, of course. If things added together are of the same substance and things separated are of different substances, what will happen? The identical things will have to be **both** of the same substance **and** of different substances. I scorn the way you pride yourself on putting things in numbered lists, as if the realities depended upon the sequence of the names. If that were really the case, what is to prevent the same things, by this argument, being both superior and inferior in worth to themselves, seeing that the same things are sometimes higher up, sometimes lower down the lists given in the Bible, just because they have an equal natural worth? I find that this same principle applies to "God" and "Lord," and even more strongly to the prepositions "from," "through," and "in,"[39]

---

[38] 1 John 5.7-8
[39] cf. Rom. 11.36

which you use to make an artificial system of the divinity, saying that
"from whom" applies to the Father, "through whom" to the Son and "in whom" applies to the Holy Spirit.

What would you have got up to if each expression **had** been given a fixed allocation? As it is, you use them as a means of introducing such a deal of inequality in rank and nature, despite the fact that it is clear, to those who take the trouble to find out, that the prepositions are used jointly of all three.

That will do for men with at least **some** intelligence! But you have made one assault upon the Spirit and so you find it hard to have your impetus checked. Boars of the fiercer kind find it hard not to struggle on to the finish, and force themselves towards the sword. So do you, till you get its thrust full in you. Come then, let us look at the remainder of your argument.

31.21 Time and time again you repeat the argument about
not being in the Bible.

Yet we are dealing here not with a smuggled-in alien, but with something disclosed to the consciousness of men past and present. The fact stands already proved by a host of people who have discussed the subject, all men who read the Holy Scriptures not in a frivolous, cursory way, but with penetration so that they saw inside the written text to its inner meaning. They were found fit to perceive the hidden loveliness; they were illuminated by the light of knowledge. We shall, so far as possible, summarize their views, building on the "foundations of others"[40]—we do not want to appear improperly and extravagantly ambitious. If the fact that the Biblical text does not very clearly or very often call him "God" (as it calls the Father, "God," in the Old Testament, and the Son, "God," in the New Testament) if this fact, I say, is the cause of your blasphemy, your inordinately verbose irreligion, we shall release you from this mischief by a brief disquisition on things and names, with special reference to Biblical usage.

31.22 Some things mentioned in the Bible are not factual; some factual things are not mentioned; some non-factual things receive no mention there; some things are both factual and mentioned. Do you ask for my proofs here? I am ready to offer them. In the Bible, God "sleeps,"[41] "wakes up,"[42] "is angered,"[43] "walks,"[44] and has a "throne of cherubim."[45] Yet when has God ever been subject to emotion? When do you

---

[40] Rom. 15.20
[41] e.g. Ps. 44(43).23(24)
[42] Jer. 31(38).26
[43] Ps. 79(78).5; cf. Isa. 5.25
[44] Gen. 3.8
[45] Isa. 37.16; Ps. 80(79).1(2)

ever hear that God is a bodily being? This is a non-factual, mental picture. We have used names derived from human experience and applied them, so far as we could, to aspects of God. His retirement from us, for reasons known to himself into an almost unconcerned inactivity, is his "sleeping." Human sleeping, after all, has the character of restful inaction. When he alters and suddenly benefits us, that is his "waking up." Waking up puts an end to sleep, just as looking at somebody puts an end to turning away from him. We have made his punishing us, his "being angered;" for with us, punishment is born of anger. His acting in different places, we call "walking," for walking is a transition from one place to another. His resting among the heavenly powers, making them almost his haunt, we call his "sitting" and "being enthroned;" this too is human language. The divine, in fact, rests nowhere as he rests in the saints. God's swift motion we call "flight;"[46] his watching over us is his "face;"[47] his giving and receiving is his "hand."[48] In short every faculty or activity of God has given us a corresponding picture in terms of something bodily.

31.23   Again, where do you get those fortresses of yours, "Ingenerate" and "Unoriginate" from—or we the term "Immortal," come to that? Show us the express words or we cross them out as unscriptural, and you will be dead as a result of your own principles, since the words, the wall of defence you trusted in,[49] will have been destroyed. Is it not plain that these terms derived from passages which imply, without actually mentioning them? The passages? What about: "I am the first and I am hereafter"[50] and "Before me there is no other God and after me there shall be none"[51] for all "is-ness"[52] (God is saying) is mine, without beginning or ending? You have taken the truths that there is nothing before God and that he has no prior cause, and given him the titles "unoriginate" and "ingenerate." The fact that there is no halt to his on-going existence means he is "immortal" and "indestructible."

The first two pairs stand accounted for. But what of the non-factual things not mentioned in the Bible—such as "deity is evil," "a sphere has four corners" or "man is not a compound"? Do you know anybody who has reached such a pitch of insanity as to venture to think, or show that he thinks, anything like that?

---

[46] e.g. Ps. 18(17).10(11)
[47] Ps. 4.6(7); 34(33).16(17)
[48] Ps. 145(144).16
[49] cf. Ps. 31(30).2(3)
[50] Isa. 44.6
[51] Isa. 43.10
[52] cf. Ex. 3.14

It remains then to exemplify things which are **both** factual **and** mentioned: "God," "man," "angel," "judgment," and "futility"—which is what your deductive arguments are, besides being an overthrowing of "the faith" and an emptying of "the mystery."[53]

31.24   There really is a great deal of diversity inherent in names and things, so why are you so dreadfully servile to the letter, so much the partisan of Jewish lore, following the syllables while you let the facts go? Supposing you mention "twice five" or "twice seven" and I infer from your words "ten" or "fourteen," or supposing from your mentioning a "rational, mortal animal" I draw the conclusion a "man," would you allege I was talking rubbish? How could I be? I am saying what **you** said. The words belong just as much to the man who gives the logical grounds for using them as their actual user. In the examples I have just given I should be considering meanings rather than words, and so, in the same way, if I hit upon something meant, though not mentioned, or not stated in clear terms, by Scripture, I should not be put off by your quibbling charge about names—I should give expression to the meaning. This is how we shall make our stand against people whose views are only half right!

I cannot say as much to you. You deny so many really crystal-clear titles belonging to the Son that it is evident you would not respect them even if you got to know a host of even plainer ones. I shall go on now to take the argument a short stage further back and explain to you (experts though you are supposed to be) the reason for all this concealment.

31.25   There have been two remarkable transformations of the human way of life in the course of the world's history. These are called two "covenants," and, so famous was the business involved, two "shakings of the earth."[54] The first was the transition from idols to the Law;[55] the second, from the Law to the Gospel.[56] The Gospel also tells of the third "shaking," the change from this present state of things to what lies unmoved, unshaken,[57] beyond. An identical feature occurs in both covenants. The feature? There was nothing sudden involved in the first movement to take their transformation in hand. We need to know why. It was so that we should be persuaded, not forced. The unspontaneous is the impermanent—as when force is used to keep stems or plants in check. The spontaneous both lasts longer and is more secure. It belongs to despotic power to use force; it is a mark of God's reasonableness that the issue should be ours. God thought it wrong to do men good against their

---

[53] cf. Rom. 4.14; 1 Cor. 1.17; 1 Tim. 3.9
[54] Heb. 12.26-27; Hag. 2.6; Mt. 27.51
[55] Ex. 20.3-5
[56] cf. Mt. 27.51; Heb. 9.3-15; Gal. 2.14ff.
[57] Heb. 12.18

will but right to benefit those with a mind to it. For this reason, he acts like a schoolmaster or doctor, taking away some ancestral customs, allowing others. He yields on some trifles which make for happiness, just as doctors do with the sick to get the medicine taken along with the sweeter ingredients artfully blended in. A departure from time-honored, customary ways is, after all, not easy. Am I making my point? The first change cut away idols but allowed sacrifices to remain; the second stripped away sacrifices but did not forbid circumcision. Then, when men had been reconciled to the withdrawal, they agreed to let go what had been left them as a concession. Under the first covenant that concession was sacrifice, and they became Jews instead of Gentiles; under the second, circumcision—and they became Christians instead of Jews, brought round gradually, bit by bit, to the Gospel. Paul shall convince you here. He progressed from circumcising[58] and keeping ceremonial cleansings[59] to the point of declaring, "But if I, brethren, preach circumcision, why am I still being persecuted?"[60] His earlier conduct was an accommodation to circumstance, his later conduct belonged to the full truth.

31.26 I can make a comparison here with the progress of the doctrine of God, except that the order is exactly the reverse. In the former case change arose from omissions; here, growth towards perfection comes through additions. In this way: the old covenant made clear proclamation of the Father, a less definite one of the Son. The new [covenant] made the Son manifest[61] and gave us a glimpse of the Spirit's Godhead. At the present time the Spirit resides amongst us, giving us a clearer manifestation of himself than before. It was dangerous for the Son to be preached openly when the Godhead of the Father was still unacknowledged. It was dangerous, too, for the Holy Spirit to be made (and here I use a rather rash expression) an extra burden, when the Son had not been received. It could mean men jeopardizing what did lie within their powers, as happens to those encumbered with a diet too strong for them or who gaze at sunlight with eyes as yet too feeble for it. No, God meant it to be by piecemeal additions, "ascents"[62] as David called them, by progress and advance from glory to glory,[63] that the light of the Trinity should shine upon more illustrious souls. This was, I believe, the motive for the Spirit's making his home in the disciples in gradual stages proportionate to their capacity to receive him—at the outset of the gospel when he performs

---

58 Acts 16.3
59 Acts 21.26
60 Gal. 5.11
61 cf. 1 Pet. 1.20
62 Ps. 83.6 [LXX]
63 2 Cor. 3.18

miracles,[64] after the Passion when he is breathed into the disciples,[65] after the Ascension when he appears in fiery tongues.[66] He was gradually revealed by Jesus also, as you too can substantiate by a more careful reading. "I will ask the Father," he says, "and he will send you another Comforter, the Spirit of Truth"[67]—intending that the Spirit should not appear to be a rival God and spokesman of another power. Later he says: "He will send him in my name"[68]—leaving out "I will ask" but retaining "He will send." Later on he says: "I shall send"[69]—indicating the Son's own rank; and later: "He will come"[70]—indicating the Spirit's power.

31.27   You see how light shines on us bit by bit, you see in the doctrine of God an order, which we had better observe, neither revealing it suddenly nor concealing it to the last. To reveal it suddenly would be clumsy, would shock outsiders. Ultimately to conceal it would be a denial of God, would make outsiders of our own people. Let me add to these remarks a thought which well may have occurred to others already, but which I suspect of being a product of my own mind. The Saviour had certain truths which he said could not at that time be borne by the disciples,[71] filled though they had been with a host of teachings. These truths, for motives I well may have mentioned, were therefore concealed. He also said that we should be taught "all things" by the Holy Spirit,[72] when he made his dwelling in us. One of these truths I take to be the **Godhead** of the Spirit, which becomes clear at a later stage, when the knowledge was timely and capable of being taken in, after our Saviour's return to heaven, no longer, because of a miracle, an object of disbelief. What greater truth could the Son promise or the Spirit teach than this one? If any promise or teaching ought to be deemed great, this ought.

31.28   Thus do I stand, thus may I stand, and those I love as well, on these issues, able to worship the Father as God, the Son as God, the Holy Spirit as God—"three distinctions in personality, one Godhead undivided in glory, honor, substance, and sovereignty," as one inspired saint of recent times wisely expressed it. May he who does not stand thus, who is a time-serving turncoat, irresolute on matters of most import—may such

---

[64] Mt. 10.1; Mark 6.7; Luke 9.1
[65] John 20.22
[66] Acts 2.3
[67] John 14.16-17
[68] John 14.26
[69] John 15.26 and 16.7
[70] Ibid.
[71] John 16.12
[72] John 14.26 and 16.13

a man, as Scripture has it, "not see the day star rising"[73] nor the glory of its heavenly brilliance! Were the Spirit not to be worshipped, how could he deify me through baptism? If he is to be worshipped, why not adored? And if to be adored, how can he fail to be God? One links with the other, a truly golden chain of salvation. From the Spirit comes our rebirth,[74] from rebirth comes a new creating, from new creating a recognition of the worth of him who effected it.

31.29 Yes, this is what one can say on the premiss that
it is not in the Bible.

But now you shall have a swarm of proof-texts, from which the Godhead of the Holy Spirit can be proved thoroughly Scriptural at least to those not utterly dense or utterly alien to the Spirit. Look at the facts: Christ is born, the Spirit is his forerunner;[75] Christ is baptized, the Spirit bears him witness;[76] Christ is tempted, the Spirit leads him up;[77] Christ performs miracles, the Spirit accompanies him;[78] Christ ascends, the Spirit fills his place.[79] Is there any significant function belonging to God, which the Spirit does not perform? Is there any title belonging to God, which cannot apply to him, except "ingenerate" and "begotten"? The Father and the Son, after all, continue to have their distinctions of personality; there must be no confusion with the Godhead which brings all other things into harmonious order. I shudder to think of the wealth of titles, the mass of names, outraged by resistance to the Spirit. He is called "Spirit of God,"[80] "Spirit of Christ,"[81] "Mind of Christ,"[82] "Spirit of the Lord,"[83] and "Lord"[84] absolutely; "Spirit of Adoption,"[85] "of Truth,"[86] "of Freedom,"[87] "Spirit of Wisdom," "Understanding," "Counsel," "Might," "Knowledge," "True Religion" and of "The Fear of God."[88] The Spirit indeed effects all these things, filling the universe with his being, sustaining the universe. His being "fills the world,"[89] his power is beyond the world's capacity to contain it. It is his

---

73 Job 3.9
74 John 3.3-5; Mt. 28.19
75 cf. Luke 1.31 and 35
76 Mt. 3.13-17; Luke 3.21-22
77 Mt. 4.1; Luke 4.2
78 Mt. 12.22 and 28
79 Acts 1.9 and 2.3-4
80 1 Cor. 2.11
81 Rom. 8.9
82 1 Cor. 2.14-16
83 2 Cor. 3.17
84 Ibid.
85 Rom. 8.15
86 John 14.17
87 2 Cor. 3.17
88 Isa. 11.2-3
89 Wis. 1.7

nature, not his given function, to be good,[90] to be righteous[91] and to be in command.[92] He is the subject, not the object, of hallowing,[93] apportioning,[94] participating,[95] filling, sustaining;[96] we share in him and he shares in nothing.[97] He is our inheritance,[98] he is glorified,[99] counted together with Father and Son;[100] he is a dire warning to us.[101] The "finger of God,"[102] he is, like God, a "fire:"[103] which proves, I think, that he is consubstantial. The Spirit it is who created[104] and creates anew through baptism[105] and resurrection.[106] The Spirit it is who knows all things,[107] who teaches all things,[108] who blows where, and as strongly as, he wills,[109] who leads,[110] speaks, sends out, separates,[111] who is vexed[112] and tempted.[113] He reveals,[114] illumines,[115] gives life—or, rather, is absolutely Light and Life.[116] He makes us his temple,[117] he deifies, he makes us complete,[118] he initiates us in such a way that he both precedes baptism[119] and is wanted after it.[120] All that God actively performs, he performs.[121] Divided in fiery tongues[122] he distributes graces,[123] makes

---

[90] Ps. 143(142).10
[91] Ps. 51(50).10(12)
[92] Ps. 50.14 [LXX]
[93] 1 Cor. 6.11
[94] John 3.34
[95] cf. Rom. 8.15; Phil. 2.1
[96] Wis. 1.7
[97] ibid.
[98] Eph. 1.13-14
[99] 1 Cor. 6.19-20
[100] 1 John 5.7-8 [variant reading]; cf. Mt. 28.19
[101] Mark 3.29
[102] Luke 11.20
[103] Acts 2.3-4; Deut. 4.24
[104] Ps. 104(103).30
[105] John 3.5; cf. 1 Cor. 12.13
[106] Ezek. 37.5-14
[107] 1 Cor. 2.10
[108] John 14.26
[109] John 3.8
[110] Ps. 143(142).10
[111] Acts 13.2-4
[112] cf. Job 4.9
[113] Acts 5.9
[114] 1 Cor. 2.10; cf. John 16.13
[115] cf. John 14.26
[116] John 6.63; Rom. 8.10
[117] cf. 1 Cor. 3.16, 6.11
[118] cf. John 16.12-13
[119] cf. Acts 10.47
[120] Acts 8.14-17
[121] 1 Cor. 12.4 and 11
[122] Acts 2.3
[123] Eph. 4.11

Apostles, prophets,[124] evangelists, pastors, and teachers.[125] He is "intelligent, manifold, clear, distinct, irresistible, unpolluted"[126]—or in other words, he is utterly wise, his operations are multifarious,[127] he clarifies all things distinctly, his authority is absolute and he is free from mutability. He is "all powerful, overseeing all and penetrates through all spirits that are intelligent and pure and most subtle"[128]—meaning, I think, angelic powers as well as prophets and Apostles. He penetrates them simultaneously, though they are distributed in various places;[129] which shows that he is not tied down by spatial limitations.

31.30 Men who speak and teach thus, who use the expression "another Comforter"[130] with almost the meaning "an additional God," men who are conscious that blasphemy against him is uniquely unpardonable,[131] who so frighteningly advertised the guilty Ananias and Sapphira, when they lied to the Spirit, as "liars to God not to man"[132]—are those men, in your opinion, preaching that the Holy Spirit is God or that he is something else? You must be literally impenetrable, utterly unspiritual, if you feel any hesitancy here or need any further instruction.

Yes, the titles are so many and so striking, what need have you of texts in full quotation? All the less exalted expressions which talk of his being given,[133] sent,[134] divided,[135] or his being a grace,[136] a gift,[137] an inspiration,[138] a promise,[139] a means of intercession[140] or anything else of the same character—all these are to be referred back to the Primal Cause, as indicating the Spirit's source and preventing a polytheistic belief in three separate causes. It is equally irreligious to make them a combined personality, like Sabellius, as to disconnect them like the Arians.

31.31 For my part, though I have examined the question in private so busily and so often, searching from all points of view for an illustration

---

[124] Wis. 7.27
[125] Eph. 4.4 and 11
[126] Wis. 7.21
[127] 1 Cor. 12.11
[128] Wis. 7.23
[129] Wis. 8.1
[130] John 14.16
[131] Mt. 12.31
[132] Acts 5.1-11
[133] Luke 11.13
[134] John 16.7
[135] Heb. 2.4
[136] 1 Cor. 12.9 and 30
[137] Acts 2.38
[138] John 20.22
[139] Luke 24.49; Acts 1.4; Gal. 3.14
[140] Rom. 8.26

of this profound matter, I have failed to find anything in this world with which I might compare the divine nature. If a faint resemblance comes my way, the more significant aspect escapes me, leaving me and my illustration here in this world. I had the idea, indeed others have had it too, of a source, a spring, and a river, and asked myself whether there were not something here corresponding with the Father, the Son, and the Holy Spirit. There is no temporal separation here, no disruption of mutual connection, even if they appear to be parted by three distinctions of personality. But I had two fears. First, of admitting the idea of an incessant stream of Deity, second that the illustration might import the suggestion of a numerical unit—source, spring, and river, though different in form, count as one thing.

31.32 Another illustration I pondered over was that of Sun, beam, and light. But here again there was the danger, first of imagining in the incomposite nature the sort of composition which belongs to the Sun and its inherent properties, second, of making the Father a substance but the others potentialities inherent in him, attributes of God not individual beings. Beam and light are not extra Suns, but emanations from the Sun, qualities of its substance. To think thus is thereby to attribute to God, to the extent that the illustration suggests the idea, both being **and** nonbeing—and that is a greater absurdity than the previous suggestions. I once heard a man describe it in terms of a sunbeam which throws its radiance on to a wall; its trembling results from the movement of water, a movement transmitted through the intervening air and caught by the beam. The beam is then checked by the resistance of the wall and becomes a quivering that surprises one with its rapidity of oscillation. It is just as much a manifold as it is a unity; it joins and parts so quickly that it is away before the eye can catch hold of it.

31.33 However, this illustration too was unacceptable to me. First, because it was quite clear what had set the sunbeam in motion, whereas nothing is prior to God to be his mover—he is cause of all and owns no prior cause. Second, because there is in this example a hint of those very things which are inconceivable in the case of God—composition, dispersion, and the lack of a fixed, natural stability. In a word, there is nothing to satisfy my mind when I try to illustrate the mental picture I have, except taking part of the image and wisely discarding the rest. So, in the end, I resolved that it was best to have done with images and shadows, deceptive and utterly inadequate as they are to express the reality. I resolved to keep close to the more truly religious view and rest content with few words, taking the Spirit as my guide and, in his company and in partnership with him, safeguarding to the end the genuine illumination I had received from him, as I strike out a path through this world. To the best of my powers

I will persuade all men to worship Father, Son, and Holy Spirit as the single Godhead and power, because to him belong all glory, honor, and might for ever and ever.[141] Amen.

---

[141] Rev. 1.6

SCRIPTURE INDEX

INDEX OF SUBJECTS AND ANCIENT AUTHORS; NAMES AND SCHOOLS

INDEX OF MODERN AUTHORS